3rd edition

retailing

GERALD PINTEL

Business Administration Department
Nassau Community College

JAY DIAMOND

Marketing and Retailing Department
Nassau Community College

PRENTICE HALL, INC., ENGLEWOOD CLIFFS, N.J. 07632

Library of Congress Cataloging in Publication Data

Pintel, Gerald.
  Retailing.

  Includes index.
  1. Retail trade—Management. I. Diamond, Jay.
II. Title.
HF5429.P57 1983   658.8'7   82-3752
ISBN 0-13-777557-1   AACR2

Editorial/production supervision and interior design by *Barbara Grasso*
Cover design by *Lee Cohen*
Manufacturing buyer: *Edward O'Dougherty*
Cover photo by *Laimute E. Druskis*

Printed in the United States of America

10 9 8 7 6 5 4 3

ISBN 0-13-777557-1

PRENTICE-HALL INTERNATIONAL, INC., *London*
PRENTICE-HALL OF AUSTRALIA PTY. LIMITED, *Sydney*
PRENTICE-HALL CANADA INC., *Toronto*
PRENTICE-HALL OF INDIA PRIVATE LIMITED, *New Delhi*
PRENTICE-HALL OF JAPAN, INC., *Tokyo*
PRENTICE-HALL OF SOUTHEAST ASIA PTE. LTD., *Singapore*
WHITEHALL BOOKS LIMITED, *Wellington, New Zealand*

contents

preface

As in the previous editions, *Retailing* continues to introduce students to the field of retailing and provide the technical and theoretical knowledge necessary for graduates who wish to enter the field.

This edition presents a considerable change in format as well as the inclusion of significant new material.

Divided into five separate sections, the book provides a logical approach to the study of retailing. They are Introduction to Retailing; Organization, Management, and Operational Functions; Buying and Merchandising Concepts; Building and Maintaining the Retail Clientele; and Retail Information Systems, Functions, and Controls.

Not only have changes been made to broaden concepts and expand upon previously presented materials, but additional areas pertinent to students of retailing have also been added. For example, an entire chapter, *Consumer Behavior*, has been added to underscore the psychology, motivations, and habits of potential retail customers. Each chapter has a new feature, *Action for the Independent Retailer*, which gives attention to the routes small and independent retailers may take to maximize the success of their operations. The chapter on credit has been expanded to a new chapter, *Credit and Other Customer Services*, which describes the various extras retailers are providing to gain their share of the market.

Another important feature that has been incorporated into this third edition is the introduction of each chapter with a set of behavioral objectives. This enables both instructor and student, alike, to familiarize themselves with what will be learned in each chapter. A summary of key points, review questions, and case problems are also presented at the conclusion of each chapter.

Accompanying the textbook is a workbook with four types of review questions, projects, and case problems. All of these provide the student with pertinent, practical challenges. They enable individuals to apply their acquired knowledge in both written and oral formats. Each exercise has been tested in the classroom numerous times and has proved to be extremely effective motivation for the student.

A teacher's manual, providing answers to the problems and cases for both the textbook and workbook, as well as sample tests, is available.

The authors wish to thank Ray Hagelman, Nassau Community College, for specific case material and illustrations, and Ms. Winnie Garrahan for the typing of the manuscript.

Gerald Pintel
Jay Diamond

I

introduction
to
retailing

1 *the nature of retailing*

3

BEHAVIORAL OBJECTIVES

Upon completion of this chapter the student should be able to

1. *Write a brief essay on the evolution of retailing in America, including the reasons for the changes.*
2. *Describe six different types of retailing institutions (such as chain stores and department stores).*
3. *Identify five future trends in retailing.*
4. *Describe the operations of six major American retailers.*

HISTORICAL DEVELOPMENT

American retailing as we know it today, with its sophisticated research methods and such decision-making devices as the computer, had its meager beginning in the early fifteenth century at the *trading post*. At that time currency was not used to make purchases; instead, goods from European markets were exchanged for the pelts of fur trappers and produce grown by farmers.

In the mid-eighteenth century this first retail institution began to expand its operation to better serve the needs of the colonists. A greater variety of merchandise was needed by the settlers, and the trading post gave way to the *general store*. This retail store operated on a cash basis, a departure from the barter system of the earlier retailer. The merchandise assortment was extensive, with offerings of foodstuffs, yard goods, feed for cattle, manufactured goods from the Old World, shoes, and such animal supplies as harnesses. The merchandise was not carefully organized as it is in retail stores today. A haphazard nondepartmentalized arrangement was typical. The general store today is still in evidence in rural areas.

In the middle of the nineteenth century there was a great variety of goods being produced in the United States, so much so that the general store was unable to carry the unlimited offerings of manufacturers. This necessitated the beginning of specialization in retailing and the introduction of the *limited line store*. This store carried a wide variety of one classification of merchandise. Shoe stores, ladies' specialty shops, jewelry stores, and groceries are examples of limited line stores. Today the limited line store, or specialty store, as it is commonly referred to, still enjoys an important place in retailing. The early specialty shops were generally individual proprietorships (individually owned). Many of them have grown into large, well-known retail empires and enjoy the distinction of having started the chain organization. A number of these great merchants will be discussed later in this chapter.

The *chain organization*, the first venture into large-scale retailing in the United States, began in the latter part of the nineteenth century. It is generally defined as two or more stores, similar in nature and having common ownership. Many of those operators of successful limited line stores opened second, third, and more units in other areas. Among the early chain organizations were J. C. Penney Co.; A&P, the food giant; and F. W. Woolworth Co., the "5 & 10 cent store."

At the end of the nineteenth and the beginning of the twentieth century the *department store,* a departmentalized retail store carrying a wide variety of hard goods and soft goods, became popular. Essentially, the department store is the bringing together of many limited line operations under one roof, with common ownership. This institution differed from the general store in that it presented an orderly arrangement of many types of merchandise, in contrast to the disorganized presentation of goods in the general store. The offerings of the department store—in addition to the typical hard goods such as furniture, appliances, and tools, and the soft goods such as wearing apparel, clothing accessories, and piece goods—often include departments specializing in groceries, baked goods, gourmet foods, pets, optics, travel arrangements, entertainment information and sales, and so on. The luxury of one-stop shopping is available to the department store customer. Branch stores, smaller units of the department store, carrying a representation of the main store's offerings, have become popular as the population has moved to the suburbs. Today in the retail field few new department stores are being established; instead we are witnessing a great expansion of the established stores through additional branches.

In an effort to better serve the needs of those people unable to patronize the existing retail institutions, either because of their distance from the stores or their lack of time to buy in person, the *mail order retailer* began to attract attention. At first, in the late nineteenth century, little was available to the mail order customer. Extensive catalogs, which since then enjoyed great popularity, were prepared and sent to customers, and the mail order business became an important part of retailing. Montgomery Ward & Co. and Sears, Roebuck and Co. were early mail order houses. Today, even with mass transportation, the extensive chain organization, and the branch store, mail order retailing continues to flourish.

The *supermarket,* a large departmentalized food store, became popular in the late 1930s. In addition to the large variety of foodstuffs, they carry an abundance of miscellaneous items such as drugs; toys; men's, women's, and children's accessories; plants; and hardware. As the department store provides one-stop shopping for the consumer, similarly the supermarket affords the luxury of purchasing all one's food needs at one location instead of making separate trips to the grocer, butcher, baker and produce dealer. Although the great majority of supermarkets are chain organizations, many independent markets are also in operation.

The most recent major innovation in retailing has been the *discount operation.* Unlike the conventional retail store with all of its services, the discounter offers limited service in exchange for lower prices. This method of merchandising is not restricted to one type of retailing organization but is found in chain, department, and specialty store operations.

MAJOR CLASSIFICATIONS OF RETAILERS

The era of the trading post belongs to history, but the other types of retail institutions that have been organized since that time are very much in evidence today. Except for the general store, they are all flourishing throughout the United States.

Retailers may be classified in many ways. As examples, they can be grouped according to their merchandising activities (the activities in the buying-selling cycle), the merchandise they carry, their dollar volume, or the number of people they employ. Although the study of each classification may be valuable, we can get a complete overview of retailing institutions by investigating small retailers and large retailers as separate categories, with further expansion into the variety of large retailers.

The Small Retailer

The small retail business as defined here grosses under $100,000 annually. Typically, there is little job specialization. The store owner is generally responsible for the overall management and merchandising tasks. The owner buys, sells, sets work schedules, plans sales promotions, secures personnel, and so forth. The "larger" small retailer, doing business at the $100,000 level, has more specialized personnel working in the organization. There might be a person responsible only for merchandising duties, which include the entire buying-selling cycle. A part-time display person might be hired for window decoration. A store manager would be responsible for the management of the physical layout of the store and supervision of personnel. But in stores of limited gross sales it is obvious that the owner must perform all activities.

The majority of small retail stores are individual proprietorships; however, included in the group are partnerships and corporations. The general store and the specialty store are the two major types of small stores, with the latter accounting for almost all small retailing institutions.

In addition to the typical small conventional retail establishments, the general and specialty stores, retailing on a small scale is gaining momentum throughout the United States. Flea markets, both the outdoor and inside variety, are flourishing and are providing opportunities for those who wish to sell at retail but have chosen not to take the traditional "store" route.

The General Store

The age of specialization, the success of the chain organization, movement to urban and suburban communities, the automobile, and the continued growth of the mail order house are some factors that have contributed to the decline of the general store.

In the rural areas the general store, which features a wide variety of unrelated merchandise, is still in operation. Management of the operation is generally haphazard. The sophisticated tools and aids of today's modern retailers are rarely employed. The proprietor engages in purchasing merchandise that is so varied as to include cracker barrel goods and ready-made apparel. The knowledge of such proprietors in any single area is so limited that they lack the ability necessary to make the right decisions. How can one individual have the product knowledge for so diversified an inventory? The limited floor space doesn't allow for wide assortment within each merchandise classification. The general store has the questionable distinction of being the most mismanaged type of retail organization. Retailers, although reluctant to agree on many things, usually concede that the general store will never regain its popularity.

The Specialty Store

The limited line store or the specialty store, as it is usually referred to today, is an establishment carrying one line of merchandise. Stores specializing in jewelry, furs, shoes, hardware, groceries, baked goods, and broader classifications such as women's clothing or men's accessories, are examples of the specialty or limited line store. The greatest number of successful small retailers operate specialty stores. Some of the factors that have led to the success of this type of organization are

1. Personalized service
2. Wide assortment of merchandise in a limited classification
3. Knowledgeable buying—the buyer must be educated only in certain lines of merchandise

The chain organization is the major competitor of the small specialty store. The chain is actually a retail organization with many units carrying specialty merchandise. The chain's ability to offer lower prices due to greater buying power, and its wide advertising to the consumer, poses the greatest threat to the small retailer.

In an attempt to meet the "unfair" competition of the chain, many small merchants have united informally. The combining of small orders to qualify for quantity discounts, particularly in groceries, small hard goods, and staple menswear such as shirts and other accessories, has enabled the small merchant to become more competitive by lowering prices. As of late, advertising, an area that the small retailer often avoids because of the costs involved, has become popular as a group activity. Where one merchant would spend a large sum for an advertisement, the group now shares the costs. A complete listing of all the stores involved in the advertisement indicates to the consumer those offering the advertised merchandise. In both group-buying and group-advertising activities, noncompeting stores are generally involved.

More formalized groups of small retailers are evidenced by the *voluntary chain* or the *cooperative chain*. The former is usually organized by a wholesaler who enters into contractual arrangements with the individual retailers, requiring that all purchases be made from that wholesaler. In addition, promotional plans, point-of-purchase display arrangements, advertising materials, merchandising advice, counter and shelf arrangements, and location selection are typical aids provided by the wholesaler. The *cooperative chain* differs in that the retailers join together and operate their own warehouse. They too are involved in many group activities that tend to lower the cost of individual operations and increase individual efficiency.

In retailing today, with the giant chain and department store organization, small retailers can more effectively compete through group activities such as group buying and advertising, which reduce costs to the individual member. Of paramount importance in the field is knowledgeable advice on management and merchandising. Whereas the large retailer can afford the luxury of specialists, the small merchants, through their combined efforts, can avail themselves of an exchange of ideas. One store owner may be expert in designing the best store layout, another might excel in the buying activity; still another might have a talent for preparing advertising copy. This exchange of information and ideas provides the special knowledge so necessary for success in retailing. Because the merchants are not direct competitors, this free exchange can be open and beneficial to all.

Since the nature of some small stores dictates a different type of management, retailing today still includes completely independent retailers who are not involved in any group arrangement. Others find this type of arrangement well suited to their needs.

The Flea Market Stall

Unlike the many small retailers who operate the general and specialty stores, these retailers function without the typical requirements of small scale retailing. Located in parking fields of racetracks, drive-in movies, and so forth, the individuals operate on a limited time basis. The days and hours of operation are scheduled during those periods in which the premises are not occupied by the racetracks and drive-in theaters. In the majority of cases business is transacted two days a week. Figure 1-1 is an example of such a flea market.

In years gone by, flea markets were established as places where people were able to dispose of the "treasures" they accumulated over a period of time. Once having accomplished this, they usually were "out of business." Today, however, the flea market is not an arena for this purpose, but a regular format for individuals to conduct retail businesses. For a modest fee, approximately $20 a day, an individual can set up shop. So successful has this format become, that acquiring a space has been as difficult as gaining a desirable location in a traditional shopping area. Stalls are generally leased for a one-year period.

Merchants at flea markets specialize in a particular type of merchandise, much the same as the specialty store. The main feature is price. Returns and refunds are usually as liberal as those in the traditional retail establishments. So effective is flea market retailing that it has caused considerable concern for retailers who are located near them. Where the large retailer has generally had the advantage over the small retailer, it is the flea market independent who is actively and successfully competing with the large retail companies.

FIGURE 1-1 A Race Track Parking Lot Flea Market

Roosevelt Raceway Flea Market—Photograph by Ray Hagelman

Today retailing is dominated by the large organization. The department store, chain organization, supermarket, and mail order house provide the majority of retail sales.

The Department Store

The department store is a departmentalized retail institution that offers a large variety of hard goods and soft goods, provides numerous customer services, has large sales volume, and employs a great number of people specializing in various tasks. Its organization will be discussed in a later chapter.

The merchandise assortment varies depending upon the size of the store. Organizations such as Macy's, Gimbels, or the Allied Stores offer enough types of merchandise in a range of prices for a consumer family to satisfy just about any of its needs. Such merchandise as men's, women's, and children's clothing, apparel accessories, musical instruments, sporting equipment, toys, furniture, hardware, perfumes, toiletries, gourmet foods, liquor, floor covering, bedding, draperies, and appliances are among those in the inventory. A Macy's shopper can buy anything from an iguana to a painting by Joan Miro, from a set of Tom Swift books to fresh Beluga caviar. In many stores, optical goods, beauty salon services, precious jewelry, religious articles, meat and poultry, silverware, and other commodities are available through *leased departments*. These departments are operated by independents or independent chain owners, generally because the nature of the goods or services warrants unusual specialized ability. The department is usually leased on a square foot rental or a percentage of sales. Department stores have found that a greater profit for the store can be realized in this way than if they operated these departments themselves. An important reason for offering these specialized goods and services is to provide the customer with one-stop shopping.

The greatest variety of services offered in retailing is in the department store. Free delivery, gift wrapping, charge accounts, return privileges, extended credit plans, and the provision of meeting rooms for clubs are among the usual services. Unusual ones include personal shoppers for foreign-speaking people, baby sitting while parents are shopping, special hours for children shoppers before holidays, and the procurement of tickets for theatrical and sporting events.

Department stores may be individually owned, belong to ownership groups such as the Allied Stores Corp., or be chains such as Macy's, which has a nationwide organization of more than fifty stores in six regional divisions.

Branches and Twigs. With the increase in the number of families moving from the cities to the suburbs, the almost hopeless traffic congestion, the shortage of adequate parking facilities, and the development and growth of shopping centers, department stores have opened additional units away from the city. The branch is a store, usually smaller than the main store, carrying a representation of the parent store's merchandise. It is geared to the needs of the community in which it is located. Some branch stores have exceeded the sales volume of the main store.

Twig stores, relatively rare in retailing today but still in existence, are very small units belonging to a department store, which unlike the branch, carry only one classification of merchandise. For example, a department store might operate a shop in a college town featuring merchandise worn on the campus.

The Chain Store

The chain store may be defined as a centrally owned and managed organization with two or more similar units each carrying the same classification of merchandise. The merchandise categories include drugs, hardware, shoes, restaurants, jewelry, variety goods, groceries, baked goods, and other types of goods and services. For example, S.S. Kresge is a variety chain; A & P is a supermarket chain; J. C. Penney is a general merchandise chain; Edison Brothers, a shoe chain; Lerner Shops, a women's chain. Each unit in these chains is similar in nature to the other units. The department store has the main store as its base of operations and it plans its purchases there, whereas the chain organization operates from central headquarters, a location that houses merchandisers, buyers, personnel administrators, advertising executives, and so on. Large chains have regional offices in addition to central headquarters. The units of the chain are generally charged with the responsibility of selling merchandise, while the central team is the decision-making body of the organization. Store managers do not formulate policy; instead they carry out the policies of the central staff.

In addition to functioning centrally in the areas of buying and merchandising, chains occasionally are centrally involved in other than the usual areas. For example, Lerner Shops, a large women's specialty chain with stores throughout the United States, has at its main offices in New York City a display department that plans window displays centrally. Windows are arranged with merchandise, photographed, and distributed for duplication by each store. Supplementary materials and directions for ease of execution are included with each photograph. In this manner, all stores are assured of having similar high-quality displays. As a result, the company projects a uniform image and has control over the individual stores' displays. Similarly, display costs are decreased since high-salaried display persons are not needed to execute the displays in each store; a store manager can easily follow the simplified plan.

The trend indicates that chains will grow larger and the individual units will increase in size.

Supermarkets

The supermarket is a large departmentalized, self-service organization selling food, primarily, and other merchandise. The merchandise assortment has grown from the usual grocery, meat, poultry, and produce categories to include hardware, toys, hosiery, drugs, books, greeting cards, and so on. A supermarket may be independently owned, belong to a voluntary or cooperative chain, or be part of a regular chain organization. The greatest number of supermarkets belong to the third category. Emphasis on lower prices, parking facilities to customers, and the luxury of one-stop food shopping are some of the more important factors that lead to their success. A & P, Safeway, and Kroger Company are presently among the largest supermarket chains.

The Mail Order Retailer

Selection of merchandise from a catalog, ordering through the mail, and delivery by similar means are the major characteristics of the mail order house. The merchandise offering of some mail order houses is so large and diversified that rarely can one find as wide an assortment in a "merchandise-stocking" store. In addition to those retailers that sell exclusively by mail, a large percentage of the total sales of department and specialty stores can be attributed to this method of retailing. Montgomery Ward & Co., Spiegel, Inc., and Sears, Roebuck and Co. are leading mail order retailers. Sears presently enjoys the status of being the world's largest retailer. The more than 140,000 items now sold by Sears include mink stoles, and sculpture priced as high as $39,500. With the exception of food, liquor, and automobiles, almost any article can be bought from Sears.

Although the chain has moved retail stores closer to the people and has perhaps made buying through catalogs not as necessary as it was in earlier times when farmers and others in isolated areas depended heavily on mail order for merchandise, this method of doing business has not disappeared. Perhaps the large number of women in the work force results in less time for shopping and encourages mail order purchasing. As is evidenced by the great sales volume of mail order houses, this form of retailing is still important.

The Catalog Store

A companion business to the mail order retailer is the catalog store. This method of retailing involves the stocking of merchandise in "warehouse" stores where customers may come in for immediate receipt of goods or may order, by way of catalog, from their homes. The catalog store has grown significantly and has become another method of large scale retailing. The main feature of catalog retailing is price. At considerably lower prices than traditional retailers charge, consumers can purchase appliances, precious jewelry, housewares, cameras, and so on. One such company that is a giant in the field is Consumers Distributing with stores throughout Connecticut, New Jersey, New York, and California. Like the traditional retailers, they offer such services as charges, gift certificates, refunds, and exchanges.

Through a combination of in-store purchases and mail order, the catalog store is continuing to grow and become a major force in large scale retailing.

THE GREAT MERCHANTS

The general investigation of the history of the retail world and the examination of the widely diversified retail operations of today suggest that many great leaders and their organizations are responsible for the various approaches to satisfying the needs of the customer. While there are many areas of retailing that all merchants have in common, there are also practices peculiar to some organizations that distinguish them from the rest.

Macy's, whose size can be appreciated by considering the amazing figures for Herald Square in New York City, the main store, of 150,000 customers a day, 400,000 items in 168 selling departments, gross sales in excess of $200 million annually, and more than 2 million square feet of space, is the world's largest store. Its overall operation boasts more than fifty separate stores operating in six regional divisions, with plans for future expansion in additional units.

Service, competitive pricing, and innovation are the key factors contributing to the store's success. About three dozen comparison shoppers check competitors' prices and if Macy's are higher for the same merchandise, the price is lowered. Its own Bureau of Standards puts merchandise through rigid laboratory tests to make certain the needs of the consumer are met. Personal shoppers are made available to satisfy any customer's unusual requirements. The Thanksgiving Day Parade was a Macy's first, an official opening for the Christmas season. This organization was even the inspiration for a well-known motion picture, *Miracle on 34th Street.*

Perhaps no other store caters to a wealthier clientele nor carries the unusual merchandise assortment found in Neiman-Marcus. Its reputation was built by the free-spending customer. His and hers Beechcraft airplanes, respectively a seven-passenger $149,000 plane and a four-place $27,000 craft, were featured in the 1960 Christmas book. Two years later a genuine Chinese junk (boat) made in Hong Kong was offered F.O.B. Houston at $11,500. Eleven of them were sold. In 1965 this store offered an Aegean cruise for ten on a chartered yacht at $145,802. Continuing with its offer of unusual merchandise, the 1980 Christmas Book features such items as a Martin D-45 guitar priced at $9,500, a limited edition of Frank Davie's book "specially produced" at $7000, and the latest His and Hers gifts shown in Figure 1-2. In order to

FIGURE 1-2 A Pair of Young Ostriches ($1500) to Keep or Give to Your Favorite Zoo

Courtesy of Neiman-Marcus

increase its volume, it has added merchandise to satisfy the desires of the customer in the $25,000 income bracket. Spectacular service and fine merchandising have made Neiman-Marcus world renowned.

Filene's of Boston is one of the world's largest specialty shops. It operates two separate kinds of retailing enterprises under one roof. The unusual part of the organization is the basement operation. Other retailers have "bargain basements" and "budget basements," but none has the unique system of merchandising developed by Edward Filene. Merchandise is reduced weekly for 30 days, and at the end of this period whatever is unsold is given to charity. Separate buyers operating in all of the world's fashion centers purchase for the basement store. Merchandise from world-famous retailers and leading manufacturers are purchased and sold with the orginal labels; Nieman-Marcus and Saks Fifth Avenue labels are found in the basement at fractions of their original selling prices. Stores overstocked because of a bad season, or manufacturers who overproduce, look to Filene's to help them. This unusual merchandising policy sells so much merchandise that less than 1 percent is given away to charity.

In the food industry, A & P continues as one of the largest food retailers, with a few thousand individual units. In addition to selling to the consumer, A & P has the country's largest food-processing plant, operates fish canneries, bakes breads and cakes for its stores, and has coffee-roasting plants and a dairy plant. Besides obtaining its private-brand merchandise, the shopper can find all the nationally advertised labels. Its policy of courteous service and low prices is generally considered the reason for its tremendous success.

Henri Bendel, the store with "the street of specialized shops," features eight small shops with separate windows on the main floor to give the customer the feeling of individual, specialized retail operations. Each boasts a different decor. This different approach, inaugurated by Geraldine Stutz, transformed a losing business into one that is financially sound.

Brooks Brothers, the oldest men's shop in the United States, boasts a clientele of former presidents, statesmen, business executives, authors, etc. Its meticulous, conservative merchandise and the personal service given to customers are chiefly responsible for this continued success. While other retailers have employed the newer scientific methods of merchandising, the century-old traditions of Brooks Brothers are still successful.

Many other famous retailers are worth investigating, but the limited amount of space allows only the mentioning of their names and their distinguishing features.

Tiffany's, the world-famous jeweler, boasts jewelry and silver treasures ranging in price from a few dollars to more than a hundred thousand dollars; Lane Bryant caters to the customer generally forgotten, the stout woman; W & J Sloan is internationally known for furniture and interior decoration; Castro Convertibles are manufacturers and retailers of the "bed hidden within the sofa"; and Bergdorf Goodman is the rich woman's retreat on Fifth Avenue in New York, where haute couture is commonplace.

CURRENT TRENDS

While many retailing procedures and practices of the past are still in evidence today, no other period in history has seen the number of innovations and trends being explored by today's merchants. Through investigating these trends, one can realize how diversified retailing has become.

Franchising

In the arrangement known as *franchising,* an organization (the franchiser) that has developed a successful retail product or service sells to individuals (the franchisees) the right to engage in the business, provided they follow the established pattern. Because of the expertise of the franchiser, the probability of success for the individual opening such an operation is greater than if that entrepreneur ventured into a completely new independent enterprise. Most retailers agree that inexperience and incompetence account for the great majority of retail store failures. The franchiser offers such services as location analysis, tested managerial techniques, knowledgeable merchandising, training plans, financial instruction, and counseling in other pertinent areas. With these services provided by the franchiser, the risk of failure is greatly reduced. Franchising got its major start in 1898 in General Motors; today it accounts for more than 10 percent of the Gross National Product through 300,000 to 400,000 outlets. Carvel, Howard Johnson, Chicken Delight, International House of Pancakes, AAMCO Automotive Transmissions, Rexall Drug Co., Hickory Farms, and Baskin-Robbins 31 Flavor Stores are examples of franchise operations which bring to the consumer a variety of goods and services. An in-depth study of franchising will follow in the next chapter.

Automation

The purpose of automation in retailing is to reduce costs by saving personnel. Some examples of automation follow.

Automatic Vending Machines

Coin-operated machines continue to grow in number and dispense many products that were originally sold over the counter. Today, in addition to the usual merchandise found in these machines, such as newspapers and cigarettes, one may purchase cooked foods, flight insurance, women's hosiery, sandwiches, and other goods. The machines are particularly successful in areas where stores are unavailable—for example, at railroad stations and movie theaters. The vending machines offer the customer the opportunity to purchase at any time, whereas in the conventional retail store the hours for purchasing are limited. Since the consumer usually requires service for expensive merchandise, the vending machine is most successful for selling inexpensive commodities.

Automatic Stores

Today the automatic checkstand has been installed in some supermarkets. The bill is determined more quickly through the use of scanners, which pick up the coded prices on the goods without the necessity of cashier assistance. This results in a speedy and more accurate tally. Better inventory control will result in automatic orders being placed with the warehouse for the replenishment of stock. In addition, customers are, in some cases, able to have money automatically withdrawn from their checking accounts and transferred to the store's account when they present an identification card to the store's computer. Some stores automatically move the goods along a conveyor belt until it reaches the customer's car. With the introduction of the new automatic services, the supermarket is certainly moving toward more complete automation.

In Tokyo, an automatic, computerized supermarket has opened. It has ended shoplifting, mistakes by cashiers, and the long line of customers waiting at cash registers. Shoppers push their carts, with plastic cards attached to them, and do their purchasing by inserting their cards into slots located near the merchandise in the windows. Automatically, after each insert the food is released and the computer adds what has been purchased. When finished, the shopper is given a bill that itemizes all of the purchases made.

Electronic Data Processing

In most stores the routine clerical duties involved in inventory control and accounting procedures are being more efficiently handled through electronic data processing. In addition, the computer is being used as a tool by merchandisers to forecast sales, fashion, color, consumer trends, and patterns. Its impact on retailing is so great that a later chapter in this book is devoted entirely to electronic data processing.

Enclosed Shopping Centers

In an effort to add to the customer's comfort and accessibility to more stores, many shopping centers have enclosed their malls. The stores have the appearance of a huge unit selling a wide variety of merchandise under one roof. Customers can park their cars, enter the enclosed center, and move freely from store to store without being bothered by extreme hot or cold weather.

Today the trend is toward even larger enclosed malls. The direction has turned to multilevel malls that not only increase the number of stores in the malls but incorporate movie theaters, restaurants, exhibition halls, and other customer attractions in the structure.

Leased Departments

This is an arrangement whereby a store leases space to an individual or chain organization to operate a small business on the store's premises. The leased departments deal in merchandise or services that require specialized merchandising. Optics, travel agencies, beauty salons, food stands, and liquor sections are typical examples of leased departments.

Shift in Hours

Since most shopping is done by women, the growing number of them in the labor force has caused a shift in retail store hours. Many retailers open later in the day and/or add evening hours to the schedule. In many stores two shifts of employees are necessary to run the operation. In states where local laws permit, Sunday openings are common. Throughout the United States some operators of supermarkets are open 24 hours a day. This arrangement allows people to shop at any convenient time.

Research

The retailer, to meet competition and satisfy the customer's needs more efficiently, is greatly involved in research methods. Questionnaires, interviews, and fashion and traffic counts are some devices used to bring pertinent data to the retailer. By better understanding what the customer wants, management should be more efficient and thus more productive. Research procedures are discussed in more detail in a later chapter.

It should be evident that retailing is in a state of flux and perhaps only those willing to accept and make the necessary changes will be successful in future retailing.

Flea Markets

The opportunity for independents to engage in retailing continues to increase through the flea market boom. Throughout the United States, the introduction of flea markets has mushroomed into a successful form of business operation. Merchandise offerings have been expanded to deliver goods to consumers as diverse as those found in department stores. Hard goods, soft goods, specialty items, and foodstuffs are now commonplace at these markets. With the enormous quantities available, with acceptance by the consumer, and to the delight of manufacturers and wholesalers selling in large quantities, the flea markets hold the promise of becoming an important force in present and future retailing.

Multimerchandise Marts

With the success of the flea market, realtors are developing giant enclosed stores that are subdivided into ministores that feature a wide variety of household goods. Many now-defunct supermarkets are being converted into this very type of retail operation. For a fixed fee, independent merchants are offered space, electricity, security, and so forth. The hours are generally restricted to evenings and Saturdays so that people with other daily occupations can be part-time merchants. So successful is this type of operation that many of the independents are expanding into "stores" at more than one mart.

Featuring Women's Wear in the Traditional Men's Shop

Many men's shops across the United States have catered solely to the male clientele for all of their years of operation. Some have been looked upon as "sophisticated shops" that have portrayed the image equal to the snobbish private men's clubs. Today, a nationwide trend is underway to open the doors of many of these retail instituitions to woo the women counterpart of their male customer. Such fashionable menswear establishments as Brooks Brothers, Robert Todd, Harold's, Mr. Guy, Leslie & Co., Caroll & Co., Wilkes Bashford, and Barney's have all successfully expanded their merchandise assortment to include women's wear. From the conservative to the high fashion and from one coast to the other, the results have been astounding. The trend seems to be gaining momentum with more and more male shops looking to convey a male-female image.

Noncompeting Cooperative Advertising

Many retailers agree that the key to success is dependent upon continuous advertising. Small retailers who wish to participate but cannot because of budget limitations have started to advertise with noncompeting merchants specializing in identical merchandise. A prime example of this is the retail liquor operation in New York. Liquor stores have organized solely for the purpose of sharing advertising expense. Only one store in an area becomes part of the group to avoid direct competition. The members decide upon the advertisement in terms of merchandise and price and equally share in the expense of this type of advertising.

Warehouse Outlets

In certain product lines, retailers have begun to move in a direction other than what is considered traditional or conventional. At this point the operations have centered upon food and furniture. One organization, Levitz, has opened multimillion-dollar furniture warehouse operations from coast to coast. These operations offer the customers immediate delivery at lower prices and are beginning to compete heavily, in particular, with popular-price furniture retailers who take months to deliver and charge higher prices. The success of these operations has prompted many regular furniture merchants to operate warehouses similar to Levitz in out-of-the-way locations that do not necessarily compete with their more conventionally operated units. Bloomingdale's, W & J Sloan, Macy's, and Abraham & Straus are some stores that operate warehouse outlets. Most recently, the trend is moving into soft goods, with manufacturers operating their own warehouses for retail purchasing.

FUTURE RETAILING CONCEPTS

Not yet actually operational, but more than merely dreams, are many new concepts that retailers will be using in the future. The expected changes necessitated by both increases in operational expenses and shortages in qualified personnel may be any or all of the following.

Joint Training Centers

Aware that it is expensive to properly train retail personnel and dangerous to place untrained people on selling floors or other store areas, merchants are beginning to talk about the creation of cooperative training centers. The plan is not really far-fetched and is operational in the advertising field. In this way, stores could continue to train employees while reducing their expenses attributable to training.

Main Street Mall Conversion

It is obvious to knowledgeable merchants that consumers are flocking to malls for the conveniences they offer. Small merchants who occupy locations on main streets are, in surprising numbers, discussing the conversion of their locations into malls. In Miami Beach, Florida, merchants on the famed Lincoln Road have done so and have convinced the city to close the area to automobile traffic. Retailing seems to be moving even closer to developing such areas resembling the giant enclosed malls. It is expected that merchants will alter their shopping streets not only to prohibit auto traffic, but also to provide interstore connections for easier access. This will somewhat eliminate the need for complete enclosure under one roof while still affording the shopper the luxury of shopping in areas that are free from the discomforts caused by cold, rain, extreme heat, and so forth.

Employee Sharing

As impossible as it might seem to many retailers, there are indications that a sharing of employees, particularly salespeople, might become a reality. The arrangement is conceivable for two reasons. First, peak sales hours are not the same in all stores—sales personnel in one store may have not much to do at the same time another store desperately needs more help. Thus, an employee sharing plan could be arranged to accommodate two or more employers' needs. Second, with the cost of transacting business becoming increasingly higher, this new arrangement could minimize expenses while maximizing profits. It might be suggested that part-time employees working exclusively for one retailer could accomplish the same goals as would be found in an employee-sharing plan. Most experienced retailers will agree, however, that those guaranteed with full-time work for which they can earn a full salary are more committed than the part-timer.

These innovative ideas, along with many others that will eventually be put to the test, will continue to assist retailers in the challenges they have yet to face.

Selling Via Cable Television

Although the practice is in its infancy, retailers have started to buy time on cable television expressly for the purpose of showing and selling products to consumers. This is not to be confused with the sponsoring of a program. The merchandise *is* the program. An item is featured, a price is quoted, and a telephone number for purchase is displayed. Upon calling, consumers may have any questions answered and at that time make arrangements for delivery.

CAREER OPPORTUNITIES

Unlike so many fields today, retailing offers the college student a variety of jobs in a wide range of institutions. With the growth of the chain organization and the increasing department store branch operations, employment opportunities are available in just about every part of the country. This coupled with the opportunity for operating one's own small business makes retailing an area of great career potential.

According to numerous personnel directors in leading chain stores, department stores, specialty stores, and resident buying offices, the personal qualities found to be most important for success are initiative, imagination, enthusiasm, and intelligence. It is hoped that students specializing in retailing will also bring to the employer the technical knowledge they have acquired in the classroom. The following discussion includes those positions one may expect to secure upon entering the field and those positions that could be reached within a few years. Separate attention will be paid to large retail organizations and small store opportunities, plus those available in the resident buying office, an institution that assists retailers with their merchandising problems. The information is intended to be a general overview of various opportunities.

The Large Retail Organization

Although students are often fascinated with the prospects of ownership, it is employment in the large retail operations that provides the setting for most retailing careers. This is not to say that the prospects of self-employment are out of reach, or that working for a small store is not possible, but those routes do not generally provide the opportunities offered by the industry leaders. Attention will be paid later in the chapter to those career opportunities, as well as those in a major retail-related enterprise, the resident buying office.

While merchandising is most often the area of interest expressed by people who are pursuing retailing careers, numerous other positions are available to prospective employees. With the continuous expansion through branches and other units, the department stores and specialty chains offer significant opportunities in personnel management, warehousing, operations, data processing, sales promotion, finance, control, and so forth.

The initial appointment within the company structure varies from organization to organization, with the most progressive stores utilizing an executive training or executive development program. Employees are nonetheless hired at every level, with the requirements for each position varied according to the specifications of the job. For example, a security guard will not enter as an executive trainee, nor will a potential buying prospect gain employment as a buyer.

While exact titles of similar positions differ from one retail organization to another, all large retailing institutions offer similar jobs. Careers in the major categories will be explored with commentary on particular jobs.

Merchandising

Without question, stores cannot function without the proper merchandise assortment to tempt the customer to buy. Such descriptive words as *glamour* and *excitement* are often present in conversations of would-be retailers when discussing merchandising and retailing. Since merchandising in its broadest definition includes numerous job titles, it is obvious why so many college graduates seek employment in one of these areas.

The best organized department and specialty chains operate executive development programs that provide both classroom and on-the-job training with a concentration on merchandising. The route that one takes in these programs to achieve the coveted buyer's job, or the length of time it takes for such achievement, varies from one company to another and according to one's own ability. Figure 1-3 depicts the career path of the executive development trainee at R.H. Macy & Co., Inc., in search of a merchandising career. The chart describes a typical advancement pattern but intentionally omits the time frame. The time spent in each position depends upon individual ability. It should be noted that the arrows stop at the buyer level. From that particular point it is assumed that people will move in almost any direction based upon such factors as personal desires, capabilities, and openings. Although the illustration is that of R.H. Macy & Co., Inc., the jobs, except for variation in title, are similar to those in most large retail operations. It is of value to use Figure 1-3 not only to depict opportunities for career growth at Macy's, but also to examine the various entry positions and eventual areas of merchandising responsibility afforded the aspiring retail executive.

Sales Promotion

In order to promote the store's image and to capture its share of the consumer market, major department and specialty chains engage in a variety of promotional endeavors. Careers in sales promotion generally attract those in-

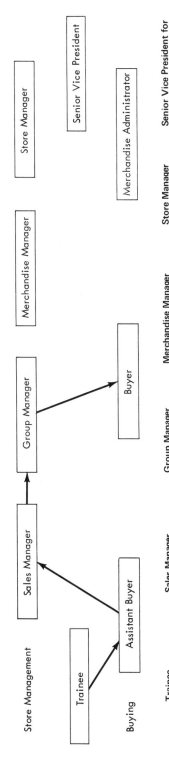

Store Management

Trainee → Sales Manager → Group Manager → Merchandise Manager → Store Manager → Senior Vice President

Buying

Assistant Buyer → Buyer → Merchandise Administrator

Trainee

General orientation to the retailing industry and the specifics of our operations through both classroom work and extensive on the job experience.

Sales Manager

Responsible for running a complete selling area in a store, including merchandise presentation, supervision of sales personnel, customer service, inventory control and all other aspects of running a business.

Assistant Buyer

Learning to be a buyer through assisting a buyer in planning, acquiring, pricing, distributing, and promoting a category of merchandise for all stores of a division.

Group Manager

Responsible for executing merchandising plans for several departments in a store and reaching sales goals; supervises, trains, and develops sales managers.

Buyer

Responsible for planning, selecting, acquiring, pricing, distributing and promoting merchandise for all stores of a division. With experience, buying responsibilities increase.

Merchandise Manager

Similar to group manager's position but with responsibility for expanded merchandise categories, coordinates the efforts among different departments; acts as major liaison between store executives and buyers.

Store Manager

Responsible for the total operation of a store, including merchandising operations and personnel, responsible for community relations, overall image of the store, and providing leadership in planning and goal setting.

Merchandise Administrator

Responsible for conceptualizing and planning overall buying in several related merchandise classifications for a division; coordinates, develops and evaluates the work of buyers, with responsibility for profits.

Senior Vice President for Merchandising

Responsible for developing and overseeing divisional objectives and policies in buying merchandise planning, advertising, promotion, and systems for large sectors of the business; direct responsibility for the overall profitability of those sectors.

FIGURE 1-3 Career Path and Job Descriptions

23

FIGURE 1-4 RETAIL SALES PROMOTION JOBS

Advertising Manager	Display Director	Special Events Manager	Publicity Manager
Art director	Window	Fashion	Public
Copy chief	display person	coordinator	relations
Copywriter	Interior	Fashion scout	director
Layout artists	display person		
Merchandise artists	Signmaker		
Production manager			

dividuals who possess both creative and artistic ability. Generally, the opportunities focus upon four specific areas—advertising, display, special events, and publicity. Employees in these positions must have a keen sense of artistic expertise, a command of the language, and an awareness of those devices that capture customer attention. Figure 1-4 shows a representation of jobs associated with promotion in the major department and specialty stores in the United States. Each area is headed by a manager who has ultimate responsibility for the positions shown in the table.

Store Operations

The responsibility of managing the day-to-day activities of the physical operation of the large department and specialty stores belongs to store operations or store management. Positions associated with the movement of goods, the recruitment of personnel, customer service, purchasing of supplies, and so forth normally are part of store operations. The range and complexity of these positions are vast. Some require only a willingness to work, while others re-

FIGURE 1-5 STORE OPERATIONS CAREERS

Personnel manager—Oversees and directs all personnel operations
Training director—Establishes training programs for employees
Employee evaluator—Evaluates employees for purposes of advancement
Purchasing agent—Purchases supplies that store needs to run operation
Security chief—Manages security staff and recommends merchandise safeguards
Adjustment manager—Handles customer adjustments and manages staff
Customer service manager—Has responsibility for directing customer services
Receiving manager—Manages and controls all aspects of receiving
Workroom manager—Has responsibility for such areas as clothing alterations
Computer programmer—Writes programs to fit needs of management
Systems analyst—Analyzes and evaluates computer systems
Traffic manager—Directs flow of goods from receiving to selling floor

FIGURE 1-6 JOB PROSPECTS, 1980s—SELECTED CATEGORIES

Job Classification	Percentage Change
Engineers	+ 22.5
Math specialists	+ 28.1
Computer specialists	+ 30.8
Teachers	− 3.7
Buyers, purchasing agents	+ 44.3
Administrators	+ 18.7
Advertising personnel	+ 42.4
Keypunch operators	− 26.7
Billing clerks	+ 59.9
Sales managers, retail	+ 54.0

Source: United States Labor Department's Bureau of Labor Statistics

quire the carefully honed skills necessary for a top flight manager. Figure 1-5 depicts various types of employment in store operations divisions.

Control

In a time when business transactions are becoming more complex and the emphasis on customer purchases is becoming more credit oriented, the number of careers in the control area is increasing. Accountants, bookkeepers, auditors, credit interviewers, charge account authorizers, and so forth, are individuals whose abilities and expertise contribute to the financial stability of the store. As the store's accounting and credit practices become more diversified, this area promises an increase in job potential.

The United States Labor Department's Bureau of Statistics Research indicates a growing need for retail employees in the 1980s. The job prospects for retail-oriented positions show enormous prospective growth when compared with other fields, many of which are showing growth, while others show a decline. Figure 1-6 shows the percentage growth or decline expected over the next ten years.

Three of the four classifications with the greatest growth potential are in retailing or directly related fields. The fourth, and leader with a potential of 59.9 percent growth, the billing clerk, is certainly a position in retailing that will increase in importance with the steady increase of credit purchasing.

Small Stores

The opportunities available in the small stores are quite limited. One important reason is that the number of successful small store operations has been declining; the chain store is offering too much competition. Another reason for limited opportunity at this level is that small store owners are either unwilling to follow the newer techniques of retail management or the costs involved in securing the services of a knowledgeable graduate are often prohibitive.

The only likely significant place in small store retailing today for the graduate is as the eventual owner of a business. While the competition of the chains has made it difficult to open and successfully operate a retail business, franchising has provided a chance for the independent retailer. In a franchise operation, an individual with enough capital might be able to operate a small store by putting to practice the theory learned in school.

Resident Buying Offices

These institutions, located away from the store's premises, generally serve in an advisory capacity to retailers. Sometimes, on authority from the stores, they place merchandise orders. Their main job is to do the preliminary work for the store buyers. Graduates of retailing programs find the resident buying office appealing as a place of employment. The regular hours without evenings and Saturdays make this job desirable. A more detailed discussion of these offices will appear in a later chapter.

For those who are serious about embarking upon a retailing career, the opportunities are certainly available. As has already been discussed, the greatest opportunity is afforded by big business. Not only do the large retailers provide excellent training programs for managerial hopefuls, but also the greatest variety of positions, due to the specialization of the various jobs. This does not, however, rule out self-employment or a career in a small company. The former requires sufficient capital and experience that many aspirants do not sufficiently possess, and the latter, little opportunity for advancement. Thus, both of these career paths are risky. Those who wish to pursue careers in these directions should be aware of the pitfalls.

Whatever the direction in retailing one is apt to take, one must understand that in order to achieve success, a real commitment must be made. Having made this commitment, one can expect many rewards from such a career.

- Advancement is rapid and is generally dependent upon one's ability.
- Salaries, although relatively low at the start, often reach the $75,000 and above range for top store management.
- Age is not a factor in retailing. The young are sought for management positions, while older indiviuals are not "put out to pasture."
- Retailing has always been a prime career for both men and women.
- Retailing trains people in modern business management techniques, which can be applied to any other management career.
- The vastness of retailing offers mobility from coast to coast. There is opportunity without individuals being limited to narrow geographic locations.

Action for the Independent Retailer

Too often, retailing textbooks and discussions by educators and practitioners alike focus on large-scale retailing. While it is true that the vast majority of retailing operations are the large organizations and that many of their practices may be adapted to the smallest in the industry, the small independent retailer and the problems associated with being an independent are usually glossed over or totally ignored by the professionals.

As we have learned in this chapter, there is still a place for the independent in this vast business, and the opportunities for self-employment are stable and, in some areas, growing. For all of these reasons, each chapter will feature a concluding section on Action for the Independent Retailer, *which will highlight those areas in which even the smallest could benefit. For example, the computer is looked upon as a tool for big business. The small independent can make limited use of such technology at modest expense, which will enable the conducting of a more efficient operation. In all of the areas such as merchandising, buying, and personnel, attention will be paid to the small retail organization.*

IMPORTANT POINTS IN THE CHAPTER

1. *The growth of retailing in America can be traced from colonial trading posts, where barter was used as the process for exchange, to the retailing giants of the present day.*

2. *The history of retailing parallels the growth of American consumer demand. As the society became wealthier and more sophisticated, retailers responded by offering a greater variety of goods and increasing the size and the number of locations at which such goods could be purchased.*

3. *To satisfy today's consumer, goods are presently offered at retail in a great variety of stores featuring an enormous range of goods and services.*

4. *A recent addition to large-scale retailing has been the catalog store, which is a companion business to the mail order retailer. It offers immediate receipt of merchandise in housewares, precious jewelry, appliances, and so forth at below traditional store prices.*

5. *Service, competitive pricing, and innovation are the key factors contributing to the successful growth of individual retailers. This may be illustrated by tracing the history of any of the retailing giants, such as Macy's, Nieman-Marcus, A & P, or Montgomery Ward.*

6. *Small-scale retailing is on the increase with the emergence and success of flea markets. Those wishing to operate independent ''stalls'' can do so in these sales arenas with a minimum investment.*

7. *Retailing of the future will be characterized by an increase in franchising, wider use of automation, and the increased use of shopping centers.*

8. *The use of research as a tool to remove unnecessary risk from retailing has become important in recent years and will become increasingly important in the future.*

9. *The challenge that retailing holds for the future will require many innovative ideas. Some that are likely to be tried include joint employee training centers, main street mall conversions, and the sharing of employees.*

10. *In comparison with other fields of employment, retailing careers hold great promise for individuals in the 1980s. While other fields show decline or little potential for career opportunities, retailing positions show a projected percentage increase of 44.3 for buyers and 54.0 for managers.*

REVIEW QUESTIONS

1. What form of retailing was the direct outgrowth of the trading post? What was the reason for its origin?

2. Contrast the general store with the specialty store. In which would the independent retailer more likely be successful?

3. What are the differences between the voluntary and cooperative chains?

4. Briefly discuss the independent retailer's opportunity in the flea market.

5. How does the department store method of management differ from chain store management?

6. Define: branch store, twig store.

7. Into what lines of merchandise have mail order houses expanded to warrant their continued success?

8. In what way has the catalog store expanded upon the mail order house concept?

9. Describe the unique basement operation of Filene's in Boston.

10. How does selling via cable TV differ from normal advertising on network TV?

11. Discuss the impact of automation on retailing.

12. How do the buying positions at the department store and resident buying office differ?

13. What are the opportunities available to individuals wishing to establish their own retail stores?

14. Besides food items, supermarkets have expanded their merchandising into different lines. What are they?

15. Even with improved transportation facilities, mail order retailing continues to grow. How do you explain this?

16. Define leased departments.

17. Why are leased department operations actively sought by large retail organizations?

18. After some "losing" seasons, which New York retailer changed its operation to a successful one featuring "a street of shops"? Why do you think the change was so successful?

19. In which types of locations are vending machines most productive? Why?

20. Discuss the trends in the shift in retail hours.

21. What are the opportunities for retailing graduates of the 80s in comparison with careers in teaching, engineering, and administration?

22. Describe some advantages of careers in retailing.

23. Do you believe retailers can satisfactorily share employees?

CASE PROBLEMS

CASE PROBLEM 1

Jane Peters, a retailing major, is graduating from a two-year college. She is a C+ student and is involved in many extracurricular activities, including the vice-president of DECA (Distributive Education Clubs of America). Her work experience has been as a part-time salesperson in the men's college shop at a local department store since entering college, and as a stock person in a supermarket during her last year in high school.

During the past two weeks Jane was interviewed on campus by representatives of three retail organizations for possible employment after graduation. The offers were as follows:

1. The first opportunity is placement in the executive training program at a well-known department store with several branches. Training would be for approximately six months on a job rotational plan in the main departments of the store, coupled with classroom instruction. Her salary would be $240 per week for that period. At the end of six months a permanent assignment would be made, with an increase in salary to $275.

2. The personnel director of a giant supermarket chain offered Jane an assistant manager's job in a local unit of the chain. She would work directly under the store manager, assisting him with employee scheduling, purchase requisitions, handling of complaints, and so forth. The salary is $175 the first year, $195 for the second year, and as a store manager, $225 the third year.

3. The third opportunity is in a large shoe chain with 600 stores throughout the country. One year of selling shoes is a requirement of all new employees, at a salary of $110 plus 2% commission. After that period there is assignment as an assistant store manager at a salary of $135 plus 2% on all shoes she sells. Her other duties would be to assist with window displays, reorder merchandise, be responsible when the manager is away, and so on. After two or three years as an assistant manager, assignment as manager is given to qualified individuals.

QUESTIONS

1. What aspects of the jobs should Jane carefully consider before making a final determination?

2. Considering the important factors, which job would you advise Jane to take?

CASE PROBLEM 2

Paul Matthews has worked for the past five years at the Elegant Lady, a fashionable, large specialty shop. After one year as an assistant department manager and two as a department manager, he was promoted to assistant buyer of active sportswear, a position he still holds at a salary of $250 per week. Three months ago Paul inherited $30,000. He has always dreamed of owning his own retail store and now, with the money he acquired, he might be able to realize his dream. After some investigation these two propositions, both fitting his finances, seem most appealing:

1. A small store located in an active shopping center is available to lease for the purpose of opening a ladies' specialty shop. The store is equipped with air conditioning but requires counters, wall cases, and so forth. The shopping center presently does not have the type of operation envisioned by Matthews. The workday is flexible in that the other stores in the center do not have uniform hours. The number of employees needed, the price range of merchandise to be carried, the store policies, and so forth, will be established by Matthews. He will be his own boss and can finally operate in a manner that pleases him.

2. "Petite Lady," a franchise organization specializing in clothing for the short female, has a new location available in the city's downtown shopping area. There are presently 70 similar units in the organization, which began its operation five years ago. They expect to complete an additional 75 stores within the next five years. The stores are all open daily from 9:30 to 6:00 and two evenings until 9:30 P.M. All merchandise is purchased from the franchiser and the rules and regulations set forth by the company must be followed. For the first two years $1,000 a month is expected as a minimum to the individual owner; after that the earnings will probably increase, as is evidenced by many other stores in the group.

QUESTIONS

1. What are the advantages and disadvantages of both situations?

2. How do the opportunities of ownership compare with his present job?

3. Which course of action should Paul Matthews take?

2 *franchising*

BEHAVIORAL OBJECTIVES

Upon completion of this chaper the student should be able to

1. *Define franchising and give examples of franchising operations.*
2. *Identify seven different types of franchises.*
3. *List and discuss eight advantages of franchising to the franchisee.*
4. *List and discuss six disadvantages of franchising to the franchisee.*
5. *List and discuss four benefits of franchising to the franchiser.*
6. *Write an essay explaining areas of conflict between franchiser and franchisee.*

INTRODUCTION

In each chapter of the text the authors have discussed the application of the principles involved to the small independent retailer. Franchising, the subject matter of this chapter, is almost exclusively concerned with small business. The possibilities for an individual to become involved in franchising are so varied that a deal can be made for as little as $1000 (Tidy Car) initial outlay to as much as several million dollars (Kampgrounds of America). Even the more expensive possibilities can be heavily mortgaged, considerably bringing down the capital requirements.

There is nothing new in the concept of franchising. It is likely that this type of agreement existed in America during colonial times. Rapid growth began after World War II, when industry grew to enormous proportions. In large part this expansion was due to the returning servicemen, some with accumulated savings, many taking advantage of the financing available through the Veterans Administration. They were eager, after years of rigid army discipline, to be their "own bosses."

The major problem faced by these young men was their lack of business experience. Their few mature years had been spent in the service, and most of them had never held full-time jobs. To tap this huge sum of money and vast store of ambition, many established business organizations undertook the franchising of their products. They offered proven products, big business "know-how," and financial help in return for a considerable expansion of their profits. The result has been a continuing boom in franchised sales that has increased in volume each year. Although statistics are not available, it is believed that franchised sales are in excess of $300 billion annually, arising from some 500 thousand franchised outlets. Since this represents about 10 percent of all American business, it is obvious that the franchising industry is one of considerable importance to the American economic scene. The amounts indicated do not represent only new franchises: automobile agencies and gasoline stations, which were franchised before World War II, are responsible for a large share of these statistics. But a glance at the business-opportunities section of any newspaper indicates that the franchising boom is still gaining momentum. Potential franchisers should, however, be aware of the risks involved in this type of venture. To proceed with caution is the best advice a prospective franchisee could follow.

DEFINITION

Because of the great variety of franchising agreements, it is difficult to define a franchise. It is estimated that there are between 2,000 and 4,000 companies offering franchising deals, and each company's contract is different. The broadest definition is one given by the Small Business Administration:

"A franchise contract is a legal agreement to conduct a given business in accordance with prescribed operating methods, financing systems, territorial domains, and commission fees. It holds out the offer of individual ownership while following proven management practices. The holder is given the benefit of the franchiser's experience and help in choice of location, financing, marketing, record keeping, and promotional techniques. The business starts out with an established product or service reputation. It is organized and operated with the advantage of 'name' and standardization."

This definition contains the great amount of information that a textbook definition should. However, all franchising agreements do not include every item mentioned. For example, many franchisers make their profit by selling the product to the franchisee, others profit by charging a commission on all franchisee sales. Only careful examination of the particular contract will indicate the agreements therein.

TYPES OF FRANCHISE ARRANGEMENTS

Conventional

This type of arrangement is usually broken down into two types, both involving varying degrees of geographical coverage.

The *territorial franchise* gives the holder the privilege of enjoying an "override" on sales of all the units within a particular area. The area might be confined to a large city, an entire state, or even a section of the country. Frequently the holder also assumes the responsibility of training and setting up the various operators of subfranchisees within the given area, which may encompass several counties or states. It is not unusual for the operating franchisee never to come in direct contact with the parent organization, but rather to deal entirely with the owner of the territorial franchise. Tastee Freeze and Service Master are typical of territorial franchises.

The *operating franchise* is held by the independent operator within any given territory who runs his or her own business within the given area allotted by the franchise (often conferred by the territorial franchiser). The operator deals either directly or indirectly with the parent organization. Such units as McDonald's and Carol's Drive Ins offer this type of arrangement. (See Figure 2-1.)

Mobile

The mobile franchise usually involves the same arrangement as the conventional franchise except that the franchisee dispenses a product or service from a moving vehicle. This vehicle is either owned by the franchisee or leased from the parent company. Tastee Freeze, a franchiser of soft ice cream stands, had such an arrangement but discontinued it after heavy losses were incurred. However, such companies as Snap-On Tools have found this arrangement very successful. (See Figure 2-2.)

Distributorship

Under this arrangement the franchisee takes title to various types of goods and further distributes them to subfranchisees. The distributor usually has exclusive coverage of a rather wide geographical area and acts as a supply house for the units that carry the company's product(s). Many firms in the appliance field operate on this basis. Eureka and the Nissen Trampoline Company operate distributorships.

Coownership

This occurs where a large capital outlay is needed. The franchiser and franchisee share in the investment and then divide the profits. Many firms in the food service industry utilize such plans, including Aunt Jemima's Pancake Houses and Denny's Restaurants.

Comanagement

In this case the franchiser usually controls the major part of the investment. The investor-manager is allowed to share proportionately in the profits. An increase in sales volume increases the owner-manager's share. This acts as an

FIGURE 2-1　Kentucky Fried Chicken—A Conventional Franchise

FIGURE 2-2　Mister Softee—A Mobile Franchise

35

incentive to further promote the firm's business. Several motel chains operate on this basis. Travelodge and Holiday Inn are examples.

Lease

In this arrangement the franchiser either backs up or takes out a lease on a satisfactory location, often receiving a profit on the rental income paid by the franchisee. Though this plan is seldom representative of the total franchise package, it is often utilized in conjunction with other stipulations. Many of the franchisers within the food service industry incorporate this plan into their overall formula.

Licensee

This again represents an arrangement often used in conjunction with others. Under this plan the franchisee is allowed to use the franchiser's trademarks, business techniques, advertising layouts, and so forth. Normally, however, the company does not provide the product but instructs the franchisee as to where it might be obtained. Often the franchiser has an agreement with a national supplier who will supply the various products to the franchisee at a specific price.

Manufacturing

In this arrangement a parent company will franchise a firm to manufacture its product(s) using prescribed techniques and materials. Often, distance and shipping costs necessitate this arrangement. The franchisee not only manufactures but also distributes the product, utilizing the marketing techniques of the parent firm.

Service

Here the franchiser sets forth prescribed patterns by which a franchise will supply a professional service. Employment agencies and any number of other service-type businesses fall within this category. An example of a service franchise is Lawn-A-Mat, a lawn preparation company.

It should be noted that many franchising firms do not fall within one specific category. Indeed, most firms offer more than one type of arrangement and exhibit a great degree of flexibility according to the situation. Counter-offers by prospective franchisees are not unusual, especially with regard to the more expensive franchises involving large capital outlays. In addition, some firms are in a constant state of reorganization in adapting their plans to the needs of the market.

An analysis of the various franchising techniques is made even more difficult in view of the increasing number of new firms that are entering the industry.

COSTS OF FRANCHISING

The cost of getting into a franchising operation varies as widely as the number of franchising possibilities available. It may run from about $1,000 for Water Care to more than $500,000 for McDonald's. It would be a mistake to believe that the higher the cost of the contract, the more successful the operation. For example, a Fort Lauderdale, Florida, outlet of Service Master, begun in 1956 at a cost of $2,500, now employs forty-five salespersons and grosses more than $500,000 per year.

HOW TO FIND A FRANCHISER

Finding a franchise deal is relatively simple. With the growth of the franchising industry there is considerable competition among franchisers in finding interested franchisees. This had led to a great deal of advertising, as evidenced by the business-opportunities section of most newspapers, which contain ads for many types of franchises. In addition, various organizations run franchise shows at which prospective franchisees are given an opportunity to discuss deals with a wide variety of possible franchisers. The *Franchise Annual*, a trade publication, lists scores of shows in major cities throughout the country.

HOW TO FIND A FRANCHISEE

Finding the right franchisee is a serious problem for the parent company. The success of the parent company depends upon the success of the outlets. Finding a person who will be successful is much more difficult than signing a contract. The careful screening process that is required to ensure success can be expensive. For example, a large food chain placed a $14,000 advertisement to recruit franchisees. Of the fifty responses, thirty-eight prospects were reviewed. Final contracts were signed by just two people. The cost of advertising alone was $7,000 per franchisee!

Not all franchisers recruit exclusively by advertising. Chicken Delight, Inc., for instance, finds franchisees among the relatives, friends, and customers of existing operators.

THE FRANCHISEE

Before going into a franchising contract, prospective franchisees should consider their own qualifications. The Small Business Administration suggests that the prospect ask such questions as the following:

1. Are you qualified, in terms of the capital and special qualifications needed, for the deal?
2. Are you willing to accept the franchiser's supervision and to abide by the rules and regulations that the franchiser requires? These can be real problems for independent-minded people who are in business for themselves.
3. Why would you want a franchised business rather than one you can start entirely on your own? Essentially, the franchisee splits the profits with the franchiser. Moreover, expansion possibilities are strictly limited by some franchisers.
4. Can you afford to be without income during the training and setting-up period? Going into business is a giant step. Selecting the correct format for oneself adds to the complications.

THE FRANCHISE CONTRACT

Franchise contracts vary according to the franchiser. In many cases it is not a fixed document but one that is changed to fit each situation. The contract is a binding legal agreement that may be very complicated to the uninformed, and since the success and happiness of the franchisee depends in large part upon the content of the document, the contract must never be signed without legal advice. Before the contract is approved, the franchisee must consider the following vital areas:

Nature of the Company

1. Has the firm been in business long enough to determine its successfulness?
2. Does it have the financial capability to stand behind its outlets?
3. Is it selective in choosing its franchisees? The more selective the firm, the better are the chances that one will succeed by associating with it.
4. What are the reactions of the other franchisees to having committed themselves?
5. How many of the outlets are company owned?

The Product

1. To what extent is it available and where?
2. What is its present status in the market?
3. To what degree is it unique?
4. Is it a repeat item?
5. Who manufactures it?
6. What is its legal status?
7. Where is it sold?

8. Is it patented?
9. Is it seasonal and to what degree?
10. Is it highly perishable?
11. What is the time element involved in getting it into a saleable state?

The Territory

1. Is it in a growing market area?
2. Is it completely and accurately defined?
3. Does it assure exclusive representation?
4. Is it subject to seasonal fluctuations?
5. Is it a highly competitive area?
6. Is it above or below the statewide average per capital income level?
7. What kind of people make up the majority of the population?

The Contract

1. Are there any prior verbal agreements that failed to show up in the written contract?
2. Is it renewable and is there a fee involved?
3. Can it be terminated? Sold? Transferred?
4. Does it assign responsibility with regard to any lawsuits that might result involving the product?
5. Does it specify all the financial conditions of the arrangement? Fee? Royalty? Is this amount fixed?
6. Is there a quota clause with regard to sales?
7. Is there a purchase clause with regard to the parent company's products?
8. Does it allow any outside business interests?
9. Does it have a return privilege permitting the holder to return unsaleable merchandise?
10. Does it provide that the holder pay part of promotional costs?
11. Is it beneficial to both parties?

Assistance

1. Is there a comprehensive training program?
2. Will the franchiser aid in such things as site selection and lease arrangements? Is there a fee involved?
3. Will guidance be given with advance planning for store opening?
4. Will you receive merchandise buying and inventory control training?
5. Will you be assisted with financing arrangements?
6. Will follow-up counseling and financial statement analysis be rendered?

In view of the preceding questions, it is evident that evaluating a franchise offer is a difficult task. The disclosure rule that the Federal Trade Commission put into effect in 1979 goes a long way in answering some of these questions. The disclosure rule will be discussed later in this chapter.

THE FRANCHISEE'S VIEWPOINT

Surveys have found that a large majority of American working people would like to be in business for themselves. Coupled with this information is the fact that three out of five people who begin small businesses fail in the first two years. The two principle reasons for small business failures are lack of business experience and insufficient capital.

Advantages

1. Franchise training programs, which run from several days to several weeks, provide business know-how to prospective franchisees. This permits the franchisee to go into a business with no previous experience.
2. Since the success of the franchised outlet is to the benefit of the parent company, the franchisee can expect support in almost every possible way.
3. A franchised business generally requires less original cash investment for fixtures and equipment than a conventional business, thanks to the credit help available from the franchiser.
4. Operating cash requirements are less since franchise inventories are less diversified than nonfranchised inventories, and the terms under which such merchandise is purchased are generally liberal.
5. The vast purchasing power of the parent company results in smaller costs and higher gross profits for the franchisee. (Some franchisees will argue this point.)
6. The advertising and promoting done by large franchisers offer benefits far in excess of those available to conventional businesses.
7. Prepared displays, kits, and other up-to-date merchandise assistance are constantly being prepared by the home office and distributed to their outlets.
8. The parent company, keenly aware of competition, maintains a constant program of research and development aimed at improving their product or service.
9. Constant assistance in the form of periodic visits by experts is available to the franchiser for normal business advice or special problems.
10. The large size of the franchising organization frequently results in savings in such areas as insurance, hospitalization, and retirement.
11. Help in record keeping, tax advice—in short, assistance in the multitude of areas that frequently plague the small business—are available at no cost.
12. Many franchisers offer scientific help in site selection.

While it is not the purpose of this book to go into detail in any of the areas of parent company help, the following illustration will indicate the depth of the location analysis performed by Mister Donut. It is part of a five-page preliminary investigation, called the "survey report."

1. The main street
2. The number of lanes in the adjacent highway
3. Whether there are dividers
4. Speed limits

5. Stop signs and stop lights
6. One-way streets
7. Traffic count
8. Anticipated highway changes
9. Foot traffic, heavy? Light?
10. Does traffic back up at peak hours? When?
11. Proportion of women in cars
12. Trucks
13. Proportion of local versus long-distance or out-of-state cars
14. Other businesses in the area
15. Schools
16. Religion by denominations
17. Population data
18. Housing data
19. Income data
20. Nearest competition
21. Summary of zoning regulations
22. Real estate taxes, on land alone? With building? Anticipated?
23. Utilities available
24. Visibility of the location from all directions; hills; corners
25. Position of neighboring buildings, feet of setback
26. Space for Mister Donut signs

It should be pointed out that this is merely the preliminary location report and by no means the total amount of data on which the location decision is based. Remember, the success of the franchiser depends upon the success of its outlets.

While the advantages to be derived from operating a franchise are considerable, the franchisee must in one way or another pay for them. The following are some of the major dissatisfactions expressed by many franchisees:

Disadvantages

1. The costs are too high. Many franchisees feel that the fees, prices for supplies, and other required charges are exorbitant. In many instances it is felt that profits could be increased if the franchiser could be eliminated. This logic is questionable since it rarely takes the advantages of the system into account. At the present time there is a class action suit (potentially 2600 McDonald's Corp. franchisees) charging that McDonald's illegally requires their franchisees to purchase only Coca-Cola rather than a different, perhaps cheaper, cola brand. The suit further charges that franchisees are forced to lease the land and building from a realty company affiliated with McDonald's at an unusually high rent. It will be some time before the suit works its way through the courts. The result will have a considerable impact, since it could lead to other charges in the fran-

chise contract. For example, if the franchisees win, will they be able to sue to change the product or marketing system as well? Would the resulting change in standards be helpful or harmful to the franchisees? After all, their success is based on customer acceptance of a specific product and system.

2. Many complaints center around the decisions made in far-off home offices with little or no understanding of the conditions at the local outlets. Thus, policies that benefit the majority of the outlets may be harmful to a few locations. As with many large centralized organizations, rigidity can be a serious problem.

3. Although franchisers know that their ultimate success depends upon the success of their franchisees, they question the amount of success. There is, after all, a certain amount of profit to be divided up between franchiser and franchisee. How that pie is divided is largely in the hands of the franchiser. Consequently, decisions that affect the profit generally favor the franchiser.

4. The franchising contract is the source of many complaints. This document is frequently long, complicated, and not fully understood by the franchisee. One of the principal problems is termination of the franchise. Some franchisees complain that their contract can be terminated for two reasons. One, as expected, is failure. The other is success, in which case the franchiser might wish to take over a lucrative location to run it as a company-owned unit. Even in cases in which the contract states that termination can only be affected for "good cause," the problem of defining "good cause" is difficult. What constitutes late payment? One day? One week? What about poor management? Who is to decide? Some states have passed legislation to control termination, but efforts to pass a national law through Congress have failed. Since no legislation can specifically cover all possible causes of termination, it is likely that the courts will continue to be an important factor in this area.

THE FRANCHISER'S VIEWPOINT

As is the case with the franchisee, the parent company benefits from a franchise operation in many important aspects.

The franchiser, by supplying a large amount of the capital needed for building new units, permits rapid expansion without decreasing the ownership of the company (as would be the case if capital were to be raised by the sale of stock), or its working capital. The latter is true because of the financing supplied by the franchisee.

A serious problem faced by expanding companies is finding management with the proper ambition, incentive, and motivation. In franchising, all unit managers are in business for themselves with their own capital to protect and future to insure; thus, each manager is vitally interested in success and anxious to operate efficiently and profitably to protect the cash investment.

The chance of success is increased because overhead is reduced, since managers need not be hired, and franchisees do not require the close supervision that is necessary in units operated by disinterested managers.

The chance of success of an outlet owned by a local person is greater than one owned by a distant, impersonal corporation. The community is more likely to accept a product sold to them by one of their own.

An example of the economic advantage available to the franchiser is the fact that in the first three years in which Kentucky Fried Chicken published their quarterly earnings, every quarter showed an increase of 80 to 100 percent over the same period of the preceding year.

SAFEGUARDS FOR PROSPECTING FRANCHISEES

All businesses, particularly those in the process of rapid growth, attract a wide variety of charlatans and fast dealers. The franchising industry is no exception. Out-and-out fraud, exaggerated advertising, and hidden costs are not unusual in franchisee recruiting . However, this sort of dishonesty, though frequently well-publicized, is not widespread. It is unfair to criticize an entire industry because of a small dishonest group.

Anyone interested in becoming a franchisee should take advantage of the available safeguards. As has been mentioned previously, the contract must be negotiated with the help of a capable attorney. Other available methods of checking the reputation of a franchiser are the Better Business Bureaus, the International Franchise Association, and any one of the many franchise consultants that are available.

Because of the many complaints by franchisees, the Federal Trade Commission requires that a disclosure document be presented by the franchiser at least ten days prior to the signing of the contract. The FTC rule requires detailed information in such areas as the business experience of the franchiser and its principal executives, as well as their bankruptcy and litigation history; the cost required to commence operations and the continuing expenses to be paid to the franchiser; a list of the persons and products that the franchisee will be required to deal with and any affiliation between them and the franchiser and its principals; information on the renewal and termination features in the contract and statistical information about the rate of termination in the past; financial information about the franchiser; and standards for making earnings claims. This last is very important. Franchisers can no longer select their most successful units and offer these as examples of profitability.

The FTC's disclosure rule offers few problems for the large, successful franchisers. They already provide most of the information to their prospective clients. The rule is aimed chiefly at the sharpshooters who have been attracted to the franchising industry.

Unfortunately the FTC is plagued by low budgets and limited manpower. It simply lacks the resources to perform effectively as a policing body.

THE FUTURE OF FRANCHISING

Since the beginning of the century, economic life in the United States has been moving in the direction of the giant corporation. The neighborhood, family-owned food and clothing stores, unable to compete with expanding supermarkets, department stores, and chains, have been slowly disappearing from the commercial scene. As a result, a constantly growing percentage of our working population is finding jobs with corporate giants, and a constantly shrinking percentage is self-employed. The franchise boom has to some extent arrested this trend. The move toward corporate bigness has not been affected, since the giant franchisers are being added to the list of large corporate enterprises. Nor can it be said that franchisees are truly "in business for themselves" since they are rather closely controlled by their parent companies. Essentially, the franchiser-franchisee relationship is a partnership with benefits to both parties. The franchisee is given the advantages of big business methods, which are basically a well-financed, scientific approach toward business problems. The franchiser, on the other hand, has the benefit of financial help in expansion and the indispensable blessing of hard work, ambition, and hustle that is generally reserved for an individually owned business. Certainly, there are conflicts of interest. No partnership is without them, but these are trivial in the overall picture. As long as the success of both parties depends ultimately on the success of each of the parties, the basis for a profitable ongoing partnership is assured, and the franchising industry will continue to grow.

Some areas of franchising are being overdeveloped, and the competition among franchisees of different parent companies is such that failures are inevitable. Fast-food franchises are beginning to feel this problem, and some major thoroughfares have franchised outlets offering similar foods (hamburgers, hot dogs, and so forth) in murderous competition.

Some of the larger franchisers are reaching the point at which there are no more territories to be found. The resulting slowdown in growth is being offset by buying up or building company-owned locations. Kentucky Fried Chicken presently operates about 250 company-owned outlets. In addition, it is presently signing up franchise locations for Kentucky Roast Beef, their newly developed fast-food program. The International House of Pancakes has been expanding by buying up other franchise companies such as United Rent-All, Orange Julius, and the House of Nine. Because this trend in takeovers is gaining momentum, the franchising industry, like other inudstries, is developing its economic giants.

Many successful franchisees have been able to expand by opening additional units. They find that multiunit operations offer certain distinct advantages, such as savings on volume buying, supervision, departmentalization training, and maintenance. In addition, as the franchisees' size increases, their clout with the franchiser rises proportionately. Such giant franchisers as

McDonalds, Pizza Hut, and Wendy's encourage multiple ownership, since they prefer selling to successful operators over finding new, unproven owners.

Action for the Independent Retailer

Since the beginning of the twentieth century, America has witnessed a slow but constant trend toward big business. Small businesses have gradually been replaced by industrial giants. Since the close of World War II, the pace has been accelerated. All of us have witnessed the replacement of the mom-and-pop grocery store by a large supermarket, and the neighborhood drugstore by a unit of a large chain. Franchising, by encouraging individuals to start independently owned businesses and by providing the expertise to compete successfully, may be reversing the trend toward big business. If so, it is not only good for individuals who want to "be in business for themselves"; it also benefits our society as a whole by safeguarding the future of the middle class.

IMPORTANT POINTS IN THE CHAPTER

1. *Franchising is an arrangement wherein an organization (the franchiser) that has developed a successful product or service sells to an individual (the franchisee) the right to engage in the business, provided that individual follows an established pattern of operations.*

2. *The growth of the franchising idea during the last twenty years has been enormous. Retail sales made by franchised dealers are an important part of the total national retail sales.*

3. *Franchise opportunities are available in almost all areas of retailing at costs ranging from a few hundred dollars to more than $200,000.*

4. *By helping the individual with "know-how" and capital, franchising permits people with limited funds and no prior experience to go into business for themselves.*

5. *The principal advantages of franchising to the franchiser are an opportunity to expand with less capital than is normally required and no problems in finding hard-working ambitious people to manage their units.*

6. *Some franchisees complain that their costs of conducting a franchised business are unnecessarily high. In addition, they feel that they are too rigidly controlled.*

7. *Franchisers are faced with the high cost of finding franchisees and the limitation on expansion brought about by the limited number of franchise locations available.*

8. *As with all rapidly growing industry, franchising has attracted many disreputable people. Proper safeguards should be taken before an individual enters a franchising agreement.*

9. *Current trends in franchising include expansion of the franchising concept, more competition among fast-food franchises, more company-operated units, and multiunit franchisees.*

10. *The FTC's disclosure requirements are an attempt to safeguard the interests of pro-spective franchisees.*

REVIEW QUESTIONS

1. Discuss the causes of the rapid expansion in the franchising industry at the close of World War II.
2. Indicate some of the factors that may be found in a franchising contract that will benefit the franchisee.
3. Compare a territorial franchise with an operating franchise. Which is apt to be more successful economically?
4. Differentiate between franchise coownership and comanagement. When are these types of franchises preferable to outright ownership?
5. What problems does a franchiser face in the recruitment of franchisees?
6. The franchiser generally makes a profit as soon as the franchise contract is signed. Mention several reasons for which a financially able prospect may be turned down.
7. What factors relating to the franchiser are important to the prospective franchisee?
8. Before accepting the territory offered by the parent company, the prospective franchi-see should check out certain facts. List as many points as you can.
9. Discuss the most important items that every good franchise contract should contain.
10. Explain the benefits of the franchise deal to the franchiser.
11. Discuss the data that should be found in a comprehensive location survey. Is a franchi-see likely to investigate a site as thoroughly as the franchiser might?
12. Since the franchiser frequently finances part of the franchisee's investment, how can franchising be considered an inexpensive means of expanding?
13. Compare the operation of a franchised store with a store operated by a manager.
14. Explain the mutual importance of the franchiser-franchisee relationship.
15. Discuss the effect of competition among franchisers in the fast-food industry.
16. Why are franchisers running out of territories? How will this affect the individual fran-chisee? The prospective franchisee?
17. How does a franchiser protect its outlets from failure?
18. Discuss the effect of franchisee failure upon the franchiser.
19. To be successful, a franchiser must be flexible. Why is this true?
20. Discuss the provisions of the FTC's Disclosure Rule.

CASE PROBLEMS

CASE PROBLEM 1

Kwik-Snak, Inc. has been franchising fast-food shops for the past seven years. Its products such as hamburgers and franks have won wide customer approval. This fact, coupled with alert, intelligent management, has made Kwik-Snak a great success. At present the company is financially stronger than ever and aggressively interested in expansion. Unfortunately, thanks to the rapid expansion of the past few years, there are no prime locations left.

A careful analysis of the existing locations revealed that many of the franchisees, though successful, are doing considerably less business than projections indicate should be done. A case in point is a site in the suburb of a large Southwestern city that is grossing $200,000 a year, in an area that the company feels should yield $300,000 per year. A location doing $100,000 of business a year is considered prime, and the wording of the contract is such that a new location could be established in the area.

Several members of the board of directors of Kwik-Snak, who realize that a major part of their success has been due to the excellent franchiser-franchisee relationship, oppose this move. Another group of directors feels that a company that stops expanding will lose its aggressiveness and spirit to the eventual disadvantage of existing franchisers.

QUESTIONS

1. Discuss the situation from the viewpoint of a stockholder of the parent company.
2. What are the points of view of the members of the board of directors? Take one point of view and defend.
3. How would a franchisee feel about this? Why?

CASE PROBLEM 2

The franchisees of a large, successful soft ice cream franchiser have formed an association at which they discuss problems of mutual interest. They feel that in cases of franchiser-franchisee conflicts of interest, the united front presented by the association strengthens their position with the home office.

The dispute in question involves buying supplies from the home office. The association agrees that the product must be bought from the home office to insure consistency among the various outlets. The product is unique and successful, and since it was developed by the home office, they are entitled to profit from it.

The purchase of paper goods (napkins, cups, and so forth) is another matter. Paper goods are not manufactured by the home office. There is nothing unusual about them, and they could be bought locally (meeting home office specifications) much more cheaply.

It is the position of the home office that it is unfair of the franchisees to favor only those parts of the agreement beneficial to themselves and oppose those areas favorable to the franchiser. The franchisees are successful and the home office is entitled to a fair share of all the profits.

QUESTIONS

1. Discuss from the point of view of the franchiser.
2. Discuss from the point of view of the franchisee.
3. What would you suggest is the best solution for all concerned?

3 *consumer behavior*

BEHAVIORAL OBJECTIVES

Upon completion of this chapter the student should be able to

1. *Discuss the psychological steps involved in decision making.*
2. *Write a short essay on learning, including the importance of drive, cues, response, and reinforcement.*
3. *Differentiate between rational and emotional motives.*
4. *Discuss attitudes and habits, giving examples of each.*
5. *Understand the importance of the family life cycle to successful retailing.*

INTRODUCTION

At its essential core, success in retailing depends upon customer satisfaction. Consequently, all of the functions of retailing must be targeted to that goal. Site selection, store layout, merchandising, services offered, and in fact every instance where retailers have options, must be resolved in favor of the choice that will maximize overall customer satisfaction. That is to say, even if a retailer decides against a particular customer service, the decision will be based upon the expectation that the reduced prices due to the savings will improve overall customer satisfaction. Those stores that are best able to satisfy customers will make the sales. Consumers who are satisfied with their purchases are likely to become loyal repeat customers.

It is obvious that the more a retailer knows about the customer, the greater the chance for success. The study of consumer behavior, the why, where, how, and when consumers buy, is of crucial importance. For example, studies show that children's shoes are bought by mothers. Since more and more mothers work, children's shoe stores need to be open on Sundays. Similarly, automobiles and major appliances are bought by husbands and wives together. Retailers of that type of merchandise must be open on weekends when both spouses are available.

Most successful retailers make decisions in this area based upon intuition, and their success indicates that they are usually correct. Whether they are aware of it or not, these people are unconscious students of consumer behavior. Like many other professionals, they have been able to learn their trade effectively through insight and trial and error. Similarly, like other professionals, they could improve their performance through the formal study of the principles that are the basis for their intuition.

The study of human behavior is probably older than retailing. In recent years, however, there are two reasons for this: first, greatly increased competition has forced individual retailers to look for an extra "edge," and second, the success of certain retailing giants has resulted in funds being available for the necessary research.

In this chapter, we shall discuss the psychology and sociology of consumer behavior. It should be noted that this is a fairly new field of research and that there are a variety of theories, which sometimes conflict, involved.

CONSUMER PSYCHOLOGY

This section of the chapter will focus on the internal thought process of an individual consumer—that is, the influence of the buyer's own personality rather than the influence of the social group to which the consumer belongs.

Decision Making

Consumer buying is a matter of decision making. Therefore, it is important to understand the internal working of the decision-making process. This process involves the following steps: stimulus and problem recognition, information gathering and selection, and finally, purchase and evaluation. An understanding of each of these steps and their application to successful retailing is necessary.

Stimulus and Problem Recognition

Decision making, like all instances of problem solving, starts with an awareness of the problem. Some stimulus is necessary to bring the problem to the attention of the future buyer. The initiation of the idea can come from a variety of sources, each of which will turn the consumer's thoughts toward resolving the problem. For example:

Self: "I have a headache, I need an aspirin."
Friend: "Let's see a movie tonight."
Business Advertisement: "All designer jeans 10% off."

Whatever the source of the stimulation, it serves to begin the decision-making process by focusing attention on the need. Of particular interest to retailers is the fact that advertising and other promotional devices, such as counter and window displays, can provide the stimulus if they are properly conceived.

Of course, the stimulus will not lead to a problem until a need arises. For example, the person with the headache who needs an aspirin will take one if it is available, and, thus, the decision about whether or not to buy is hastened. If, on the other hand the response to the stimulus, "I have a headache, I need an aspirin," is, "I took the last one in the bottle last week," then the problem is recognized and the decision-making problem goes on. Similarly, if the response to the friend's suggestion is, "I have too much homework," or to the advertisement is, "I have all of the jeans I need," then there is no problem. If, however, the response to the stimulus is positive, then the decision-making process continues.

Information Gathering

In the event that the problem recognized is of sufficient importance to the consumer to require a solution, the next step in the decision-making process is gathering information and making the selection. Even in the simplest case, many decisions must be made. "Shall I buy an advertised, popular brand of aspirin or the generic brand, which is cheaper and, I'm told, just as good?" "Shall I buy the one advertised on T.V. as stronger or my own brand?" "Shall I stop in the next drugstore I come to or wait until I get to my neighborhood drugstore?"

As the intended purchase becomes more expensive and complicated, the information gathering becomes more intensive. For example, a person needing a new car must first decide on standard size, compact, or subcompact. Then, having decided on a compact, two-door or four-door? Blue or gray? Automatic or shift? Which maker? The list is endless and the complications so great that outside help is frequently needed. For such expensive purchases people usually visit many showrooms, have discussions with friends who have made similar purchases, and consult literature such as *Consumer Reports* magazine before making a decision.

Retailers, in order to turn the information-gathering phase of the decision-making process to their best advantage, must be prime providers of information. Advertising, displays, and knowledgeable sales personnel are of great importance in getting the message across. The consumers, after all, are faced with alternatives and must be convinced that the retailer's product is more likely to satisfy their needs than is the product of a competitor.

Purchase and Evaluation

After the prospective purchaser has evaluated the information that has been gathered, the next step in the decision-making process is the actual purchase. It is at this point that the retailer's involvement is most intense because the decision to purchase a specific product involves the selection of the specific store from which the purchase is to be made. The buying decision may have had as a stimulus an advertisement stating, "All designer jeans 10% off," but that does not mean that the purchase will be made from that particular advertisement. All that the ad did was start a reaction that resulted in a consumer's decision to buy a pair of jeans. Among the information gathered was: Is a 10 percent deduction enough, or is another store offering more? What is the store's image? Convenience? Return policy? and so on.

The availability of the required merchandise is another important factor to the retailer at this time. Once the decision to purchase a particular item is made, the purchaser wants the goods to be available in the selected store. If the merchandising of that particular store has not anticipated the customer's desire, not only will the sale be lost, but also the selection of that particular store in the future is jeopardized.

The decision-making process does not end with the purchase. There is still the problem of satisfaction. The satisfied purchaser may be an immediate customer for accessories. The shirt buyer may select a tie—the woman who bought a handbag may be interested in matching shoes. In addition, the contented customer may become a loyal repeater, and that is the bottom line of successful retailing.

On the other hand, a dissatisfied customer can be a serious problem. Not only is the future business of the dissatisfied customer lost; also endangered is the business of friends who may hear the story. How to guard against dissatisfaction? For one thing, no high-pressure selling; for another, follow-up calls or letters on expensive items such as automobiles and high-priced appliances helps. Honest advertising and liberal merchandise return policies are steps in the right direction. Finally, money-back guarantees if the consumer is not satisfied are offered by many large retailers who recognize that a satisfied customer is worth more than a lost sale.

Learning

Basically, decision making is a learning process. Having made the buying decision by the steps indicated above and achieved satisfaction, the consumer is likely to repeat the purchase when the need arises again. Decision making then is a response to a stimulus. Some years ago Ivan Pavlov, a Russian psychologist, found that with the proper conditioning, he could teach a subject to respond in a particular way to a given stimulus. In other words, he could guide the learning procedure. His work was simple: each time he fed a dog, he would ring a bell. After repeated trials, the dog would salivate at the sound of the bell, without the presence of food. He had taught the dog to salivate on cue. This work is the foundation of learning theory and provides the basis of much of today's retail advertising and sales promotion.

Modern behavioral scientists have refined Pavlov's work by breaking it down into four steps: drive, cues, response, and reinforcement.

Drive

The first step in the learning process is a drive. By definition, a drive is an individual's awareness of an internal tension that is caused by a need from within. Basic drives may be to satisfy needs for humor, shelter, or warmth.

Other drives may be to obtain a new tie, hair style, or sweater. The drive creates a tension in the individual, which will only be appeased by taking action. If the drive is strong enough, the individual will seek to satisfy it.

Cues

The manner in which an individual responds to the drive depends upon cues that individual has been made aware of. These are ideas and other bits of information that have been stored in memory. Advertising is an example of an important generator of cues. An individual who is interested in buying a pair of slacks may remember a recent advertisement for just the sort of merchandise that will be suitable. Another, anxious to satisfy a drive for food, may remember a Chinese restaurant or Burger King nearby. Advertising, window displays, conversations with friends, and store decor are all cues of sorts.

Response

A positive action taken, as a result of cues, to satisfy a drive is called a response. This would be the actual making of the purchase that will ease the tension caused by the drive. Purchasing the slacks or ordering the food would be examples of responses in the illustrations just given.

Reinforcement

When the response to the drive proves satisfying, reinforcement occurs. When a similar need arises in the future, the reinforced response is likely to return as an important cue for future satisfaction. Those who enjoy McDonald's hamburgers return again and again. Popular brands are established through positive reinforcement, as is store loyalty.

It may seem a long jump between Pavlov's dogs and successful retailing, but consider the worker who glances at a clock at 12:00 and becomes hungry for lunch. Is that response unlike the salivating dogs? How about the individual who is deluged by television commercials for designer jeans? Isn't that an effective way to start a drive and suggest a brand name as a cue?

Buying Motives

The more retailers know about their customers, the more likely they are to satisfy the customers' needs. One major piece of information is why people buy and what motivates them. Different people buy for different reasons. Consider this: An individual decides to buy a car. The alternatives from which the selection is to be made are enormous. To understand the reason for a particular choice, we must first understand why the decision to buy the car was made in the first place. Has the old car broken down? Does it look tacky? Is it in the repair shop too often? Is it a gas-guzzler? If we can understand the motivation for the purchase, we can direct our total sales pitch, including advertising, merchandising, personal selling, and other promotion, in that direction.

Rational versus Emotional Motivation

One common way of classifying motives is by differentiating between rational and emotional buyers.

Rational buyers do their homework. In the case of the car buyer, comparative data will be obtained on the cost of the automobile, gas mileage, frequency of repair, estimated life, and so on. The actual purchase will be based upon the outcome of careful study.

In contrast, the emotional buyer bases the buying desicion on style, pride of ownership, romance, and so on.

For example, any jacket will provide warmth. The rational buyer will select the product that provides the best construction, durability, and economy. The emotional buyer will buy the high-fashion, designer-labeled jacket that looks best. It should be pointed out that we are discussing buying motives, not intelligence. The rational buyer may gather the wrong information, interpret it incorrectly, and for any of a number of reasons make a totally irrational purchase.

It must be understood that the borderline between rational and emotional motives is frequently crossed. That is, some individuals, usually rational buyers, take an occasional flyer for an emotional product that strikes their fancy. Moreover, an individual who buys clothing on an emotional basis might put considerable research into the purchase of a lawn mower.

The point for retailers is that when selling products that appeal to emotional purchasers, use an emotional sales pitch. Do not, for example, use the same advertising and sales promotion for a Cadillac as one would use for a Chevette. Also, alert retailers must change their message as their products move from one category to another. Consider Volkswagen advertising over the years. Originally the automobiles were offered as a low-cost, efficiently operating machine, ideally suited to the rational buyer. In recent years costs have increased, styling has improved, and the stripped-down version is hard to find. The down-to-earth advertising has changed to one with snob appeal. The cars now appear outside of mansions, fancy country clubs, and expensive art galleries. The ads are peopled by cultured, well-spoken individuals, who can well afford a Cadillac or Mercedes-Benz. The focus is no longer targeted to the down-to-earth rational buyer, but to the status-seeking, prestige-conscious, emotional buyer.

Maslow's Hierarchy of Needs

Abraham Maslow proposed an order in which needs are fulfilled, which has become an important part of the literature of motivation. His proposal provides a listing of the relative importance of each motivating need in relation to other needs. The following explains his view of motivational needs in order of their importance:

Necessities for Survival. Obviously, these needs that are required for survival are more important than any other type of motivation. Those who need food, water, shelter, or sleep will not be motivated to satisfy any other needs until those are satisfied. In affluent societies, such as ours, motivations to ensure survival are rarely an important factor.

After the basic survival needs have been satisfied, an individual turns to the satisfaction of a need for the safety and protection of self, family, and friends. This drive for self-preservation is often capitalized upon by retailers of such products as vitamin pills, security devices, and the like. Consider the advertising for smoke detectors that provide safety for the family, or the automobiles that provide the greatest safety in the event of an accident. The need for safety and security is basic, and the retailer must bear that in mind when making product selections, making advertising and sales promotion decisions, and planning the training of sales staff.

Social Motivation. Next in Maslow's order of importance is social motivation. Man is by nature a social animal. That is, happiness depends upon a successful adjustment to society. An individual must love and be loved by a family and be an accepted member of a group. Included in this motive is the need to attract a mate and care for a family. We are constantly bombarded by advertisements that offer satisfaction of this need. Cosmetics, clothing, and furniture, as well as membership in organizations, and home entertaining are appeals to the satisfaction of this motive.

The need for self-esteem and recognition by society is next in Maslow's order of importance. The longing for status and recognition is frequently satisfied by the ownership of certain products that are the proof of success. The sale of expensive cars and furs, the choice of the "right" school for one's children, shopping in high-image stores, and having the "right" label on one's clothes are examples of attempts to satisfy the need for self-esteem. When Ford Motors advertises, "Step Up To A Lincoln Continental," this is exactly what they are talking about.

Maslow's final level of motivation is self-actualization. It refers to the development of one's self by realizing one's full potential for understanding and gracious living. Books, records, objects of fine art, and colleges offering cultural courses to nontypical students are examples of the products sold to satisfy the need for self-actualization.

When Maslow theorized his hierarchy of needs, he did not intend it as a hard and fast rule. In fact, some people buy expensive cars before fully satisfying all of the previous needs outlined. However, Maslow's categories provide a good rule of thumb to retailers. Stores, or departments within stores, by understanding the underlying purpose behind a consumer's buying decision, can focus their efforts toward satisfying that particular need by adjusting their offerings and sales pitch to a specific area.

Attitudes

An attitude is an individual's feeling toward a particular object. These preconceived opinions are often crucial to a store's success. Attitudes are learned; they are the result of, for example, an individual's experience, conversations with friends, and reactions to advertising and sales promotion. The importance of attitude to retailing success can be illustrated. For example, an individual has several friends who have had negative experience with the return policies of a particular store. As a result, the individual may never try the store. A positive attitude can result if the experiences with a particular retailer are good. Attitudes can be shaped from a wide variety of sources. Even such information as the personal life of the store's owner can have an effect on a prospective customer toward a store. Attitudes can rarely be easily changed. For example, the perception of Sears has always been that of an organization that gives value, and the store's emphasis has been on hardware, housewares, and appliances. An ongoing attempt to include fashion clothing as part of the store's image has met with only fair success. Or consider the perception that small, independently owned retailers do not acccept returned goods easily. It is doubtful that a small retailer that advertises a liberal return policy would change many consumer perceptions.

A retailer's image (the way that it is perceived by customers and potential customers) is vital and difficult to alter. Consequently, every effort must be made to minimize customer discontent. The slogan, "The Customer is Always Right" has a more beneficial effect on the store than it does on the customer.

Habits

Another important factor in consumer behavior is the buying habits of the retailer's market. When, where, and how much will be purchased are pieces of information that the successful retailer must blend effectively if customer satisfaction is to be achieved.

Conforming to the consumer's "time" habit, that is when the consumer buys, requires that the retailer have the merchandise on hand, the staff available, and the advertising geared to consumer wants. Christmas tree ornaments must be available in December, and bathing suits, in the spring and early summer. Advertising must inform customers of the availability of the goods, and the store's operation must be geared to handle peak loads whenever necessary. In the case of supermarkets, whose peak day is Friday, advertising usually appears in the Thursday newspapers and the shelves are fully stocked by Friday morning.

Satisfying the "time" habit is usually learned quickly and conformed to easily. It is not a habit that can easily be changed. The "where" habit, the store from which a consumer buys a particular item, is another matter. In recent years, this habit has been changed. Supermarkets now carry a line of nonprescription drugs, large drugstores display housewares and small appliances, and even prestigious men's shops carry women's ready-to-wear. This is not to indicate that the "where" habit is easily changed. It requires a considerable investment in inventory and promotion and patience. But it can be done.

The quantity habit is easily adjusted to. It depends upon the area that the retailer services. In suburban areas where shoppers travel by automobile, supermarket shoppers buy in huge quantity. Not so in urban areas where supermarket purchasers must hand-carry the goods. They shop more frequently and buy smaller quantities. Similarly, in economically deprived areas, food marketers must be prepared to sell eggs individually rather than by the dozen.

Conforming to customers' behavioral habits is relatively easy. However, many retailers do not seem to realize that these habits are in a constant state of change and that frequent adjustments may be necessary. For example, the growing number of working women has been changing buying habits. For one thing, since shoppers who work are not able to shop during the day, evenings and Sundays have become increasingly important for shopping. Also, the unavailability of working women during shopping hours has increased the number of men shoppers for goods that have traditionally been the responsibility of their wives. Promotional displays, merchandise, and sales presentations that had been successful with women must be adjusted to this new breed of customer. Where people shop is another changing habit. For example, the success and continued growth of the flea market has been causing serious problems to traditional retailers. As more people get into the habit of buying at these low-overhead, cut-price retailers, the competition is forced to adjust to this new threat by means such as carrying different lines of merchandise or lowering prices.

CONSUMER SOCIOLOGY

Understanding another influence on consumer behavior, which gives insight into their buying habits, requires the study of individuals as members of groups. We have already discussed the psychological influences on buyer motivation. These were the individual, internal thought processes of a person that result in a particular behavioral pattern. They are not the whole story. Individuals are also influenced by the groups to which they belong. This is the work of sociologists. These behavioral scientists are concerned with the influences that family, friends, and groups have on an individual's activities.

Similar people tend to congregate together. The similarity can be based upon economic success, educational achievement, religion, ethnic background, and a host of other factors. Since people within a group have a tendency to act in a similar fashion, it is worthwhile to study these groupings. Retailers generally focus their efforts on a particular segment of the market. Understanding the characteristics of this segment or group, its likes, dislikes, needs, motivations, and buying patterns, will improve the retailer's ability to ensure customer satisfaction.

The problem with sociological grouping is that there are simply too many ways to define the boundaries of groups and there may be serious overlaps. One generally accepted system of classifications is based upon economics and similarity of outlooks, goals, and attitudes.

Upper-Upper

These are the socially elite. They comprise 1 percent of the population. Their great wealth is inherited and is used to purchase mansions in exclusive neighborhoods, summer homes, education in the "best" schools, and so on.

Cost is not an important factor in their purchases. They are conservative in dress and inconspicuous in spending habits. Since traveling takes much of their time, a considerable amount of their purchasing is done abroad.

Lower-Upper

These are the newly rich. They amount to 2 percent of the population. They are professionals, executives of large corporations, or owners of successful businesses. They are active in social affairs and free and conspicuous spenders.

Members of the lower-upper class are wealthy people who do not worry about costs. Labels are important to them, so they shop in exclusive shops and high-image department stores. They own boats, swimming pools, and large homes. They are proud of their wealth and enjoy displaying it.

Upper-Middle

This group consists of 12 percent of the population. They are the best educated in the society, career oriented, and concerned with status. They are frequently professionals, middle-level executives, or owners of successful businesses.

At this level of income, the cost of purchases begins to be important.

They are careful, rational buyers. They buy quality merchandise and although they are conspicuous spenders, they try not to appear that way. Their goal is a "gracious" way of life.

Lower-Middle

This group of white-collar and highly paid blue-collar workers consists of about 30 percent of the population. These "typical Americans" are respectable, conscientious, and conservative. They are do-it-yourself homeowners and respectable church-goers.

Members of the lower-middle class are very price conscious. They are careful, rational shoppers who buy from a wide variety of nonexclusive stores.

Upper-Lower

This is the largest segment of our population, consisting of about 35 percent of the population. They generally hold blue-collar jobs and are not well-educated. Job security is more important to them than upward mobility.

These are impulsive, emotional buyers who are very susceptible to advertising, and loyal brand users. They shop at low-end stores where credit is available. Being poor shoppers, they frequently overpay.

Lower-Lower

This class of poorly educated, unskilled workers comprises 20 percent of the population. They are present-oriented and generally disinterested in upward mobility. They populate slum areas and are frequently welfare recipients.

Members of this class shop locally where credit is available. They are impulsive buyers who frequently overpay. An unusually large proportion of their income is spent to improve their personal appearance.

Family Life Cycle

Another way to categorize individuals into groups is according to their stage in the family life cycle. Newly marrieds, or couples with young children usually have similar needs and motivations for their purchases. (See Figure 3-1.)

Action for the Independent Retailer

It is likely that understanding consumer behavior and capitalizing on that knowledge is more important to the small retailer than to the giant competitor. For one thing, the small retailer can less afford to lose a sale.

FIGURE 3-1 FAMILY LIFE CYCLE

Stage	Distinguishing Features	Buying Patterns
Single	Low earnings. Small financial responsibilities. Interested in romance and recreation.	High-fashion clothing. Automobiles, vacations, cosmetics, furniture and appliances, entertainment.
Newlywed	Two earners. Small financial responsibilities. Free spenders.	Durables for new home. Vacations, entertainment. Clothing.
Full Nest I; Youngest child under 6	One earner. Tight financial position. Desire home ownership.	Careful spenders. Practical housewares and appliances; durability and safety are prime factors.
Full Nest II; Youngest child over 6	Improved financially. Wife works. Less advertising influence. Concerned with future.	Home buyers. Child-oriented products and vacations. Savings. Some luxuries.
Full Nest III; Grown children still home	High income level. Financial independence. Skeptical of advertising.	Quality replacement in durable goods. Vacations and retirement homes. Travel, boats, books.
Empty Nest I; Still working	Financially secure. Wife retired. Children independent.	Retirement home. Luxuries. Travel, recreation, self-education, gifts, clothing.
Empty Nest II; Retired	Cut in income. Worry about future finances. Keep homes but cut spending.	Medical care and other health improvements. Few luxuries. Price conscious. Travel, inexpensive recreation.
Sole Survivor I; Employed	Good income. Present-oriented. Active in job. Friends. Often sell homes.	Health services. Travel. Clothing. Recreation.
Sole Survivor II; Retired	Poor income. Depressed.	Health. Security. Careful shopping. Join social groups.

Small retailers generally suffer from limited amounts of space and capital. These assets, therefore, must be utilized with care and accuracy. Only the largest stores have the space and financial ability to carry goods that will appeal to a wide variety of customers. Because of these limitations the small retailer must aim at a relatively small specialized segment of the market. To try to do otherwise will result in too narrow an inventory in any one category of goods to be effective. Once having decided which section of the population to service, small retailers will increase their chance of success by learning as much as possible about that class of individuals. Failure to do so might result in so impossible a situation as locating a children's shoe store in a neighborhood peopled by retired individuals. The large store, of course, faces a far less severe problem. Space and sufficient financial strength to enable the store to carry a huge inventory permit them to appeal to broad classes of individuals, which allows their thrust to be broader and less subject to error. In brief, behavioral scientists have much to say to the small retailer, who would be wise to pay attention.

In conclusion, it should be noted that sociologically speaking, there are many ways in which consumers with similar habits and motivations can be grouped. Race, religion, ethnic background, earnings, and educational achievement are only a few ways in which people with similar characteristics and, of importance to retailers, similar buying habits and motivations can be grouped. Moreover, people with similar characteristics tend to live in the same neighborhood. Small retailers must understand as much as possible about their clientele. They all do it by trial and error, but one wonders if they don't miss something. Some research or formal study in this area might be of considerable value.

IMPORTANT POINTS IN THE CHAPTER

1. *Customer satisfaction, the key to successful retailing, depends in large part upon the retailer's understanding of the psychological and sociological effects on the consumer's buying decision.*

2. *Consumer psychology deals with the effects of customers' personality on their buying decisions.*

3. *Decision making can be broken down into the following steps: stimulus and problem recognition, information gathering, and purchase and evaluation.*

4. *The steps in the learning process are drive, cues, response, and reinforcement. A satisfactory purchase provides reinforcement and leads to repeated purchases.*

5. *A rational purchase is one based on a study of cost efficiency. Emotional purchases are based on pride, romance, style, and so forth.*

6. *Maslow theorizes that needs are satisfied in the following order: first, necessities for survival; then, social motives.*

7. *An attitude is an individual's feeling toward a particular object. Attitudes are more easily learned than changed.*

8. *Retailers must adjust their operation to comply with their customers' buying habits.*

9. *Sociologists have found that consumers can be grouped into broad categories that have similar habits and motivations.*

REVIEW QUESTIONS

1. Why might a retailer, aware of the importance of customer satisfaction, decide on an "all sales final" policy?

2. Discuss the types of stores that benefit greatly from being open on Sundays and those that can remain closed.

3. One of the steps in decision making is stimulus and problem recognition. Define and give examples.

4. How does a consumer gather information for the buying decision? How can a retailer get involved in that process?

5. Discuss the importance of post-purchase evaluation.

6. Define the use of the word "drive" in the learning process. Give examples.

7. How does Pavlov's work with dogs relate to retailers?

8. Define the term *reinforcement* as it relates to the learning process. Provide examples that indicate its importance to the retailer.

9. Define rational motivation. Give examples.

10. Define emotional motivation. Give examples.

11. You are selling ski jackets. Differentiate between the presentation that you would make to a rational buyer and that you would make to an emotional buyer.

12. Explain the theory of Maslow's Hierarchy of Needs and list them in proper order.

13. What is an attitude? How may it be learned? How changed?

14. Give examples of the effect of the how, why, and where of consumer habits on retailers.

15. What information can sociologists provide to retailers?

16. Discuss the buying motivations of the upper-middle class.

17. Describe the upper-lower class. How can a retailer reach them?

18. Discuss newlyweds as customers.

19. What are the buying interests of a middle-aged couple with independent children?

20. Is the understanding of the sociological makeup of the area important to the small retailer. Why?

CASE PROBLEMS

CASE PROBLEM 1

John Sawyer, age 42, has a fine job with a major firm of stockbrokers. He earns in excess of $50,000 per year and his prospects for advancement, both in earnings and position within the firm, are excellent.

The Sawyers live in a house in a distant, middle-class suburb of New York City. John commutes to work by car. The house is small and unspectacular. The Sawyers and their children, aged 16, 12, and 8, find it quite crowded and have decided to sell the house and move to larger quarters.

After a great deal of searching, the Sawyers have decided upon a house in an exclusive suburb, which costs $250,000. This is more expensive than the Sawyers can afford, but Mr. Sawyer, thanks to the excellent banking connections he has developed at work, can raise an unusually high mortgage that will swing the deal. Although he realizes that he cannot really afford the house, John Sawyer plans to go ahead with the deal for these reasons:

1. The whole family loves the house.
2. If he can hang on for a few years, promotions and salary increases will make everything come out satisfactorily.
3. Entertaining both his business superiors and customers in the new house will have a favorable effect on his future earnings.
4. New friends from the new affluent neighborhood may prove to be valuable customers.
5. The new friends his children will make will have a positive effect on their future.

QUESTIONS

1. Is this a rational or emotional motive? Why?
2. Which of Maslow's Hierarchy of Needs does this purchase satisfy? Discuss.
3. To what social class do the Sawyers belong?
4. Discuss the purchase in terms of the decision-making process.

CASE PROBLEM 2

Younglife Builders, Inc. is in the process of completing a large apartment complex in a nearby suburb of San Francisco. The complex has been designed to attract young singles and newlyweds. The apartments are of one, two, and three rooms and are designed to appeal to the prospective clientele. Included in the plans are tennis courts, jogging tracks, and other athletic facilities. There will also be public rooms for social activities and small gymnasiums and saunas. Because of the unique appeal of the proposal, the apartments have all been rented prior to completion and there is a waiting list to cover cancellations. Naturally, the rents are quite high.

Centralized within the complex is a large shopping center that will be operated by the builders. Because of the size of the complex and the distance to competing stores, it is a "can't miss" location for retailers. As a result, the builders are in the enviable position of having long lists of fully qualified applicants to choose from.

Leases for this sort of situation frequently include clauses under which the rental is based, in part, upon the tenant's gross income. Therefore, Younglife Builders Inc. will increase its profits by selecting from the retail applicants the stores that will be most successful. Another consideration to be taken into account is that the apartment renters must have all of their reasonable buying needs satisfied by the shopping center.

QUESTIONS

1. What types of stores (in terms of specific merchandise carried) should be selected?
2. Why?

organization, management, and operational functions

II

store organization

4

67

BEHAVIORAL OBJECTIVES

Upon completion of this chapter the student should be able to

1. *Prepare a simple organizational chart and explain the importance of such a chart.*
2. *Define specialization and departmentalization and give examples of each.*
3. *Discuss three theories for the grouping of functions into separate departments.*
4. *List seven duties of the merchandise manager.*
5. *Give three arguments for and three against the separation of buying and selling.*
6. *List six of the responsibilities of the store management function.*
7. *List the three responsibilities of the control function.*
8. *Identify four characteristics of a chain store.*
9. *Define and give examples of the centralization and decentralization of chain stores.*

INTRODUCTION

Any human effort that must be done by more than one person will be accomplished more effectively if it is organized. If all individuals involved have a clear idea of their duties and responsibilities, there will be less chance of duplication of work, or tasks being omitted. A small luncheonette run by a husband and wife must have organization. If there is no clear understanding of who is responsible for making the egg salad, there will be days in which twice the amount of required egg salad is made and other days in which none is made. Of course, a very small enterprise needs no formal organization. Where there are few people involved, each person's tasks and responsibilities are quickly and easily understood. An enterprise involving thousands of employees is another matter.

The organization of a retail store is accomplished by the identification and separation of all of the similar functions (activities) of the enterprise, and the assignment of the responsibility for the performance of these functions to specific groups of individuals. The lines of authority and control must be clearly established and thoroughly understood by every worker in the organization. In other words, all individual workers in the organization must know what their jobs are, the people they supervise, and to whom they are responsible.

THE USE OF CHARTS

Many complicated problems can be more easily understood by the use of diagrams. The use of a map in a geography lesson gives a much clearer picture of relative positions than could possibly be given by words. The use of an organization chart to describe the functions of a retail establishment and the responsibilities of its personnel greatly simplifies the understanding of the position of each individual in the establishment. Naturally, since the chart is brief and concise, it must be backed up by descriptions, duties, and responsibilities of each job or job classification. All employees, by glancing at the organization chart, can understand the relationship of their jobs to the overall picture and the lines of authority above and below their positions.

Unfortunately, organization charts do not take into account the personal relationships that exist between employees as a result of the teamwork and cooperation that is the keynote of a successful retailing operation. While the organization chart gives a brief sketch of how an institution operates, it is doubtful if any retailer follows the minor details of the chart to the letter.

Another disadvantage of organization charts is that they always seem to be out of date. No two retailers are apt to have exactly the same organization chart. Even an individual retailer, considering the speed at which retailing constantly changes, is not apt to use the same organization chart for a long period of time. It has even been said that organization charts are generally obsolete on the very day that they are published. While day-to-day changes are generally of a minor nature, the charts must be constantly revised if they are to be used effectively.

Constructing an Organization Chart

The construction of an organization chart requires the operation of the enterprise to be broken down into functions. A function is a type of activity that can be differentiated from other activities. Buying, selling, and receiving are examples of functions. Not all stores perform the same functions. Those that maintain charge accounts will have a credit function, which is unnecessary to a cash-and-carry store.

Once the functions have been separated, the next step is to arrange them in lines of authority. In some retail operations sales personnel are responsible to assistant buyers, who are responsible to buyers. On an organization chart this would appear as in Figure 4-1.

The buyer, assistant buyer, and salesperson all are in decision-making positions. They appear in a vertical line on the chart and are called line positions.

In the chart shown in Figure 4-2, the research unit makes no decisions. It

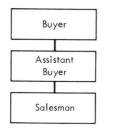

FIGURE 4-1   Line Relationship

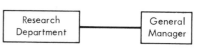

FIGURE 4-2   Staff Relationship

acts in an advisory capacity to the general manager. This is called a staff position and is indicated by horizontal placement.

SMALL STORE ORGANIZATION

All stores, regardless of size, require organization. The difference between large and small store organization lies chiefly in the numbers of employees involved. In essence, both the large and the small store conduct the same type of operation. The major difference from an organizational point of view is that the small store, with few employees, must require each employee to perform many functions. The large store, with many more employees than functions to be performed, assigns groups of employees to do a single function. The greater the number of employees, the greater the amount of possible specialization. In drawing up an organization chart, it is useless to define a function for which there are no available specialist employees. The organization chart of a small employer is relatively simple. Figure 4-3 shows an organization chart for a store whose personnel consist of an owner and four employees.

Note that the chart gives all employees a clear understanding of their responsibilities (impossible to indicate on extensive organization charts), and the lines of authority from the salesperson through the manager to the owner. In addition, the owner is able to control all employees by knowing the exact nature of each person's responsibilities. This serves as a basis for tightening up shoddy work or rewarding outstanding effort. Because of lack of understanding or laziness, few small retailers construct such charts, although it would be to their advantage to do so. By clearly defining the responsibiity of each employee, the employer would minimize "passing the buck," neglect of duty, and the evasion of responsibility.

It should be understood that the fixing of responsibility by the organization chart should not preclude cooperation among the employees. Thus, while one particular employee is given a certain responsibility, the other workers are expected to help that employee if the situation warrants such cooperation. Giving a person the responsibility for seeing that a task is done is not meant to indicate that that individual is the only one who should perform that task.

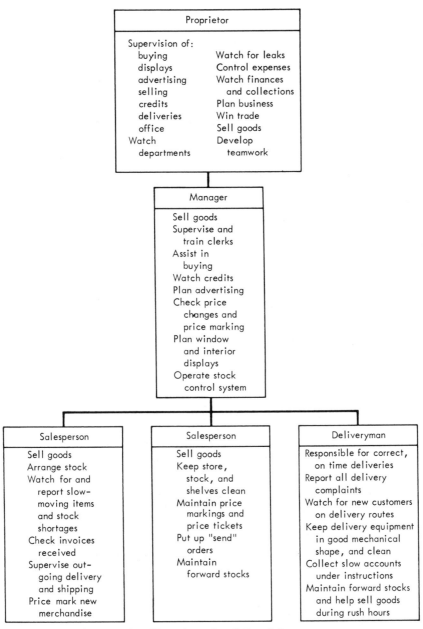

FIGURE 4-3 Organization Chart for a Small Retail Store

EXPANSION OF A SMALL STORE

As the size of a retailing operation grows, the number of employees increases. This permits the store to operate more efficiently by providing for specialists in the work force. For example, when the volume of receiving, maintenance work, and stockroom activities becomes heavy enough to be done by full-time employees, new functions may be identified and staffed. The work will then be done by properly trained experts devoting full time to the job rather than by salespeople to whom the job is a burdensome chore. The growth of the small store typifies this. As the store's sales volume increases, new personnel must be employed.

An example of this change in operations may be seen by looking again at Figure 4-3. If the store's sales volume required the hiring of a fifth person, the new employee's responsibilities would be taken from the work previously delegated to the original four. This would result in a lessening of each worker's duties. If the new person, for example, were a part-time bookkeeper, that employee would take over all of the clerical tasks that previously were performed by the other workers. The result would be a specialist doing all of the clerical tasks. Since the original workers would no longer be required to perform clerical duties, in which they are probably poorly trained and disinterested, the performance of their other tasks would be improved. The organizational chart pictured in Figure 4-3 would be amended to indicate a new box to the right of the box labeled "proprietor" (connected by a horizontal line, since clerical work is a staff function). The new box would be headed by the title "bookkeeper" and would list all of the clerical functions, which would be deleted from the boxes indicating the responsibilities of the other employees.

The point is that the basic functions of a large retailer are not very different from those of a small store. Therefore, as the number of personnel increases, the functions that each person is responsible for can be decreased until the point is reached in which specialists or teams of specialists can be employed for each function. This is called *specialization* and is one of the principal reasons for the success of American big business.

Departmentalization

As a retail store increases in sales volume and the number of persons it employs, there is a constant increase in the amount of specialization possible. This is true even in specialty shops, where specialization of similar types of merchandise may be found. Large ladies' specialty stores consider coats and dresses as two distinct specialties.

In all but the smallest stores, related functions are grouped into departments. There are several advantages to departmentalization, among which are specialization and managerial control.

Specialization

By limiting the responsibility of an employee to one specific function, that employee's knowledge of that function and, therefore, ability to perform that function, is increased. A person who is responsible for major appliances soon becomes expert in the buying and selling of such articles. In a small store the major appliance and furniture functions may be grouped together. This arrangement is preferable to no departmentalization at all.

Managerial Control

As a store grows in size, it becomes more and more difficult to control. The owner of a small store knows precisely the profitability of each type of merchandise the store handles. In a medium-sized or large-volume store it is impossible for management to have this information without referring to accounting reports. Income statements (reports prepared by accountants that show profits and losses) can be made for the entire store, or for the various types of merchandise within the store. If the selling functions are divided into departments, the profitability of each department can be determined. In this way weaknesses can be identified and improved, while strong points can be rewarded. Where departmentalization occurs, separate records of sales, inventory, and, frequently, operating expenses are maintained. This permits managerial control over all of these items. A store that does not departmentalize finds itself in a situation similar to that of a person owning three stores in separate locations who does not keep individualized records for each unit. Although unlikely, it is possible under such conditions to find that one store is losing money.

When to Departmentalize

The number of departments that are to be found in a store range from three to four departments in a small store to more than 150 separate departments in a large organization. The problem of deciding whether or not to set up a special department is a difficult one that can be solved only by a thorough understanding of the purposes of departmentalization. The principal advantages of departmentalization are specialization and control. When the volume of a specific class of merchandise is so great that managerial control requires exact information, and when the quantity of personnel available permits specialization, a separate department should be set up. Since the quantity of personnel and the amount of control required generally depend upon sales volume, the total sales of a particular item is the one most important factor to be taken into account in making the decision of whether or not to departmentalize.

The Changing Departmental Structure

The departmental structure of a store is in a constant state of change. New high-volume items such as skis and ski accessories may require new departments. Expansion of sales volume may necessitate the splitting up of old departments. Some departments, such as cruisewear and beachwear, are seasonal in nature. It is an important duty of management to constantly review the departmental setup so that they make the organizational changes when they become necessary. Rigidity in the area of departmentalization of sales departments can be very damaging to retail operations.

Partial Departmentalization

Managerial control can be improved by partial departmentalization, even in stores that lack the required number of personnel for full departmentalization. This can best be shown by means of an illustration. The Hicksville Upholstery and Slip Cover Company is a small suburban retailer of drapery and upholstery fabrics. The working organization consists of four salespeople grouped in one department. A year ago a decision was made to add a line of venetian blinds and window shades. This required an expenditure of $2,000 for inventory. It was further decided that $50 per month would be spent on directory advertising and occasional ads in a local buyer's guide. At the end of the first year the advertising commitment had to be renewed, increased, or decreased. Without some sort of control, a decision such as this could not be effectively made. Although there are too few employees for full departmentalization, record keeping for the new line can be accomplished with little effort. By keeping records of all sales and purchases of venetian blinds and window shades, the proprietor could with little extra effort get an excellent idea of the profitability of that area.

Other Departments

Because the most important function of a retail store is selling, the selling departments are given the most attention. This should not be taken to mean that selling departments are the most important in the store. A department store is operated through the cooperative action of many different departments, and the failure of any of the departments to function effectively is damaging to the overall success of the store. Those in top management in many stores frequently have backgrounds and interests in the field of merchandising, sales promotion, and selling. Care must be taken in such cases that these executives do not emphasize the departments in which they are interested at the expense of the supportive departments.

SMALL DEPARTMENT STORE
ORGANIZATION

The principal difference between the operational plan of a small retailer and a small department store is that the increased sales volume and the necessary additional personnel of the small department store permits more specialization of workers. The organization chart of the small department store is pictured in Figure 4-4.

A comparison of this chart and Figure 4-3 shows several striking changes. The most important difference is that the organization chart of the small department store recognizes two functions—that is, two vertical lines of responsibility of equal authority; neither the director of merchandising nor the director of store operations has authority over the other. Dividing the store into two major functions has the effect of freeing all the merchandise personnel from the chores listed under the operations functions. In other words, although the small department store has too few employees for full specialization, there has been a grouping of functions into two major classifications.

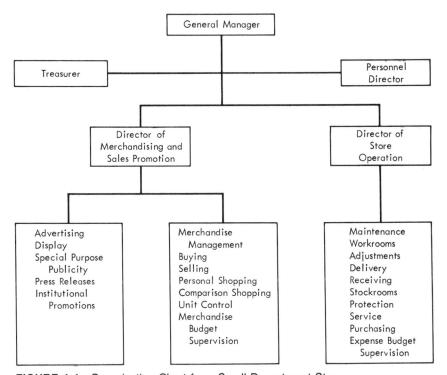

FIGURE 4-4 Organization Chart for a Small Department Store

It must be borne in mind that an organization chart is a graphic representation of a store's operation. As such, it is the result of a great deal of study and debate. For example, many stores include the personnel function under the responsibilities of the director of store operation. This would have the effect of giving that director a great deal of power in the area of hiring the personnel required by the merchandising function. Note also that the manager of publicity is as important an individual as the merchandising manager. By this arrangement, neither person has the final say on publicity. They must cooperate on decisions or appeal to the director of merchandising for decisions that they cannot work out between themselves. Note that the treasurer is a staff function reporting directly to the general manager. Since the financial control of both major functions is the responsibility of the treasurer, to place this position under either of the other two departments might put the treasurer in the impossible position of complaining to the boss of the boss's incompetence.

As a store grows in size and increases in the amount of possible specialization, a third function may be added to the two-function plan pictured in

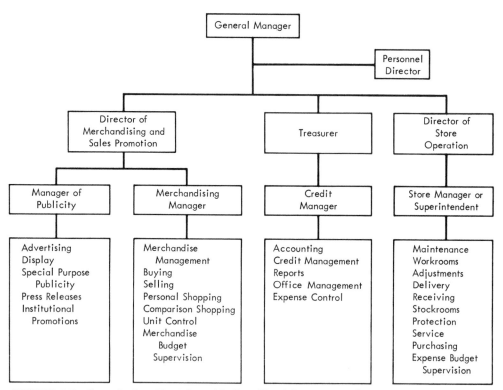

FIGURE 4-5 Organization Chart for a Medium-Sized Department Store

Figure 4-4. A store in which credit sales are an important consideration may be operated under the three-function organization plan pictured in Figure 4-5.

In this medium-sized department store, the office of the treasurer has been elevated to an equal standing with the merchandising and operations departments. Many stores of this size that are heavily involved in publicity might break the publicity department away from the director of merchandising and set it up as a separate function.

In comparing the two-function organization chart of the small department store with the three-function chart of a medium-sized department store, note the increase in the number of management and middle-management positions that become necessary as a store grows in size. The director of merchandising and sales promotion of the small store cannot solely fulfill that responsibility in the larger store. The medium-sized store requires a manager of publicity and a merchandising manager to work with the director of merchandising and sales promotion to get the job done.

LARGE DEPARTMENT STORE ORGANIZATION

The large department store with its great number of employees has no trouble in achieving a high degree of specialization. The very size of a large department store complicates its operation and makes operational planning extremely important.

Following the business recession of 1921 to 1923 the National Retail Dry Goods Association (now known as the National Retail Merchants Association) formed a committee to study the operational plans of a group of successful stores and determine a sound plan for effective department store organization. Paul M. Mazur, an authority on the subject, was commissioned to work with the committee. After eighteen months, in which thirteen stores of varying sizes were studied, the Mazur Plan was evolved. The Mazur Plan had a considerable effect on department store organization from the time of its first publication. Although there have been many variations of the plan since its inception, it still forms the basis of most large department store operations. The organization chart for a large department store based on the Mazur Plan is depicted in Figure 4-6.

As is indicated in the organization chart, the Mazur Plan proposes a four-function operation, with the lines of authority grouped under the controller, merchandise manager, publicity manager, and store manager. The Mazur Plan offered several advantages that were unique at the time of the proposal and have since been gradually accepted as basic to the field of retailing operations.

1. It divided the store into four highly specialized divisions of store operation—control, merchandising, publicity, and store management.

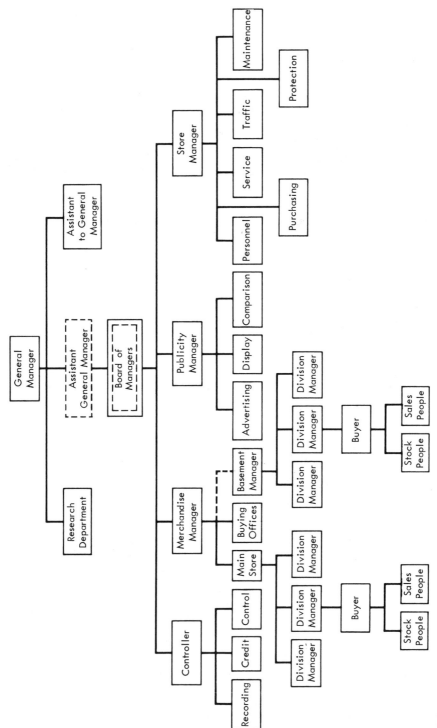

FIGURE 4-6 Mazur's Four-Function Organization Plan

2. The Plan indicates the position of each employee group in relation to every other employee group in the store. All employees know their responsibilities and the lines of authority through which they must operate.

3. The board of managers, consisting of the heads of each of the four functions, provides a meeting place in which the heads of each specialty can get a perspective of the store as a total unit. This promotes cooperation between the various functions.

The most serious criticism of the Mazur Plan is that it fails to recognize the prime importance of the merchandising division. While the merchandising division is responsible for selling merchandise, it has no control over the publicity department, which has equal status. Similarly, the merchandising division is charged with selling but has no direct voice in the training of personnel, which falls under the responsibility of the store manager. Many large stores operate under adaptations of the Mazur Plan in which the merchandising, personnel, and publicity departments are all responsible to the merchandise manager. Other stores have separated the personnel department from the responsibility of the store manager and elevated it to a major function. They operate under a five-function system. These stores leave it up to the general manager and board of managers to maintain the necessary cooperation between functions.

It is doubtful if any stores can be found that operate exactly as Mazur suggested. On the other hand it would be difficult to find a store whose organizational setup is not based upon Mazur's idea.

Whatever the organizational plan, there are certain features that are universally found. Following is a brief discussion of the characteristics of the four functions suggested by Mazur.

The Merchandising Function

The function of the merchandising manager and his or her department is to maintain the inventory offered for sale in accordance with the requirements of the consumer. The people responsible for the merchandise function can be evaluated by comparing the stock of goods offered for sale with consumer demand. In many stores the sale of goods is also included among the responsibilities of the merchandise function.

Unquestionably, merchandising is the most important function of a retail store. A three-function organizational plan has even been suggested in which the merchandising function is responsible for sales promotion, publicity, and personnel, as well as the normal merchandising responsibility. Under this plan the retail organization is focused on buying and selling, with all other functions serving in a staff or advisory position.

The merchandise manager is probably the most important executive in the store. That person's duties and the duties of the various departments under his or her control are as follows:

1. See to it that the major policy decisions affecting the store's image, price range, and quality, which are set up by top management, are properly carried out.
2. Control all buying and selling so that a cooperative effort is made to consistently give the store the image that is required by top management. For maximum effectiveness their decisions must be uniformly met throughout all of the divisions and departments in the store.
3. Assist buyers to understand up-to-date market conditions and business trends.
4. Set up and administer a system for merchandise budgeting and control, that will accurately indicate the inventory position of the store at all times. This will aid buyers in their purchase planning and provide reports from which departmental effectiveness can be determined.
5. Give whatever assistance is necessary to individual buyers to help them in carrying out their individual duties.
6. Cooperate fully with the sales promotion and publicity departments in carrying out sales promotion schemes, and see to it that the various merchandising departments cooperate as well.
7. Supervise the buying and selling activities of each department to insure compliance with the policies that have been established.
8. Provide help to buyers in finding new resources.

One of the characteristics of sound management is that the number of persons reporting to a supervisor should never be so great that the supervisor is unable to give adequate personal attention to each individual. As a department store grows in size and the number of departments in the store increases, it becomes impossible for the merchandise manager to give adequate attention to each area. It is customary in large stores to group similar departments into divisions under the authority of a divisional manager. For example, the women's wear division of a large department store would include all departments carrying women's clothing.

To carry out these responsibilities, the merchandise function is broken down into various areas. Figure 4-7 indicates the manner in which this may be done.

It can be seen that a high degree of specialization exists within the merchandise function. Some of the specialized areas such as budgeting, merchandise statistics, fashion, comparison shopping, and testing serve the merchandise manager as advisors, while those areas concerned with buying and selling are organized in a line or decision-making capacity.

As is typical of many department stores, the organization plan pictured in Figure 4-7 indicates a basement store as a completely separate entity from the main store. The basement manager is responsible for a group of departments that are parallel to and equal in importance to the main store. Note that both the basement store and the main store managers are responsible to

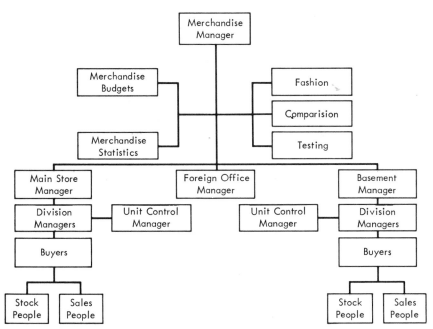

FIGURE 4-7 Organization of the Merchandising Function

the merchandise manager. One of the most serious faults in showing the operation of a department store by means of organization charts is that the chart cannot show the cooperation between separate lines of responsibility that are necessary for a successful operation. In this case, the two units must cooperate very closely with each other to insure that the same merchandise is not offered in both areas at different prices.

The placing of comparison shopping under the responsibility of the merchandising manager is not always found in department store organization. There are two theories concerning the purpose of comparison shopping. The first is that such shopping acts as an aid to merchandising by providing information regarding styles, quality, and prices being offered by competitors. If this theory is accepted, then the service provided by comparison shoppers should be reported to the merchandise manager.

The second theory is that comparison shopping is a means of measuring the effectiveness of the merchandising function. When this theory is followed, the comparison shoppers would naturally make their reports to some other executive.

In Figure 4-7 it should be noted that buying and selling are under the jurisdiction of the store's buyers. There are, however, those who advocate their separation.

Separation of Buying
and Selling

In most department stores the responsibility for both buying and selling rests with the buyer. The effectiveness of this procedure has resulted in a continuous debate for many years. Those who feel that the two responsibilities should be split between two separate individuals offer the following arguments:

1. In today's complex buying market there is simply too much time spent buying to permit a buyer to do an adequate job as a supervisor of the sales force. As a result, buyers who are forced to spend part of their time on the selling floor cannot perform either their buying or their selling duties with maximum effectiveness. Often, it is the important selling function that suffers more.

2. The characteristics required of a good buyer are quite different from those required of a competent director of sales personnel. The skills, personality, and training of a buyer should be directed toward a knowledge of the wholesale market, current style trends, and the ability to negotiate with manufacturers. On the other hand, good sales managers must understand the consumer market and consumer personality. They should be interested in people, speak fluently, and be persuasive and imaginative. Because it is difficult to find both sets of characteristics in one person, the functions should be separated and the responsibilities of buying and selling should be split between two people.

3. Although it is true that a buyer cannot operate effectively without a hand on the "customer's pulse," computerized inventory reports make available to the buyer a much more scientific analysis of consumer demand than can be obtained by spending a few hours each week on the selling floor.

Despite the arguments mentioned above, most stores favor a combination of the buying and selling responsibilities in a single person. They offer these arguments:

1. It is not vital for a buyer to spend a great deal of time on the selling floor. Therefore, the buyer need not be a great salesperson. If buying requires long periods of absence from the floor, the buyer's assistant should be available.

2. Computerized reports give scientific sales analyses, but they do not indicate other vital information. For example, while the data processing department may indicate that blue is the best-selling color for blouses actually sold, it will not reveal the number of requests that were made for red blouses that the department does not carry in stock.

3. Probably the most important argument against splitting the buying and selling responsibilities is that managerial control suffers from such a separation. When one person is charged with both areas, that person is also individually responsible for the department's profit. A department with falling profits that is operated under the joint responsibilities of a buyer and a sales manager is frequently the focal point for friction, conflicts of interest, and "passing the buck."

The majority of experts seem to favor the division of the buying and selling areas. They feel that a system of standards can be set up to measure the effectiveness of each of the areas and that the division of the responsibilities allows both areas the benefits of specialization. In most stores, however, the buyer is also responsible for the department's selling.

Those stores that separate the buying and selling areas do so by removing the selling responsibilities from the merchandise function and placing it under the responsibility of a manager of personal selling, who in turn reports to the director of sales promotion.

The problem of separation of the buying and selling areas will be discussed later in this chapter in relation to branch and chain store organization, where the problems involved are somewhat different.

The Store Management Function

All of the functions related to the physical operation of the store are grouped together under the supervision of the store manager, superintendent, or director of store operations. The organization chart pictured in Figure 4-8 is not typical of the responsibilities of all store managers in that it limits the duty of the function to purely operating jobs. In many stores such areas as customer claims and personnel fall under the supervision of the store manager.

The responsibilities of the various departments that fall under the supervision of the store manager are as follows:

Protection Department

1. Detectives
2. Service shopping
3. Outside protective agencies
4. Insurance

Workrooms

1. Clothing alterations
2. Merchandise repairs

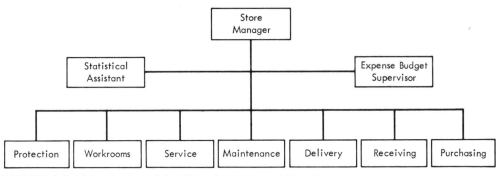

FIGURE 4-8 Organization of the Store Management Function

3. Restaurants
4. Soda fountains
5. Beauty parlors

Service

1. Adjustments
2. Floor services
3. Cashiers
4. Wrapping

Maintenance

1. Repairs
2. Maintenance of mechanical equipment
3. Ventilation
4. Heating
5. Housekeeping
6. Construction and alteration

Delivery

1. Delivery room
2. Central wrapping
3. Garages
4. Warehouses

Receiving

1. Receiving room
2. Marking
3. Checking
4. Stockrooms
5. Invoice and order

Purchasing

1. Equipment
2. Supplies

The Control Function

The control function, under the supervision of the controller or treasurer, is charged with the responsibility of safeguarding the company's assets. To insure unbiased reporting, the control function should never be subordinate to any of the other functions. Instead it should operate as a function in its own right or as a staff function reporting directly to the general manager. As is the case with other functions, the controller's duties are performed by a separate

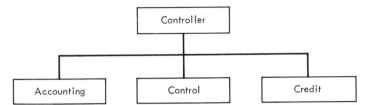

FIGURE 4-9 Organization of the Control Function

department. Figure 4-9 indicates the various departments that make up the control function in a typical department store.

The responsibilities of the control department are as follows:

Accounting Office

1. General accounting
2. Accounts payable
3. Insurance and taxes
4. Incoming mail
5. Payroll
6. Inventory planning and supervision
7. Reports

Control

1. Expense control
2. Budget control
3. Sales audit
4. Merchandise statistics and reports

Credit

1. Invoicing customers
2. Cashiers in credit office
3. Charge accounts
4. Credit authorization
5. Credit interviews
6. Deferred payments

The Publicity Function

Publicity, a function that is often referred to as sales promotion in some retail organizations, has as its chief a publicity (sales promotion) manager. The responsibilities of this function are sometimes divided into the three areas, as indicated in Figure 4-6, of advertising, display, and comparison. Some companies relegate the comparison responsibility to the merchandising division (see

Figure 4-7) and organize the function into the four specific areas of advertising, display, special events, and publicity.

The importance of this division is underscored and significantly discussed in Chapter 14, *Sales Promotional Activities.*

BRANCH STORE ORGANIZATION

Since World War II great masses of urban population have moved to the suburbs of the large metropolitan areas. These people were generally of the economic class that provided the downtown department store giants with an important segment of their customers. To offset the resulting sales loss, many large stores followed their customers to the suburbs by locating branch stores in prime suburban areas.

The branch store is usually one of several such units operating under a parent store and in many cases accounting for more than 50 percent of the total volume. In addition to increasing the sales volume, the typical branch operates more inexpensively than the main store. This savings is due in part to the branch store's use of many of the facilities of the parent, such as the data processing department. Similarly, many of the branch store's office functions and much of its advertising can be taken over by the parent with a relatively small increase in overall expenses.

The organization of branch stores depends in large part on the size of the branch, the distance between the branch and the parent store, and the policy of top management concerning the splitting up of the responsibility for buying and selling between two individuals. It is likely that every branch store handles its own physical operations under an independent store manager. The personnel function of the branch is also generally under the independent control of the branch unless the distance from the parent is so small that the parent can take over the personnel responsibilities efficiently. The control function of the branch is generally split between the branch and the parent, with the branch performing the operating details and the parent doing the analyses and report making.

The manner in which the merchandising function is handled requires more discussion, since the success or failure of the branch depends upon effective merchandising. The method of organizing the merchandising function of the branch varies considerably from store to store. Among the problems that must be faced are

1. Is each individual department within the branch large enough to warrant a full-time buyer?
2. If each department is of sufficient size to require an independent buyer, can one be found in the area in which the branch is located?
3. If the branch departments are too small to each support an independent buyer,

shall groupings be made that will result in one buyer in charge of several departments?

4. Can parent store buyers, who may not be completely aware of the branch's customer demand, effectively service the branch?

5. What is the top-management attitude toward splitting the buying and selling functions? It is unlikely that the parent store buyer can spend time on the selling floor of each branch.

6. Can effective communications be maintained between the branch and the home office, or will something be lost when managerial directives are transmitted to the branch?

There are three methods of organizing branch merchandising functions.

The Dependent Branch

Where the branch stores are few in number, located near the parent, and much smaller than the parent, parent store buyers generally take over the merchandising function of the branch. This can work quite effectively where the distance between stores is so small that the clientele is roughly the same for both units and the amount of extra work that must be done by the buyer is not burdensome. It must be borne in mind that as the time the buyer spends in the wholesale market increases, the time spent on the selling floor must decrease. The resulting lack of supervision becomes magnified as the number of branch selling floors increases. In situations in which parent buyers take on the responsibility for branch buying, it is generally necessary to split the buying and selling functions. Under such a plan the branch salespeople are responsible to a branch department sales supervisor.

The Independent Branch

As the number of branches and the sales volume of the branches increase, it becomes obvious that the parent buyers cannot handle the increased workload. In such situations separate buyers are employed by each branch. Bullock's in Los Angeles operates very successfully under this plan. Top management at Bullock's believes that the clientele at every store is different and that only by employing independent buyers will each store be able to offer merchandise that is unique to its customers' demands. Part of Bullock's success in this operation is due to the fact that each new unit is large enough to support independent buyers. The chief obstacle to a more rapid expansion on the part of Bullock's is the lack of trained buyers. This has resulted in the occasional use of one buyer for two of Bullock's units. Not every department store has been as successful as Bullock's in this type of branch independence. Marshall Field, for example, opened their Milwaukee branch with independent buyers and was forced to withdraw them.

Equal Stores

Many stores, particularly those with many branches or large successful branches, have adopted chain store merchandising principles. This is the exact opposite of Bullock's system in that it requires a central buying headquarters that is completely divorced from selling responsibilities. This does *not* mean that it gets no feedback from the selling floors. Quite the contrary, to be successful, the central buying headquarters must receive a constant stream of information from the selling floors. As branch sales volume and the number of branch units increase, it is likely that the equal store concept will become more common.

Such successful stores as Burdine's of Miami operate with considerable success with centralized buying, while other retailers maintain a successful operation with an exactly opposite point of view. Perhaps the organizational plan is less important than the personnel who make it work.*

CHAIN STORE ORGANIZATION

Chain store organizations are among the most economical methods of retail distribution; the enormous volume that they do in similar types of merchandise permits the use of scientifically determined economical methods of performing many retailing functions. We have already discussed the independent store, in which each function is performed individually, and the branch store, in which some of the functions of groups of stores can be economically grouped at one location. The chain store is a further extension of the movement toward retailing centralization. Some of the characteristics of chain store organizations are

1. Centralization and control of most of the operating functions are administered in central or regional offices.
2. The operation is generally broken down into a greater number of functions than are generally found in department stores. Chain store operation requires such additional functions as real estate, warehousing, traffic, and transportation.
3. There is an increase in the relative importance of the personnel function.
4. Carefully constructed reports must be frequently filed with the home office to permit adequate control of the various chain units.

The most important decision that must be made in the area of chain store organization is the amount of independence that should be granted to the managers of the individual chain outlets.

*This discussion of department store branches should not be confused with ownership groups of stores such as the Federal Department Stores. These are groups of stores whose ownership is the same but whose operations are almost completely individualized.

Centralization

The argument favoring a highly centralized operation, in which most of the decisions are made at the home office, is that the home office provides highly trained specialists for decision making who are certain to be more competent than the individual managers. For this reason having a weak store manager need not necessarily result in a poorly run store. The most serious disadvantage of centralization is that the home office, often a great distance from a specific outlet, cannot understand the local problems involved. Conditions vary considerably from store to store, particularly when fashion merchandise is involved, and only the store manager is able to make decisions concerning the unique requirements of the store's particular clientele. Those favoring centralization argue that the home office experts are available for advice and that the close control of the home office tends to minimize errors.

Decentralization

As more responsibility and authority are delegated to the store managers, each store becomes more individualized to the requirements of its specific clientele. Moreover, managers, as their degree of control increases, have more incentive to improve their stores' profitability. True, a weak manager cannot be carried by a decentralized system, but the detailed system of control used by most chain store organizations permits the rapid identification of weak stores and quick corrective action.

An objection to decentralization is that it frequently leads to a duplication of buying and other functions. The degree of decentralization depends in large part upon the type of product handled. The buying function of a food chain, for example, is apt to be more highly centralized than the buying function of a fashion merchandise chain.

Regional decentralization is found in almost all nationally organized chains. Under a regional plan, the units in the chain are organized into semi-independent groups according to geographical location. The organization chart of a nationally organized grocery chain which operates thousands of stores throughout the United States is pictured in Figure 4-10.

The annual gross sales volume of the chain is in excess of $3 billion. As may be seen on the chart, the company is divided into six geographical areas, each of which operates as a distinct entity, carrying out all the functions within its territory, including buying. Within each geographic district, the required number of warehouse units are operated. Each warehouse is supervised by a vice-president or general superintendent, who is aided by two or three assistant general superintendents. These assistant general superintendents supervise the activities of assistant superintendents, who operate with the help of six assistants, each of whom is responsible for from twelve to fourteen store managers.

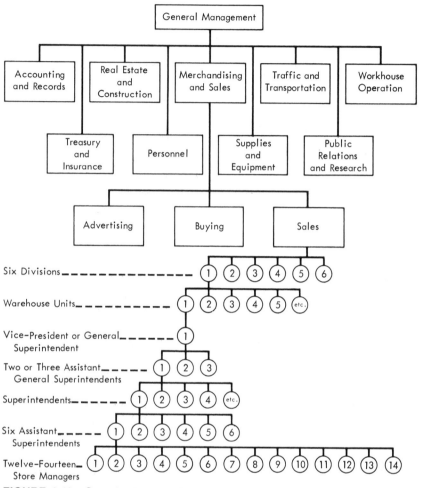

FIGURE 4-10 Organization of a Grocery Chain

CURRENT TRENDS IN STORE ORGANIZATION

The major organizational trends in retailing operations seem to be having the effect of canceling out the differences between the operations of multiunit department stores and chain stores. In the case of chain stores there is a decided movement toward decentralization, with more and more decisions being left to the discretion of the individual store buyers and managers. The reverse has been happening in the multiunit department stores, where the trend seems to be toward more centralized control, and the savings inherent in centralized buying.

As the department stores move toward centralized buying, the question of the division of the buying and selling functions becomes academic. A buyer for a group of department stores is simply too busy to be held responsible for selling. So along with centralization of buying there is a growing movement to separate buying and selling functions.

Once it has been established that the buyers are not responsible for the sale of the goods they have bought, attention must be turned to departmental organization. When the buyer was responsible for sales, it was necessary to group all sales and salespeople into departments organized according to the merchandise that one buyer purchased. If the buyer is no longer required to supervise selling departments, merchandise may then be classified along the lines of customer need. Dresses and the accessories that go with specific dresses need no longer be separated into two different departments. Similarly, classifications may be made according to the sex, age, and size of the customer. Many department stores maintain "shops" that cut across traditional lines with great success. Ski shops, bath shops, swim shops, and the like are generally supplied by several different buyers. Where the sales of such shops must be split between different departments, the accounting for profits becomes difficult, but if buyers are not responsible for selling, such problems do not exist. Once the concept that there might be different classifications of buying and selling departments becomes widespread, a situation may exist in which, say, eighty buying departments might supply merchandise for hundreds of selling centers.

Action for the Independent Retailer

Lack of proper organization can be costly to both small and large retailers. However, because an institution increases in complexity as it grows in size, the problem of proper organization is less compelling for the small operator. But considering the competitive disadvantages faced by independent retailers, this is one area in which they cannot afford to be lax. Any time two or more people cooperate toward the same goal, efficiency can be improved if their efforts are carefully organized. Each individual must be assigned and have a clear understanding of his or her duties and responsibilities, or some functions will be unnecessarily duplicated while other chores are not done at all. Naturally, in a small store, some functions must be shared, specialization is minimized, and clear lines of responsibility are difficult to establish. Certainly organization charts and job descriptions are not necessary in a small store, but no matter how informally the organization is run, its efficiency will be improved if the employees know exactly what is required of them.

IMPORTANT POINTS IN THE CHAPTER

1. *No organization of two or more people can operate effectively without a clearly understood organization of the duties and responsibilities of each person. The larger the working force, the more important clear lines of authority and duty become.*

2. *An organization chart is a device that indicates at a glance the duties and responsibilities of each person in the organization.*

3. *Large stores with many employees are able to limit the responsibilities of each employee to a specific area. This is called specialization and it results in increased worker efficiency.*

4. *Small stores have too few workers to afford specialization. Consequently, each worker is responsible for more than one function. As a store grows in size, the opportunity for specialization increases.*

5. *Departmentalization is a form of specialization that includes all similar merchandise and services in separate categories or departments.*

6. *Departmentalization is a customer convenience in that it groups similar merchandise in one department. Managerial control is improved by departmentalization, since departmental records may be kept and used to judge efficiency.*

7. *The first serious effort to organize department stores scientifically was done by Mazur, who divided the store into the four functions under the control of the merchandise manager, the controller, the publicity manager, and the store manager.*

8. *Variations of the Mazur Plan are found in all large stores. No two stores are organized in exactly the same way since organizational plans are constantly changing.*

9. *In most large department stores the merchandise function is responsible for the acquisition and sale of all of the goods required by the store's customers.*

10. *The physical operation of the store is the responsibility of the store management function.*

11. *The control function includes all record keeping and the safeguarding of the company's assets by means of various bookkeeping devices.*

12. *Advertising, special promotions, and publicity are the responsibility of the publicity function.*

13. *Branch stores may be operated independently, under their own department managers, or dependently, under the jurisdiction of the main store's department managers.*

14. *In chain store operation the functions are usually divided between the home office and the chain unit, with the merchandise, control, and part of the publicity function in the hands of the home office. There is a trend toward decentralizing chain operations with more responsibilities in the hands of the individual managers.*

REVIEW QUESTIONS

1. What are the first steps in organizing a retail operation?
2. Define a line position on an organization chart. Give an example of a line position.
3. What is specialization? How does it affect operating efficiency?

4. Discuss the advantages of departmentalization in the areas of efficiency of sales personnel.

5. List several advantages that may result from setting up departments according to similarity of merchandise. Give examples

6. Explain the principal differences between the operational organization of a small department store and a small nondepartmentalized retailer.

7. What are the four major line functions of the Mazur Plan?

8. Describe the responsibilities of the merchandising manager.

9. The organization chart pictured in Figure 4-7 indicates that the basement store is a separate line unit from the main store. What are the advantages of this?

10. Give the principal arguments against the separation of the responsibility for buying and selling.

11. What are the principal responsibilities of the store manager?

12. Explain the disadvantage of placing the control function under the responsibility of the merchandise manager.

13. Discuss the reasons for the increase in chain store operations.

14. Explain the conditions under which the personnel function of the branch can be taken over by the main store.

15. Discuss the considerations that must be taken into account in determining the organization of the merchandising function of the branch.

16. Under what conditions should the branch maintain its own buyers?

17. What is the effect of central buying offices servicing both branch and parent on the division of buying and selling responsibilities?

18. Describe the characteristics of chain store organizations.

19. Present arguments favoring the decentralization of decision making in chain store organizations.

20. Explain the trend toward decentralization of chain store organizations.

CASE PROBLEMS

CASE PROBLEM 1

Cee-Jay's is a small men's shop that has been operating successfully for several years in a suburban shopping center. The store's clientele has grown to a point at which the proprietor has decided to hire a high school student as a part-time stock clerk and another employee as a part-time bookkeeper. The organization chart of the present operation is pictured in Figure 4-3.

QUESTION

1. Prepare a new organization chart that indicates the responsibilities of both the old and the new personnel.

CASE PROBLEM 2

Clifford's, Inc. is a large, successful downtown department store that is constructing its first branch store at a suburban location 50 miles from the parent store. Top management has been meeting to determine the place of the new unit in the store's organization. The main store is organized under the four-function system pictured in Figure 4-6.

QUESTION

1. Explain how you would reorganize the organization chart to include the branch. In your solution treat each of the following four functions separately, describing the work to be performed by branch personnel and the work to be performed by parent personnel.

1. Control Function
2. Publicity Function
3. Store Managing Function
4. Merchandising Function

5 *the management of personnel*

BEHAVIORAL OBJECTIVES

Upon completion of this chapter the student should be able to

1. *List five functions of the personnel department.*
2. *Differentiate between in-store and outside sources of personnel supply, giving three examples of the latter.*
3. *Give five steps in a typical selection procedure.*
4. *List four areas of testing.*
5. *Discuss five advantages of a training program.*
6. *Write a short essay on personnel evaluations, indicating four reasons for this procedure.*
7. *Achieve the grade of 75% on an examination consisting of problems in finding the earnings under the following methods: hourly basis; straight commission; salary plus commission; and salary plus quota bonus.*

INTRODUCTION

The organization chart provides the skeleton of an enterprise. Covering the bare skeleton with flesh and blood to give it life is the responsibility of the personnel department. It is up to the personnel department to provide the people who will make the organization chart work effectively. The bare chart, no matter how brilliantly conceived, can be effective only if capable people are employed to carry out the responsibilities set forth in the plan.

POSITION OF THE PERSONNEL DEPARTMENT IN THE ORGANIZATION

The importance of personnel management to the retail operation does not depend upon the size of the store. No store, regardless of its size, can operate effectively without capable people. In a small store the personnel function can easily be handled by the proprietor. However, the personnel problems of a major retailer become so massive that specialists are required to do the job efficiently.

Theoretically, the personnel department performs a staff, or advisory, function. For example, salespersons hired by the personnel department are sent to the selling departments for final approval. In practice, however, thanks to the personnel department's excellent record, the selling departments rarely dispute their judgment. In effect, with lower level employees, the final hiring decision is made by the personnel department. Consequently, while shown on most organization charts as staff (advisory), the personnel department sometimes actually performs a line (decision-making) function.

THE LAW AND PERSONNEL PRACTICES

In recent years, an ever increasing awareness of the law and how employees are protected has become necessary for personnel managers to understand and follow. On the federal level, government has concerned itself with such areas as salaries, hiring practices, and minority discrimination. Prior to the current legislation, retailers were guided by their own selection procedures and instincts without concern for penalties. Although such practices as race discrimination and lesser pay for women were often standard practice, the violations of the individual's rights were more socially unacceptable than legally based.

At the federal level of government, significant legislation has been enacted to protect citizens. The Fair Labor Standards Act, most recently amended in 1974, addresses minimum salaries and hours per work week for employees in stores grossing more than $250,000 per year. The Equal Pay Act of 1963 requires equal pay for equal work. Title VII of the Civil Rights Act prohibits discrimination on the basis of race, color, and religion. The Age Discrimination in Employment Act protects individuals from bias in hiring because of age. In addition to this legislation many states and municipalities have enacted legislation for the further protection of their inhabitants.

With the passage of these laws, retailers have been required to keep records concerning their hiring practices, which could be legally scrutinized by governmental agencies. Unfair practices are frowned upon by these agencies and carry a variety of penalties.

FUNCTIONS OF THE PERSONNEL DEPARTMENT

The overall function of the personnel department is to provide the store with capable workers. This is done by performing duties in the following areas:

1. Recruitment
2. Training
3. Evaluation
4. Compensation
5. Employee Services and Benefits
6. Labor Relations

Recruitment

Before any steps can be taken to hire people, the personnel department must have a clear and exact understanding of the job to be filled. An analysis of every job in the store must be made to ensure that the characteristics of the person hired to do the job match the requirements of the job. Recruitment and training, to be effective, must be tailored to a specific set of requirements for each job. Those duties required for the job are called job specifications. The requirements of the individual are called man specifications.

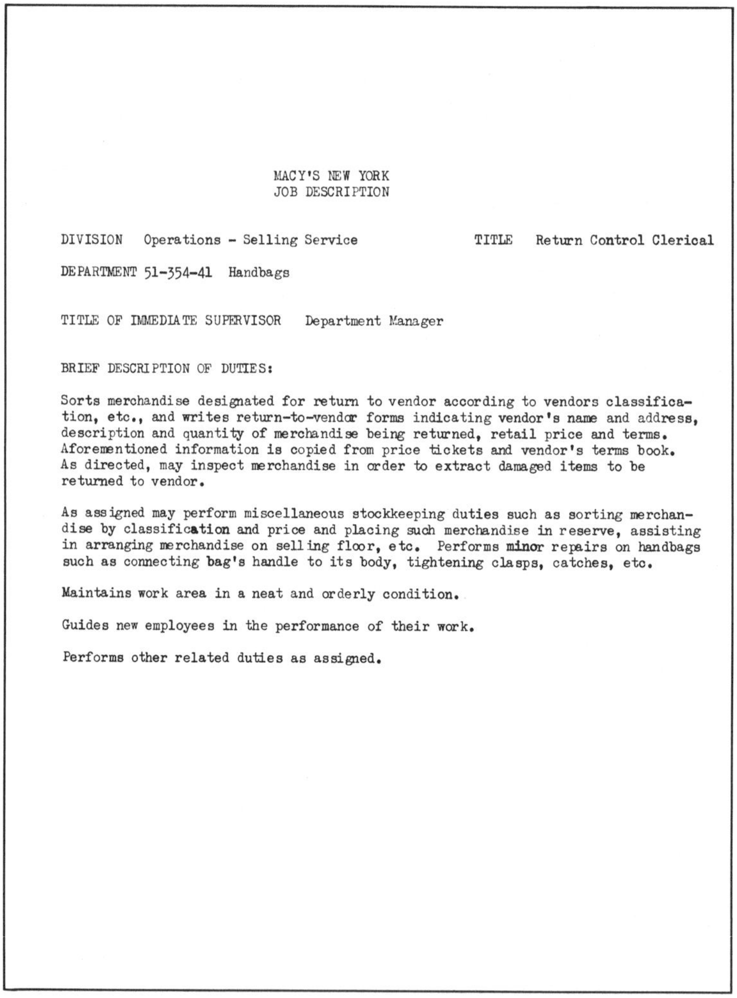

```
                         MACY'S NEW YORK
                         JOB DESCRIPTION


DIVISION   Operations - Selling Service          TITLE   Return Control Clerical

DEPARTMENT 51-354-41  Handbags


TITLE OF IMMEDIATE SUPERVISOR   Department Manager


BRIEF DESCRIPTION OF DUTIES:

Sorts merchandise designated for return to vendor according to vendors classifica-
tion, etc., and writes return-to-vendor forms indicating vendor's name and address,
description and quantity of merchandise being returned, retail price and terms.
Aforementioned information is copied from price tickets and vendor's terms book.
As directed, may inspect merchandise in order to extract damaged items to be
returned to vendor.

As assigned may perform miscellaneous stockkeeping duties such as sorting merchan-
dise by classification and price and placing such merchandise in reserve, assisting
in arranging merchandise on selling floor, etc.  Performs minor repairs on handbags
such as connecting bag's handle to its body, tightening clasps, catches, etc.

Maintains work area in a neat and orderly condition.

Guides new employees in the performance of their work.

Performs other related duties as assigned.
```

FIGURE 5-1 Job Description—Return Control Clerical

Job Analyses

Scientific analysis of each job in the store must be cooperatively accomplished by the personnel department and the supervisors of each department. Then, a job description should be formally printed and available to the recruiting staff of the personnel department. (See Figure 5-1.) Jobs are usually analyzed by observation, questionnaire, and personal interviews with top and middle management. The anlaysis should include

1. Description and title of job
2. The exact duties required by the job
3. Compensation range
4. Working conditions
5. Necessary training
6. Possibilities for advancement
7. Physical characteristics required of the workers
8. Mental ability required by the job, including desired educational level and experience
9. Personal characteristics required, such as appearance, maturity, initiative, and ability to get on with others

From the job analysis, the personnel department is able to formulate training programs and develop interview techniques and recruiting practices for each job. Furthermore, the job analysis focuses management's attention on working conditions and gives the prospective employee a clear picture of the job's responsibilities and chances for job improvement.

Sources of Personnel Supply

One of the most important personnel problems of a large retail operation is the high rate of employee turnover. This is due, in large part, to relatively low wages, many young employees, a large number of part-timers, and the effect of the seasonal nature of retailing on personnel needs. Whatever the causes of turnover, it is a constant problem that can be met only by establishing sources of supply that will provide workers when they are needed.

In-Store Sources. The high rate of retail personnel turnover is not restricted to sales personnel. Top and mid-management jobs are constantly becoming available through turnover or expansion. Most stores prefer to fill such jobs by promotion. Moving people up to a higher job builds morale by indicating that a person who has been in the store for a while will not be passed over for promotion by an outsider. Since managerial training programs are expensive, it is important that a store select managers that are not likely to leave.

The in-service promotion of one person opens a chain of promotions to the work force. For example, the promotion of a buyer to the position of assistant merchandising manager may be followed by the promotion of an assistant buyer to buyer, a department manager to assistant buyer, and a salesperson to department manager. In each case the new job holder is a person whose personality, skill, and ability are well-known to management. The most sophisticated personnel department cannot learn as much about a new job applicant as the information they have available from the personnel records of an in-service applicant. The chance for a happy marriage between worker and job improves as the information about the worker improves.

Stores depending upon promotions from within to fill vacancies have relatively simple recruitment problems, since they need only to worry about hiring for the lowest-level jobs. Although the requirements of low-level jobs are modest, care must be taken that some entry jobs are filled by people of high qualification who will become the raw material for later in-service promotions.

Another advantage of in-service promotions is the ability of a store to attract highly qualified people for lower-level jobs. A store with a reputation for having a good promotion policy will get more high-quality applicants than an organization in which promotions are rarely given. Such stores as Gimbels and the Edison Brothers chain of shoe stores mention in-service promotions in the brochures printed to attract job applicants.

Although it is generally agreed that in-store promotions merit a great deal of attention, it should be understood that a policy that is strictly based 100 percent on promotion from within can actually act as a deterrent for new ideas. Very often this policy of inbreeding results in a reaffirming of "old hat" ideas. It is desirable for the growth and vitality of the organization to recruit managerial talent from other retail orientations; these people can often breathe needed fresh ideas into the company. A blending of applicants from within the organization and from outside sources is most beneficial.

Outside Sources.   Among the outside sources of personnel are advertisements, employment agencies (both private and governmental), schools and colleges, and transient applicants (persons coming directly to the store for work). Since retailing is highly seasonal, it is necessary for the personnel departments to know exactly which outside sources to use for the type of personnel required.

1. *Want ads.* Advertising for help in the local newspapers is probably the most effective method of attracting large numbers of job applicants. The disadvantage of using this source is that there is no preliminary screening for qualifications. Applicants supplied by any of the other sources mentioned have had some of their qualifications checked before coming to the store. In answer to an ad there is frequently a deluge of applicants, many of whom lack necessary qualifications. The want ads are most useful when large numbers of relatively unqualified workers are needed. Two types of ads are used, blind ads in which only the job is listed and the store's identity is concealed by using a P.O. box number, and open ads

that indicate both the position and the company name. Some retailers employ both techniques or choose the one that is believed to be most appropriate for the particular company.

2. *Employment agencies.* Private and government-sponsored employment agencies are available to supply needed personnel. Employment agencies do not produce as great a number of applicants as advertising. However, the agency matches the applicant's qualifications with the job's requirements and thus saves a considerable amount of personnel department's time in interviewing.

Many employment agencies specialize in specific types of personnel, such as office workers or managerial executives. Personnel departments should keep records of the various employment agencies in their areas, so they can fill sudden vacancies in a minimum amount of time.

3. *Schools and colleges.* Student recruiting generally begins at the high school level. Most high schools and colleges maintain a job placement office to help find part-time employment for interested students. It is important for the personnel department to keep close contact with the neighboring educational institutions even in times of slow recruitment. The seasonal nature of retail recruitment makes it imperative that large numbers of part-time people be available when they are needed.

Many schools and colleges include cooperative work experience programs among their course offerings. Under this plan retailing students are given the opportunity to spend part of their school days at the work for which they are being trained. This affords the students an opportunity to learn under actual business conditions, while helping the store fill needed positions. Perhaps the most important feature of the cooperative work experience program is that it gives the store the opportunity to work with the student before an actual hiring decision must be made. Upon their graduation, the store is able to employ those students who have been found to be satisfactory under actual working conditions.

Many of the larger stores compete for college graduates. It is felt that these people will eventually fill the top and mid-management positions. Personnel managers regularly attend college career days specifically for this purpose.

Miscellaneous Sources. There are additional means of recruiting qualified personnel in addition to the foregoing.

1. *Recommendations.* The use of current employees to help find new people is common. Posting job vacancies on the bulletin board or circulating the information by word of mouth generally results in job applications from friends and relatives of the working staff. One of the causes of job turnover, particularly during the first week, is that the job is not what the newly hired worker expected. Hiring by recommendation may reduce turnover, since applicants come to the store fully informed by their friends or relatives about what to expect from the job.

2. *Transient applicants.* Certainly the cheapest and probably the most widely used means by which jobs are filled are casual (transient) applicants. These are people who show up at the employment department, fill out an application, and either go through the employment procedure if there is work available, or have the information placed on file for later use in the event that no job is available.

Selection Procedures

A series of procedures must be undertaken by the personnel department to screen individuals and ensure a proper match-up of applicant and job requirements. Not only must this process provide the right worker for the job to be performed, but it must also make certain that attention is paid to the prospect's integrity. With the continuing increase in internal pilferage, management must concern itself with careful screening procedures. Management has any number of devices available to determine honesty. One is the checking of references, which will be discussed later. The use of the polygraph or lie detector test is also being used in the selection procedure as a deterrent to infidelity. While it has been argued that polygraph usage is an affront to prospective employees, it has nonetheless proved to be beneficial to its users. Whatever the process used for screening applicants, care must be exercised to avoid costly errors in employment. Only careful attention, without the pitfalls of hasty decisions, can provide satisfactory employees.

It should be understood that not all stores follow the same procedures. Moreover, the procedures followed within a store may vary from job to job. Thus an applicant for a low-level job might not require reference checking, whereas a person interested in a managerial position would undergo a careful system of reference checking. In addition, the order in which the selection procedures are performed may vary, with supply and demand often the determining factor in how carefully a prospective worker is screened.

The typical steps in the selection procedures of most retail stores are (1) application blank, (2) preliminary interview, (3) checking references, (4) testing, and (5) final interview.

Application Blank. Some stores require that an application blank be filled in before an interview, some interview first, and others do both simultaneously. In any event, the application blank serves several purposes:

1. It obtains necessary information from the applicant.
2. It provides a basis upon which the interview can be conducted.
3. If the applicant is hired, it becomes part of his or her permanent file for future reference when necessary.
4. If the applicant is not hired it may be kept for future use when a worker is needed.

The information found on an application consists of identification data (name, address, personal history), education (schools attended, degrees achieved), prior employment record (jobs held since graduation, reasons for termination), and references (persons to be contacted for further information). In recent years, to eliminate bias, antidiscrimination laws have forbidden the use of photographs and questions relating to race and religion. An example of an application may be found in Figure 5-2.

The prime function of the application is to match applicants with job requirements. Consequently, it must be carefully constructed.

Preliminary Interview. The preliminary interview, sometimes referred to as a "rail interview" (it is a short, stand-up interview that may be done over the railing of the personnel department), has the function of correcting the application, and weeding out those applicants in whom the store is not interested. The preliminary interview should be conducted by an experienced person who is thoroughly acquainted with available positions and the requirements for such positions. Although the preliminary interview must be short, time should not be saved at the cost of efficiency. This may result in qualified people being turned away and jobs given to those of mediocre abilities. Weeding out undesirable applicants requires a great deal of tact. Disappointing people without proper regard for their feelings may cause a loss of good will to the store. Some stores give the rail interview before requiring the application to be filled out. This is undoubtedly an economy measure, but most progressive stores give every job applicant the right to an interview and an application, to ensure customer good will.

A successful preliminary intervew should result in such important knowledge as voice, diction, and grooming.

Checking References. Checking the background information given on the application is time-consuming and expensive. Therefore, it is often ignored in cases of applicants for low-level jobs. The references given are from friends of the prospective employee who have no experience with the applicant's work habits. It is unusual to get a bad response from a reference supplied by an applicant. Thus, retailers must exercise caution when checking references.

An applicant's background can be more accurately checked by contacting prior employers. Although this can be done by mail, a telephone call can be more informative. The information supplied from former employers on work habits, attitudes, and quantity and quality of a prospect's work can be much more important in the hiring decision than the knowledge gathered by the application blank or interview. With all of the expense incurred as the result of internal theft, management who ignore careful reference checking could pay dearly in the long run. A discussion on internal pilferage in Chapter 8, *Store Security*, underscores the need for checking references.

Testing. At best, the questionnaire gives raw facts that cannot always be verified, and the results of the interview are little more than the personal views of the interviewer. In an effort to get more objective information about prospective workers, many large retailers are turning to various types of testing. Among those used are tests of ability, aptitude, intelligence, and personality.

1. *Ability testing.* For many jobs, ability testing has always been used to rate performance. For example, a secretary is rarely hired without some sort of a typing or stenography test. Aside from some nervousness on the part of the applicant, for which allowances may be made, such tests give an accurate indication of secretarial skills. Wrapping, filing, and machine operation are other areas in which skills may be effectively tested. The major disadvantage of such testing is a lack

| F. 240A-4-67 | APPLICATION FOR EMPLOYMENT | | MACY'S HERALD SQUARE | DO NOT WRITE IN THIS SPACE |

APPLICATION FOR EMPLOYMENT MACY'S HERALD SQUARE

DO NOT WRITE IN THIS SPACE
P 1 2 3 4
E 1 2 3 4
R 1 2 3 4

IN THE EVENT THAT YOU ARE EMPLOYED THIS BECOMES PART OF YOUR PERSONNEL RECORD, THEREFORE IT IS IMPORTANT THAT YOU ENTER ALL INFORMATION NEATLY, ACCURATELY AND COMPLETELY.

| Last Name (Print Clearly) | First Name | Middle Name | Maiden Name | Husband's or Wife's First Name |

| Number and Street | City, Postal Zone and State | Tel. No. | Social Security No. |

| Date of Birth | Age* | Single ☐ Divorced ☐ Separated ☐ Married ☐ Widowed ☐ | No. of Dependents | Height Ft. in. | Weight | American Citizen | Yes ☐ No ☐ |

* APPLICABLE LAW PROHIBITS DISCRIMINATION IN EMPLOYMENT BECAUSE OF RACE, COLOR, RELIGION, SEX, NATIONAL ORIGIN OR AGE.

| Schedule Preferred: | Full Time ☐ Mid-Day ☐ | Evenings ☐ and Saturdays ☐ | Other: | Position Desired: | Sales ☐ Office ☐ | Other: | State Salary Desired (Optional) |

| Relative in our employ? | Yes ☐ No ☐ | If so, in which store or dept. | Name of Relative | Read ad in which paper | Referred to us by Macy Employee Name of Employee |

| Have you ever been employed by Macy's before? | Yes ☐ No ☐ | If yes, under what name were you employed? | Position and Dept. | Dates Employed |

EDUCATION

SCHOOL	NUMBER OF YEARS	GRADUATED YES	GRADUATED NO	NAME AND LOCATION OF SCHOOL	MAJOR SUBJECT OR SPECIALIZATION	DATES ATTENDED
Grammar						
High School						
College						
Other						

PREVIOUS EMPLOYMENT

PLEASE ACCOUNT FOR ALL TIME SINCE LEAVING SCHOOL, INCLUDING **CURRENT EMPLOYMENT AND PERIODS OF UNEMPLOYMENT**. STATE IF ANY OF THESE EMPLOYERS ARE RELATED TO YOU.

DATES EMPLOYED	BUSINESS NAME AND ADDRESS	JOB TITLE AND DUTIES	REASON FOR LEAVING	SALARY
From: To:	Last or Present Employer Address			
From: To:	Previous Employer Address			
From: To:	Previous Employer Address			
From: To:	Previous Employer Address			
From: To:	Previous Employer Address			
From: To:	Previous Employer Address			

PLEASE ANSWER ALL QUESTIONS ON REVERSE SIDE

| Referred by | Test Scores | Second Interview |

FIGURE 5-2 Application for Employment—Macy's, Herald Square, New York City

GENERAL INFORMATION

No of children,
if any, and ages_____

Were you ever arrested (other than Traffic Violations)?

Yes ☐   No ☐

Date and purpose of
last physicial exam._____

If yes, indicate date_____

Names of personal aquaintances who work for Macy's

place_____

_____

offense_____

_____

Were you acquitted ☐   convicted ☐

Husband's (or Wife's)
Occupation_____

In case of accident notify:

Business
Address_____

Name_____Relationship_____

Father's
Occupation _____

Home
Address_____   Tel.
No._____
Street and City

Business
Address_____

Business
Address_____   Tel.
No._____
Street and City

Please list any hobbies, training or work experience you have not indicated on the other side of application.

U. S. MILITARY RECORD

Branch of Service	Rank or Rate	Duties or Assignment	Date Inducted	Date of Separation or Discharge

Are you a member of a U. S. Service Reserve Corps? Yes ☐   No ☐   Army ☐   Navy ☐

Inactive?_____   Active?_____   Marine ☐   Air Force ☐

DO NOT WRITE BELOW THIS LINE

Test for: FT ☐   PT ☐   SO ☐   H.B ☐   R   (   )

☐ SALES   ☐ M.C./CHECKER   OTHER: C   (   )

☐ CLERICAL   ☐ M.C. CASHIER

☐ TEL. ORD. BD.   ☐ STOCK/PACKER   P   (   )

AGREEMENT

I hereby certify that to the best of my knowledge all statements I have made on this application are true and correct. I understand that any misrepresentation of facts on this application is sufficient cause for dismissal.

I understand that certain departments have union shop agreements and that if I am assigned to one of these departments I must abide by the terms and conditions set forth in the collective bargaining agreement applicable to that department.

I agree to observe all rules of the store and faithfully perform whatever duties may be assigned to me.

Signature_____   Witness_____

FIGURE 5-2   (Cont.)

of standardization. Different applicants may be given different tests under a variety of testing conditions. For best effect, ability testing should be scientifically administered, with all applicants given the same test under the same conditions.

2. *Aptitude testing.* Aptitude tests are generally written and are used to determine an applicant's capacity for a certain type of work. While most aptitude tests are designed for testing mechanical ability, work has been done on the design of aptitude tests for salespeople.

3. *Intelligence testing.* Some large department stores feel that intelligence testing is important to successful employment and require all applicants to take a written intelligence test. They believe that every job classification should be filled by a person having an I.Q. falling within a certain range. All people falling below the minimum I.Q. are ruled out as not having enough intelligence. Those whose scores fall above the maximum are ruled out, since it is believed that they would become bored with the job and quit or perform ineffectively. Intelligence testing is not widespread among retailers. Probably fewer than 25 percent of the stores require such tests.

4. *Personality testing.* There is little doubt that such personality characteristics as friendliness and sociability are advantageous to a salesperson. There are few who would argue the premise that knowledge of personality is important in personnel placing. However, there are excellent arguments to the effect that personality tests have little or no validity. The fact is that none of the tests, with the possible exception of skill tests such as typing, are as yet anywhere near perfection. Although testing has a very promising future in personnel work, the tests available are far from being perfect instruments. The greatest disadvantage of personnel testing is that too much reliance may be placed on the results. An applicant's test scores are valuable, but should only be used as one of many factors in making a decision

Final Interview. After all of the preliminary interviewing, application, reference checking, and testing have been completed, the final or secondary interview is held. This interview may be conducted by a senior interviewer or the head of the department for which the applicant is slated to work. It has the dual purpose of informing the applicant of the duties and responsibilities that will be required by the job, and of permitting the interviewer to judge the applicant's knowledge and personality in relation to the specific job opening.

Some stores require that a physical examination be taken by all new employees. It would be wise for all stores to adopt this requirement. Retail work is difficult and can only be performed by persons who are physically fit. Screening out those who do not have the physical stamina for the work reduces personnel turnover. To offset the high cost of physical examinations, many stores require their new employees to have their own doctors fill out a medical form. Many insurance carriers require physical exams of prospective employees.

Training Employees

A new worker in a small store requires very little time in which to "fit in" to the organization. Soon after an employee is hired, the proprietor introduces

FIGURE 5-3 New Employee Orientation Literature

the worker to the exisiting personnel. After a few days the worker learns the details of the job's responsibilities and working conditions. In a large store the orientation of new employees is done in a more formal manner. New employees may be given guided tours of the store, lectures on store regulations, and literature on the history of the store. (See Figure 5-3.) Learning about the store to help the new employee "feel at home" is a part of the training program.

The training program itself can be informal, as in the case of a small store where a new employee is "broken in" by an experienced worker. It can be short, as it would be for a new unloader in the receiving department of a large store, who might merely have to be told where to put the cartons taken from the truck. In short, every new job requires a training period that is adapted to the specific job.

The training of employees in a large store is generally the responsibility of the personnel department. (See Figure 5-4.) It is an expensive procedure, both in terms of the time spent by personnel people and the nonproductive time spent by the employee during the training period. Since employees are fully paid during this nonproductive period, the expense of training employees is considerable. A great deal of pressure is put on the personnel department, since management insists upon demonstrable results in return for the

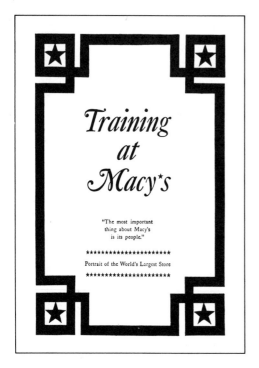

FIGURE 5-4 A Kit Complete with Training Aids for New Employees

expense involved. The following are some of the advantages of a training program:

1. As a worker becomes more skilled at the job, both the quantity and quality of work increase. A training program, by shortening the learning process, brings a worker to a high competence level much more quickly than could be done by informal learning.

2. As the productivity of individual workers increases, fewer employees are needed to handle any given volume of work. The training program lessens the time during which a new worker "doesn't carry his or her weight," and by increasing worker skills, the total work force may be decreased.

3. There is a best way to perform every task. Employees cannot be expected to learn this way by themselves. An organization that has set up standardized procedures must be sure that all of its employees are trained to follow these procedures. Work that is not done in conformity with standardized procedures is apt to lead to errors and customer dissatisfaction.

4. A well-trained worker needs less supervision than a poorly trained person. The worker's knowledge and skill reduce dependence on supervisors. This permits a reduction in the amount of supervisory help needed and frees supervisors for other tasks.

5. The well-trained employee is confident and capable, feels secure at the job, and has good chances for advancement. A poorly trained employee, on the other

hand, is nervous, lacks confidence, and, as a result, frequently hates the work and is likely to quit.

6. Employees who have benefited from an expensive training program are made to feel that the store has a high regard for their potential. In addition, during the training period, the training personnel always show the store in its best light and attempt to improve morale.

Persons to Be Trained

Since the training program must be given to employees with a wide range of prior experience, the programs given must vary with the needs of the individual workers. Generally speaking, training groups may be broken down as follows:

Inexperienced Sales Personnel. The training of inexperienced sales personnel is usually done in two or three full days or spread over a few hours a day for several weeks. The work includes a full explanation of store policies concerning employees, such as dress regulations, employee discounts, and absence from work. In addition, such store procedures as policy on returned merchandise, credit handling, filling out sales slips, and C.O.D. sales are explained at length. Product information on the goods to be sold is given by the buyer or department manager.

Many retail organizations believe that the training of sales personnel is the most important of all the training programs and provide handbooks that can be studied by the new employees at their leisure. The actual course work usually includes such up-to-date teaching procedures as role-playing, slides and movies, and programmed instruction.

Large stores frequently call in outside experts to assist in their training programs. Since this can be an expensive procedure, particularly for smaller stores, it is not unusual for small and medium-sized stores to band together in setting up a training center. By doing this, they minimize the cost of expensive training to the individual store.

The sponsor system is commonly used for breaking in new personnel for both the selling and nonselling departments. Under this system an experienced employee is given the responsibility of greeting new workers and introducing them to the existing staff, explaining departmental procedures, giving product information and the location of stock, and improving the new person's selling techniques. It is the sponsors' further task to periodically evaluate their charges and try to keep the new employees' morale at a high level. In most stores the sponsor receives an increase in salary for these efforts.

Inexperienced Nonselling Personnel. Inexperienced nonselling or support personnel such as stock clerks and office workers have somewhat different training needs from salespeople. In the area of store policy concerning employees (employee benefits, discounts, and so on) the educational needs are the same for all employees and they can be taught together, either by lecture, handbook, or some combination of the two. Training in the duties of the specific nonselling jobs is usually done in the department by the sponsor system. Generally there are too few nonselling people hired at any one time for formalized class training. Care should be taken that support personnel are being properly trained; much customer dissatisfaction is caused by errors made by nonselling personnel.

New, Experienced Personnel. Naturally, the training of experienced personnel will be of relatively short duration. These people have already learned the skills required by their jobs and need only to be given instruction in the store's policies and procedures. Of course, people who have gained their experience at another store must be carefully supervised until the department manager can be sure their job skills are equal to those required by the store.

Follow-up Training. Progressive retailers are becoming increasingly aware of the fact that job capability depends upon constant educational growth. Brief introductory training rarely results in maximum job capability. New methods and questions are always coming up and there must be an occasional meeting for discussion.

The training of regular personnel generally takes the form of individual conferences or small discussion seminars. At such small group meetings the teacher does little more than guide discussion. The workers discuss their problems, suggest new approaches, and arrive at conclusions. When new methods or procedures are to be initiated, the instructor must take a more central position.

Follow-up training is eagerly sought by workers anxious for promotion. It provides them with an opportunity to improve the job skills upon which their promotion will be based.

Part-Time Personnel. The training of part-time help presents the store with a serious problem. Extras seldom work long enough to make an expensive training program worthwhile. On the other hand, it is impossible to put a poorly trained salesperson on the floor. Frequently, a compromise is made. The necessary training period is shortened, and the new employee is turned over to a sponsor as soon as possible. The inadequate training period frequently results in errors. The training of extras is one of the biggest problems a personnel department has to face, since as much as one-third of a store's total sales may be done by part-timers.

Executive Training. Since most large retailers fill many executive vacancies by promoting people from within the store, it is vital that they have well-trained persons available. This can be achieved by means of an executive training program. (See Figure 5-5.)

The training of executives generally includes conferences, sponsors, work-study arrangements with colleges, evening courses at colleges, rotation of trainees in various departments, correspondence courses, and lectures. The training period for executives may take several years to accomplish. The individuals to be given executive training may be found among present employees or, more often, recruited from among college graduating classes. The earning of a college degree either prior to or during executive training is often mandatory.

Personnel Evaluation

If an organization is to be assured of maintaining a high standard of employee performance, it must evaluate its personnel periodically. Some of the reasons for employee evaluation are as follows:

1. Nothing encourages workers more than rewards for good performance. Only by an evaluation of an employee's performance can management make a fair decision on the rate of pay to which a person is entitled. Evaluation that is used to set fair salaries becomes an important source of employee good will.
2. Constant employee evaluation earmarks those employees who are deserving of promotion and who would do well in an advanced job. Without proper evaluation, promotion tends to be haphazard. This can result in poor supervisory performance.
3. If employees are to improve their effectiveness, they must be informed of their areas of weakness. Such knowledge enables them to seek out means of improvement by training courses, self-help, or conferences with knowledgeable people.
4. All stores have on their payrolls people who have the necessary qualifications for the job, but lack the interest or capacity to meet the required standards of proficiency. Job evaluations are an aid in the process of weeding out such individuals.

Small Store Employees

Probably the most effective job evaluation is done by the proprietor of a small store. Through constant contact with all of the store's employees, the proprietor has thorough knowledge of their merits and shortcomings. The basic disadvantage of evaluations of this kind is the likelihood that the boss's prejudices will make the evaluation personal rather than scientific. As a result bosses might promote the persons they like rather than the ones best fitted for the jobs.

Large Store Employees

Large retail organizations evaluate their employees by using printed forms at periodic intervals. Figure 5-6 shows an example of an evaluation report. It is usually filled out by the buyer or department head, and at a meeting of the employee, the supervisor, and a personnel department representative, before being forwarded to the personnel department.

Macy*s Executive Development Program

"RETAILING'S MOST COVETED SHEEPSKIN IS STILL AWARDED ON HERALD SQUARE *Alma Mater of what is probably the most distinguished alumni in American business generally, and in retailing specifically, is no duly accredited college or university. It's a store. It's Macy*s"*

—From Women's Wear Daily,
—the trade paper with the country's largest circuiation

ON THE JOB TRAINING

While there is some "classroom" work, Macy*s training is primarily learning by doing. Theory is translated into action, as it always is at Macy*s.

If you are selected for Macy*s Development Program, you will be placed on the company's payroll as an executive as soon as you report for work. During the first 5 weeks, you will be in the company's special Sales Supervision program that includes:

Executive orientation and store tour	*Introduction to sales supervision*
Conference on executive leadership	*Meeting on budgeting and scheduling*
Preparation for sales training	*Conference on safety*
Introduction to assigned selling area	*Practice supervision*
Sales training	*Discussion of job reviews*
Conference on employment practices	*Merchandising procedures*
Seminar on shortages	*Conference on adjustment policy*
Role of the sales manager	*You and your job*
Conference on labor relations	

FIGURE 5-5 Macy's Executive Development Program

EXECUTIVE CONFERENCE PROGRAM

A series of conferences with top executives of the company will be scheduled during your first 3 months. The subjects and the speakers might be as follows:

"The Store Division": President of the Division
"Function of Divisional Personnel": Vice President for Personnel
"Function of Divisional Control": Vice President for Control
"Merchandising Policies": Vice President for Merchandising
"Merchandising for Volume and Profit": Vice President and Store Manager
"Function of Divisional Sales Promotion": Vice President for Sales Promotion and Public Relations
"Function of Divisional Operations": Vice President for Operations
"Development of the Division to a Multi-Store Group": Vice President for Stores

COUNSELLING

Throughout the Sales Supervision program, you will be assigned to an experienced supervisor who will provide direction and answer your questions about the work and your progress. During your early development, the Executive Personnel Department provides continuous counselling on your career.

PERFORMANCE REVIEWS

After completing each training assignment, your supervisor will appraise your over-all performance. The supervisor's recommendation as to the kind of responsibility that most suits you will be discussed with you, and areas of work where you may need strengthening. At all times, you will know how you are doing.

POSITION ROTATION

During your early days at Macy*s, every effort will be made to make your work practical rather than theoretical or academic. Your assignments will be varied, and selected on the basis of your progress. We are anxious to find out as soon as possible whether your future with us lies in the world of fashion, basic merchandise, hard or soft goods, or in store management. Naturally, you will have a say in this, too, because you will soon discover for yourself which area you find most interesting.

FIGURE 5-5 (Cont.)

Salesclerk
Performance Rating

DIVISIONAL PERSONNEL

Store No.	Dept. No.	Job No.	Employee Ident. No.	Name

RATING FACTORS	EXCELLENT	GOOD	MEETS ACC. STANDARD	BELOW STANDARD	UNSATISFACTORY
1. MANNER AND INTEREST IN CUSTOMER	Most pleasing and interested manner to all	Shows sincere interest in customer's needs	Businesslike, courteous, attentive	Indifferent; shows little interest; sometimes brushes off customer	Rude; abrupt; antagonizes customer
2. ALERTNESS TO SERVICE	Immediately approaches waiting customers and acknowledges other waiting customers	Quick to approach waiting customers	Usually prompt in approaching customers	Frequently slow to approach waiting customers	Frequently waits for customer to approach him or ignores customers
3. MERCHANDISE KNOWLEDGE (INC. CONSTRUCTION, USES, MATERIALS, AND AVAILABILITY)	Expert knowledge for salesclerk	Knows merchandise well	Has basic working knowledge	Has only limited knowledge	Lacks fundamental knowledge needed to sell in department
4. SKILL IN USING MERCHANDISE KNOWLEDGE	Outstanding skill in determining customer's needs, selecting selling points, and presenting merchandise convincingly	Capable in determining customer's needs and arousing interest by methods of presenting merchandise	Generally determines what customer wants and gives adequate information about merchandise	Just an order taker; unconvincing; has some difficulty closing sales	Does not show proper merchandise or present merchandise to advantage; gives incorrect information; has great difficulty closing sales
		SATISFACTORY ☐		UNSATISFACTORY ☐	
5. GROOMING					
6. COOPERATION	Goes out of way to be congenial and helpful; gets along unusually well with others	Willingly does what he is told to do and does fair share of work; gets along well with others	Does what he is told; assumes his share of work without question	Avoids his share of work in department; reluctantly does what he is told; sometimes causes minor friction	Resents direction; causes serious friction
7. SYSTEM	Thoroughly knows system and makes almost no errors	Knows system well; makes very few errors	Working knowledge of system; makes only normal amount of errors	Has difficulty with system; makes more errors than he should	Makes unusually large number of errors; careless
8. STOCK WORK	Excellent housekeeper; takes initiative in stock work	Keeps stock in very good condition with little supervision	Neat and orderly; performs expected stock duties with normal supervision	Requires more than normal supervision to complete stock duties	Does not perform assigned stock work; careless and untidy in stock work
9. RELIABILITY (inc. adherence to policies and regulations – promptness in returning from lunch absences due to illness)	Can always be relied upon; does what is expected with minimum supervision	Can be relied on with few exceptions to do what is expected; needs little supervision	Usually can be relied on to do what is expected; requires only normal supervision	Requires more than normal supervision; frequently interferes with department operation by failing to do what is expected	Seriously hampers operation of department by unreliability on any phase of job; needs constant supervision

NO. OF ILLNESS ABSENCES _____ ON _____ (number) _____ OCCASIONS.

NO. OF PERSONAL ABSENCES _____ NO. OF LATE ARRIVALS _____ NO. OF LUNCH LATES _____ NO. OF FAILURES TO CLOCK _____

NO. OF WEEKS COVERED _____ (From _____ to _____) RATING _____

EXCLUSIVE OF _____ WKS. VAC.; _____ WKS. L. of A.; _____ WKS. ILLNESS ABSENCES

10. ATTENDANCE — NO. OF WEEKS COVERED, Exclusive of Vac.& L.of A. _____ (From _____ to _____)

ENTER COMMENTS, DISPOSITION AND SIGNATURES ON REVERSE SIDE

F.2278R 1-65

FIGURE 5-6 Sales Clerk Performance Rating—An Evaluation Report Form Used at Macy's, New York

PERTINENT COMMENTS

Below Standard or Unsatisfactory ratings on any factor should be explained by a statement of specific criticisms.

DISPOSITION

1. O.K. FOR INCREASE ☐

2. WARN FOR WITHHOLDING OF AUTOMATIC INCREASE ☐

3. WARN FOR WITHHOLDING OF AUTOMATIC INCREASE AND/OR DISCHARGE ☐

4. DISCHARGE ☐

OTHER (SPECIFY) _____

Signature of Rater _____ Date _____

Telephone Extension _____

Dept. or Group Mgr's Signature _____ Date _____

Approved by Job Review _____ Date _____

Interviewed By _____

FOR USE OF RECORD OFFICE

RECORD CARD POSTED ☐

WARN FOR WITHHOLDING NOTED ☐

FIGURE 5-6 (Cont.)

115

Outside shopping service organizations are used by many stores to evaluate salespeople. These people, posing as ordinary customers, prepare a "shopping report," which evaluates such characteristics as a salesperson's courtesy, ability, grooming, and compliance with the store's procedures.

Personnel evaluation if poorly handled, can be destructive to morale. Employees must be clearly made to understand that the purpose is not to hurt them but to improve their effectiveness and, by so doing, their jobs and their pay.

Compensation

Probably the most important consideration of a person looking for a job is the amount of salary being offered. For persons on the job, a fair compensation plan is one of the important keys to high morale. It is likely that the principal cause of employee turnover is the worker's ability to find a better-paying job elsewhere. In short, the maintenance of a sound compensation policy is a vital responsibility of the personnel department. Unlike the areas of recruitment and training, where the personnel department serves in a line or decision-making function, the responsibility of the personnel department in setting compensation policy is strictly staff or advisory. However, top management who make compensation decisions rely heavily on the personnel department for advice and planning in this area.

Requirements of a Compensation System

To be effective, the compensation plan must be drawn up with the following factors in mind:

1. The level of earnings should be such that the employees can maintain a decent standard of living. Salaries must be equal or slightly better than the salaries offered by competitors if a high quality work force is to be maintained.
2. An effective earnings plan must be so easily understood by the employees that they can predict their weekly earnings with accuracy. A simple earnings plan has the additional benefit of reducing the office help required to make up the payroll.
3. Earnings must be keyed to productivity. The worker must be made to feel that increased effort will result in increased compensation.
4. Similar jobs should receive similar compensation and the level of compensation should be fair. Of equal importance, employees must be made to believe that they are being fairly paid.
5. Since employee living expenses are stable from week to week, their salary requirements should be paid regularly. When salary rewards are offered as an incentive to better work, they must be paid promptly if they are to maintain their effectiveness. Salaries should be paid on a specific day of the week and there should be absolutely no deviation from this date.

Salaries of Salespeople

There are four principal methods of compensating salespeople: straight salary, straight commission, salary plus commission, and salary plus quota bonus.

Straight Salary. The payment of salespeople by a straight salary is the most widely used of all compensation methods. A person being paid a straight salary receives a specified, unvarying amount each pay period. It can be paid on a weekly or an hourly basis.

Illustrative Problem

Calculate the earnings of a salesperson who worked 35 hours during a week and was paid at the rate of $4.25 per hour.

Solution

Hours worked $\times$ pay rate $=$ earnings
35 $\times$ $4.25 $=$ $148.75

Advantages

1. It is easily understandable to the employee.
2. Salary payments are definite, permitting the employees to budget their expenses.
3. Workers do not lose income for time spent at nonselling or training tasks.
4. Bookkeeping is simplified.

Disadvantages

1. There is no direct incentive to better productivity. An increase in straight salary as a reward for better production frequently lags far behind increased productivity. This can be the cause of employee resentment.
2. To insure the fairness of individual salaries, employee evaluation must be undertaken frequently.
3. Salaries are not keyed to sales levels. This results in the retailer paying higher salaries than he can afford in slow periods and lower salaries than he can afford in peak periods.

Straight salary, because of its simplicity, is probably the best payroll system for a retail store. However, it can be used effectively only if constant worker evaluation keys salaries to individual worth.

Straight Commission. Under this system, which is unusual in retailing sales, people are paid only on the basis of the amount of merchandise they sell. At the end of a pay period each employee's total sales are added and multiplied by a commission to determine the worker's earnings for that period.

Illustrative Problem

Calculate the earnings of a salesperson whose sales for the week were $4,824.00 at the commission rate of 7%.

Solution

Sales   × commission rate   = earnings
$4,824.00 ×   7%   = $337.68

Advantages

1. It is easily understood by the employee.
2. A straight commission system can be converted to a regular weekly plan by permitting a drawing account.
3. Since income is calculated on the basis of production, this system is an incentive to increased production.
4. Customer service is speeded and sales help may be eliminated since a salesperson's earnings increase with the number of customers that employee handles. Therefore, each salesperson will handle more customers.
5. Salary expense increases when the store can afford high expenses (peak periods) and decreases during a lull in sales activity.

Disadvantages

1. Competition among sales personnel for high-ticket customers can lead to hard feeling among salespeople.
2. Customer service suffers, since the salespeople is in a hurry to finish and "grab" another customer. The result is high-pressure selling, avoiding low-price buyers, and ignoring browsers.
3. Employees resent nonselling chores since it keeps them from selling and reduces their earnings.
4. Employee morale suffers during slow periods, when their earnings are less than their drawings.

Straight commission systems are not generally used in retail stores. The incentive provided by such a plan is so strong that it becomes destructive to customer servicing and employee morale.

Salary Plus Commission. The use of a straight salary plus a small commission on all sales is an attempt to combine the best features of the straight salary and straight commission plan. Under this system each salesperson is paid a salary that is slightly less than would be received under the straight salary plan. In addition, a commission is paid on *all* sales. Commission rates used under this system are low, usually running between 1 percent and 2 percent.

Illustrative Problem

A salesperson who earns $4.00 per hour plus 1% commission on sales worked 35 hours during the week and had sales of $2,400.00 for that period.

Solution

Regular pay 35 hours $\times$ \$4.00 $=$ \$140.00
Commission \$2,400.00 $\times$ 1% $=$ <u> 24.00</u>
Total earnings \$164.00

Advantages

1. It provides some incentive toward greater productivity.
2. The workers can expect fairly stable regular earnings.

Disadvantages

1. Salary plus commission is somewhat more complicated to calculate. It is often impossible for employees to keep track of their sales and they occasionally feel that they were cheated.
2. The commission is frequently too small to act as an incentive to some people. To others, it is a great incentive despite its size. This may result in customer dissatisfaction and employee rivalries.

By and large the salary plus commission wage plan seems a satisfactory compromise between the advantages and disadvantages of the straight salary and straight commission systems. As a result, this form of compensation is widely used by retailers.

Salary Plus Quota Bonus. Another compromise between the straight salary and straight commission plans is the salary plus quota bonus system. Under this method employees are paid a fixed weekly amount. In addition, a weekly or monthly sales quota is determined. At the end of the quota period they are paid a commission on the amount by which their sales exceeded their quotas.

Illustrative Problem

A salesperson earns \$220.00 per week plus 4% on sales made in excess of \$2,000.00. Calculate the weekly earnings for an employee whose sales equaled \$3,000.00.

Solution

Regular earnings   \$220.00
Quota excess (\$3,000 − \$2,000) \$1,000 $\times$ 4% <u> 40.00</u>
Total earnings \$260.00

The advantages and disadvantages of the salary plus quota bonus system of compensation are similar to those of the salary plus commission compensation method. The salary plus quota bonus system is widely used and the trend seems to be toward greater acceptance of the plan.

Salaries of Nonselling Personnel

It is rare in retailing to find nonselling personnel who are paid on other than a straight hourly or weekly basis. This is due to the difficulty involved in finding a yardstick with which to measure their productivity. An occasional store may pay bonuses to people who do repetitive work such as markers, stenographers, or wrappers based on their production. Most stores shy away from this because each piece marked, typed, or wrapped offers special problems. As a result, although most retailers recognize the importance of incentive payments, no sound basis for such remuneration has been found.

Other Compensation

To improve employee morale and loyalty, many larger stores offer their selling and nonselling employees a wide variety of monetary benefits.

P.M.'s. Prize money is frequently offered to sales personnel for selling particular types of merchandise. While such prizes usually take the form of extra commissions, they may also be in the form of vacation trips, appliances, or other merchandise. Such rewards may also be given for the winning of contests or the performance of certain tasks.

Employee Discounts. Employees are generally given discounts of 10 percent to 20 percent on purchases of the store's merchandise. It is estimated that as much as 4 percent of the total sales of a department store are made to employees. An employee discount policy is an effective way to sell merchandise as well as a method of improving employee morale. R. H. Macy and Company allows employee dicounts of 20 percent on merchandise an employee can wear to work, and 10 percent on all other purchases.

Profit Sharing. Many larger retailers such as Montgomery Ward & Co., the J. C. Penney Co., and Sears, Roebuck and Co. maintain profit-sharing plans for all of their personnel. It is felt that such compensation involves the workers in the success of the store by making employees partners in its profits and losses. The management of Sears, Roebuck and Co. have indicated that they consider profit sharing to be an important part of their success.

Managerial Compensation

The most frequently used method of compensating managerial personnel is the straight salary plan. To increase the incentive of managers, most stores rely upon bonuses, which may be based on any of the following methods:

Based on the Total Operation. Under this plan, bonuses are paid in relation to the profit of the entire store. When the store has a successful year, bonuses are high. Low total store profits for the year will result in reduced bonuses. This method attempts to interest department executives in the over-all success of the store rather than just of their own specific department.

Based on Department Sales. Bonuses may be based on departmental sales. This plan can work in several ways: the bonus percentage may be taken on total department sales, in which case a small percentage (1 percent) of the sales is paid as a bonus. Frequently, this type of bonus is calculated on the amount by which the department's sales exceed a predetermined quota. In such cases the percent used would be higher.

Based on Net Income. Bonuses of from 1 percent to 10 percent are sometimes given on total departmental net profit, or on the amount by which the department's net profit exceeds a set quota. Basing managerial bonuses on net profit rather than sales has the advantage of focusing the manager's interest on high profits instead of high sales.

Chain Store Management. Discount and variety chains generally pay their managers a straight salary plus 10 percent to 15 percent of their store's profits as a bonus. Other firms, believing that the manager is entitled to as much as 20 percent of the profits, deduct the manager's salary from 20 percent of the profits and give that manager the difference as a bonus.

Whatever managerial bonus plan is used, it should be sufficient to attract outstanding people and reward them for out-of-the-ordinary achievement.

Employee Services and Benefits

Both governmental statutes and union contracts provide other employee benefits than appear in a worker's pay envelope. Employer payments for social security and unemployment insurance are required by statute. Many union contracts require employer contributions to union welfare and hospitalization plans. Most retail stores, to build employee good will, offer many other services and activities. These include profit sharing (Sears contributes more than $60 million per year for this), clubs, athletic facilities, savings and loan arrangements, life insurance, and many other features.

While many of the benefits and services to be discussed come as the result of government legislation or from the expertise of the union negotiator at times of contract renewal, these additional earnings are often the basis for the prospective employee to accept the job. It is certainly true that salary is the greatest motivational factor for employees, but all too often, the salaries from one company to another are similar for particular job titles. This is particularly true at the lower levels, where wages may be set by unions whose involvement may transcend many retail organizations.

For these reasons, jobs are often refused or accepted because of the available benefit or service package. Very often it is the benefit plan that entices an employee who has served a company well to move to another operation. A salary cannot be the only consideration for employment. The extras are often as valuable as the actual take-home pay and are a significant part of the reasons for joining a particular retail organization.

Medical and Health Services

It is not unusual to find a doctor or nurse in continuous attendance at a large store for the benefit of the employees. In addition, visiting nurses are made freely available for the assistance of employees confined to their homes. Retailers that are not large enough to afford full-time medical staffs may offer them on a part-time basis.

Hospitalization, dental, and life insurance are often arranged by the store in order to offer their employees a low group rate. The cost of such plans may be borne by the store, the employee, or both.

Social, Educational, and Athletic Activities

Many larger retail establishments provide facilities for employee clubs and equipment for a wide variety of employee activities from baseball teams to dance bands. Generally, these activities are conceived and sponsored by groups of employees, who find management more than willing to encourage any activity that might promote loyalty and enhance employee morale.

Savings Plans

Typical of an employee savings plan is one operated by Montgomery Ward & Co. That retailing giant contributes some $2 million per year to a plan in which they deposit 25 percent to 50 percent of the amount their employees deposit in a savings account (the employees may deposit up to 3 percent of their annual earnings).

Many such savings plans permit low-cost employee loans to be made, which may be paid back by payroll deduction.

Other Employee Services

The employee services discussed above are far from the complete range of benefits offered by retailers. Typical of other benefits are

1. The F. W. Woolworth Stock Purchase Plan, which permits employees to purchase company stock at a savings of 15 percent.
2. The Gertz Cooperative Education Grants, which offer direct financial payment to employees satisfactorily completing job-related courses
3. Sick leave, life insurance, pensions, profit sharing, and other benefits that are available to employees of most large retailers

The growth of the labor movement has added a new dimension to the responsibility of the personnel department. Retail workers have generally lagged behind the rest of the labor force in the increase in union membership, but the growth has been real, if slow, and union contract negotiation has become an area of considerable importance.

The personnel department continues to play a growing role in dealing with the labor unions. Perhaps more than any other part of management, the personnel specialists are employed to make certain that the employees deliver services for which they were hired.

While there frequently seem to be management–employee problems, a company can only be successful if the needs of their customers are served. Unhappy workers lead to a decrease in productivity, with profits often affected. Although personnel directors are a part of management, their roles are seen as buffers between management and labor. How to satisfy employee demands without giving the store away perhaps best sums up personnel's most difficult function.

Prior to contract negotiations, the personnel department's team is often charged with the responsibility of examining employee demands and recommending avenues that would provide the best productivity for the store. In areas such as employee compensation methods and benefits, personnel provides insights on which top management can base negotiations.

Once a contract has been settled, the personnel department is usually called upon to participate in contractual disputes with employees and their unions. Although a contract is in evidence, the translation of legally worded passages is almost always an ongoing practice. Compromises between management and labor must be reached in the contract.

The work of personnel management is delicate. Only through tact and diplomacy can both sides of a labor dispute be satisfied. Personnel managers who appear to be too management oriented can lower employee morale, while too much employee appeasement can hurt the company's role in managing the organization. A delicate balance must be struck.

Action for the Independent Retailer

No matter what the size of the organization, its success is directly dependent on its employees. Small stores cannot afford the services of personnel specialists but must be aware of the appropriate practices necessary to manage even one or two employees.

The selection of employees in the smaller organization often requires even more attention than in the larger retail companies. Not only might individual employees in smaller stores be required to perform a greater variety of duties than the specialists in large stores, but they are also more personally involved with the customers. Where the big retailer has an extensive clientele, and less-than-diligent workers might get lost in the shuffle, the small store employee must often relate to everyone who happens to pass through the doors.

With these factors in mind, care must be directed to screening prospective employees. Although ads and agencies might be used to find people, small retailers often find their best candidates to be the transient applicants who seek employment because of a "help wanted" sign at the store's entrance. This method is simple and inexpensive and can be utilized at a moment's notice. A complete interview will provide much of the information necessary to find the right individual. It will provide such pertinent information as experience, personal qualities, and required salaries. Training for the small store is best on the job under the watchful eye of the owner or manager. This training is a plus when compared with large companies where owners and management are usually far removed from lower employee levels. Periodic evaluation, and informal is usually best, provides motivation for improvement. Although the smaller independent store cannot offer the typical benefits of larger companies, it can provide great incentive in larger employee discounts, something the giants simply cannot afford to do.

Careful involvement of the store owner can easily prompt better employee performance. Correction can be made quickly before costly errors result in customer loss. Small stores usually have little employee turnover if workers are carefully selected.

IMPORTANT POINTS IN THE CHAPTER

1. As a store grows in size, the problems involved with personnel become so great that specialists are required to handle them.

2. In recent years the federal government has enacted a significant amount of legislation that has necessitated personnel managers to reevaluate their stores' employment practices.

3. The personnel department is responsible for the organization's recruitment, training, evaluation, compensation, special services, and labor relations.

4. Recruitment, based upon a careful job analysis, requires a knowledge of the sources of labor supply in the area.

5. Interviews serve the double purpose of informing the applicant about the job and the employer about the applicant.

6. After an applicant has been selected, it is the responsibility of the personnel department to provide the training necessary for effective job performance.

7. To ensure the maintenance of a high standard of employee performance, personnel must be periodically evaluated. This evaluation is the basis for promotion, additional training, salary adjustment, and discharge.

8. Employee earnings is one of the most important factors in the establishment of good worker-management relations. Retail workers are generally compensated on one of the following bases: straight salary, straight commission, salary plus commission, salary plus quota bonus.

9. *The most frequently used method of compensating managerial personnel is the straight salary plan. To increase the incentive of managers, most stores offer bonuses.*

10. *Employee morale may be increased by offering a wide variety of special services, which may include profit sharing, clubs, life and health insurance, and tuition reimbursement.*

11. *The personnel department is responsible for the negoitations and interpretation of labor-management employment contracts.*

REVIEW QUESTIONS

1. Discuss the function of recruitment that is performed by the personnel department. Is it a line or a staff function?

2. Why must the recruitment function begin with a careful analysis of the job to be filled?

3. List nine items that should be included in a job analysis.

4. What are the advantages to the store cooperating with schools in cooperative work experience programs?

5. Discuss the kinds of recruitment in terms of cost to the store. Which is most expensive? Cheapest?

6. What is the purpose of the application blank? What sort of information should it require of an applicant?

7. Discuss reference checking. Describe another method of checking on a prospective candidate.

8. Why are personality tests rarely used in personnel work?

9. Differentiate between the training necessary for new inexperienced personnel and the training necessary for new experienced personnel.

10. Describe the methods in which training of regular personnel is accomplished.

11. What are the problems involved in the training of part-time personnel? Why is this area of training important?

12. List and discuss the reasons for employee evaluation.

13. Discuss the advantages and disadvantages of paying sales personnel on the basis of straight salary. Given an example of the straight salary plan.

14. Discuss the advantages and disadvantages of paying sales personnel a straight salary plus commission. Give an example of the salary plus commission plan.

15. What are the problems involved in giving incentive pay to nonselling personnel? Give examples.

16. Explain the manner in which a store benefits from the payment of P.M.'s to its employees.

17. Explain and discuss several methods of paying buyers incentive money based on sales.

18. Discuss the paying of buyers' incentive bonuses based on profits rather than on sales?

19. Why do department stores provide expensive employee services that they are not required to do by law or contract?

20. Explain the function of the personnel department in the area of labor relations. Is it a line or a staff function?

CASE PROBLEMS

CASE PROBLEM 1

Dale's Department Store is a medium-sized establishment located in the downtown section of an urban center. The store is progressively run and has grown in the past ten years from a small appliance store to a department store with twelve departments and 80 employees. As yet there is no furniture or hardware department, but negotiations are currently underway for additional space in which to house these departments. The profit picture is excellent and all signs indicate a continued period of growth and expansion.

The personnel department consists of three people, one of them a secretary. Their only function is to bring in job applicants by placing want ads, contacting employment agencies, and so on. The actual interviewing and hiring is done by the selling departments, who are also responsible for employee training. All sales personnel are paid on a straight commission basis.

The top management of the store is aware of the advantages of having a full-scale personnel department but feels that the store's profits are inadequate to support such a non-producing staff organization. Preliminary estimates indicate that a full personnel department would reduce annual profits by 20%. Much of this cost would be wasted, since a store the size of Dale's never hires enough employees at one time to form an economically worthwhile training class.

A group of small and medium-sized retailers in the area have banded together to set up a school for all of the members of the group. By using a single school for all of the cooperating stores, classes would be large enough to handle employee training at a fairly low rate per student.

Dale's is considering an invitation to join the group.

QUESTIONS

1. What are the advantages and disadvantages of joining the group from the point of view of effective store operations?

2. What are the advantages and disadvantages from the point of view of the mid-management in the selling departments?

3. What are the advantages and disadvantages from the point of view of the veteran salespersons in the departments?

4. The sales school will teach only areas of interest to all of its students. For example, it will teach "how to sell," but not "how to handle returns," since each cooperating store might have a different system. Outline those areas that should be taught by the sales school and those that should be taught by the store.

CASE PROBLEM 2

The Plainview Paint Store is a large individually owned retailer. The store is located in a suburb of a large metropolitan center that over the past fifteen years has grown from a farming area to a heavily populated town. The store has grown with the surrounding area and has reached a size at which it makes a comfortable living for the owner and pays good salaries to its twelve salespeople.

The store serves a population made up of middle- and lower-middle-class homeowners and most of the sales are to do-it-yourself workers. As a result, the individual sales are small, but the markup on each sale is excellent.

Salesmen are well paid on a straight salary basis. The owner, who has always worked on a 10-hour day, 6-day week, no-vacation basis, has decided to reduce his business activities. He was on vacation during the whole month of January, leaving responsibility for the store's operation in the hands of one of the salesmen, whom he appointed as manager with a $25 per week raise.

When he returned from vacation he found that January sales were 20% below the sales of the previous January. The year's sales up to January had been running slightly ahead of previous figures; the weather was good and the competition was unchanged. A spot check of the inventory indicated that no merchandise was missing. He rightly attributed the decline in business to the fact that he was not on hand to motivate the salespeople.

QUESTIONS

1. Indicate two compensation plans under which the salespeople might be motivated while the proprietor is away.
2. Indicate two plans under which the manager might be motivated while the proprietor is away.
3. Which plan or combination of the above plans would you use? Support your reasons for this choice.
4. Can you think of a noncash type of remuneration that might improve the salespeople's incentive?

CASE PROBLEM 3

Soon after her promotion at Barnard's Department Store, Miss Wagner began to encounter a serious problem as manager of the men's department. Competition among sales personnel has become so fierce that frequent arguments take place on the selling floor. Miss Wagner is certain the root of the problem is that salespeople are paid on a straight commission basis and are out to make as much money for themselves as possible.

Coupled with this problem, the manager finds it extremely difficult motivating her sales force to perform nonselling tasks such as stockwork, floor moves, and handling returns.

"I just don't know what to do about it anymore," Miss Wagner explains to her divisional manager. "I'm seriously considering asking management to take them all off commission and start using a straight salary plan."

QUESTIONS

1. Do you agree with Miss Wagner's suggestion?
2. If you were the divisional manager, what other recommendations might you offer?

store location
6 and layout

BEHAVIORAL OBJECTIVES

Upon completion of this chapter the student should be able to

1. *Discuss the importance of population analysis to site selection. Include five population factors that must be considered.*
2. *Identify eight nonpopulation characteristics involved in site selection.*
3. *List five reasons for the growth of suburban shopping centers.*
4. *Describe a controlled shopping center, indicating three characteristics of such establishments.*
5. *Discuss four current trends in shopping centers.*
6. *List five principles regarding the location of selling departments.*

STORE LOCATION

One of the most common causes of failure of new retail stores is management error in the location of the store. In recent years there has been a considerable amount of research done in this field. Despite this, the number of retailers that actually subject proposed sites to a scientific survey is still very small. It is not the purpose of this chapter to go into the complicated mathematics of scientific site evaluation. Instead, the discussion will be limited to the important factors that must be weighed before a decision can be made, first on the general area for a new retail operation, and then on a specific site within that area.

Selecting the General Area

A logical approach to store location is to begin by selecting the general area in which the store is to be established. In making this decision, one should carefully analyze the following factors.

Geography of the Area

The size and shape of the proposed area must be analyzed to determine the boundaries within which the customer population will fall. The population within this area can then be studied.

Population

Any analysis of future customer demand must begin with an understanding of the nature of the typical customer. Population size and density is generally agreed upon to be a most important factor affecting retailing success. A detailed study of an area's population should include the following considerations:

1. It is important to know the predominant age of the population. Since young people's needs and wants differ from those of older people, the success of many types of retail operations depends upon the careful analysis of age data.

2. Differences in sex and marital status have much the same effect on retail sales as age differences, and care must be taken to determine any unusual facts concerning the population's sex and marital status.

3. The size of the population may be subject to seasonal variations. This is true of summer resorts. If the area in question is likely to be affected by such seasonal changes, the information is vital to the location selection.

4. The various religious affiliations, education levels, and national origins of the population must be determined. These differences frequently indicate variations in prejudices, needs, and preferences.

5. The income level of the population can be estimated in many ways. Data on per capita and family earnings are obtainable from the census bureau. Information about the number of telephones and auto registrations per house, and on the value of the dwellings themselves, is available. Since retail volume depends upon income level, the investigation of the earning power of the area must be extensive. Such information as the source, stability, and seasonal nature of the income must be determined and weighed before the decision to locate can be made.

6. The buying needs of homeowners are considerably different from those of apartment renters. Although these differences may not be obvious in the buying of food and clothing, they certainly would be important to the sales of major appliances and gardening tools. Moreover, the buying needs of the new homeowner are considerably different from those of the established homeowner.

Characteristics of the Area

In addition to the study of the characteristics of the population, certain information about the trading area itself is required.

1. An alert, progressive community whose members are willing to tax themselves for a quality school system and other local improvements will probably attract new families for years to come. Such a community is frequently the home of an active chamber of commerce and other clubs. A test of progressiveness is the rate of new development, both of commercial enterprises and of new homes. Active growth is generally a by-product of progressiveness.

2. Of great interest in the location of new retailing outlets is the competition in the area to be selected. Both the quality and quantity of the competition should be judged. The fact that there are several conventional appliance stores might not rule out the introduction of a discount appliance store.

3. The area should have features that attract out-of-the-area customers. Such attractions as parks, theaters, zoos, and athletic events frequently bring transient retail business into an area.

4. Judgment should be made upon the accessibility of the area. The roads should be good, the traffic bearable, and after a fairly fast trip the customer should have no trouble finding a parking space. In these times of serious road congestion this

factor has become of prime importance. In addition to being easily accessible to automobiles, a good shopping area should be fed by public transportation.

5. Proper banking help is important to the retailer. Sound audit control requires the daily deposit of cash sales. In addition, banks are needed to make temporary working capital as well as long-term improvement loans. With the recent wide expansion of commercial banks, lack of banking facilities is rarely a problem.

6. Present-day retailing requires the store to grant its customers speedy credit on demand. To do this, extensive credit checking must be done by outside agencies. It is vital that such credit-checking agencies be available in the area in which a new store is to be located.

7. Those retailers that depend upon advertising to promote their merchandise must be certain that the required advertising media are available in the area in which they decide to locate.

8. The retailing area selected should be within short delivery time of the store's major sources of supply.

9. Many retail customers demand that their purchases be delivered. Facilities for delivery must be available if the store is to offer this service.

10. There must be an adequate labor force in the area to staff the store at a salary level within the store's budget. If the prospective labor force is unionized, the union requirements must be studied.

11. Local laws must be studied to determine sales taxes, necessary licenses, days in the week the store may remain open, and so on. In addition, such possible problems as difficulty in obtaining insurance and local crime rate should be determined.

12. The history of the area should be analyzed to determine current trends. Is the area the same as it was ten years ago? Five years ago? If it has deteriorated, is it likely to continue to do so? Is any improvement likely to continue? Are the characteristics of the population changing? In what way?

It should be understood that a trading area does not have to score perfectly in all of the areas listed. Few successful stores would have that perfect a report. However, each of the areas indicated should be *considered* before a decision to locate is made.

Selecting the Shopping District

After the general area has been selected, the specific shopping district within the area must be decided upon. Like the decision on the general area, this decision must be based on a considerable body of facts. There are many types of retail locations, and the relative merits of each type must be carefully weighed.

Downtown Areas

The central shopping district located in the hub of a large city has always been the focal point for the strongest retail establishments. It is at this point, where the area's population is at its densest, that the highest volume of sales per square foot of selling space is made. This attracts the retailing giants and the largest department stores. High-promotion stores are characteristic of such areas; the great potential of available customers almost guarantees the success of any worthwhile promotion. Central business district locations are usually at a premium, and the rentals are very high.

Shopping Centers

Although downtown central shopping districts are still of great retailing importance, recent years have seen a trend toward decentralization. The downtown stores are being subjected to more and more competition from large regional shopping centers located in the suburbs. Many metropolitan department stores have been both adding to and taking advantage of this trend by locating branch stores in suburban shopping centers. The success of the suburban shopping center has been due chiefly to the following factors:

1. Since 1945 there has been a massive population exodus from the cities. Since the shift in population has been among the upper- and middle-class families, the disposable income loss from the city to the suburbs has been great. As a result, the per capita income of the city families has declined, while the purchasing power available in the suburbs has skyrocketed. Retailers, anxious to tap this mine of purchasing power, have moved to suburban locations.

2. As a result of the increased use of the automobile, downtown shopping areas are marked by their awful traffic congestion and unavailability of inexpensive parking facilities. These transportation difficulties greatly favor suburban stores, where traveling and parking are relatively effortless.

3. As the trend toward suburban living continues, nearby suburbia becomes crowded and homeowners are forced even further away from the city. As a result, many homeowners are simply too far from the city for convenient shopping.

4. Competitive downtown stores are generally so close to one another that the shopper is able to compare quality and price before making a purchase. But comparison shopping has been less important in recent years, partly due to the fact that a few pennies saved by such methods are not important to our inflation-oriented society. Moreover, improved communication techniques, such as television and newspaper advertising, have lessened the importance of comparison shopping.

5. The availability of space in the suburbs has played a part in the increase in retailing activity in the outlying districts. Downtown locations are generally poorly planned, overpriced, and difficult to find. In contrast, suburbia offers building to order, cheaper rents, and a choice of locations.

Controlled Shopping Centers. Controlled shopping centers are those that have been planned and are operated by developers. (See Figure 6-1.) The centers are organized and controlled to a point at which the amount of competition is limited. Through research, for example, the developer determines that the potential consumer market in that area will require six ladies' shoe stores, two children's shops, three men's clothing stores, and so forth to satisfy shopping needs. Not only does it offer maximum shopping satisfaction to consumers, but it also guarantees a certain amount of shoppers who are restricted to the available retail shops in the center. Ultimately, the shopping center

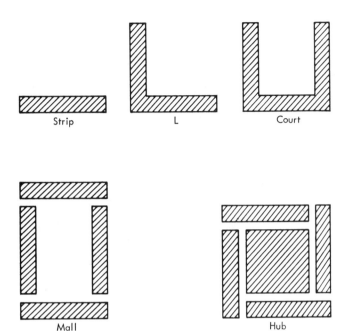

Strip

L

Court

Mall

Hub

FIGURE 6-1 Types of Planned Shopping Center Layouts

developer is faced with less failure of the retailers involved and greater profit for himself.

Controlled shopping centers may be found in a variety of sizes, shapes, and locations:

1. Occasionally, as a result of an urban renewal project, a controlled shopping center may be found in the downtown shopping district of a large city. Such shopping centers are generally characterized by high-rise large stores.

2. Large regional shopping centers, serving the needs of a large area, are frequently in direct competition with downtown shopping districts. Regional shopping centers are generally built around one or more department store branches, which attract customers. These are surrounded by a variety of small and medium-sized stores that take advantage of the traffic.

3. Community shopping centers are generally built around a junior department store or specialty shop. They service fewer families than the regional centers and do not compete directly with them.

4. By far the most common type of shopping center is the "strip" type. This is a neighborhood center built along a main traffic street. The principal tenant is usually a supermarket, and many of the stores offer services to the immediate neighborhood.

See Figure 6-2 for a list of factors to consider in determining shopping center locations.

133

FIGURE 6-2 CHECKPOINTS FOR EVALUATING SHOPPING CENTER LOCATIONS

1. Who is the shopping center developer?
2. How long has he been in the business of developing real estate?
3. What are his financial resources?
4. With whom has he arranged for the financing of the center?
5. What is his reputation for integrity?
6. Who performed the economic analysis? Does the report cover both favorable and unfavorable factors?
7. What experience has the economic consultant had?
8. Has an architectural firm been retained to plan the center?
9. Has the architect designed other centers? Have they been successful from a retailing standpoint?
10. Who will build the center? The developer? An experienced contractor? An inexperienced contractor?
11. Has the developer had experience with other centers?
12. What is, or will be, the quality of management for the center?
13. Will the management have merchandising and promotion experience? (Some developers are large retailers rather than real estate operators.)
14. What percent of the leases have been signed? Are they on a contingent basis?
15. Has every facet of the lease been carefully studied?
16. Is the ratio of parking area to selling area 3-to-1 or more?
17. Has sufficient space (400 feet) been assigned to each car?
18. Is the parking space designed so that the shopper does not walk more than 300 to 350 feet from the farthest spot to the store?
19. What is the angle of parking space? (Ninety degrees provides the best expacity and circulation.)
20. What is the planned or actual car turnover? (3.3 cars per parking space per day is the average.)
21. Is the number of total spaces adequate for the planned business volume? (Too many spaces make the center look dead; too few openly invite competition around the center.)
22. Does the parking scheme distribute the cars so as to favor no one area?
23. Is there an adequate number of ingress/egress roads in proper relationship with the arrangement of parking spaces?
24. For the larger centers, a ring road is preferable. Is this the case?
25. Is the site large enough for the type of center?
26. Is the size sufficiently dominant to forestall the construction of similar shopping centers nearby?
27. Is the center of regular shape? If not, does the location of the buildings minimize the disadvantage of the site's shape?
28. Is the site sufficiently deep? (A depth of at least 400 feet is preferred; if less, the center may look like a strip development.)
29. Is the site level? Is it on well-drained land?
30. Does the center face north and/or east?
31. Can the center be seen from a distance?
32. Are any structures, such as a service station, located in the parking area? (If so, do they impede the site's visibility?)
33. Is the site a complete unit? (A road should not pass through the site.)
34. Are the buildings set far enough back on the site that the entire area may be seen?
35. Are all the stores readily accessible to each other, with none having an advantage?

Source: J. E. Mertes, "Site Opportunities for the Small Retailer," *Journal of Retailing,* Vol. XXXIX, No. 3, p. 44.

The following is a partial list of the advantages of a controlled shopping center:

1. *Adequate parking.* It is not unusual to find four times as much parking space as floor space in a shopping center. Since suburban locations offer no parking other than that provided by the shopping center, adequate parking is mandatory.
2. *Controlled competition.* In a situation where a single individual or group makes all of the decisions concerning tenancy, it is possible to select only those tenants who will make the shopping center an independent unit, able to satisfy the consumer's every need. To do this, stores that complement each other would be substituted for stores that compete with each other, in an attempt to attract the greatest possible number of buyers.
3. *Unified promotional activities.* Because of its minimal competition and the similarity of geographic location, the retailers that make up the shopping center often cooperate in promotions and advertising for their mutual benefit.

Current Trends of Shopping Centers. The shopping center is a relatively new idea that has not yet reached its final stage of development. Trends seem to indicate that certain changes will take place.

1. *Enclosed mall.* There is presently a strong trend toward enclosing the larger shopping centers. This is true both of newly constructed centers and as improvements in older centers. The enclosed mall allows for climate control throughout the shopping center and gives the shopper the feeling of being in one immense store. The walkways between the stores of the mall and the storefronts themselves are generally beautifully and uniquely landscaped. (See Figure 6-3.)
2. *Expansion.* A growing portion of new retail building, and expansion of present facilities will be in shopping centers.
3. *Size.* Shopping centers will continue to increase in size. The one department store as a traffic builder is being replaced with centers containing four or five department stores and additional levels to better utilize the available space.
4. *Total customer convenience.* Offices, theaters, banks, and other nonretailing customer attractions are being added to shopping centers to increase consumer dependence upon them.
5. *Future locations.* Shopping centers are being located in sparsely settled areas, along major turnpikes, in high-rise locations where land is expensive, and in downtown areas through urban renewal. In short, wherever a retailing area is needed, the shopping center is being considered.

Free-Standing Stores

The success of the large suburban free-standing store indicates that this recent development will be increasingly important. Generally, such stores are discount stores, chain specialty shops, or department store branches. They are generally found along major automobile arteries where they may attract clientele from considerable distances. They are easily reached and offer adequate parking. Since single free-standing stores cannot attract as much traffic as a shopping center can, they rely on heavy advertising and promotions for their customers.

FIGURE 6-3 Walt Whitman Shopping Center—Enclosed Mall

Neighborhood Clusters

In most towns a number of small stores ranging from those carrying food items to units dealing in ready-to-wear can be found grouped together on a main street. Generally these are family-owned stores that appeal to the local population.

Off the Beaten Path

Away from the general mainstream of retail establishments, warehouse outlets of manufacturers as well as conventional retail store operators have begun to gain prominence. Throughout the country, menswear, ladies' wear, furniture, carpets, and other merchandise have become available for sale at locations that are neither considered convenient for shoppers nor generally appropriate for retailing. The key to this location is *price*. In order to attract the people to out-of-the-way locations, real bargains must be offered.

The Specific Site

Once the general area for store location and the particular type of shopping district within that area have been decided upon, the remaining step is the selection of a specific site. The decision on specific site is a sensitive one, since

100 feet can mark the difference between an excellent and a poor site. Similarly, a successful high-priced men's shop can fail in an area perfectly suited to a low-price operation. Several factors must be considered.

Analysis of the Population

The analysis of the population for a specific site requires more than a specific name count. Differentiation must be made between potential customers and disinterested browsers. For example, only one in thousands of commuters may be likely to stop at a men's haberdashery on the way to work, but a far greater number may stop at a luncheonette.

Neighboring Stores

The nearby stores must be compatible if the site is to be a successful one. Many stores do well by locating near department stores and attracting customers whose prime purpose is to shop at the department store. Similarly, ladies' clothing, accessory, millinery, and shoe stores tend to complement one another, particularly if they appeal to the same economic level. The opposite is also true. A high-priced shop in an area catering to low-income customers is unlikely to be successful. The wrong sort of neighbor may be damaging. A fine restaurant should not be located next to a garage, or a children's shop next to a bar.

Traveling Convenience

If the site selected is in an urban center and if success depends upon non-local customers, convenient mass transit systems must be available. In the case of suburban retailing locations the same logic requires good roads and sufficient parking for a successful location.

STORE LAYOUT

Once the final selection of a site has been made, attention must center upon how to use its interior and exterior most efficiently. The enormous amount of competition in soft goods, hard goods, and foodstuffs, for example, necessitates careful store layout planning. Even in the smallest retail organizations the store layout is not left to chance. Suppliers to these smaller organizations are only too happy to lend their assistance. Remember, the more efficient the retail store, the more successful are the vendors. Large retail organizations, including the franchisers, go to great lengths to scientifically plan store layouts. Some aspects of layout (the overall plan) are the work of top management and often outside consultants. Middle managers are involved in their respective departments' physical arrangements.

The term *layout* does not signify only physical arrangement; it also involves the selection of merchandise displays, lighting fixtures, and the location of selling, service, administrative, and staff areas.

Exterior Layout and Design

The store's exterior structure and its surrounding parts must be carefully designed to attract the consumers' attention. However, not only must these facilities be appealing to the eye, they must also be functional. The convenience of the customer cannot in any way be sacrificed to the aesthetic quality of the structure. In some types of retail operations the building itself is extremely important as an attention-getting device. However, as is the case in advertising, merely attracting attention is insufficient—holding the attention is important. The store that attracts the consumer passing by in an automobile but doesn't provide the necessary parking facilities will not bring that consumer in to shop.

Today's newest retail structures are as individualistic as the interiors of our homes. (See Figure 6-4.) Effort is made to incorporate the image of the operation into its exterior structure. For example, the ivy league shop featuring tweeds and bulky sweaters often chooses an exterior of "hand-split wooden shakes" for its building material. The franchisers develop definite personalities for their units and incorporate them into the structure. Kentucky Fried Chicken, a fast-food franchise, is quickly recognized by the passing consumer merely because of its façade.

An extremely important aspect of exterior planning is the provision for parking facilities. Typically, the large department stores and supermarkets, and often small stores, provide parking in large fields surrounding the store. With the need for more auto space, some stores, such as the Abraham & Straus branch in Hempstead, New York, have gone to multi-level parking facilities. Alexander's in Valley Stream, New York, has two-level parking with access to the store on both levels. Other retail organizations have installed underground and rooftop parking. In an effort to bring the customer right to the selling floor, Macy's, at one of its branches, has introduced an innovation in parking facilities. The main parking area is located around the selling floors of the store. Through the use of ramps, a customer can drive to a particular floor, park the car, and enter the selling area without leaving the building. This arrangement attempts to combine artistic design and function.

Outdoor selling areas have served to expand the selling facilities of retail stores. Outdoor furniture and garden supplies are just two examples of merchandise sold outside of the store. Many stores hold special sales on sections of their parking fields.

Windows and entrances vary in retailing. The gamut is run from the windowless store to the store with many windows. Image, store policy, and location are just some factors that will determine the types and number of win-

FIGURE 6-4 J. W. Robinson's, Santa Barbara, California—An Example of Individualistic Department Store Design

dows and entrances. A more in-depth discussion of windows will be found in Chapter 13, *Display*.

Interior Layout and Design

The appearance of a store naturally affects one's first impression upon entering it. Years ago the retailer was satisfied with selecting "nice" colors and materials; today's entrepreneur relies upon expertise. Seldom does one find a colorless decor and wooden or other standard floors and lighting in today's retail stores. These have been replaced by newer materials and color arrangements conducive to shopping.

Wall, Floor, and Ceiling Materials

Paint still seems to dominate a store's walls and ceiling. Even the supermarkets compete via store attractiveness. Bold colors, with different departments using different color schemes, separate the store into clearly defined areas. It is not unusual to see food stores painted in bright reds, yellows, and oranges. Some food markets even have "wood-panel" areas for both a change of pace and function—wood being just about maintenance-free. In the department and specialty stores walls are adorned with paint, paper, fabric, wood, mirrors, and textures such as cork. Of course, image is a tremendous factor in the selection of these materials.

Floors have taken on a new look and have also become more functional. There has been extensive use of carpeting in many retail stores. With the creation of a rubber-backed, 100-percent nylon-face carpet that is cemented to the floor, stores are improving their appearance and soothing tired feet. This carpet conceals soil (because of its color combination and construction) and releases it with easy laundering. It is so durable, it is being used in hospitals, theaters, restaurants, and other heavy-traffic areas. Textured vinyl tiles, pretreated wooden planks that resist scratching, poured seamless vinyl floors, and conventional carpeting have replaced the ordinary store flooring.

Lighting and Selection of Lighting Fixtures

Because the fluorescent light is most economical to use, a large number of retailers choose to light their store in that fashion. The stores seeking to project atmosphere, such as those selling high-fashion merchandise, do not use fluorescent fixtures. Most stores employ experts to help them select the proper lighting fixtures and their locations. In an effort to maximize the effectiveness of lighting, one branch of Ohrbach's engaged the renowned theatrical lighting director Louis Feder to design their lighting plan.

Lighting, if used intelligently, can show the store's offerings to their best advantage. This includes merchandise that is hanging on a rack, folded on a counter, displayed inside the store or in a window, being tried on by a customer, or being checked out by the wrapping clerk. Proper lighting will also ensure that departments and merchandise can be easily seen and that employees and customers can read merchandise tags.

Today's modern retail establishment makes use of the incandescent bulb (the type found in most homes) and houses it in a wide variety of fixtures. The bulbs may be recessed into the walls and ceilings (either in stationary or swivel fixtures) or used as illumination in the most contemporary or elaborate chandeliers. Many retailers are using track lighting systems similar to those originally used in museums. They provide the retailer with flexibility in movement as well as beauty. Whatever the choice, it must be appropriate for the particular retail establishment.

Merchandise Fixtures

Fixtures can help to project a store's image; but more important they must help to properly stock, display, and finally sell merchandise.

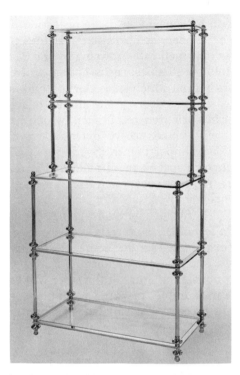

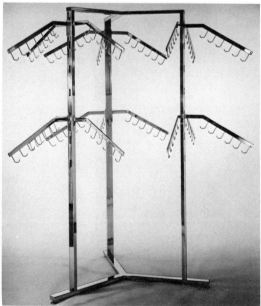

FIGURE 6-5 Merchandise Fixtures Designed for Self-Service

Perhaps the most important factor to be considered in the selection of fixtures is whether the store is a service or self-service operation. Needless to say, the self-service store employs fixtures that facilitate browsing by the customer. (See Figure 6-5.) Counters accessible on all sides, racks not separated from the customer by the narrow counters behind which sales clerks stand in service stores, and merchandise cases free of glass doors are examples of fixtures found in self-service units. The service-oriented retail shop, which requires the assistance of a salesperson, will make use of enclosed cases, hanging racks behind counters, and enclosed compartments. (See Figure 6-6.) Each type of operation and product has its own special requirements. For example, precious jewelry, by its very nature, requires separation from the shopper, while containers of coffee belong on open shelves.

Fixtures come in many materials. Wood, formica, wrought iron, plastic, glass, and combinations of these are just a few of the materials that are used. The styles have as wide a range as do furnishings for the home. Particular types again depend upon image, cost, taste, and the merchandise.

Specialized equipment used in many nonselling areas of the store will be discussed in the appropriate chapters. For example, marking equipment is discussed in Chapter 7 and electronic data processing equipment in Chapter 20.

Locating the Departments

Of all the departments, the selling departments are the most important to a store's success. Where to locate them, particularly when a store has

FIGURE 6-6 Merchandise Fixtures Found in Service Stores

many, is a problem that management must concern itself with. Not as important, but also necessary to the store's success, is the location of the "supporting departments." The receiving department, stockrooms, checkout counters, administrative offices, display department, and advertising offices are just a few to be assigned space.

Some of the factors that must be considered in locating the departments are total space available, assortment of merchandise to be carried, type of merchandise, the number of floor levels, the number of entrances, elevator and escalator locations, and type of operation (service or self-service).

The small retail store should plan the location of its merchandise as carefully as its large counterparts do. While it is true that the small store will not have the same amount of merchandise to display, there is a more limited amount of space available. Many small retailers stock their goods haphazardly. This ultimately leads to a less efficient operation; poor layout planning reduces the amount of merchandise that can be displayed.

Selling Departments. The principles regarding the locating of departments should be understood by anyone entering retailing. Some general rules are

1. Convenience goods (merchandise that requires little effort in purchasing, such as cigarettes), impulse goods (goods that are bought without much contemplation, such as umbrellas in a rainstorm), and inexpensive merchandise in general should be located in high-traffic areas. These include locations at store entrances, next to elevators and escalators, or next to the refund department. A large New York specialty store opened a ladies' hosiery department next to the refund area and quickly doubled its hosiery sales.
2. Shopping goods (those that require more careful consideration, such as clothing and furniture) should be located at the rear of single-level stores and upstairs in multilevel stores. Generally the more expensive and less-frequented departments, such as furniture, are located at the furthest points to reach in a store.
3. If the store has many levels, it is often wise for a department to display a representation or a portion of its offerings on the main floor. These are called split departments. For example, men's clothing might be located on the second floor but might have a small area selling just shirts and ties on the main floor. This part of its merchandise offering is usually less expensive than the rest and therefore might be purchased impulsively. It also may make the potential customer aware of the type of menswear available in the store, encouraging a trip to the main department in another location.
4. Storage areas used to stock additional goods may have a central location in a store (the basement, for example) or may be located within each department. The trend today is for showing as much as possible without great reserve space. In any case, reserve merchandise is best located close to the selling floor, where it can be secured for the customer quickly. Bulky merchandise, such as furniture and appliances, generally necessitate large storage areas away from the selling floor.
5. Department space allocation should be keyed to the percentage of the store's total sales expected for each department.

6. Those departments with related merchandise should be next to each other. For example, the handbag department should be near the shoe department. This allows for the customer to easily purchase a pair of shoes and coordinating handbag and thus leads to increased total sales for the store.

This list is by no means complete. Different types of stores might require other factors to be considered.

Nonselling Areas. The prime space in a retail establishment is designated as the selling floor, but without the sales-supporting and administrative departments, retailers could not be successful. These departments are usually located to the rear of single-story units and on the upper floor of a multilevel shop. The further away from the entrance, the less desirable the space for selling.

Department Layout

After a department is assigned space and the appropriate fixtures have been selected, the physical organization of the department takes place. Each department must consider any factors peculiar to its merchandise before deciding upon an arrangement. For example, a precious jewelry department might assemble four counters at right angles to each other, forming an island in the center that may house another, taller floor case (see Figure 6-7). This arrangement permits maximum security and yet enables the customer to see the merchandise. In a budget department open racks and aisle tables (see Figure 6-8) may be placed so that the merchandise receives maximum exposure. Supermarkets generally arrange their shelves back to back in long aisles that permit a continuous flow of traffic (see Figure 6-9). This arrangement allows for mass stocking of merchandise that can be easily selected by the customer without the necessity of frequent replenishment.

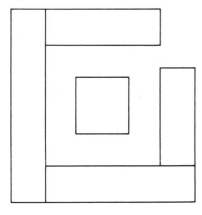

FIGURE 6-7 Four Counters at Right Angles with Center Floor Case

FIGURE 6-8   Open Rack and Aisle Table

Whatever the retail establishment might be, care must be exercised to allow for a smooth flow of customer traffic while at the same time leading individuals throughout the store. Aisles should be easily accessible. Narrow lanes tie up traffic and add to confusion in peak selling periods.

Traffic Movement

Seasoned retailers know that few customers will use the staircase as a means of going to upper and lower floors. Elevators and escalators have until recently been the main customer-moving devices. Over the last few years an innovation in moving the customer from floor to floor has been in evidence. Times Square Stores, in a multilevel unit in Brooklyn, makes use of a moving ramp on which the customer can ascend with a shopping cart. As a general rule, the smaller store is best off using an elevator; it requires less space than the escalator or moving ramp and can be installed less expensively. The retailer not wishing to make an investment in any of these automatic devices might be wiser to confine the selling area to one floor or stock a second story with desirable merchandise that is unavailable elsewhere.

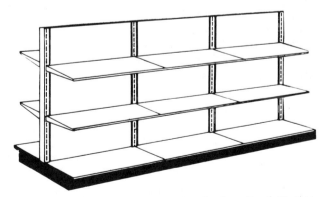

FIGURE 6-9   Island Unit Featuring Back-to-Back Shelving
for Maximum Exposure—Used Extensively in Supermarkets

Action for the Independent Retailer

Site selection typifies the advantages of size. Large successful stores not only have a financial advantage; they also have the know-how and the willingness to scientifically survey a prospective location. While it is true that most small businesses cannot afford the expense of a truly scientific survey, few make any attempt to evaluate all of the information available to them. All too often, a location is picked by hunch. In addition, many sites are selected with more attention paid to the ease of commuting to the proprietor's home than to the needs of the neighborhood in which the store is to be located. As a result, an important cause of small retail failure is poor site selection. The pity is that much of the necessary information is available, free of charge, to anyone willing to spend a little time at the library studying census reports and the like.

The interior and the exterior layout of the small store is important. Since lack of sufficient space and financial strength results in a relatively small inventory, it is important that it should be shown to its best advantage. We have all seen inviting, beautifully set up small stores that have been designed with a minimum of expense. All it takes is the proprietor's understanding of the importance of proper layout, taste, and effort.

IMPORTANT POINTS IN THE CHAPTER

1. *One of the principal reasons for the failure of new retail stores is poor site selection. Despite this, many retailers select locations in an unscientific manner.*

2. *Site selection should begin with an appraisal of the general area, with particular attention paid to the size and characteristics of the area's population.*

3. *After the general area has been decided upon, the specific location within that area must be determined. Choices between the relative merits of downtown areas, shopping centers, or neighborhood areas, must be made.*

4. *During recent years shopping centers, particularly the controlled type, have undergone dramatic growth. Some of the reasons for this expansion are one-stop shopping, adequate parking, controlled competition, and unified promotional activities.*

5. *Current trends indicate a continued growth of shopping centers, particularly the enclosed mall types.*

6. *To ensure maximum use of facilities, store layout should be scientifically determined.*

7. *Competition for the customer's attention begins with imaginative exterior layout and design. Exterior design should be tasteful, eye-catching, and functional.*

8. *Interior design begins with wall, floor, and ceiling materials. These should be attractive to the eye, useful in separating areas, and in keeping with the store's image.*

9. *Lighting fixtures should be attractive, be adequate for good overall visibility, and have the additional function of setting off the store's merchandise to its best advantage.*

10. *The store's image may be emphasized by the selection of the merchandise fixtures. Self-service stores must display merchandise in a manner that encourages customer browsing. Service-oriented stores usually feature enclosed cases and inaccessible racks.*

11. *The location of the various departments depends, to a large extent, on store traffic. Convenience goods and inexpensive merchandise should be located in high-traffic areas. Goods that require careful consideration are usually placed in less highly used areas. Such departments frequently display samples of their stock in high-traffic areas.*

12. *Service departments such as stockrooms are located in areas of light traffic as close as possible to the departments they serve.*

REVIEW QUESTIONS

1. Most small retailers do not select sites for their stores effectively. Why?

2. Indicate six characteristics that should be studied in a location analysis. For each of the factors mentioned, suggest a type of store for which this informtion would be important.

3. Give examples of the types of retailers that require newspaper space and radio time. What types of stores would not have such requirements?

4. What sort of retailers would do poorly in a high-rent downtown area? Name several that would do well.

5. Why are downtown shopping centers generally of the high-rise variety?

6. Name three advantages of locating in a controlled shopping center.

7. What are the advantages of an enclosed mall?

8. Indicate four pairs of stores that would make poor neighbors.

9. From whom can small retailers get assistance in planning their store's layout?

10. Which classification of department in a store requires the most consideration in the physical layout?

11. Besides visual appeal, what must a retailer consider in planning the store's exterior space?

12. How have some stores converted limited exterior shape into more adequate parking facilities?

13. What are some of the departments that stores have located outside of the building proper?

14. Discuss those factors that contribute to the number and type of windows a store has.

15. Besides paint, which materials do modern retailers use for their walls and ceilings?

16. In addition to beauty, why have retailers covered their selling floors with carpeting instead of wood and vinyl tile?

17. What are some advantages of fluorescent lighting?

18. Why do self-service and service departments require different merchandise fixtures?

19. Define convenience goods. Where should they be located?

20. What are shopping goods? Is there anything to consider in determining which of these should be located nearest and furthest from the entrance?

21. Where should storage areas be located?

22. Discuss how a store allocates the amount of space for each department.

CASE PROBLEMS

CASE PROBLEM 1

Jill Watson has just sold a highly successful supermarket in a suburban location. She opened the store ten years ago as a neighborhood grocery, and because of her ability and the growth of the area she was able to expand the store to a medium-sized supermarket, for which she received in excess of $100,000.

She is seriously considering a small supermarket in a midtown high-density location in which, in addition to the regular supermarket activities, she will make sandwiches and coffee (not to be eaten on the premises).

QUESTION

1. Discuss the following:
   a. Traffic count
   b. Prices she can get
   c. Probable rental
   d. Working days and hours
   e. Competition
   f. Breakfast and lunch business
   g. Local competition
   h. Effect of suburban competition
   i. Difficulty of obtaining personnel
   j. Employee salaries

CASE PROBLEM 2

All the department managers of Belldocks Specialty Shop were called to a meeting requested by top management. The purpose of the meeting was to discuss the establishment of a special department in a separate location to handle customers' returns and refunds. At the present time each department is handling its own adjustments. The main reasons for the proposed change are:

1. Customers returning merchandise often take up a salesperson's time, which might be better spent in selling other merchandise.
2. At peak periods departments often become overcrowded with adjustments.
3. Dissatisfied customers making returns sometimes disrupt order in the departments.
4. The number of people working in each department could be cut down and the money used to hire a few experts on returns and adjustments.

Belldocks is a four-level retail store (including a basement selling floor) selling men's, women's, and children's clothing. Last year they grossed $14 million in their twelve selling departments.

QUESTIONS

1. Are there any advantages in having each department handle its own returns? Discuss them.
2. If the decision was reached to centralize returns, where would you locate this new department? Carefully outline and discuss the factors to be considered in the selection of the location.

7 *merchandise handling*

BEHAVIORAL OBJECTIVES

Upon completion of this chapter the student should be able to

1. *Discuss five advantages of a centralized receiving department.*
2. *Explain the importance of the location of the receiving department.*
3. *List eight ideas that can improve the effectiveness of a receiving department.*
4. *Differentiate among blind, semiblind, and direct checking.*
5. *List six purposes served by marking.*
6. *Write a brief essay on marking principles. At least five of the principles indicated in the text should be included.*

INTRODUCTION

In a small retailing operation the problem of getting the merchandise that has been ordered into stock or onto the selling floor is relatively simple. The person who ordered the goods is generally on hand when the merchandise is unpacked. This enables that individual to supervise the checking of merchandise, mark it with the selling price, and see to its placement in stock or on the selling shelves. Since the receipt of merchandise generally takes place directly on the selling floor, the handling of incoming merchandise is rapid and efficient.

The large retail establishment, where buyers cannot personally check the merchandise received, and where selling floors may be far from the receiving area, faces special problems. Effectively solving these problems results in both financial savings and rapid movement of goods from the receiving department to the selling floor. In periods of high activity, such as the Christmas season, making goods quickly available to the customer is important.

THE CENTRALIZED RECEIVING DEPARTMENT

Because the receiving of merchandise is part of the buying function, it should be part of the buyer's responsibility. This setup works well in a small store. However, as the size of the operation increases, individualized departmental receiving becomes impractical and a centralized receiving department (an independent department responsible for all receiving) is necessary. Some of the advantages of the centralized receiving department are as follows:

1. *Better physical control of merchandise.* There is always the possibility of goods disappearing between the time the merchandise arrives in the store and the time

it appears on the selling shelves. When the receiving operation is the chore of sales personnel, the procedures tend to be haphazard. Since receiving is not the prime job of salespeople, they are disinterested and careless. In addition, the frequent interruptions that occur on the sales floor practically guarantee errors. In contrast, a properly set up receiving department with standardized routines requires paperwork and signatures for both the receipt of goods into the store and the transfer of goods to warehouses and selling departments. The responsibility of specific individuals is clearly defined. Under such conditions, goods are unlikely to disappear.

2. *Better financial control of merchandise.* By standardizing procedures and fixing responsibilities, which can only be done with thoroughly trained personnel, the receiving deparment can be closely tied in with the accounting department. In this way, proper credits for damaged goods, shortages, and discounts can be achieved.

3. *More efficient use of equipment and supplies.* The centralized receiving department, thanks to its large volume of activity, can effectively use labor-saving machinery, which the relatively small, departmentalized receiving activities would not have sufficient volume for. For example, an expensive ticketing machine capable of great labor and cost savings would not be practical for the small amount of receiving done by an individual selling department. Similarly, if receiving and marking supplies are to be spread throughout all of the selling departments in a store, there is apt to be considerable waste and an unnecessary investment in the inventory of supplies.

4. *Relieving selling departments of receiving responsibilities.* Since the prime responsibility of sales personnel is selling, any job that distracts them from customers or possible customers is apt to reduce their selling effectiveness. Not only will their sales effectiveness be lessened, but the receiving operation will suffer as well since it will be treated with boredom and disinterest.

5. *General advantages of specialization.* The advantage of mass production is that when the volume is large enough for a task to be broken down into its various parts and performed by separate individuals, the task can be done more effectively. In a large receiving department, where each worker does a specific job repetitively, that employee becomes proficient at it. This enables standardized procedures, individual responsibility, and the use of specialized machinery. As a result of this specialization, the centralized receiving department is capable of more effectively performing the receiving operation than the individual selling departments.

THE LOCATION OF THE RECEIVING DEPARTMENT

The location of the receiving department in a store varies according to the physical structure of the particular store. There are, however, certain factors that must be taken into account by all stores before the decision on locating the centralized receiving department can be made.

1. *Value of the space.* Since the success or failure of a store depends, in large part, on its ability to sell merchandise, the location of the various selling departments must be given more importance than the location of the receiving department. In

some large department stores located in the central business districts of large cities, the sales space is considered so valuable that many of the receiving functions are carried on in warehouses located a considerable distance from the main store. In this way the store is able to use a larger portion of its valuable space for selling. As a general rule, the receiving department should be placed in a low sales-value area. This can be in the back of a small store, or the upper floors of a large store (accessible by elevator to an unfolding platform at ground level).

2. *Amount of space.* The amount of space to be used by the receiving department depends upon the anticipated volume of the store. The department must be large enough to handle the receiving operation during peak periods, when additional personnel are required. Insufficient space results in sloppy procedures and damaged merchandise. In addition, there are frequently delays in getting goods from the receiving department to the selling departments. This results in lost sales. Since the receiving department does not bring in any profits, there is frequently a tendency to allocate too little space to the receiving department. This can be a serious managerial error.

3. *Type of merchandise received.* Merchandise of high bulk is frequently stored away from the main selling area. This is particularly true with such goods as furniture or appliances, which are sold by means of samples on the selling floor and shipped to the customer from warehouses. Small, high-value merchandise is generally received and stored as close to the selling floors as possible.

4. *Convenience to stockroom, elevators, and selling areas.* After the goods have been received, checked, and marked, it is necessary to transport them either directly to the selling floors or to stockrooms. The location of the receiving department should be such that the flow of merchandise to its destination should be as efficient as possible. This requires taking into account the availability of freight elevators, stockrooms, and so on.

5. *Availability to common carriers.* The loading platforms required for receiving merchandise should be easily accessible to trucks, and large enough to enable the unloading crew to perform its job quickly and effectively. In large downtown shopping areas the glut of traffic has dramatically worsened this problem. Even the substantial structural changes that many mid-city stores have undergone have only partially alleviated the problem. During the peak Christmas rush it is not unusual for a truck to wait hours to be unloaded at the receiving department of a large urban department store. This results in increased freight costs and delay in getting merchandise to the selling departments.

EQUIPMENT AND LAYOUT

In small and medium-sized stores, receiving functions can be efficiently handled with no special equipment or strictly followed procedures. Incoming packages may be delivered to the selling floor or the back of the store. When time permits, the goods are unpacked, checked, marked, and put on the selling shelves and racks or in the storeroom. As the store increases in size, the volume of receiving becomes so great that more scientific methods are needed to prevent costly errors or serious time loss in getting the merchandise to the selling floors. It is impossible to completely standardize receiving operations in a large store; the receiving department must be prepared at any time to handle a shipment of pianos or spools of thread and, obviously, they must be handled differently. However, there are certain broad principles which, if carefully followed, will improve receiving effectiveness. The Dennison Manufacturing Company suggests that the following ten ideas will improve the effectiveness of any receiving department:

1. *Straight-line movement of all materials with as little backtracking as possible.* Goods should be unloaded from the trucks and the receiving operations performed in such a manner that the first operation to be performed should be done closest to the unloading platform and the last operation to be performed should be done closest to the selling floor or storeroom. In other words, the unpacking operation should be done nearest to the truck, then the goods should be checked at a point closer to the selling floor. Finally, the price-marking operation should be located nearest the selling floor. Such an operation would require a minimum of merchandise handling. (See Figure 7-1.)

2. *Movement of all material through the shortest possible distance and with the fewest possible motions.* While the layout of an individual store depends upon the amount and shape of the available space, careful study must be made of the use of the space to ensure maximum effectiveness.

3. *Maximum machine operation, minimum hand operation.* By mechanizing operations wherever possible, the receiving department may be assured of considerable time savings. Moreover, in these times of high labor costs, machines can generally do a job more inexpensively, as well as more effectively. An example of this is the use of conveyor belts that bring the goods to workers rather than having the workers do their own carrying of goods.

4. *Determination of the most efficient methods of performing specific repetitive operations, and standardization of these methods.* Most receiving operations consist of simple repetitive tasks. If these tasks are done in any but the most efficient way, time will be lost. It is necessary to determine the best way to do the job, and to do it that way every time.

5. *Careful attention to working conditions.* Improper working conditions can contribute to deficiencies and result in lost time. Such factors as proper table and chair heights, adequate lighting, and good machine layout are very important. Not only must equipment be scientifically laid out, but attention must be given to human production as well. Care must be taken to ensure that working conditions, worker comfort, and worker efficiency be maintained at as high a level as possible.

6. *Careful selection and training of personnel.* Wherever possible, the same operation should be performed by the same people. Receiving department workers require specific talents and must be selected with this in mind. That is to say, a person responsible for unpacking must have the physical qualifications necessary for the job. In stores with a large volume of receiving and many receiving department employees, it is possible to specialize the working force. Rather than training a person to be a jack-of-all-trades, workers should be taught to do specific jobs. Doing the same operation repetitively increases a worker's efficiency.

7. *Adequate supervision.* To ensure that standard methods and standard quality are maintained, careful supervision is required. If procedures are not carefully supervised, there is always the likelihood that the most perfect planning will not be followed. Receiving departments must be set up in such a way that all of the fore-

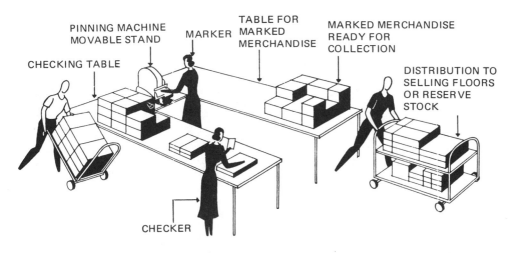

Flowchart labels:

PINNING MACHINE MOVABLE STAND

CHECKING TABLE

MARKER

TABLE FOR MARKED MERCHANDISE

MARKED MERCHANDISE READY FOR COLLECTION

DISTRIBUTION TO SELLING FLOORS OR RESERVE STOCK

CHECKER

This method of operation is based on parallel stationary tables, with attaching machine on movable stand between them. Tables and machine stand are exactly the same height (about 36″) and space between tables is just wide enough for marker and machine. Overhead electric connection permits machine to move the length of the table. The operating method is as follows:

1. Receiver or stockman brings packages containing merchandise to be machine-marked to checking table.

2. Checker matches invoice to package, opens, piles merchandise on table, invoice checks, leaving retailed invoice with merchandise.

3. Marker moves pinning machine opposite merchandise, and machine-marks, piling marked merchandise on the table at her right. As piles of boxes are marked, she moves machine so that merchandise to be marked, and space to pile it after marking, always are right at hand.

4. Stockman collects marked merchandise from table, takes to forward or reserve stock.
   This operating plan shows a single unit for one attaching machine. It is capable of indefinite expansion by increasing the length of the tables and adding more pinning machines. It is adaptable to portable table operation by using lines of portable tables in place of the stationary tables; or to a combination of the two systems by having the checking table stationary and the tables for marked merchandise portable.

FIGURE 7-1 Flow Chart Showing Checking and Marking Operation with Stationary Tables

Courtesy of Dennison Manufacturing Co.

man's responsibilities, both for workers and for machines, are always in plain sight and easily supervised and controlled.

8. *Sufficient equipment.* The efficiency of a large receiving department depends upon the efficiency of its equipment. There must be enough equipment to take full advantage of machine operation even in times of peak production. It is particularly vital that carefully set up procedures be used during rush periods. If the amount of equipment on hand does not have the capacity to handle peak production quantities, procedures are apt to break down, and the errors and inefficiencies that they were designed to overcome will occur.

9. *Standby equipment.* The fullest possible use of equipment, taking into consideration the importance of standby equipment for emergencies, must be insisted upon. The major problem in the receiving operation is errors. The best defense against errors is strict adherence to carefully designed procedures. Machine breakdowns can be very serious, not only in terms of lost production, but more important, because the carefully set up procedures must be altered. Since the personnel have been carefully trained in specific procedures, any change in procedures is apt to cause serious errors. It is vital that, wherever possible, standby equipment is available.

10. *Enough records for adequate control.* Paper work is perhaps the most annoying function of the receiving department and it should, wherever possible, be eliminated. On the other hand, a certain minimum amount of records must be kept for proper control.

Although all of the above principles are obvious, they are not simple. It is not unusual for a large store to use engineers and time and motion experts to set up their receiving departments.

Frequently, separate receiving areas are used for specific types of goods. Where the volume of receiving of appliances or ready-to-wear is great enough, the use of special receiving areas permits the adaptation of procedures specifically designed for those specific goods.

Stores rely upon one or several types of equipment in their handling of merchandise.

Stationary Tables

The most commonly used piece of equipment in a receiving room is the stationary table. This type of table is well-suited to a small store because it is compact and requires little space. Incoming packages are first brought to the table. The merchandise is unpacked and sorted as it is placed on the table. Then the goods are checked, marked, and taken to the selling floor.

Portable Tables

Where the volume of incoming goods is so great that the operations of unpacking and checking are separated from marking, portable tables are used. The merchandise is placed on tables on wheels, where it is unpacked and checked. Then each table is wheeled to the marking area. After being marked, the goods, still on the same table, may be moved to the selling floor. The use of the portable table minimizes the handling of goods. The design of the portable table depends on the merchandise to be handled. Racks may be substituted for tables if ready-to-wear merchandise is involved. The portable equipment eliminates the handling necessitated by the use of stationary tables.

Bins

When bins are to be used in a receiving department, the floor is generally divided into two sections: (1) unpacking and checking and (2) marking. The two sections are separated by a wall of bins. After the merchandise is unpacked and checked on tables in the receiving section, it is put into the bins and then onto tables in the marking section for the second operation. The objection to the bin system is the unnecessary extra handling, and the errors in marking due to mixing all the merchandise in the same bin.

Conveyor Systems

Large-volume stores can make considerable savings in receiving costs by use of conveyor systems. Under such systems the goods are unpacked on to a large

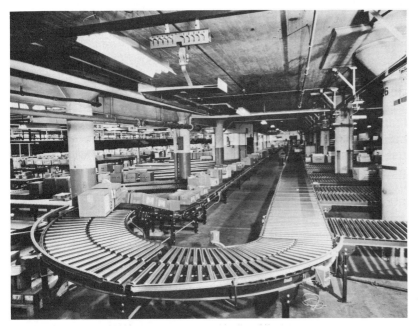

FIGURE 7-2 A Roller Conveyor System in Combination with Live Roller Lines and Belt Conveyors—Particularly Suited for Rapid and Efficient Transport from and to Store Areas and Dispatch Points

FIGURE 7-3 Handler Removes Needed Stock from This 125-Foot Conveyor—
The Remainder Accumulates on the Conveyor

conveyor belt. The belt moves the goods to a line of checkers, who place the goods on stationary tables alongside the conveyor. After being checked, the goods are replaced on the belt and move to the markers. The goods are once more transferred to small tables, marked, and replaced on the conveyor for removal to the sales floors and stockroom. (See Figures 7-2 and 7-3.) In stores that feature hanging soft goods, a different type of conveyor system is used. The merchandise is placed on hangers and put on a rack-like conveyor system. The merchandise automatically moves along, on hangers, to the checking and marking areas and finally to the designated selling areas. Stores using this system have "spurs" that terminate in certain areas of the selling departments so that little physical handling of merchandise is required between the receiving and selling areas.

Receivings in a department store are of a wide variety, and none of the four types of equipment described above is best for every type of goods. As a result, most large stores use a combination of methods.

RECEIVING OPERATIONS

The receiving operation begins with the delivery of merchandise from the carrier to the unloading or receiving platform. Ideally, this should be done indoors to protect against damage by weather, unnecessary handling of cartons, and interference with outside traffic. But because any use of indoor space is likely to reduce the space available for selling, mid-city stores, in which space is at a premium, frequently provide for outdoor unloading of deliveries.

Receiving operations include inspection, recording, checking, and marking of merchandise.

Inspecting

The first phase of the receiving operations is the inspection of the delivered packages or cartons. The newly delivered packages should be inspected (not unpacked) immediately upon unloading from the truck. This should be done in the presence of the driver. The number of cartons and condition of the cartons should be checked. Any open or damaged cartons or shortage of cartons should be noted on the trucker's receipt. This information should also be noted on the store's copy of the freight bill, which the trucker must sign as confirmation. The trucker's signature attesting to the discrepancy is necessary if damage claims are to be filed.

Since freight costs are generally paid by the store, it is necessary to check the amount charged for the delivery. Checking freight costs frequently requires weighing the delivered goods. If this is not always possible, spot checks should be made from time to time.

The still-unopened cartons are then marked with department numbers so they can be taken to the particular area of the receiving department designated for the unpacking of that particular type of merchandise.

The Receiving Record

Before the cartons are sent on for unpacking, a receiving record is made out. The form of the receiving record varies from store to store, but it generally contains the following information:

> Date and hour of arrival
> Weight
> Form of transportation
> Number of pieces
> Receiving number
> Invoice number
> Condition of packages
> Delivery charges
> Name of deliverer
> Amount of invoice
> Department ordering goods
> Remarks

A small store, in which the proprietor has complete knowledge and control of the operation, can frequently do without a formal receiving record. In a large store the receiving record is an important document, for the following reasons:

1. In the event of a disagreement between the vendor and the store over a particular shipment, the receiving record provides necessary information. In a small store the proprietor can either trust his or her memory in such cases, or make an informal note on each shipment.
2. The vendor's invoice number on the receiving record ensures that no invoice is paid unless the merchandise has been received. This is done by matching up invoices and receiving records prior to payment. The person paying invoices in a small store need not worry about whether or not the merchandise was received. That individual was there when the delivery was made. In a large store the person signing the check depends upon the receiving record for proof of delivery.

Checking

The next step in the receiving process involves checking the incoming goods. This includes determining if the goods are in agreement with the purchase order, removing the merchandise from the shipping container and sorting it, checking the quantity of the merchandise, and checking the quality of the merchandise.

Unpacking and Sorting

Many stores have the policy of not opening a container until the invoice arrives. Unpacking and sorting without an invoice results in faulty operations because shortages and incorrect shipments become difficult to ascertain. Even when lists of the merchandise received are made out, discrepancies with the invoice are difficult to recheck, since goods delivered to the shipping floor cannot be recounted.

Quantity Checking

There are several methods of checking the quantity of incoming merchandise. Most stores use either the blind check method or the direct check method. There are also combinations of these methods and variations of them. Occasionally a store uses the spot-check method in which a few random items are checked. Since many errors slip through a spot-checking system, this method is not recommended.

The Direct Check. This system provides for the checking of the quantity of incoming merchandise directly against the vendor's invoice. Shipments for which no invoice has arrived from the vendor are held unopened until the invoice is available. Frequently, the pile-up of unopened packages becomes so great that they must be quantity-checked without an invoice. In such cases, "dummy" invoices are prepared and used as though they were real.

The following are the advantages of the direct check method:

1. With no paperwork to do other than checkmarks against an invoice, the checker can work speedily and economically.
2. In the event of a discrepancy between the invoice and the checker's count, a recheck can be made quickly and efficiently.
3. The description of the merchandise is stated on the invoice and not left up to the imagination of the checker.

Direct checking is the most widely used method of quantity verification in small stores and probably in large stores as well. The problem of not always having the invoice on hand can be overcome by insisting that vendors include duplicate invoices in their packing containers.

The most serious disadvantage of the direct checking method is that it may lead to careless checking. Checking is a boring task and subject to carelessness. When the checker is told the quantity in advance (from the invoice) it is possible to check too quickly or, in a rush period, not to check at all.

The Blind Check. The blind check method is designed to minimize the checking errors that occur with direct checking. The system provides for the checker to prepare a list of the items being received, without benefit of the invoice. Standardized forms are provided to ease the paper work, but much paper work remains to be done. This has the effect of slowing down the checking process. The blind check requires the checker to describe the merchandise. When the checker's description does not match the invoice description, costly delays may develop. This method does reduce the handling (and sometimes loss) of invoices.

The Semiblind Check. The semiblind check method combines the best features of the direct check and the blind check methods. By providing the checker with a copy of the buying order, in which all of the paper work is already included with the exception of the quantity, the unnecessary paper work of the blind check method is eliminated. Because they are not told the quantity, the checkers are forced to determine the quantity by carefully counting the merchandise.

Whichever quantity checking method is used, discrepancies must be noted so that claims may be made for short shipments and returns made for overshipments.

Quality Checking

Generally speaking, checkers cannot be held responsible for any quality checking other than obvious errors. Close quality checking is the responsibility of the buyer, the buyer's assistants, or department managers. In practice, branded merchandise that is frequently reordered is rarely subject to quality checking. Merchandise that is to be stored in its original containers (men's shirts in plastic bags) is rarely quality checked. The decision is made by the buyer, who must decide whether the time saved by not checking is offset by customer dissatisfaction with an occasional poor quality item that slipped through unchecked.

Marking

With the exception of single-price stores, or merchandise that has been pre-marked by the vendor, all merchandise must be marked with its selling price before being offered for sale. This can be done with a variety of pinned tickets or gummed labels, by hand or a machine process. (See Figures 7-4 and 7-5.) Frequently merchandise control can be improved by including other information than the selling price on the ticket. Some of the purposes served by marking follow:

1. When the selling price is clearly marked on the merchandise, it helps customers to make the buying decision. Moreover, since price and quality are closely relat-

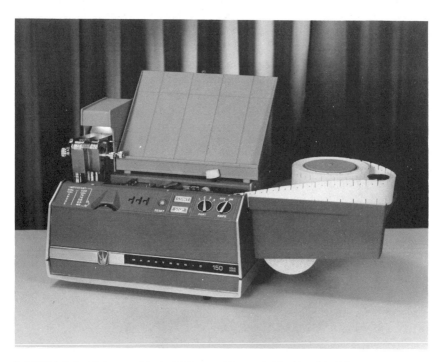

FIGURE 7-4 Ticket and Label Printer—Monarch Marking Machines

FIGURE 7-5 Dial-A-Pricer Marking Machine—Monarch Marking Machines

ed, a clearly displayed retail price helps customers locate the quality of goods in which they are interested.

2. Marking improves the service of salespersons. Customers who are interested in spending a certain amount for an item can be easily directed to a section of the store in which that price range may be found, and then be left to help themselves while the salesperson goes to other customers.

3. In self-service stores such as supermarkets, it is imperative that the customer know the price in order to make the buying decision.

4. Since the value of the merchandise on hand must be calculated several times a year, it is important that the selling price of the goods be easily determined. In another chapter of the book there will be a discussion on finding the cost of the goods when the selling price is known.

5. The marking tag, showing the price and department, enables the accounting department to determine the total sales and profits of the store, by department.

6. Information on the tag showing the date it was first offered for sale helps the buyer make decisions on markdowns and reorders.

7. Customers like to believe they all pay the same price for a store's merchandise. While price marking doesn't guarantee this, it helps give the impression of a single selling price for all customers.

Marking Principles

Setting up a sound system of marking procedures requires close attention to certain basic rules.

Neatness. The growing use of machine printing and rubber stamping has to a large extent solved the problem of neatness and legibility. In stores where marking is done by hand, care must be taken that the information marked is clear and easily read.

Location. The placing of the tag on the merchandise should be carefully planned. A salesperson or prospective customer should be able to locate the tag easily. The tag should always be located in the same position on similar merchandise. That is, it is helpful if all men's jackets are tagged on the right sleeve.

Damages. Careless marking can result in tearing or soiling of the merchandise. Care must be taken to avoid this. In addition, the price tag should be designed so that removal of the ticket at the time of sale will leave both the ticket and the merchandise undamaged.

Permanence. The marking system must be designed to protect against being lost, altered, or switched. Tickets attached by machine are generally more permanent than those that are attached by hand.

Standardization. Where possible, the number of different types of tickets should be kept to a minimum. This reduces the cost of ticketing and increases the efficiency of the marking operation.

Control. Proper marking is vital. A dress with a mismarked size will never be sold. Price errors lose both sales dollars and customer good will. Therefore marking must be carefully supervised by means of exact, clearly defined channels of responsibility.

The Price Tag

The information to be found on the tag varies with the needs of the individual store and the type of merchandise involved. (See Figure 7-6.) In a small store the person who makes the decision on the selling price is generally available when the goods are being marked. Larger stores face the problem of channeling price and other data to the markers.

One way of getting the sales price to the marker is by having the buyer mark the selling price on the invoice after it has been checked. Although this is a common method, it has the disadvantage of the invoice potentially being lost because of the excessive handling.

Frequently the buyer may mark one piece of the incoming goods, and have someone else duplicate the tag on the balance of the shipment. This has the advantage of having the buyer see the merchandise just before it gets to the selling floor. Unfortunately, this method requires the buyer to be in the receiving department every time a shipment arrives.

Staple merchandise that is rarely subject to price change can be marked from lists supplied to the marker in advance.

The central offices of chain stores prepare lists of retail prices and send

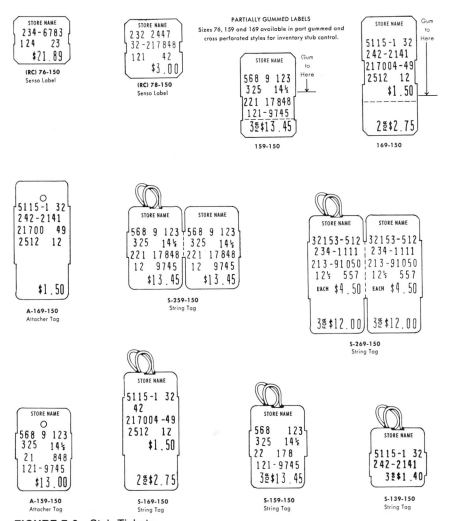

FIGURE 7-6 Stub Tickets

Courtesy of Dennison Manufacturing Co.

them to the individual stores. (Store managers may change these prices in a few cases to meet local competition.)

In some stores the price and other information to be marked are placed on a duplicate copy of the buyer's order, which is sent to the receiving department. In such cases, the information is available to the marker when the merchandise comes into the store.

Coding the Cost. In many small stores it is desirable to mark the cost of the merchandise as well as its selling price. Some stores, such as jewelry and appliance stores, whose merchandise does not have a fixed selling price, tag their merchandise with the cost and do not indicate the selling price. Naturally, if the cost is to be marked, it must be done in such a way that it can be easily read by the salesperson and not understood by the customer. A common coding system is the use of a word or phrase containing ten letters, each letter representing a number. The numbers are substituted for the letters to determine the cost.

$$1 \quad 2 \quad 3 \quad 4 \quad 5 \quad 6 \quad 7 \quad 8 \quad 9 \quad 0$$
$$C \quad O \quad S \quad T \quad M \quad A \quad R \quad K \quad E \quad D$$

By using the code indicated above, an item marked C S R M has a cost of $13.75. Any ten-letter word or phrase in which no letter appears more than once can be used for a costing code.

Other Information. The balance of the information placed on the price tag depends upon the type of merchandise and the merchandise control systems used by the store. A large department store using up-to-date data processing procedures may put extensive information on the tag. Tags may be designed in such fashion that sales informational reports on color, style, and size may be available to the buyer. This can have an important effect on future buying decisions. This topic is discussed fully in Chapter 20.

Bulk Marking

Low-price items that are subject to frequent price variations need not be marked until they are placed on the selling floor. This procedure is frequently followed by supermarkets. Goods are received in large cartons and the price is marked on the outside of the carton and stored. Not until the goods are brought to the selling floor are the individual items marked. In this way, price changes during the storage period do not require remarking. This procedure is sometimes called delayed marking.

Nonmarking

Certain types of goods need not be marked at all. In all cases of nonmarking, the checkout counters must be provided with lists of selling prices.

1. Merchandise that can be effectively displayed on shelves, counters, or tables can be priced by a sign. This shortcut in the marking function saves time and money.
2. In the case of very inexpensive merchandise, the cost of marking in relation to the profit may make marking illogical.
3. Certain products such as fruits and vegetables may be damaged by marking.
4. Promotional goods or other merchandise subject to constant price change are not usually marked because constant remarking is too time-consuming.

Premarking

As a means of saving space, time, and money, many large retailers have the manufacturers do the marking for them. This is most commonly found in staple goods such as men's shirts or hosiery, where price fluctuation is relatively uncommon.

Outside Marking

Many large stores, such as Gertz, Gimbels, Marshall Field, and Montgomery Ward, have their marking performed by their freight carriers. As in the case of premarking, the retailer must supply all the marking information and specifications to the outside marking firm. In the case of high-fashion merchandise, where every day is important, some retailers feel that outside marking permits a time saving of several days between the day of receipt and the day the goods appear on the selling floor.

Remarking

Many factors may require the remarking of merchandise—markdowns; additional markups; soiled, torn, or lost tags; merchandise returned by customers, and so on. Large retailers that keep track of the retail value of the inventory require special forms to be made out to enable the accounting de-

FIGURE 7-7 Reprice Markers—Monarch Marking Machines

partment to make the necessary changes on their inventory control records. This is frequently unnecessary in smaller stores.

There is a difference of opinion on the manner in which remarking is to be done. Many stores draw a line through the old price and write in the new price above it. This may give some customers the impression that they are getting a bargain. On the other hand, there are customers who believe the merchandise was overpriced to begin with. Such customers tend to look with suspicion on other goods in the store that have not been marked down. As a result, many stores handle markdowns by removing the old ticket and replacing it with a new ticket containing a new selling price. In this way, the customer may not be aware of the markdown. (See Figure 7-7.)

BRANCH AND CHAIN STORE RECEIVING

A large portion of the merchandise received by chain store operations is processed by the receiving departments of centrally located warehouses. Since the centralized location handles vastly more volume than would be required of any individual unit, centralization permits savings and efficiency not available to the small units. The vast volume enables the maximum utilization of expensive merchandise handling and marking equipment, and the large work force permits specialization and standardization of procedures in the most scientific manner. In addition, centralized receiving saves duplication of expensive machinery, supplies, and labor. By minimizing the receiving function of the individual units, more chain selling space becomes available. (In effect, inexpensive warehouse space is being traded for prime selling space.)

The disadvantages of centralized receiving are

1. *Extra shipping costs.* Goods must go from the vendor to the central warehouse to the store, rather than directly to the store.
2. *Duplication of checking.* Goods are checked at the warehouse (from the vendor) and at the selling outlet (from the warehouse).

RECEIVING DEPARTMENT PERSONNEL

No other department in a large retail operation has as many varied job qualifications as the receiving department. That is, the work performed by the various receiving, checking, and marking clerks requires strength for moving packages, the ability to handle tools and equipment for unpacking cartons, and the capacity for doing the vast amount of repetitive work without carelessness that is required of markers. In short, most of the lower-level jobs in the receiving room are primarily physical.

At the management level, job qualifications are another matter. The following is a list of the more important requirements of receiving department managerial personnel.

1. *Being well-organized.* Activities in the receiving department during a rush period can be hectic. There are always mislaid invoices, merchandise with which discrepancies have been found, and so on that may disrupt the normal flow of work. This, coupled with insufficient space at peak periods, requires careful, well-organized management if the receiving department is to work effectively.
2. *Tact.* Receiving room management is always under pressure from department managers or buyers to rush needed goods to the selling floor. Frequently, requests are made for "one piece" to satisfy a waiting customer. Anything that may disrupt receiving procedures can be the cause of receiving, checking, or marking errors. Explaining this fact to an angry buyer requires a considerable amount of tact and diplomacy.
3. *Ability to handle workers.* As is the case with all retail operations, there are never enough people to handle peak periods. The result is that the existing personnel must be asked on occasion to do far more than the normal amount of work. In areas in which the work required is largely physical, considerable managerial skill is required to get the extra effort from already tired personnel.

Action for the Independent Retailer

Merchandise handling is another area in which the small retailer has an advantage over the high-volume competitor. Inspecting, checking, and marking of goods can be closely supervised, and the merchandise can be stored or placed on the selling floor with a minimum of errors. In addition, because of the relatively small space involved, there is little time lost in getting goods from storage to the selling floor.

The only time the small store gets into trouble with merchandise handling is in periods of peak selling activity, when the inventory is at its highest level and customer activity demands instant access to goods. At such times the independent retailer must plan the allocation of storeroom space carefully. Stored merchandise must be organized so that all goods are easily accessible and readily found. Naturally, the fastest moving merchandise must be stored in the most accessible locations.

IMPORTANT POINTS IN THE CHAPTER

1. *Active stores that receive a large volume of goods find it advisable to set up centralized receiving departments. This frees the sales personnel of a burdensome nonselling duty* and improves the receiving function by providing specialists who use specialized equipment in that area.

2. The effectiveness of the receiving department can be measured by the amount of time that is required to move goods from the incoming trucks to the selling floor. The location, layout, and equipment used by the receiving department are crucial to effective receiving.

3. The receiving department is responsible for the receipt and inspection of incoming goods, sorting and checking, and marking the goods for sale.

4. Many large retailers have their incoming goods premarked by the supplier or freight forwarder. This procedure saves space, time, and money.

5. A large portion of the merchandise received by chain stores is processed by the receiving departments of centrally located warehouses. Although this procedure increases shipping and handling costs, the amount of selling space at the retail outlets is increased.

REVIEW QUESTIONS

1. Differentiate between receiving functions at a large and a small retail operation.
2. Centralized receiving departments use equipment and supplies more efficiently than individual departments. Why is this so?
3. List several disadvantages of using salespeople for receiving.
4. Why do downtown receiving departments frequently perform the bulk of their activities at a location some distance from the store?
5. The nature of some goods is such that they are more easily received at nonselling locations. List several examples of such merchandise.
6. Explain and discuss the importance of a straight-line operation in the layout of a receiving department.
7. Discuss the effect on standardized receiving procedures of inadequate equipment to handle pre-Christmas volume.
8. Does the layout of the receiving room have any relationship to the quality of the department manager's supervision?
9. What are the advantages of a portable receiving table over a stationary table?
10. Discuss the advantages of a conveyor belt in a receiving department.
11. Why is there not one best method of receiving all goods?
12. Discuss the importance of having the trucker sign the freight invoice on which a damaged carton was noted.
13. What are the advantages and disadvantages of checking the freight charges on incoming goods?
14. Explain the importance of a receiving record to a large retailer.
15. Discuss the advantages and disadvantages of the direct checking method of quantity checking.

16. Describe the blind check method of quantity checking.

17. Why are checkers not responsible for quality checking?

18. List six principles of good marking.

19. A jewelry store that uses the word *blacksmith* to code its cost has an item marked "CSLH." What did the item cost?

20. Describe and discuss four types of goods that are not usually price-marked.

CASE PROBLEMS

CASE PROBLEM 1

The Roffis Store began operations twenty years ago in the quiet suburb of a large city. Since its opening, there has been a tremendous amount of suburban growth. This expansion, coupled with capable, aggressive management, has resulted in phenomenal growth. At present, the store consists of twenty departments whose annual volume exceeds $8 million.

When the store first opened, deliveries were made through the front and immediately unpacked, checked, marked, and placed on the selling shelves. As the store expanded and responsibilities were divided among departments, receiving and storeroom space was provided in the rear of the store. At present, packages are received in the rear of the store. They are then delivered, unopened, to the various departments, where the balance of the receiving functions are performed.

The proprietor's son, recently employed by the store, argues for the setting up of a centralized receiving room. Mr. Roffis objects to this, pointing out that selling space, already in short supply, will be wasted, that centralized receiving operations would require new personnel (the work is presently being done by salespersons), and that checking and marking can best be done by the departments since only they know the specific merchandise.

QUESTIONS

1. Support the son's argument.

2. How would you go about setting up a centralized receiving department?

CASE PROBLEM 2

The buyers of a large suburban department store, P. W. Brennan's, are extremely unhappy about the receiving department's procedures. A petition of grievances, signed by every buyer in the store, has been presented to management. The following are some of their grievances:

1. Two full days are required for goods that have been delivered to the store to reach the selling floors.

2. A recent receiving department policy no longer allows buyers to take goods from the receiving department to satisfy specific customers. This loses sales and frequently results in loss of customer good will.

3. The success or failure of the store depends on sales. It is a serious mistake to allow receiving functions to take precedence over sales or customer good will. Top priority should be given to the sales departments rather than the receiving department.

4. Some of the goods coming through have not been properly checked for quality. For example, a large shipment of ladies' sweaters was sent to the selling floor with loose buttons.

QUESTIONS

1. As the manager of the receiving department, how would you respond to the above arguments?

2. As the merchandise manager, how would you handle this serious problem?

8 *store security*

BEHAVIORAL OBJECTIVES

Upon completion of this chapter the student should be able to

1. *List six techniques for deterring shoplifting.*
2. *Discuss five deterrents and controls of internal theft.*
3. *Explain the use of polygraph testing.*
4. *Discuss the duties and responsibilities of security personnel.*

INTRODUCTION

Merchants throughout the world are constantly in search of new merchandise as well as techniques to ensure themselves a competitive position in their quest for the customer's dollar. In this, the age of sophisticated retailing, there is one severe problem that continues to plague the retailer at an alarming rate. Simply stated, business executives have not yet been able to prevent merchandise from "walking out of their shops." Reports from all corners of the globe indicate that the pilferage rate is on the move. Not only does this inventory shrinkage aggravate the merchant and significantly cut profits, but it also has an enormous impact on consumer prices. Who must bear the burden of merchandise loss? Certainly, in the long run it must be the everyday, honest consumer!

The National Coalition to Prevent Shoplifting estimates that $16 billion was lost to shoplifters during 1979. Since these, like all other costs, are passed along to the consumer, the cost of shoplifting was $200 per American family.

In an attempt to curtail these illegal activities, merchants have resorted to a number of precautionary measures while still searching for more appropriate techniques. Since different retailers have different security problems, there are numerous methods that might be employed to reduce their losses. In this chapter emphasis will be placed upon the problems associated with inventory shortages, techniques by which employees as well as customers steal merchandise, and the security systems that merchants use to curtail shoplifting and internal theft.

INVENTORY SHORTAGES

The problem of inventory shortage is not strictly limited to shoplifting. Shoplifting, the theft of merchandise by children, parents, and so on, as well as professionals who "steal to order," is just one cause of shrinking inventories. In fact, many reliable sources agree that the bulk of store thefts is attributable to dishonest employees. At a Mass Retailing Institute conference it was reported that about 75 percent of the $850 million stolen the previous year from mass merchandisers was taken by employees. More recently it was estimated that more than $5 billion, 2 percent of all general merchandise sales, is lost because of internal theft. Perhaps the most startling recent news concerning internal theft is in a *Women's Wear Daily* article that reports 5,000 employees' "resignations" at Montgomery Ward because of signed confessions of internal theft. The total shrinkage figure for 1975 at Montgomery Ward reached $10 million. Although the figures do vary from one study to another, it is quite obvious that the problem is monumental and continues to plague the retail industry since profits decline dollar for dollar as inventory shortages increase.

SHOPLIFTING

Who are the culprits involved in stealing from retailers? Are they drug addicts, people from disadvantaged backgrounds, schoolchildren out for kicks, or people who are forced to thievery because of economic pressures? The answer certainly is all of these. However, stealing is by no means limited to the aforementioned. The police chief of a large metropolitan city reported that within a few months his police force had arrested a mayor, the wife of an army general, and two clergymen, all of whom had been caught in the act of illegally removing merchandise from stores. Thus, it is not a simple matter for merchants to be on the lookout for the stereotyped shoplifter.

In addition to understanding that shoplifters come from all walks of life, it should also be understood that the merchandise stolen is not restricted to a particular type of retail operation or a few geographic locations but is evident in all retail organizations as well as every conceivable location. Department stores, specialty shops, discount operations, supermarkets, and chain stores alike, located in downtown areas, shopping malls, and neighborhood clusters on free-standing areas from coast to coast have to cope with this serious problem.

The modern shopping mall with its completely "open fronts" is generally regarded as the shoplifter's paradise. How conducive it is to stealing! Crowds of people milling around in virtually unprotected store entrances make the shopping mall a haven for shoplifters. As the success of this type of retailing center has increased, so have the numbers of reported merchandise thefts. And what about those who are not caught?

Some interesting information concerning shoplifting is available from studies prepared by Commercial Service Systems, Inc.

1. The most significant month for shoplifting is December for all stores except supermarkets. Most stores realize a substantial amount of their business during the shopping period just up until Christmas; thus the increase in shoplifting. Supermarkets, however, show no appreciable change in business from month to month and are therefore uniformly plagued throughout the year.

2. Supermarkets also differ from the rest of the field in terms of the most active day of the week for shoplifting. While they are most frequently plagued on Thursdays, the traditionally busy day for household "supermarketing," the other retailers generally find Saturday the most troublesome day.

3. The hours in which most apprehensions are reported for all stores are during the 3:00 P.M. to 6:00 P.M. period, with the evening hours next in importance.

4. The merchandise involved runs the gamut from the inexpensive pack of cigarettes to such high-priced items as furs, precious jewelry, and major appliances. You might wonder how an item of great bulk can be shoplifted. The ingenuity of the shoplifter has never ceased to amaze even the most seasoned store detective. A story that has been told for many years about the baby grand piano shoplifted from a well-known downtown New York department store should point up the creativity of the professional shoplifter. The story is as follows.

   Two men dressed in workmen's coveralls came onto the selling floor of a large piano department. They waited for the manager to leave for lunch and descended upon the salesperson who had been left in charge. They showed a "proper-looking" carefully executed requisition form for removal of a baby grand piano from the selling floor for transfer to a branch store. Not only did the salesman sign the authorization form, but he proceeded to assist the two "movers" onto the freight elevator, where the piano moved quickly past the security guard (he checked the signature on the form) onto a waiting truck and off to the person who probably requested such a piano. Although it might be difficult to believe, the story is true and should underscore the fact that every conceivable type of merchandise is vulnerable to shoplifting.

5. There is no age that is considered typical for a shoplifter. Incredible as it might seem, approximately 10 percent of the shoplifters apprehended in supermarkets and drugstores have been under twelve years of age. Most studies agree that approximately 70 percent of shoplifters are under thirty.

6. Popular opinion has it that the female has an edge over her male counterpart in terms of who shoplifts more. It is generally agreed by research groups, however, that the distribution among males and females is just about equal.

FIGURE 8-1 FREQUENCY OF SHOPLIFTING

City	No. of Tests	No. of Shoplifters	Ratio of Shoplifters to Customers	% Shoplifters	Average Theft
N.Y. Store #1	500	42	1 out of 12	8.4	$7.15
N.Y. Store #2	361	19	1 out of 19	5.2	5.36
Boston	404	18	1 out of 22	4.4	3.69
Phila.	382	30	1 out of 13	7.8	4.86
TOTAL	1,647	109	1 out of 15	6.6	$5.26

City	Males Followed	Males Shoplifters	%	Females Followed	Females Shoplifters	%
N.Y. Store #1	156	10	6.4	344	32	9.2
N.Y. Store #2	135	7	5.7	226	12	5.3
Boston	149	4	2.6	255	14	5.4
Phila.	132	8	6.0	250	22	8.8
TOTAL	572	29	5.0	1,075	80	7.4

FIGURE 8-2 PROFILE OF AVERAGE SHOPLIFTER

City	Caucasians Followed	Caucasians Shoplifters	%	Nonwhites Followed	Nonwhites Shoplifters	%
N.Y. Store #1	360	30	8.3	140	12	8.5
N.Y. Store #2	253	15	5.8	108	4	3.7
Boston	336	12	3.5	68	6	8.8
Phila.	248	19	7.6	134	11	8.2
TOTAL	1,197	76	6.3	450	33	7.3

	Under 21		21–35		Over 35	
	No. of Thieves	% of Age Sample	No. of Thieves	% of Age Sample	No. of Thieves	% of Age Sample
N.Y. Store #1	8	7.8	18	8.0	16	8.4
N.Y. Store #2	4	6.1	4	3.2	11	6.3
Boston	5	4.1	7	7.1	6	3.2
Phila.	9	10.9	13	8.6	8	5.4
TOTAL	26	7.1	42	7.0	41	6.0

An informative study was undertaken by Management Safeguards, Inc. concerning shoplifting in New York, Boston, and Philadelphia department stores. Emphasis centered upon the frequency of shoplifting in downtown areas, the profile of the average shoplifter, frequency of shoplifting, and the methods employed in the stealing of goods. The results are shown in Figures 8-1 through 8-3.

Analysis of the survey shows that all age groups, with minor exceptions, steal with equal frequency, that there is virtually no difference between caucasians and nonwhites, and that one out of every fifteen "shoppers" actually steals.

FIGURE 8-3 METHODS EMPLOYED IN SHOPLIFTING

City	Shopping Bags	Pocketbooks	Concealed in Clothes or Wore	Other
N.Y. Store #1	25	3	12	2
N.Y. Store #2	7	5	6	1
Boston	5	5	8	0
Phila.	9	9	11	1
TOTAL	46	22	37	4

Control of Shoplifting

Once having realized that shoplifting is a serious problem that eats into company profits and ultimately drives consumer prices upward, retailers must develop a program to deter or minimize the amount of merchandise that is stolen. Different stores are faced with different control problems because of the nature of the goods handled, the method of operation (service or self-service), and the layouts and geographic locations. Whatever the circumstances, however, retailers must begin initially with a program of employee involvement. This does not mean that an abundance of security guards must be hired to safeguard the goods. This could prove to be too costly and might also create an atmosphere not psychologically conducive for shopping. The regular employees—such as department managers, sales personnel, stock people, and cashiers—should be informed about the severity of the shoplifting problem, the store's policy in this regard, and how they can be effectively involved in the security program. This employee awareness is generally accomplished at sessions directed by the store's chief security officer. Typically, the training is twofold. First, employees are generally instructed to make customers feel that they are not alone but are very much in view. This is accomplished by greeting the customer and making oneself thoroughly conspicuous. Second, if the customer's action arouses suspicion, a procedure to follow is outlined. Some stores use a procedure in which a number is dialed on the telephone to alert the security department of the location of the "lurking shoplifter." Other stores use a "code" announcement over the loudspeaker system to indicate a possible shoplifting episode. There are many systems. What is most important is for the store employee to be aware of the shoplifting possibilities, and the proper handling of these situations. The latter is important because improper detention of a suspect could cause the retailer problems of greater severity than that of stolen goods.

Deterrent Techniques

In addition to properly informing and training employees about shoplifting, there are a number of techniques and devices that assist either in the apprehension of a shoplifter or in the psychological prevention of the crime.

Surveillance Systems

Many stores have attributed their successful decreases in shoplifting to closed-circuit television and camera systems. Not only have they actually recorded the criminal's actions but they have also proved to be excellent psychological deterrents. The very prominent display of a surveillance camera can almost ensure that many planned thefts will not be tried. In fact, most security specialists agree that the electronic surveillance systems are the best fighters of shoplifting.

The systems available are many. They range from the simple to the sophisticated. In addition to their use as spotters of shoplifters, they are frequently used to "record" issuers of checks. This often prevents the passing of bad checks and the apprehension of individuals who actually have written bad checks. Figure 8-4 shows the Diebold CL-16 surveillance camera system which, in addition to providing internal surveillance, detects holdups and bad checks. Its sophistication and versatility permits automatic camera filming at specific hours, specific days, or all the time. The system can also be connected to an alarm system.

Figure 8-5 shows a sophisticated surveillance system, the Diebold VSS-2, which can accommodate as many as eight video cameras and can provide videotape instant replay from any one of them at the touch of a button. Essential-

FIGURE 8-4 Diebold CL-16 Surveillance System

FIGURE 8-5 Diebold VSS-2 Video Surveillance System

ly, the system is one of many camera installations that tie into a control console that can be situated in any convenient location. It also can be tied into the store's alarm system for appropriate activation.

Two-Way Mirrors

Much merchandise that is stolen from department and specialty stores is hidden under the clothing of shoplifters. What place provides more convenience and privacy than the store's try-on room? This area is one that provides many soft-goods retailers with a severe problem. In order to curtail merchandise concealment in try-on rooms, some retailers have resorted to the "watchful eye." The installation of two-way mirrors, one side for the customer to use as an ordinary mirror and the other side monitored by a store employee without customer awareness, has assisted retailers in apprehending many would-be shoplifters. The problems created by these devices are many, however. They are considered to be one of the most controversial shoplifting prevention devices on the market. Opponents of the two-way mirrors believe that they are an infringement on people's privacy. Proponents believe that retailers have every right to safeguard their own merchandise. At present, they are still being used, but many legal battles are being fought to determine whether or not their use interferes with constitutional rights.

Merchandise Price Labels

A problem that plagues retailers in just about every type of store is the switching of price tags—the "customer" changes the price on the merchandise by substituting new tags with lower prices. Instead of actually stealing the article, the individual actually makes the purchase, but at a significantly lower price. Stores that are hardest hit are those with large sales volume, a wide variety of merchandise at varied price ranges, and centralized checkout locations. These are easy prey for criminals since the cash register operator is generally not familiar with the merchandise.

Merchants have tried many different types of mechandise tags to thwart the offenders. For "hanging" goods, where all else has failed, tickets with heavy nylon filament string that must be attached by special machines are being effectively used. Although the string may be cut with a pair of scissors, it is impossible to replace it unless the machine, which is cumbersome, is used.

For merchandise that must be labeled directly with a "sticker" tag, would-be label-switchers have found the latest switch-proof label virtually impossible to tamper with. Pictured in Figure 8-6 is the "Switch-Gard™" label created by the Dennison Manufacturing Company. It employs a tough, broad-range adhesive that can only be removed through total destruction. It has been a boon to security-minded retailers who require labels that are capable of sticking to any surface.

Pilferage Detection Systems

If you walk through any modern enclosed shopping mall you are immediately aware of the "open" storefronts and their accessibility to shoplifters. Merchants who believe that the open front is motivation for the shopper to enter the premises are not about to return to traditionally conventional store entrances. In order to maintain the open feeling, many retailers have installed systems that are similar to the security installations at most major air terminals.

The system requires that merchandise be "tagged" with special rectangular-shaped solid plastic discs. Removal of the disc can only be accomplished by means of a special machine. Once the merchandise has been paid for and the disc removed by the cashier, the customer can freely leave the store. Exit

FIGURE 8-6 Security Labels

from the premises is by way of an installation that resembles a door frame (without the door). But if someone steals an item, the disc has not been removed; passage through the security door frame sets off a very loud alarm that alerts store personnel. The system does require continuous additional expense to the retailer, since each piece of merchandise must be tagged twice, once for the price ticket and again for the security tag. The thwarting of shoplifting by the use of this alarm system has been so successful that it is now being used in more traditionally built stores.

Fitting-Room Control

As mentioned earlier, the shoplifter's favorite place is often the fitting room. Here a great deal of merchandise can be concealed and lost to the store. Many security-conscious stores use a system that involves placing guards at fitting-room entrances. Typically, individuals are restricted to a limited number of articles in the dressing rooms at any one time. They are given a color-coded plastic device that indicates the number of items brought into the try-on cubicle. (For example, green might represent two items.) When they have finished trying the articles on, the customers must return to the "checker" with the number of garments designated by the color-coded device. Some stores have found that even with this system, resourceful shoplifters sometimes substituted their own garments for the merchandise they wished to steal.

Magnifying Mirrors

Stores that wish to spend minimal amounts on security but also want to minimize shoplifting install circular magnifying mirrors at out-of-the-way areas on the selling floor. By strategic positioning, store personnel can watch potential shoplifters in these otherwise concealed areas. In addition to providing some view of these areas, the mirrors act as psychological deterrents.

Locking Display Systems

Illustrated in Figure 8-7 is an antitheft locking display system manufactured by Securax, Inc. of Santa Ana, California. These systems are used for high-value merchandise, such as jewelry and leather jackets, in self-service areas. While they all require a salesperson to free the goods for really careful scrutiny, they do permit customer handling and even the preliminary trying on of clothing on a self-service basis without fear of theft. By the time the salesperson's presence is needed, the customer is pretty well sold. These are high-priced items, and even self-service stores prefer salesperson involvement in the final stages of the sale of such goods.

The number of devices employed by stores vary from company to company. With the enormity of the shoplifting problem, even those considered to be

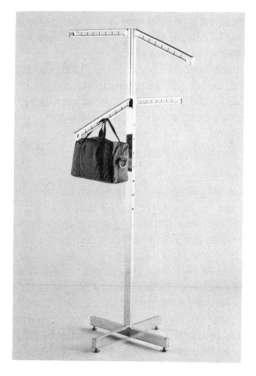

FIGURE 8-7 Securax Locking Display System

as secure as possible are always seeking new devices to use on their selling floors. Evidence of the continuous need for safeguard devices is the continuous growth of producers of loss-prevention devices throughout the country.

INTERNAL THEFT

As indicated earlier in the chapter, many retailers report that internal theft accounts for greater inventory shortages than shoplifting. The factors attributable to internal theft are numerous. First there are the general motivational factors associated with stealing. Kleptomania, an irresistible urge to steal; impulsiveness, the act of stealing without planning; and a monetary need and social acceptance (strange, but true, particularly in teenage groups) are some reasons for internal (as well as shopper) stealing. In addition to these factors, an employee may feel underpaid; or simple hatred for the employer may be the motive for theft. Whatever the reasons, retailers must be aware of the problems inherent in internal theft, deterrents, and internal control.

The University of Minnesota recently surveyed thirty-five companies employing 5,000 workers in the Minneapolis area to determine the workers that are most likely to steal. They found the following:

1. Internal theft is most likely to be found among those who have the least to lose. These include unmarried people in low positions with little seniority to lose or dependents to worry about.
2. Dissatisfied workers are prime candidates for theft. The anger brought about by layoffs, insufficient raises, increased productivity demands, and reduced overtime frequently triggers theft.
3. The most ambitious workers, those who set the highest achievement goals and are most concerned with self-improvement, are also the most likely to steal.
4. Where employees congregate after working hours, the likelihood of cheating increases.
5. Organizations that allow their employees to get away with extended coffee breaks and abuse of sick day privileges, and that show other signs of laxity, suffere more from internal theft than companies that insist on rigid compliance to the rules.
6. Internal security personnel are so involved with external sources of theft that employee theft frequently goes unnoticed.

Deterrents and Controls

In order to avoid as much stealing by employees as possible, retailers must carefully charge those in positions of hiring with the responsibility of sound screening procedures. If prospective employees are scrupulously screened before beginning their employment, the company will almost certainly run less risk for internal theft. This by no means should make the reader believe that prescreening completely eliminates thieves, but that it could substantially reduce the number of illegal incidents.

Application Forms

One of the most important screening devices used in hiring employees is the application form. Careful use of this device can be helpful in determining the possible shortcomings of the prospective employee in terms of honesty. The application form in Figure 5-2 requires the applicant to give information on any arrests, convictions, and previous employment. These sections should not be lightly passed over but studied for possible deficiencies. Employers with special security problems could design an even better application to collect more pertinent information. Whichever form is used, it is important to follow up the information so that appropriate action may be taken.

Polygraph Testing

Some retail employers believe that the only appropriate means of determining an applicant's honesty is by means of a polygraph, better known as a lie detector test. Although many employees as well as employers object to this device, it is being used in many types of hiring situations throughout the United States. There are approximately 1,500 trained polygraphists active today; they administered between 250,000 and 350,000 tests during 1975, of which a significant number were retail-oriented.

Generally, the polygraph examination consists of two or more tests, with approximately a dozen questions each. The duration of a typical test is three minutes. Before questioning, the individual to be tested has a blood pressure cuff attached to the upper arm (identical to the system employed by physicians). Another attachment is placed around the trunk of the body. Finally, a third attachment is placed on one or two of the individual's fingers. In order to assist the examinee to relax and become accustomed to the device, a control test is used. When the tests are administered, the responses are recorded to indicate changes in pressure. Experts, through careful analysis, can determine the questions about which a person may be apprehensive. From this, a final determination is made about the individual's fitness in terms of honesty.

It should be understood that retailers are using polygraph testing not only during the preemployment period, but also during employment, for such uses as trying to uncover serious causes of internal theft and in circumstances that would involve promotions and transfers to more responsible positions.

References

Some retail organizations require the listing of references on the application form or at the time of interview. They include both personal and business references. From these, management can make certain decisions regarding the honesty of the prospective employee. Often, instability and dishonesty are discovered through reference checking.

Shopping Services

Many years ago, retailers engaged outside shopping services expressly for the purpose of evaluating employees on the basis of customer courtesy. In recent years, with the ever-increasing problem of internal theft, shopping service emphasis has shifted to the area of employee honesty.

Shopping services are generally secured on a contract basis. The service regularly "checks" employees by sending "shoppers" into the store. Employees are checked several times by these investigators to determine, among other things, their honesty. For example, there might be an indication that some sales are not rung up on the register.

It is important for the shopping service to have many shoppers and rotate them so that store employees are unable to detect them and differentiate them from real customers.

Smuggling Control

A very serious problem involves employees smuggling merchandise off the premises. Although it is difficult to completely prevent this, cautious retailers have made inroads into this problem.

Stockpersons, in particular, have caused serious stock shortages for retailers. For example, merchandise can be hidden in trash containers for later retrieval outside. In order to correct this situation, some retailers have installed "through-the-wall" security systems. These systems, as pictured in Figures 8-8 and 8-9, require that employees dispose of empty cartons, refuse, and so on through the wall that connects with a compactor on the outside of the building. In this way, if an employee tries to pass merchandise outside, it will be destroyed by the compactor.

The system, or similar types, is widely used today in all classifications of retail organizations. Reports from users indicate significantly fewer losses in merchandise.

Another preventive measure taken by numerous retailers to prevent the illegal removal of merchandise is the institution of a policy that requires employees to check coats, handbags, briefcases, lunch boxes, and so on in lockers before they proceed onto the selling floors. Women requiring personal items such as combs, handkerchiefs, and so forth are permitted to carry them in

FIGURE 8-8 Through-the-Wall Security System—Outside

FIGURE 8-9 Through-the-Wall Security System—Inside

small, transparent vinyl purses that are provided by the store. To ensure that the procedure is carried out, a guard is usually stationed at the employee entrance to the selling floor. Any violations or suspicious acts are reported by the guard to security.

SECURITY PERSONNEL

In order to properly coordinate the controls and deterrents to shoplifting and internal theft, retailers must secure the best available security staff. The size of the staff and the responsibility it has varies from company to company according to the merchandise offered for sale, the number of employees, geographic location, and so forth. The dollar investment in security personnel should be in line with the seriousness of the store's problem. Many retailers have as their security heads retired police chiefs or detectives. Their responsibility includes not only management of their personnel, and so forth, but the training of all people in the store to make them security minded. Specifically, the duties of security heads generally include

1. Training their staff members
2. Organizing systems to alert store personnel of potential shoplifters
3. Conducting seminars on do's and dont's of apprehending shoplifters (if any individual isn't properly confronted, the store could face a possible legal suit)
4. Selecting appropriate deterrent devices
5. Performing liaison with outside shopping services
6. Interrogating suspected shoplifters and dishonest employees
7. Advising management on security matters
8. Making recommendations on store layout changes to guarantee better security

Legal Deterrents

One of the problems faced by security personnel is the possibility of a lawsuit if the shoplifting charges cannot be proved in court. In most retail establishments, nothing that can be stolen can be as costly to the store as a lawsuit for false arrest. As a result most shoplifting arrests are made outside of the store because people arrested inside of the store can always claim that they intended to pay before leaving, and the courts generally support their contention. Recently the courts in several states have declared that shoplifters may be found guilty if they are apprehended before leaving. For instance, a New York court recently found that concealment of merchandise, furtive or unusual behavior, and heading toward a store exit might establish the fact that a crime had been committed.

Although the vast majority of security problems is associated with shoplifting and internal theft, the reader should be aware that retailers are also plagued by such things as armed robbery, burglary, and physical security problems.

With the proper systems and effective personnel recruitment the retailer's security problems, although impossible to eliminate, can be reduced.

Action for the Independent Retailer

Shoplifting is not confined to large retailers. Small businesses, which can least afford it, suffer from this evil as well. However, this is one area in which the small business has a decided advantage. Generally, shoplifting thrives in an atmosphere of self-service, and this is much more likely to be found in large stores. Moreover, because of the limited space available to the small retailer, constant surveillance is possible. There are no unpopulated corners in which the shoplifter can operate. In addition, the personnel in a small store can be trained and supervised in the area of theft prevention, at least more effectively than their large store counterparts.

Internal theft occurs in small stores as well as large. It can be minimized by checking the cash register tapes against the sales slips daily to determine that all sales have been rung up and by spot-checking inventory constantly. For example, the owner of a small liquor store goes to lunch, leaving the clerk in charge. Before going, she glances at a shelf of a popular brand and sees eight bottles. After returning, there are six bottles left. The sales slips should indicate that two bottles have been sold. If not, the clerk has some explaining to do. Different goods should be checked during each absence. The clerk should never know which goods are being checked. Where there are items kept in a storeroom, these should be included in the count.

IMPORTANT POINTS IN THE CHAPTER

1. *Most inventory shortages are due to shoplifting and internal theft.*
2. *Most studies indicate that shoplifters come from all walks of life. The group includes teenagers, parents, economically disadvantaged people, and kleptomaniacs.*
3. *The most significant shoplifting month is December; Saturday is the most active day of the week for theft.*
4. *Surveillance systems, two-way mirrors, tamper-proof merchandise tags, pilferage detection systems, fitting-room control, and magnifying mirrors are used to deter shoplifting.*
5. *Prescreening of prospective employees is essential in the control of internal theft.*
6. *Polygraph testing, reference checks, outside shopping services, and smuggling control devices are widely used to prevent employee theft.*
7. *Stores are spending more money in proper security control than ever before and are often hiring retired police chiefs to head their programs.*
8. *An effective security program requires that all employees be sufficiently trained so that they will become security conscious.*

REVIEW QUESTIONS

1. Do merchandise shortages affect the customer? Explain your answer.
2. Define shoplifting.
3. To whom are most merchandise thefts attributable?
4. Describe the typical shoplifter.
5. Why do "customers" steal merchandise?
6. At what time of the year do shoplifters cause the most trouble? Why?

7. What is a surveillance system? How does one operate?

8. Discuss the use of two-way mirrors. Do you believe that they are being appropriately used in retailing?

9. Customers, as well as employees, have often resorted to switching price tags. How can this now be avoided?

10. Describe the widely used store entrance pilferage detection system.

11. Why are fitting rooms so conducive to shoplifting?

12. In what way have merchants reduced fitting-room thefts?

13. Define kleptomania.

14. It has been said that the employee application form is an excellent device to control internal theft. Do you agree? Defend your answer.

15. Briefly describe polygraph testing.

16. Are employee references aids in controlling internal theft? Defend your position.

17. What is a shopping service? How does it assist the store's security program?

18. Discuss compactors and their role in the prevention of employee merchandise smuggling.

19. Explain some of the duties and responsibilities of real security chiefs.

20. How large should a retail security staff be? Defend you answer with sound reasoning.

CASE PROBLEMS

CASE PROBLEM 1

Some people believe that the cost of store security is too expensive to be practical for the smaller independent retailers. Such a retailer, the Just Jeans Company, is located on the main street of a midwestern suburban community. Just Jeans has been in business for five years and has experienced shoplifting problems that seem to be out of proportion to the amount of business transacted. As business has increased and the crowds in the store have increased, shoplifting has gotten out of hand. One problem confronting the store is its self-service method of operation. People on the selling floor are at a minimum. The store has a manager, an assistant manager, and a cashier. The owner, Mr. Davis, has considered hiring salespeople who would keep a watchful eye on the customers as well as sell. The manager, Eric Shafler, insists that the store's clientele, mainly teenagers, would adversely react to salespeople and that the store would be risking a decrease in sales. The assistant manager, Richard Pearl, suggests a full-time security guard; Mr. Davis has vetoed this idea as too costly.

At the present time security is limited to circular magnifying mirrors at strategic positions. The operation must now decide which route to take before the shoplifting problem leads to the store's failure.

QUESTIONS

1. Do you agree with any of the suggestions made thus far by the store principals?

2. Suggest a security plan to help reduce shoplifting in Just Jeans. Keep in mind the costs involved and whether they can be afforded by the company.

CASE PROBLEM 2

For the past twenty years, the Shelby Company, a full-time department store, has equipped its premises with the most sophisticated systems to deter shoplifting. After considerable research, the company has discovered that although shoplifting has declined, inventory shrinkage is still plaguing the company. The problem seems to indicate a significant amount of internal theft. Particular difficulty centers around the soft-goods departments. Not only is merchandise taken by the employees, but much price-tag switching is taking place so that lower prices are actually being paid for merchandise that should sell for more.

Many suggestions have been made by the management. One involves the polygraph testing of presently employed personnel. Another suggestion is to have a manager at each register who is familiar with merchandise prices and can prevent selling at lower prices. The last point suggested is to gradually replace all personnel with new people who could be better screened before employment.

QUESTIONS

1. Do you agree with any of the suggestions? Evaluate each and defend your answers with sound reasoning.
2. Suggest your own plan to assist the company in fighting internal theft.

III

buying and merchandising concepts

9 *the buying function*

BEHAVIORAL OBJECTIVES

Upon completion of this chapter the student should be able to

1. *List five responsibilities of the buyer.*
2. *Explain the duties of an assistant buyer, indicating five areas of responsibility.*
3. *Write an essay on "What to Buy." This should include at least six sources of buyer information.*
4. *Achieve a grade of 70% on an examination containing four open-to-buy problems.*
5. *Differentiate, giving advantages and disadvantages, between buying from wholesalers and buying from manufacturers.*
6. *List six reasons for buying from foreign sources.*

INTRODUCTION

Whenever retailing students are asked about their future aspirations, invariably a great number respond that they would like to be buyers. The buying function seems to be the most glamorous aspect of the retail operation. Perhaps to the inexperienced it is a chance to spend a great deal of money in sums that one could never spend for one's own needs. While the buying job does often present glamorous and exciting moments, few jobs in retailing require more ability and disciplined training. In this chapter emphasis will be placed upon the *store* buyers and how they select merchandise. The next chapter will deal with the role of *resident office* buyers and their relationship to store buyers.

The responsibility for buying does not always belong to an individual called the *buyer*. In most small stores the purchasing of merchandise is usually a responsibility of the proprietor. Since sales volume is low and employees, if any, are few in number, the store owner is a jack-of-all-trades who buys merchandise in addition to performing many other tasks. Buying for this type of operation is generally less carefully planned than is the purchasing for a larger organization.

The small retailer, who is becoming important once again as part of a franchise organization, is often not responsible for the purchase of goods. Merchandise is often selected by the buyer of the franchise company and shipped into the different franchisees' locations. For example, Different Drummer, a franchise operation specializing in kookie merchandise, will buy all the merchandise for a unit for a percentage of purchases.

As the store organization grows, the responsibility for purchasing becomes greater. The chain organization and the department store with branches buy such great quantities of merchandise for distribution that the buyer's job becomes one of the most important in the operation. Only those individuals with skill and competence can become successful buyers. In order to make students aware of the dimensions of this job, an overview of some of the buyer's duties as well as the qualifications necessary to carry out these responsibilities are discussed. Since most buyers have assisted a buyer before they assumed full responsibility (and since many students will be assistants a few years after graduation from college), the roles of the assistant and the buyer will be discussed separately.

DUTIES AND RESPONSIBILITIES

Buyer

The responsibilities of the buyer generally include the following:

1. The most important duty of a buyer is the actual purchasing of the goods. The buyer is faced with the perennial problems of what merchandise to choose from which vendors, in which quantity, and the correct timing of delivery to meet with customers' demands. Included in these tasks are negotiating the price, shipping terms, and extra dating (additional time in which to pay for merchandise). Since these are areas of great significance, an in-depth study of each will be made later in the chapter.

2. After buying arrangements have been worked out, the buyer must price the merchandise to conform with the policies of the store and the markup to be achieved by the particular department. Included in this area are the pricing of the individual items and the repricing of goods that have moved slowly, in the hope the lower price will move them faster. New merchandise can then be put on the selling floor in place of the slow-moving goods.

3. After goods are received and marked and come to the selling floor (ticketing of merchandise, checking of quantities against invoices, and the moving of goods is done at either a warehouse or a receiving department in large stores), the placement of the goods is usually determined by the buyer. Such decisions as whether to display folded merchandise on shelves or put them on merchandise racks are left to the buyer's discretion. The buyer, who usually knows more about this merchandise than anyone else in the store, knows how best to visually feature the merchandise in the department.

4. In most department stores managing the department is the responsibility of the buyer. Buyers are involved in the final selection of employees for their departments, the supervision of selling, and the arranging of sales meetings.

5. The buyer selects merchandise for promotion, merchandise that should be displayed, and merchandise that should be advertised; the buyer also plans fashion shows, when relevant, and any special events that might promote goods.

6. Selling on the floor during peak periods is another buyer responsibility. This provides buyers with actual customer contact, which enables them to determine customer wants firsthand.

Assistant Buyer

Most buyers have assistants to help with the many chores of buying for a store or a department. Some of the more typical duties and responsibilities an assistant will perform are the following:

1. Most reorders of merchandise are placed by assistant buyers. This is merely a replenishment of fast-selling merchandise that has sold in the departmnet.
2. Assistants often "follow up" orders that have not as yet been delivered. Often these are orders that were especially placed for individual customers and if not delivered on time will be canceled.
3. The purchase of some new merchandise is done by assistants. Occasionally when a department is large, the buyer will allow an assistant to purchase some lines. Generally the purchase is limited to staple goods.
4. When the buyer plans to purchase goods for a new season the assistant is included in the decision-making group. This arrangement allows for another opinion plus excellent on-the-job training in preparation for a full buyer's job.
5. By selling merchandise in the department, the assistant buyer acts as liaison between the buyer and the customer. This contact with the customer provides the assistant with information concerning the customer's wants.

BUYER QUALIFICATIONS

In order to aspire to managerial positions in retailing, particularly buying careers, individuals must possess certain qualifications and characteristics. Following are some of those deemed most important by many of the leading retailers who were interviewed:

1. A college degree, preferably in the area of retail business management, is necessary. It is rare today for a high school student to climb the ladder of success from stock clerk to manager. The sophistication of retailing today demands a knowledgeable individual to step into positions of authority. The success stories often told by oldtime "self-educated" retailers are part of the history of retailing and not of its future.
2. An enthusiastic attitude is a must for buyers. Buyers (unless the responsibility is not theirs, as in central purchasing for chain stores) are usually responsible for the sale of merchandise in their departments. Enthusiasm is one of the most effective methods for motivating employees to sell goods. The buyers' enthusiasm seems to transfer to their subordinates. *Many stores will overlook some of an individual's shortcomings, but few, if asked, will choose an unenthusiastic individual for a buying position.*
3. Product knowledge is extremely important in buying efficiently. It is just about impossible for one to have complete knowledge of every item stocked by department stores. An understanding of style and textiles for the fashion buyer and a knowledge of grades of fruits and vegetables for the produce buyer in a supermarket is almost mandatory for success. Too many people de-emphasize the importance of product knowledge, but the individual with the ability to

knowledgeably examine goods and make discerning decisions will certainly be ahead in the buying game.

4. A simple working knowledge of retailing mathematics is a must for every buyer. The buyer must be able to quickly determine markup, markdown, open to buy, and other often-used computations.

5. Leadership ability is extremely important. The buyer not only is a purchasing agent but is responsible for subordinates as well. Assistant buyers and salespeople under the buyer will be as good as the leadership over them.

6. The ability to get along with people is an important quality a buyer must have. In addition to the people in the department, buyers continually meet with merchandise managers, vendors, and buying office representatives. Ability to get along with these different parties helps to guarantee a more efficient operation.

7. While students agree that such characteristics as ability, knowledge, and leadership are important qualities that a buyer should possess, they often underestimate the importance of appearance. The buyer's appearance sets an example for the staff, makes a lasting impression on customers the buyer comes into contact with, and often sets the tone in relationships with the vendors from whom the buyer purchases. Rarely does an individual successfully complete an interview and receive an offer for a managerial position in retailing without satisfactory appearance.

ORGANIZATION FOR BUYING

Not every individual buyer has the same overall responsibilities. The duties required will depend on the policy, size, and scope of the operation and geographic separation of the units for which the buyer is responsible.

In department stores with branches, buyers usually have headquarters in the main store and do the purchasing for that store plus the branches. The number of lines each buyer is responsible for varies according to the volume for each line. For example, a smaller department store might have one children's wear buyer responsible for all purchases of children's clothing, while a very large store would probably have a separate buyer for children's shoes. Some department stores have separate buyers for departments in branches when the branch operation is dissimilar to that of the main store.

In most chain organizations buyers do not operate from a main store but from central headquarters located some distance from the individual units. For example, Lerner Shops, a large specialty chain with several hundred units, houses its buyers in New York City along with the other divisions' executives (advertising and display, for example). In this type of situation the buyer is responsible only for purchasing and not for sales within the units, as are most of the department store buyers. In fact, we see that the department store buyer generally has more responsibilities. The central buyers rely chiefly on reports from the various units to plan purchases. Since they are far removed from the selling floor, direct customer contact is impossible. The manner in which quantities and styles are determined varies. Some central buyers make all purchases, determine each store's needs, and distribute these goods to the various units. In other chains the buyers select the merchandise for the units, and the store managers or department managers determine the quantities needed. Still another arrangement has the central buyer select styles and negotiate price arrangements and terms with vendors. Then a catalog or list of goods available to the stores is published, and the store's managers pick the goods they desire. Stores using the latter system usually require that all units carry certain specified lines, with the balance to be selected by individual managers.

Whichever system is used, to a certain degree each buyer is faced with all the elements of the buying procedure. In the systems where store managers determine quantities and sometimes the items to carry, they too may be considered buyers since they are involved in the selection of merchandise.

MODEL STOCK DEVELOPMENT

The particular assortment a department has to offer is most important to its success. The buyer must carefully plan the proper merchandise assortment in terms of depth and breadth. The inventory that contains an appropriate assortment at the time customers are ready to purchase is known as a model stock. Development of the model stock varies significantly from department to department, with those that are fashion oriented presenting the most involvement and planning by the buyer. Fashion departments are concerned not only with assortment in terms of price and variety of products, but also with color, style, and so forth.

A model stock is accomplished through the buyer's ability to evaluate both the customer's needs and the demands dictated by store management. By paying close attention to these forces, the buyer must plan the most perfect assortment possible. Large stores, and even some smaller operations, provide their buyers with pertinent information in the form of computerized reports. These reports, which make the task of model stock development simpler, are explored in Chapter 20, *Electronic Data Processing*.

Before such planning can take place, the buyer must be knowledgeable in the essentials or elements of buying. Armed with this pertinent information, the buyer will have a better insight into model stock development.

ELEMENTS OF BUYING

Whether one buys for a small store, a department store with branches, a large specialty store, or a chain organization, four major areas are of concern to all buyers. Sometimes called the elements of buying, they are *what to buy, how much to buy, from whom to buy,* and *when to buy.*

What to Buy

The decision of which merchandise to select from all that is made available by vendors is not made by guessing. While some misinformed or uninformed individuals feel that buyers are lucky when they choose the right merchandise, those who are knowledgeable understand the great deal of care that is exercised in the planning of purchases.

A buyer tries to determine, before purchasing, the customers' wants and needs, and attempts to satisfy these desires by purchasing the right merchandise. Sound marketing tells us that products should be designed and produced with the customer in mind. Good buyers, too, purchase with the customer in mind. In order to determine what the customer wants, the buyer gathers information from a number of sources.

While not all buyers use all the sources available to them, all of them study past sales records. An investigation of past sales reveals which price lines sold best, which sizes were most popular, which were the peak selling periods, which vendors had the fastest-moving merchandise, and any other information that has been recorded by the store.

The method used to record the pertinent information varies from store to store. The smaller the operation, the less sophisticated is the system used. One system used by small stores is to hand-record all goods received in an inventory book and include whichever information might be meaningful for future purchasing (Figure 9-1). For example, included might be the vendor's name, style number of item, cost price and selling price (to show markup), color, sizes, number of pieces, and when goods were received. At the end of each day the sales receipts or merchandise tags (Figure 9-2) (either of which should record any information kept in the inventory book) are used to check off the items sold. Whenever the buyer desires, she or he can immediately check the records to see how the merchandise is selling. In addition, this book serves as a perpetual inventory and shows what merchandise is still available for sale.

In the larger retail organizations a more sophisticated system of recording sales is kept. The computer, used by most large retailers today, keeps the same records as those kept by hand, but does it more quickly and usually more efficiently. Buyers are given all sorts of past sales data by the computer either daily, weekly, monthly, or at any interval necessary for the efficiency of the operation. Food store buyers, for example, often require daily sales information because their merchandise turns over so rapidly. Furniture store buyers, on the other hand, require less frequent information because of the nature of the goods. With the introduction of the point-of-purchase register, which is tied into the computer in many stores, the past sales information is always available. An in-depth study of use of the computer in retailing and how it helps the buyer is covered in Chapter 20.

Surveys of different varieties are used by buyers to determine customers' wants. Stores often interview people to determine taste and buying habits,

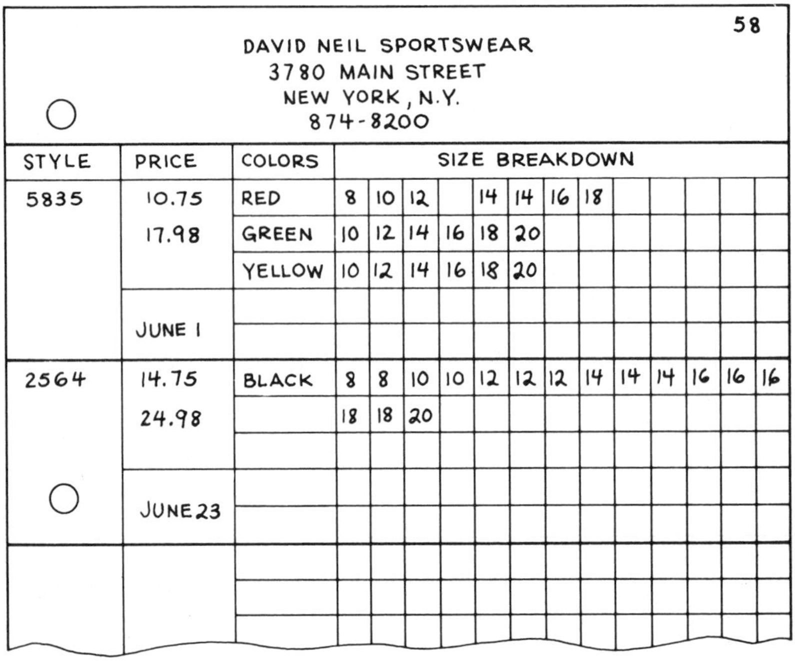

DAVID NEIL SPORTSWEAR
3780 MAIN STREET
NEW YORK, N.Y.
874-8200

STYLE	PRICE	COLORS	SIZE BREAKDOWN													
5835	10.75	RED	8	10	12		14	14	16	18						
	17.98	GREEN	10	12	14	16	18	20								
		YELLOW	10	12	14	16	18	20								
	JUNE 1															
2564	14.75	BLACK	8	8	10	10	12	12	12	14	14	14	16	16	16	
	24.98		18	18	20											
	JUNE 23															

FIGURE 9-1 Inventory Page (Small Store)

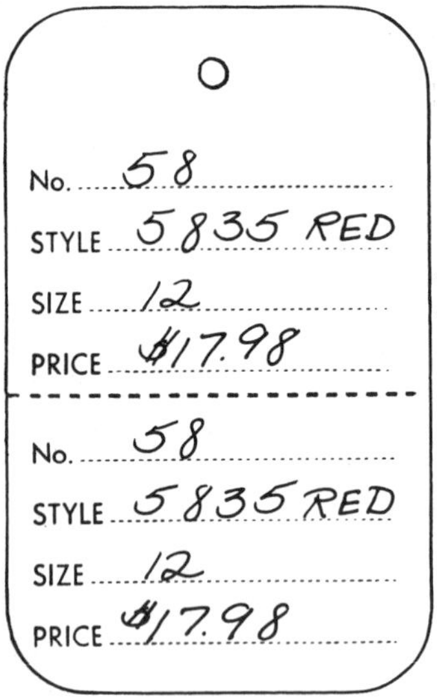

No. _5 8_
STYLE _5835 RED_
SIZE _12_
PRICE _$17.98_

- - - - - - - - - - - - - - - - - - - -

No. _58_
STYLE _5835 RED_
SIZE _12_
PRICE _$17.98_

FIGURE 9-2 Merchandise Tag (Small Store)

send out questionnaires to charge customers to inquire about merchandise that might interest them, hold consumer panels to discover likes and dislikes, and conduct fashion counts to discover what people are wearing. Through these techniques buyers find out firsthand what their customers or potential customers desire. Chapter 19 explores the use of research in the retail store.

Buyers constantly scan trade periodicals to keep up with what's current in their field. Supermarket buyers generally read *Chain Store Age*; fashion buyers faithfully scan *Women's Wear Daily* for women's fashions and *The Daily News Record* for men's clothing. Each segment of the retail store industry subscribes to the papers and magazines of its trade. These periodicals offer important information to buyers, such as new merchandise available for sale, information about consumers (from surveys taken), best-seller reports (Figure 9-3 shows the activity of a specific vendor's "hot" item with various retail stores), trends in the market, and merchandise forecasting.

Market research is undertaken by some of the trade papers, as well as by newspapers and consumer magazines, and is reported on a weekly or monthly basis, or in special editions.

Fashion reports by such companies as the Fairchild organization offer significant statistics to buyers. Fairchild, publisher of *Women's Wear Daily*, has a worldwide staff to cover the latest news on fashion changes and trends. Its reporters attend showings of fabric and garment manufacturers and of Parisian, Italian, Israeli, and other internationally known designers.

Among other widely read trade publications are *Drug Topics, Home-Furnishings Daily*, which covers the home furnishings field, and *Footwear News*.

Consumer newspapers and magazines provide buyers with much information. By merely reading the daily newspapers, food buyers can learn the goods their competitors are promoting and at what prices. Fashion buyers could learn about the styles that have been selected by the consumer magazines to be shown to its readers. Because many readers are influenced by magazines, the store certainly should know the merchandise to which their customers are being exposed.

Salespeople provide buyers with information. Since salespersons are actually the ones who speak to customers, they know the customers' demands. Such items as price information, styles desired, and qualities wanted are examples of the information salespeople can give their buyers.

Want slips are used by most large retail stores (see Figure 9-4). These are slips of paper that are completed by either the customer or salesperson for merchandise requested but not available. The want slips can be analyzed by the buyer, and a determination can be made to add new merchandise or increase particular assortments. This information must be used wisely, since action on each slip can lead to such merchandise diversification that the department can become filled with too much merchandise that is not really desired by many.

Resident buying offices are extremely important aids to store buyers. Because their role is so great in some aspects of retailing, the next chapter will be completely devoted to them and how they help retail store organizations.

A very important factor for all buyers to be aware of in making their selections is the store's image. The image might be that of fashion innovation, such as in the case of Saks Fifth Avenue, conservative styling for the discriminating male, as is the Brooks Brothers image, or perhaps high fashion at rock bottom prices, as in Filene's Basement Store in Boston. Complete awareness of their store's image by all of its buyers will guarantee a unified impression to

HOT ITEMS

LOS ANGELES

SPORTSWEAR

WARM WEATHER BRINGS OUT A YEN FOR CASUAL COTTONS AND BLENDS. PANTS AND SKIMMERS ARE SELLING AT A FAST PACE IN COOL FABRICS.

FOR THE PATIO AND AROUND THE POOL. The scramble is on for the printed skimmer, pantdress a n d built-in bra skimmer in brown, bright blue and gray print on white background. Easy care cotton makes them i d e a l for summer wear. Comes in sizes 8-16 at I. Magnin. Retail for $36-38. From: Tori Richard, Honolulu.

CRISP PANTSUITS LOOK NEAT AT MAY CO. Made of Celanese - Fortrel polyester, they come in lilac, blue, navy and oyster. One style has v-neck tunic with collar and matching belt. The other has wrap top with collar and matching belt. Pants are straight - legged, with elasticized waist. Retail at $30-33. From: Internationale Set, Los Angeles.

AT CONTEMPO CASUALS, BLOUSES A R E GOOD SELLERS. A shortsleeved acrylic knit with turtleneck is on reorder. Comes in multitude of colors. Re-

tails at $13. From: Leroy, Los Angeles. Also soaring is a Victorian - looking, long sleeve voile floral print blouse. Comes in beige and retails for $13. From: Tootique, Los Angeles.

BIRMINGHAM

SCRAMBLE FOR SPORTSWEAR IN WARM SUNSHINE. PANT, VEST AND LONGUETTE COAT NEWEST MOVE IN THE FASHION GAME. T-SHIRT DRESSES REORDERING ALL OVER THE PLACE. JEANS GYRATING. PANT DRESSES, PANT SKIRTS SCURRYING. SWIM SUITS SIZZLE IN COIN DOT MIDIS.

TRIPLE TREAT IN PANT, VEST AND LONGUETTE COAT at the 6-store Pizitz chain. An ad on this wowed its viewers. Pants and vest in muted tones of gray, cream, brown. Coat, belted back, is in rich cream. The whole "she-bang" only $76 retail. Customers galore, according to sportswear buyer, Ruth Alford. From: Carnival, New York.

T-SHIRT D R E S S E S A SMASH at Loveman's, in the Junior department. Buyer Barbara Porter kept busy reordering these. Cotton knit stripers. Primarily navy and red. $10 each, retail. From: Bobbie Brooks, Cleveland.

LEVI'S F O R G A L S a knockout at Loveman's these days too. Checks, stripes, solids. Denims. Flare or straight legs. $7 to $12 retail. Levi's for Gals, San Francisco.

PANTS DRESSES PERKING UP T H E SALES SCENE. at Parisian. Assorted prints. Assorted colors. $11 retail. From: Byer out of California, these are all cottons.

PANT SKIRTS SELLING AT PARISIAN TOO. Flappanel fronts, back zipped, modified A-lines. Assorted stripes, solids, prints. Cottons, and cotton blends. $5 and $6 retail. From: Byer, out of California.

SWIM SUITS IN THE BIG SALES SWIM at Burger-Phillips. Cheerily checking, according to sportswear buyer, Jane Tabor, are the coin dot midi, at $27 retail, and the twin dot panel midi at $28 retail. Both are in red and white, black and white, red and black. But the red and black flew out first. From: Elizabeth Stewart out of California.

S N A P P Y S H O R T SLEEVED TOPPER charming all comers at Burger's. BanLon, V-neck, in red, white, navy, yellow, and black. $14 retail. From: Vera, New York.

FIGURE 9-3 "Hot Items"

Reprinted by permission from *Women's Wear Daily,* Fairchild Publications, Inc.

SALES CLERKS	If you could not supply an item exactly as the Customer wanted it,—record the item the customer described immediately after the customer leaves—even though you sold a substitute.					
ITEM CUSTOMER DESCRIBED (Style—Fabric—Etc.)		Color	Size	Price	No. Calls	Buyer's Disposition
ITEMS LOW IN STOCK						
CUSTOMER WANT SLIP		Sales Clerk No._____			Date_____	
		Name_____				

FIGURE 9-4 Want Slip—Abraham & Strauss

the customer. If buyers go off on their own and move in different directions, the entire operation will suffer.

How Much to Buy

While the ability to select items from all those available is important in purchasing, the wrong quantities in stock may mean a loss for the department. Many students are aware of the dangers inherent in overbuying, but few realize the dangers in not buying enough. There is nothing quite as aggravating to the buyer as having requests for certain merchandise but not enough pieces to suit the customers' demands.

Generally, the initial step in determining how much to buy is to estimate the retail sales for the period of purchase. This is usually a job encompassing the entire organization and is the responsibility of top management. The buyer is interested in the sales estimate for his or her department and has important input in the planning stages. The estimate or forecast is for a designated period of time, the time varying according to the merchandise. For example, buyers of perishables might be concerned with daily requirements, whereas purchasers of staple goods might just need a semiannual picture. Although the purchase periods differ, the key items analyzed in forecasting retail sales are about the same for all retailers. Such factors as disposable income (that which is available to be spent after taxes), unemployment, and shifts in population are of great importance to top management. At the buyer level estimating future sales is usually based on a comparison of how much is being sold this year with last year's sales. By determining the percentage of increase (or decrease) a buyer can add (or subtract) that percentage to last year's purchases for the same upcoming period. In many retail stores these figures are readily available through the proper programming of the computer. The buyer is also concerned with those factors that have a local effect. For example, a purchaser of men's workclothes, whose customers work principally for a large plant, must carefully watch that plant's progress. If it is apparent that the factory will lose certain contracts, layoffs will be inevitable. The small retailer is generally more concerned with local conditions than those of national importance.

Other factors that must be considered at the department level are expansion plans for the store (new branches or units), enlargement of the department's selling space, change in selling practices (service to self-service or the reverse), the size of the department's promotion budget (for display, advertising, special events), the possibility of a more diversified offering, and more specialization.

Although it would be easier for buyers to purchase only at the beginning of a new season, they must constantly add merchandise to their initial purchases throughout the period. Goods that were sold must be replaced and inventories kept at the designated levels.

Open to Buy

Buyers, in order to effectively control their inventories, must carefully plan the amount of merchandise they are going to add at a given time. Since inventory needs vary from month to month, depending upon the season, sale periods, holidays, and so forth, the buyer must always adjust the amounts of merchandise needed. The amount of merchandise that can be ordered at any time during a period is the difference between the total purchases planned by the buyer and the commitments already made. The amount of this difference is called *open to buy*, or as it is referred to in practice, the O.T.B. The formula used is:

Merchandise needed for period — merchandise available = open to buy

Illustrative Problem

The retail inventory for dresses in the budget department of Haring's Department Store figured at $42,000 on September 1, with a planned inventory of $36,000 for September 30. Planned sales, based upon last year's figures, were $22,000 with markdowns of $2,000, for the entire month. The commitments for September were $6,000 at retail. What was the open to buy?

Solution

Merchandise needed (Sept. 1–30)		
End-of-month inventory (planned)	$36,000	
Planned sales (Sept. 1–30)	22,000	
Planned markdowns	2,000	
Total merchandise needed		$60,000
Merchandise available (Sept. 1)		
Opening inventory	$42,000	
Commitments	6,000	
Total merchandise available		48,000
Open to buy (Sept. 1)		$12,000

The above illustration indicates how a buyer can determine his or her open to buy for a period of a month. Very often, buyers must determine their needs within the monthly period. By slightly adjusting the procedure outlined to include the sales actually recorded and the goods actually marked down, the open to buy for any specific date may be obtained.

Illustrative Problem

On March 14, the blouse buyer for Kent's Specialty Shop decided to determine her open to buy. The following figures were available:

Present inventory at retail (March 14)	$12,000
Inventory commitments (March 14)	3,000
Planned end-of-month inventory (March 31)	15,000
Planned sales	6,000
Actual sales	3,000
Planned markdowns	500
Actual markdowns	200

What is the buyer's open to buy?

Solution

Merchandise needed (March 14–31)			
End-of-month inventory (planned)		$15,000	
Planned sales	$6,000		
Less: actual sales	3,000		
Balance of planned sales		3,000	
Planned markdowns	$ 500		
Less: actual markdowns	200		
Balance of planned markdowns		300	
Total merchandise needed			$18,300

Merchandise available (March 14)

Present inventory	$12,000	
Commitments	3,000	
Total merchandise available		15,000
Open to buy (March 14)		$3,300

From Whom to Buy

In most types of merchandise classifications the number of resources available from which to choose merchandise is practically limitless. The store buyers are not only faced with the problem of selecting particular resources, but also must decide whether to purchase directly from the manufacturer (or grower) or a middleperson, or sometimes perhaps even produce their own merchandise (if the retail business is very large).

The specific vendor from whom to buy is determined by investigating those same sources mentioned in the section of this chapter dealing with what to buy. Other sources are the shopping of competing stores, trade directories such as those published by Fairchild, reporting services, and discussions with buyers of noncompeting stores (stores carrying the same type of goods but far enough away not to be a competitor).

Figures 9-5 and 9-6 are examples of forms used by buyers to record information about vendors from whom they have purchased. The vendor information card gives the buyer a quick glimpse of the company in terms of sales representatives, factory location, terms, and discounts. The buyer's bible information card shows the buyer's past experience with the company's particular merchandise items. Both are important references for buyer use.

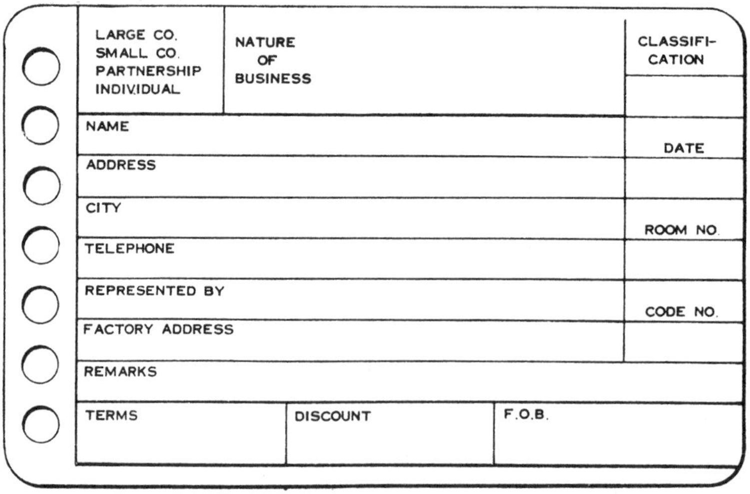

FIGURE 9-5 Vendor Information Card

NAME			ADDRESS				
MERCHANDISE	STYLE NO	COST	RETAIL	M.U.%	M.D.%	MNTD M.U.	RATING

FIGURE 9-6 Buyer's Bible

The main channels of distribution for consumer goods (those goods that are purchased for personal use), simply stated, are

1. Manufacturer (grower)__________Consumer
2. Manufacturer________Retailer's own stores________Consumer
3. Manufacturer________Retailer________Consumer
4. Manufacturer________Wholesaler________Retailer________Consumer

In the first situation the manufacturer actually skips the most common type of retail selling, in a store, and sells directly to the consumer at the producer's factory (or farm, as the case may be) or at the consumer's home. Examples of this distribution technique are the Fuller Brush Company selling door to door and the suit manufacturer selling to the consumer at the factory. This latter situation is becoming more popular with producers throughout the United States.

The second channel presents a situation in which manufacturers, in addition to their production chores, also set up their own retail stores from which they sell their own merchandise. An example of this method is the Castro Convertible Company selling the merchandise it produces in its own retail stores.

The first two distribution methods do not involve store buyers. It is through the last two channels of distribution that most consumer goods flow. In one the retailer buys directly from the producer. The other involves purchasing from a middleperson. The decision of whether to buy from the manufacturer or wholesaler is not always up to the buyer's discretion; some manufacturers, no matter how large the retail organization, sell only through middlepersons. Where the manufacturer distributes to both the wholesalers and retailers, the decision from which type of resource to purchase is the buyer's.

Buying from Manufacturers

The purchase of merchandise directly from the manufacturer is generally restricted to large retailers, except in the distribution of fashion merchandise, where even the small retailers purchase directly. The very nature of fashion merchandise, with its constant changes due to consumer demand and the seasonability of the goods, necessitates this route. These goods must reach the retailer quickly and the use of the wholesaler would slow down the process. The direct purchase of merchandise usually affords the buyer lower prices (than at the wholesaler) and a chance to make suggestions about changes in the manufacturer's design. A typical manufacturer's purchase order is shown in Figure 9-7.

Buying from Wholesalers

Outside the fashion world, purchasing from wholesalers is important. Some factors that persuade the buyer to purchase from middlepersons are

1. *Quick delivery.* One of the main duties the wholesaler performs for the retailer is the storage of merchandise. With the wholesaler's warehouse stocked with goods, the retailer can expect prompt delivery, sometimes even same-day service.
2. *Smaller orders.* Most manufacturers require minimum orders that are too large for the smaller retailer. Wholesalers sell in smaller quantities than do manufacturers.
3. *Wide assortment.* While manufacturers sell only their own products, the wholesaler carries the offerings of many manufacturers. This affords the retailer a comparison of goods and also saves the time it would take to shop many manufacturers' lines.
4. *Easier credit terms.* Generally wholesalers offer more liberal credit terms than manufacturers.

The wholesaler is really a service organization. It manufactures nothing. When the buyer feels one or a number of the services the wholesaler offers is more important than price, the buyer will purchase from the wholesaler although it will mean paying more for the goods. Even the largest of retailers, able to buy direct, use wholesalers when they need immediate delivery and the manufacturer cannot accommodate them. In other cases where, although their overall volume is large, some items are sold infrequently or do not move rapidly, they turn to wholesalers for small quantities.

♥ *The Look You Love* ♥

KAY WINDSOR

1400 BROADWAY, NEW YORK, N.Y. 10018 – 212–736-3900

SPECIAL INSTRUCTIONS ☐ CODES ☐☐☐☐☐

SPACES BELOW FOR OFFICE USE

ORDER # ______ CUSTOMER # ______

SALESMAN # ______ STATE ______

TERMS ______ 8/10 EOM

AD ☐ REORDER ☐ OTHER: ☐

SHIP TO:

NAME ______

LOCAL ADDRESS ______

CITY ______ STATE ______ ZIP CODE ______

CHARGE TO:

NAME ______

LOCAL ADDRESS ______

CITY ______ STATE ______ ZIP CODE ______

ORDER DATE ______

START DATE ______

COMPLETION DATE ______

CUSTOMER ORDER # ______

DEPT. # ______

UPS ☐ PP ☐ EXPRESS ☐ AIR ☐

ZONE ______ OTHER ☐

INSURE YES ☐ NO ☐

ALL SHIPMENTS F.O.B. NEW BEDFORD, MASS.

IF REQUESTED METHOD OF SHIPMENT IS NOT AVAILABLE, VENDOR RESERVES RIGHT TO SHIP IN MOST EXPEDITIOUS MANNER AVAILABLE TO AREA.

SPECIAL INSTRUCTIONS: ______

X X	STYLE	COLOR	COLOR #	DESCRIPTION	QUAN.	8	10	12	14	16	18	20	PRICE

THE ABOVE ORDER IS SUBJECT TO ACCEPTANCE OF THE SELLER AND TO CONDITIONS ON THE REVERSE SIDE OF THIS CONTRACT.

BUYER'S SIGNATURE ______

NO GOODS ACCEPTED FOR RETURN WITHOUT WRITTEN CONSENT. ALL RETURNS MUST BE MADE TO OUR FACTORY.

LOS ANGELES OFFICE
110 EAST NINTH STREET
TEL.: 627-4694

"The Most Advertised Name in Fashion"

DALLAS OFFICE
NEW APPAREL MART
ROOM 1223 – MELROSE 1-7124

F.O.B. — FACTORY

FACTORY: TABER MILL—NEW BEDFORD, MASS. WYMAN 9-6205

FIGURE 9-7 Purchase Order

When to Buy

When to actually purchase goods can vary from every day (small retailers of perishables) to as infrequently as semiannually. In any case, the timing is of utmost importance.

Buyers must buy sufficiently early to allow enough time for the goods to reach the selling floor. The purchase from wholesalers allows buying merchandise very close to the time the consumer will purchase goods. It is the purchase from manufacturers, coupled with such elements as seasons, weather, and perishability, that poses problems for buyers.

The buyer of seasonal merchandise such as swimsuits, nearly always bought from manufacturers, purchases well in advance of the season. This is necessary because production takes a couple of months and the store wants the goods early enough to whet the customer's appetite. In the case of seasonal merchandise, manufacturers, as an inducement to retailers, often "date" the purchase orders. That is, they extend the period for payment of the invoices. The buyer of seasonal goods who purchases too late might not get delivery. Also, if the customers don't have enough advance exposure to the merchandise, they might be tempted to buy elsewhere.

The weather poses a special problem. Abundant snowfalls will sell snowblowers just as durations of extreme heat will sell air conditioners. While it's difficult to determine weather, it is an important factor to buyers.

Perishability also plays havoc with buyers. Perishable goods must be purchased as frequently as possible and in carefully determined quantities. There is nothing as unsalable as sour milk or wilted roses.

The efficiency of the buyer is extremely important to the store's success. We have discussed how important it is for this person to receive as much help as is available in order to do an effective job. There is, particularly in the fashion field, an aid without whose help many retailers would fail. This is the resident buying office, which will be discussed in detail in the next chapter.

Negotiating the Purchase

After one has prepared a purchasing plan that carefully considers all of the elements of buying, the next step is to seek out the appropriate vendors for the purpose of negotiating an order.

Negotiating with the vendor involves a number of purchasing decisions that require a knowledge of the particular market, product information, discounts, transportation arrangements, and so forth.

Negotiating price requires an understanding of a piece of legislation known as the Robinson-Patman Act. This was enacted to limit price discrimination and protect the small businessperson from the industrial giants who could get lower prices. Basically, under the law, all buyers must pay the same price except in instances where

- the price reduction is made to meet competition.
- the price is lowered because cost savings result from sales to particular customers.
- the merchandise is obsolete or part of a "job lot."

Once these guidelines are understood, it is the buyer's knowledge of the market and product that enables attainment of a satisfactory price.

A variety of discounts enter into a purchase negotiation. Cash discounts for prompt payment, quantity discounts, seasonal discounts, advertising discounts, and promotional discounts must all be explored to gain the best possible deal.

An important aspect of the negotiation lies with transportation costs. An astute negotiator can often convince the vendor to assume costs of shipping the goods and can thereby actually reduce the cost of the merchandise.

Other negotiating considerations include ventures in cooperative purchasing, where individual orders can be combined for better prices, and consignment buying, which permits payment of goods only when they are sold to the consumer.

Negotiation involves a great deal of expertise and understanding of psychology. Buyers must establish limits for goods they expect to purchase, justify the reasons for the price offered, be willing to split the difference in price when an impasse is reached, and develop relationships that would assure the best possible future deals.

FOREIGN PURCHASING

Scanning the newspapers at almost any time, one sees such advertising headlines as "imported from Hong Kong," "made in Great Britain," and "copies of original French and Italian designs." Because the public is attracted to imported merchandise, and for other reasons, the amount of space allocated to imported merchandise seems to increase each year. Although Paris was once considered the prime market for fashion imports, today buyers are also scouting and purchasing from markets in Italy, England, Scotland, Germany, Hong Kong, and Taiwan, among others. The arrangements by which they purchase vary according to the size of the retail organization and the amount of foreign goods purchased. Some of the methods used in the procurement of imported merchandise are

1. *Periodic trips by store buyers.* In the case of large users, it is common practice for a buyer to visit the foreign markets in person. These trips are made frequently.

Buyers of fashion merchandise go even more frequently. The use of this method demands careful preplanning since the time spent abroad is limited. Hotel reservations, transportation arrangements, and buying appointments must all be planned in advance. Buyers, particularly of merchandise manufactured by the foreign haute couture houses, plan their trips to coincide with the couturiers' "openings." In order to make certain that the leading fashion houses can be visited in the short time spent in Paris, "Chambre de la Syndicale" regulates the times of the showings in France.

2. *Commissionaires or foreign resident offices.* This representation is similar to our own resident buying offices. Further discussion will be presented in the next chapter.

3. *Import wholesalers.* These are middlepersons who carry samples of merchandise available from foreign countries. The smaller retailer wishing to avoid the expense involved in direct visits to foreign countries can purchase his or her needs from the importers. The cost is a little more than if purchased directly, but since the purchasing power of the small retailer is limited, this arrangement is satisfactory.

4. *Privately owned foreign offices.* Organizations such as the American Merchandising Corporation maintain offices in the foreign markets. This allows for maximum time to be spent in these markets in which to seek out the best goods, by professional buyers, at the best prices. Naturally, only the giant retail organizations can avail themselves of this arrangement.

The reasons for purchasing goods from foreign resources are many. Besides prestige, some of the other reasons are

1. In general, goods of comparable value cost less in foreign countries. By purchasing abroad, retailers can offer better value to their customers while at the same time achieving higher markups. One ready-to-wear buyer for a well-known department store revealed that a markup of 70 percent was realized on his foreign purchases. This is well above the usual markup for American-made clothing of equal quality.

2. Some merchandise is not available at home. For example, the label-conscious "Jet Set" spends enormous sums for original designs. Such names as St. Laurent, Givenchy, and Ungaro command prices from some customers that other (American) designers do not. Such merchandise is only available abroad.

3. For purposes of copying designs, stores spend great sums in foreign countries. Rather than sell the originals, stores visit the foreign fashion houses to purchase styles for the express purpose of copying them. This arrangement permits the average American to purchase copies of famous original designs at a fraction of the original's cost. This market has become increasingly important in fashion retailing.

A retailer must weigh the advantages against the disadvantages before embarking upon a program of purchasing imported goods. Some of the disadvantages offered by retailers who oppose buying from foreign resources are

1. The expense incurred from a buying trip abroad may be too costly to reap profits from the merchandise purchased.

2. The delivery period is generally uncertain, owing to the distance involved and the limited shipping facilities.

3. The outlay of cash often necessary at the time of shipment might be extensive. Since the shipping period is so long, capital is tied up without having the goods available for sale.

4. Owing to the time lag, purchases must be made far in advance of the selling period, when such considerations as color and size may not be made with knowledgeable certainty.

5. Sometimes the initial duty assessment is inaccurate owing to change. This may result in higher tariffs.

6. Reorders are generally impossible on imported goods, particularly in fashion, since the time it takes for delivery may be long.

7. Goods bought according to specification may fall short of what was expected. Since the distance between the vendor and the purchaser is great, return of imperfect goods is often impossible.

8. Damaged goods are costly to return to the foreign manufacturer.

Action for the Independent Retailer

Very often it is the taste and feel for appealing merchandise that prompts an individual to begin a retail business. Creative buying is an important factor contributing to a store's success and this is where the independent can compete with even the largest retailer.

The small businessperson who operates a store is generally its buyer. In addition to purchasing, the individual is often on the sales floor within earshot of the customer, if not actually making the sale. Where the buyers for large stores rely heavily upon printouts and other buying tools, the independent is getting firsthand buying information. If it is believed that the consumer determines the inventory necessary, who then is better informed than the independent retailer who interfaces with the customer daily? The independents also have the advantage of faster reaction to customer needs. That is, there is no need to clear through management changes in merchandising philosophy that seem worthy. The independent can adjust quickly to the customer's needs.

It is the creative buyer who can motivate customer purchasing. This is one area where store size does not play a significant role.

IMPORTANT POINTS IN THE CHAPTER

1. *In most large stores individual buyers are responsible for all purchasing and selling activities carried on by the department they head.*

2. *The effectiveness of a selling department depends in large part on how successful the buyer is in satisfying customer demand.*

3. *The basic elements of buying are what to buy, how much to buy, from whom to buy, and when to buy.*

4. *While some of the buyer's choices are a matter of taste, buyers have many sources of information available that help them make selections. Among these are past sales records, inventory records, surveys, trade periodicals, and newspapers.*

5. *Top management sets budgetary restrictions on buying. The buyer must carefully plan purchases to remain within the budget.*

6. *Open to buy is the difference between the buyer's planned purchases and the buying commitments she or he has already made.*

7. *In the decision of from whom to buy, the buyer weighs the advantages and disadvantages among various producers, and types of sources (wholesaler or manufacturer).*

8. *Recent years have seen an increase in the amount of foreign purchases made by retailers. Foreign producers, although subjected to many disadvantages, frequently offer unusual styling and reduced costs.*

REVIEW QUESTIONS

1. Who purchases goods for those stores unable to afford buyers?
2. In what situation can a small retailer actually receive the services of a seasoned buyer? What is the usual financial arrangement for this service?
3. What are some responsibilities of the store buyer other than purchasing merchandise?
4. What duties are performed by assistant buyers?
5. What does "following up" an order entail?
6. Discuss some of those characteristics necessary to a successful buyer.
7. Who generally buys the merchandise for department store branches?
8. Under what circumstances does a branch buy independently of the main store?
9. Explain central buying.
10. How do the chain store buyer's responsibilities differ from those of the department store buyer?
11. Discuss the variations of central buying practiced in the chain organizations.
12. What should the first thought be when a buyer plans purchases?
13. Which source of information is used by all buyers when planning purchases?
14. Describe two forms used by retailers to record vital sales information?
15. How can the large retail store quickly provide its buyers with sales information?
16. Why do buyers scan consumer newspapers and magazines?
17. What factors should be considered in determining how much to buy?
18. Discuss open to buy. Why are buyers constantly determining their O.T.B?
19. From whom are most fashion goods purchased, manufacturers or wholesalers? Why?
20. Discuss the reasons for the growth in foreign purchasing.

CASE PROBLEMS

CASE PROBLEM 1

The Time-Rite Appliance Company is a small retail chain with three units located in New Jersey. It carries a general line of appliances such as refrigerators, washing machines, dishwashers, toasters, and electric can openers. It plans the addition of another line of merchandise, air conditioners, because of consumer demand. Most of the items carried are purchased from manufacturers (unless a particular manufacturer distributes exclusively through wholesalers), and some from wholesalers in an emergency situation. All inventory sells throughout the year, with Christmas the peak period. Since the company does not sell any of the newer "fashion type" styles of appliances extensively, you might say its inventory was stable. The problem confronting it now is from whom to purchase the air conditioning units—manufacturers or wholesalers. Time-Rite is unsure of the sales volume to anticipate from this line and thus the appropriate quantities to stock.

QUESTIONS

1. Compare air conditioners with the company's other lines. What factors must it consider?
2. How advantageous would purchasing be from manufacturers? From wholesalers?
3. How would you suggest Time-Rite proceed with its first year's merchandising of air conditioners?

CASE PROBLEM 2

The Men's Shop at Lustig's Department Store is one of the organization's busiest departments. One reason is that, in addition to the great ability of the haberdashery buyer, the store is located in an area occupied by many large firms employing vast numbers of male employees. These include advertising firms, sales organizations, insurance companies, and so on.

During the past two months, while the rest of the store continues to meet and beat their sales figures, the business shirt sales in the Men's Shop have declined considerably. The buyer at this time is uncertain of how to rectify the situation but knows he has to begin with his customer in mind.

QUESTION

1. If you were that department's buyer, what methods would you use to secure customer information that might change the present situation?

10

resident buying offices

BEHAVIORAL OBJECTIVES

Upon completion of this chapter the student should be able to

1. *Explain the difference between a privately owned resident buying office and an independent one.*
2. *Write an essay on the selection of a resident buying office. This should include at least four factors that should be considered.*
3. *List and discuss ten services performed by a resident buying office.*
4. *Indicate the importance of foreign resident buying offices, pointing out four services they perform.*

INTRODUCTION

In the preceding chapter an overview of most of the store buyer's sources of information was presented. Perhaps the single most important aid to the buyer's procurement of merchandise (particularly in soft goods) is the resident buying office. Unlike retail stores, which for the most part are located away from the wholesale markets, the resident offices are located in these markets. Through affiliation with a resident office, the store personnel can feel the pulse of their market without making many costly and time-consuming trips. By selecting the appropriate office, store buyers can carry out their duties and responsibilities at the store with the security of knowing that someone is constantly scanning the market for new resources and new merchandise for them.

TYPES OF RESIDENT OFFICES

There are two major types of resident buying offices, the privately owned office and the independent office.

Privately Owned Offices

In the strictest sense of the word, the private office is owned by and exclusively aids a single retail organization. Since maintaining a buying office is costly, there are few private offices. Not completely private but certainly more so than the independent offices are those resident offices that are owned by a group of stores. This arrangement allows for expenses to be shared by the members of the group, much like a cooperative. The members of the group are noncompeting stores and can thus safely aid each other in many ways without the fear of jeopardizing their own operations. In the completely private office this information exchange is unavailable since ownership is exclusive. There are several group offices in New York City. One of the best known is AMC, The American Merchandising Corporation, with such members as Abraham & Straus and Bloomingdale's, both large New York-based department stores.

Independent Offices

The independent office has as its members many different, noncompeting, retail stores. These offices run the gamut of representing fairly small retail organizations to the larger retailers. The fees charged for the many services afforded customers vary according to sales volume, remuneration generally being a percentage of the sales figures. The fees also vary from office to office, depending upon the services offered. Stores generally enter into contractual agreements with the resident buying offices for periods of one year. Some of the better known independent offices are Atlas Buying Corporation, Independent Retailers Syndicate, Certified Buying Service, and Ark Wright, Inc.

SELECTION OF AN OFFICE

Few retailers really have a choice as to the category of office to which they can belong. Only a very small percentage are large enough to warrant a privately owned or semiprivately owned company. The remainder of those retailers needing market representation must choose from the several hundred independent resident buying offices now in existence. Selecting the right office is extremely important. Buying decisions are often based upon an office's recommendation, and poor advice can lead to a store's failure.

One important point to consider in the selection of an office is its size. The office must be sufficiently large to give the store adequate assistance. For example, some offices are so small that their staff members cannot specialize in any one capacity. Perhaps one individual may be responsible for covering both the sportswear and the dress markets in all price ranges. This monumental task surely does not give one individual sufficient time to completely investigate either of these markets. The store cannot then be confident of the office's recommendation.

The other stores that deal through the resident buying office require careful investigation. First, it is important to be certain that competitors are not members. Since the resident buying office is a great place for exchanging information with other store buyers, the inclusion of competition at the same office could be disastrous. Second, the other retail organizations being represented should be similar to one's own. Clientele, merchandising policies, price ranges, and image are just some areas of significance. If the other stores are unlike your own operation, the information exchange will be meaningless.

Some resident offices represent a number of different types of retail operations. This is fine, as long as it is large enough to employ enough people to cater to all the different needs.

The merchandise in which an office specializes is an important factor in its being selected by a store for representation. Only the very large offices run the gamut of hard goods and soft goods. Others specialize in particular merchandise. For an operation that encompasses all types of merchandise (for example, a department store), membership would be most beneficial in an office whose offerings are more diversified. The more specialization in a store, the more specialized the office that is chosen should be. Both the office and the organization should be interested in the same type of retailing.

The services offered by resident buying offices vary from office to office. Naturally, these services are important to consider in selecting the right office.

SERVICES OF AN OFFICE

It is imperative to select the office that offers those services needed to help your operation. Very small stores, unable to afford the fees of the full-service resident offices, often join a small office which only advises about new resources and new merchandise available. Most retailers join an office for many additional services. Following are some of these.

Placing Orders

Stores often satisfy their customers by reordering out-of-stock merchandise for them or merchandise not usually carried at all. The resident office will place these "special orders" and make certain that the vendors deliver the item within the specified time period. Sometimes buyers are in need of new merchandise and are unable to visit the market. Given approximate specifications, resident buyers will actually make purchases for the store.

Most retailers' businesses thrive on reorders of merchandise that has sold successfully. Since the timing of receipt of reordered merchandise is extremely important (it might be needed for an advertisement or a window display), store buyers often depend upon the resident office to place the reorder. With the office located in the market, the resident buyer can carefully check with the vendors to make certain that delivery promises are kept. Only the retailer who has run a newspaper advertisement and not received the merchandise when promised can appreciate this responsibility that is undertaken by the resident offices. An order form similar to that in Figure 10-1 is used for order placement.

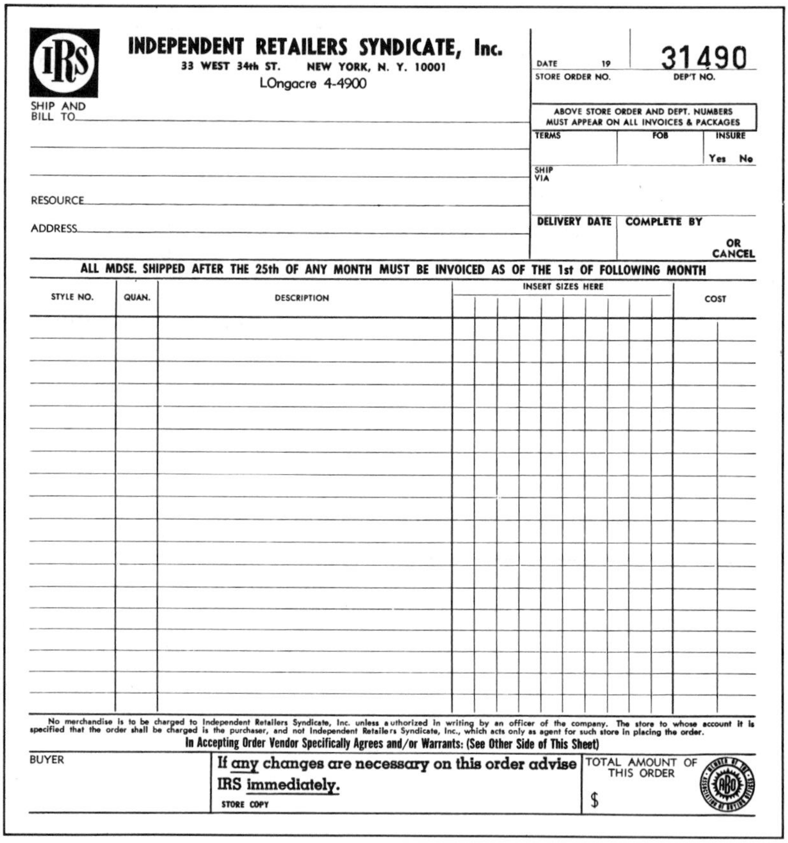

INDEPENDENT RETAILERS SYNDICATE, Inc.
33 WEST 34th ST. NEW YORK, N. Y. 10001
LOngacre 4-4900

DATE 19 — STORE ORDER NO. — 31490 — DEP'T NO.

ABOVE STORE ORDER AND DEPT. NUMBERS MUST APPEAR ON ALL INVOICES & PACKAGES

SHIP AND BILL TO

TERMS | FOB | INSURE Yes No

SHIP VIA

RESOURCE

ADDRESS

DELIVERY DATE | COMPLETE BY OR CANCEL

ALL MDSE. SHIPPED AFTER THE 25th OF ANY MONTH MUST BE INVOICED AS OF THE 1st OF FOLLOWING MONTH

STYLE NO.	QUAN.	DESCRIPTION	INSERT SIZES HERE	COST

No merchandise is to be charged to Independent Retailers Syndicate, Inc. unless authorized in writing by an officer of the company. The store to whose account it is specified that the order shall be charged is the purchaser, and not Independent Retailers Syndicate, Inc., which acts only as agent for such store in placing the order.

In Accepting Order Vendor Specifically Agrees and/or Warrants: (See Other Side of This Sheet)

BUYER | If any changes are necessary on this order advise IRS immediately. STORE COPY | TOTAL AMOUNT OF THIS ORDER $

FIGURE 10–1 Purchase Order Form—Independent Retailers Syndicate, New York City

Arranging Adjustments

It is not unusual for a store buyer who has carefully ordered merchandise, paying strict attention to style, color, and size selection, to receive goods that were not wanted. A completely different fabric from that which was seen in the sample merchandise is not uncommon in shipments. Handling these adjustments through a resident office is much wiser for the retailer. Vendors are unlikely to ignore the resident buyer's complaints as they might an individual small retailer, since the resident offices are so influential through their recommendations. Sometimes the buying office can convince the vendor to accept a return of merchandise that has been ordered but is not selling satisfactorily. In this case, the retailer handling the situation alone usually doesn't stand a chance. Other adjustment situations include poor fit, inferior workmanship, and poor wearability.

Foreign Market Information

In both hard goods and soft goods, foreign markets are becoming increasingly important. A tremendous amount of merchandise is being imported each year at prices below those found in the United States. The larger resident buying offices have branches in many of these foreign countries. Because few stores can send their buyers abroad, the information about the merchandise available is becoming an extremely important service. (Foreign buying is discussed in detail later in this chapter.)

Locating New Resources

Retailers are always looking for new resources. Since many vendors begin on a small scale with little sales help and advertising, it is difficult for stores away from the market to hear about the newcomers. Through the resident offices (every new firm tries desperately to be recommended by them) retailers are made aware of new resources.

Recommending New Items

Buyers purchase sufficient goods prior to each selling season to complete their opening inventories. They generally visit their markets, either alone or assisted by the resident buyer, to select the goods they desire. During the season, when store buyers are involved in duties at the store, they find that they generally need new merchandise to spruce up the inventory. The resident office will scout the market and suggest such merchandise that will fit the bill. Often this recommendation by the resident buyer turns out to be a "hot item."

Preparing Displays and Promotional Materials

In large stores the display department is charged with the responsibility of creating dramatic, timely windows and interior displays. The smaller shop either periodically engages a free-lance display person or trims its own windows. In the latter instances, catchy ideas are always being sought by store buyers. Many resident offices arrange displays in typical window-size settings so that the retailer can copy them. This gives retailers new ideas to bring back to their stores. Similarly, copy for advertisements is prepared. Some offices even provide mats (paper composition printing plates of complete advertisements) to which the store's name is added, for newspaper advertisements.

Preparing Fashion Shows

Resident buying offices typically present fashion shows to their member stores during "market week," a time when most buyers visit the market to begin purchasing for a new season. In addition to these shows, many of the offices prepare complete fashion show "packages" for their retailers to present at their stores. These packages include such important elements as the commentary, suggested musical selections, and background recommendations. Following these prescribed plans makes the presentation of a fashion show a routine job.

Training Salespeople

Some offices aid in the training of salespeople. They provide training materials such as booklets, brochures, and recordings, which describe the art of selling. In addition, some even send counselors to the store. By using this service, the buyer makes certain that once the purchases arrive at the store, the salespeople will be sufficiently knowledgeable in the dissemination of the proper information concerning the merchandise.

Preparing for the Store Buyer's Visit

The frequency of visits a store buyer makes to the market varies from store to store. Distance from the market, size of the department, and the store's need for the buyer's presence on the selling floor are just some factors that help determine how often the market is visited. Whenever the buyer does decide to come to the market, the resident buying office goes to work to make certain that the trip will be fruitful and that as much as possible can be condensed into that brief period (generally one week). The office's preparation includes

1. Locating the most desirable merchandise.
2. Publishing the "buyer's arrival" in such papers as *The New York Times* and the appropriate trade papers. This notifies all interested vendors about the buyers that are in town, the length of their stay, and their temporary residence. In this way advance appointments can be made through the offices.
3. Arranging hotel accommodations.
4. Providing working space at the resident office to study their puchasing plans and to see salespersons and their merchandise.
5. Assigning a resident buyer to accompany the store buyer to market to help with the selection of merchandise.

Market Week

Although the resident offices must have their services available to the retail store members at all times, it is during the regular visits to the market that the resident buyers are busiest serving the store buyer's needs. These periodic visits are generally made during the "market weeks." They are times when the manufacturers of particular industries "open" and show their lines to the store buyers. Because the period is extremely hectic and the store buyer's time away from the store is generally limited to a week, the resident office planning must be perfectly organized. It is during this period that the previously mentioned buyer preparations must be made.

Making Available Private Brands

A private brand is one that bears either the store's label or the resident buying office's name. Private brand merchandise permits the store to gain a high markup without the fear of price cutting by competitors, because exact comparison shopping is impossible. Few retailers are large enough to market private brands by themselves. By joining a buying office, small individual orders can be consolidated into large orders. To obtain large orders, manufacturers will gladly produce merchandise to specification and affix private labels. This merchandise usually costs less because of the great quantities manufactured. In this way, the store makes a better profit and the customer gets good value.

Pooling Orders

On merchandise other than private brands, resident offices often pool orders. This frequently enables a small user to qualify for a quantity discount.

The Resident Office Contract Form in Figure 10-2 summarizes the terms of the agreement made between the resident buying office and the retailer.

EXAMPLE OF AN INDEPENDENT OFFICE'S RELATIONSHIP WITH ITS MEMBER STORES

In an attempt to make certain that retailers are obtaining the maximum benefits of belonging to their office, IRS (Independent Retailers Syndicate, 33 West 34th Street, New York, N.Y.) distributes a booklet to its members entitled, *How to Make Full Use of IRS Services.* This simple booklet, the text of which follows, points up many of the advantages of joining this resident office and the means of maximizing the benefits of its offerings.

> The IRS Management Team, vitally concerned that *all* clients derive maximum benefit from IRS service, has coordinated their thinking and your review and follow-through will bring you tangible results. To construct the base for your campaign to get all you can out of IRS, it is necessary to define the five principles of IRS service.

New York _____

To: Atlas Buying Corp.
     500 – 7th Avenue
     New York, N.Y. 10018

This confirms your agreement to represent us as resident buyer in the New York market and to furnish us information regarding market conditions on the following terms:

Office space in your office will be furnished to our visiting personnel without extra charge. You will charge us at cost for forwarding packages, telephone tolls, and telegrams and other similar items. A flat charge of $ _____ per month will be made for postage. We shall pay you the sum $ _____ per annum at the beginning of each contract year this agreement remains in effect. We shall have the privilege of paying said sum in equal monthly installments of $ _____ each on the _____ day of each month during the term hereof. Should we default in the payment of any such installment, the entire unpaid sum for the whole remaining term of this agreement shall immediately become due and payable without notice or demand. This agreement is binding to heirs and successors.

You will also make available the merchandising facilities of your affiliate ABC Distributing Corp. On any merchandise purchased by said Distributing Corp. three per cent (3%) of the net purchase cost to cover billing, bookkeeping and other similar expenses involved in the handling of such transactions in addition to the net cost of the merchandise. We will pay for all such merchandise within ten (10) days from date of invoice.

The term of this agreement shall be for _____ year beginning _____ 19 ____.
This agreement shall be automatically renewed from year to year unless, on or before sixty (60) days preceding the end of any contract year, notice in writing is given by either party of the intention not to renew.

STORE _____

ADDRESS _____

CITY _____ STATE _____ ZIP CODE ___

              BY _____

We accept and agree to the above contract:
        ATLAS BUYING CORP.
By _____

FIGURE 10-2 Resident Office Contract Form

First, IRS renders uniquely *personalized service.* We are staffed and equipped to provide it. IRS merchandise managers cover one division rather than two or more and our buyers cover markets the way the markets are organized. IRS are specialists. They are in the market every day, seeing it more thoroughly and making judgments that are more extensive than your most energetic buyer could possibly cram into a perfectly planned trip a few times a year.

Second, *intercommunication* is the final criterion by which our people have to be judged. It simply is not enough for an IRS buyer to be diligent, a good reporter and right. The outcome is less than satisfactory if store buyers do not respond with buying reaction to bulletins and consultations. Communication is lacking if they do not make long-distance phone calls regularly or if they do not review their classifications, resources, price lines, and turnover.

Third, *merchandising counsel* is a cornerstone of IRS service. When your buyer or merchandiser has troubles that are bigger than picking up a couple of hot items, he has a lot of friends at IRS. There is an IRS merchandise manager, with depth of background in retailing and full information on the market, who can help him. There is also a principal of IRS, waiting with an open door to discuss the major problem and set wheels in motion to develop strategies and solutions. If you think your buyer is too shy to walk through the supervisory doors at IRS when he feels he is not getting the help he needs, tell him his prestige with everyone at IRS goes up every time he details a problem to the first and second echelon of the office and asks for the full measure of help he needs. We will respect him for doing it.

Fourth, *orientation sessions* for new personnel and reorientation meetings for those who have been around for a while are established IRS techniques for assuring the realization of full service. When you are sending or bringing a new buyer to market for the first time, tell us in advance and we will see to it that he receives a thorough indoctrination with regard to our services. We will tell him about every facility, every program and make sure he meets everyone he should know. Our people will then be informed to give him special attention.

You may conclude that you have buyers who have been with your store ten years and still do not know how to use IRS correctly, or some who have forgotten. Whether you have 2 or 20 such people, your recognition of the fact is all we need. We will set up a program of reorientation for your entire staff, if necessary. With new buyers, alert IRS staff members can originate the suggestion for an orientation effort. When old hands are involved, the initiative will generally have to be yours. Just tell us what you want, whom you want and how thoroughly you would like the job done.

Fifth, *in the absence of management initiative, supervision, and backing, the first four principles of IRS service mean nothing. Without your insistent and persistent effort, none of them will get done.* And if you will ask the right questions, the job of supervising your staff's full use of IRS services takes on some definite shapes.

IRS service rests on these five principles. During our discussions in Management Team meetings, one question we posed was: How does an astute IRS buyer or division head spot deterioration in his rapport with store counterparts? The following are the telltale signs on which everyone on the Management Team focused:

A. Store personnel who maximize the services of the office get to the office early. Store principals who get the most out of the office set a contagious example by walking in on IRS Divisional Managers well before official hours begin in the morning, and their buyers arrive with them.

B. Even though some store personnel come in just to make an appearance, between visits the mailbag is light and the phone is silent. Despite our pressure, there is no reaction. Constant communication is essential if you are going to maximize our services. We were the first to dramatize the upsurge of the "Country Corner" trend—the very first office in New York to urge fast action. We also sounded the alarm on storage sheds well ahead of the crest. But too many of you responded only after your competitor led the way. Perhaps some responded only under the pain of being left out, rather than to assure being the first with it.

C. Generating excitement is hard work and not strictly one way. The IRS staff strives mightily to light a spark in your buyer, and to create excitement in retailing.

D. The after-trip market follow-up is conspicuously absent. When the IRS buyer and your buyer talk the same language, the store buyer wants the latest possible updating before he feels his market mission was executed properly. He phones a couple of days after he returns home and says, in effect—"I am about to finalize the results of my trip. Has anything turned up since I spoke to you? Do you want to change any of your recommendations?" This follow-up can be the finishing touch on a successful trip.

E. Without advance notice, the store buyer arrives in New York. Here he is with no specific event or promotion or fill-in need communicated beforehand. What we might have had ready for his review is now the subject of a time-consuming discussion. When he does not let us know what he needs, and whom he needs, before he comes in, he simply puts us at a disadvantage. Without advance notice a store buyer also puts himself at a disadvantage.

In order to make full use of our service, pose these questions to your merchandise staff as they head for New York, when they come back, and in between.

As Your Buyer Is Leaving for the Market:

Have you informed the IRS merchandise manager and your counterpart buyer (or buyers) that you are coming?

Have you told them why you are coming in?

Have you told them about your specific needs in items or planning counsel?

Do you have a copy of your merchandising plans to discuss with them?

When Your Buyer Comes Back from New York:

Did you review your plans and purchases with your IRS counterparts?

Did they offer constructive suggestions for changes?

Did you pick up any unexpected bonus items?

What is being featured in the IRS Fashion Office display?

Are we heavy on any goods IRS has earmarked for fast decline?

Are we light on styles IRS reports on the upgrade?

Did you look at any new resources suggested by IRS? Did you ask?

What are the two or three most important trends that were reported to you by your IRS counterparts? Did you ask?

Were you offered a chance to participate in any special purchases? If you declined, why did you turn it down?

If you asked for help and did not get it, whom did you tell at IRS? What were the results then?

Here Are Some Questions Which You Might Pose at Merchandise Meetings Between Market Trips:

When did you speak to your IRS counterparts last by phone?

What are the IRS people excited about right now? Have you bought it?

Have you briefed your people on the recent "Fashion Sales Tips"?

Has the Colt Wholesale Division offered any special values to you?

If you are not buying, what is your reason?

Has IRS bulletined you on any new items we do not show?

Have you tested any bulletined items in the last month?

Some of These Questions Have to Be Directed at You as Well as Your Buyer—For Example:

If you have a weak department or classification, have you discussed the possibility of organizing a Crash Program to reverse a bad trend while there is still time to make corrections?

If your store is being held back by a department with declining volume or profit, IRS executives, skilled merchandisers with strong retail background, can custom design a Crash Program that will telescope the vitality and growth of five years into two.

Have you challenged IRS to cope with that kind of problem in your store?

Are you branching out or adding space by construction or doing a face-lifting job? Have you asked for a meeting with IRS management to draw the blueprint for a special IRS project while you are in the blueprint stage?

If your store has no classification committed to Unit Control Service, have you seen some of the hard-to-believe-but-true figures of Unit Control operations within this group? We are not going to belabor this point. We will just let the figures do the talking.

We are not going to detail what "Operation Kidstuff" has done for participating children's departments in the four years since it was launched, or the undisputable superiority of IRS catalogs and enclosures—all of them now consistently over-subscribed, or the nonmerchandising services of the well-manned IRS operations departments, or the unique counseling available to store management in many areas of retailing. These are tremendously important extras that are available to you in top management, and our original purpose was to suggest how you can best ensure that your staff is getting all the service that IRS can deliver during, and between market visits. These services are wide and deep and the capability is provided by skilled professional IRS personnel, whose number and special knowledge are just as wide and just as deep.

What we have presented to you has not been a set of abstract ideas or possibilities. What we have offered are our carefully considered suggestions on how you can make sure that your store makes full use of our people. You must diligently check your people to be sure they are using the office properly. In this way, IRS can serve you fully, efficiently, and profitably.

FOREIGN RESIDENT BUYING OFFICES

In addition to the prestige merchandise made available by the leading couturiers, a great deal of other merchandise is finding its way onto the selling floors of American retailers. There are a number of arrangements available to the retailer for the procurement of merchandise for import. Since only the very large retail organizations will invest in trips to foreign lands for purposes of purchasing, other methods are employed by smaller entrepreneurs for the importing of goods.

Similar to those resident offices operating in the United States are the resident buying offices located in foreign countries. Some of the offices, called commissionaires, are completely independent (without American affiliation) and are designed to service the buyers from other countries. Other offices are affiliated with the American resident buying offices and their services are available to member stores, as is any other R.B.O. service. Whichever type of office represents the American retailer, the services afforded the buyer are the same. Some of the services offered are

1. The purchase of new merchandise. Purchasing in this manner is somewhat risky for the store because the foreign office must use its judgment and the store must accept what has been purchased. Sometimes, if time is available, photographs or samples of goods are sent to the United States for approval. This eliminates some of the risk.
2. The placement of reorders. Much the same as our own resident buying offices, those in foreign countries place orders and follow up reorders. Even though the office somewhat facilitates purchasing in foreign countries, the reordering of merchandise must be contemplated with caution. Shipping delays, strikes, and so forth can cause merchandise to be delivered too late to be meaningful in terms of sales.
3. The arrangement for shipment of the merchandise.
4. Assistance to those stores wishing to visit the foreign markets. They arrange such things as hotel accommodations and appointments with vendors.

The commissionaires, for their services, are paid a commission on the cost of the purchases they make. The commission charged is approximately 7 percent of the foreign cost.

Although the cost of goods in foreign countries may be considerably less than comparable domestic goods, there are additional costs that must be considered before a purchase is completed. An example of the computation involved in determining the true or landed cost, as it is technically called, follows:

Initial Cost	50 sweaters @ 3000 lire each	150,000
	100 sweaters @ 6000 lire each	600,000
	Total Initial Cost	750,000
	Less 3% Discount	22,500
		727,500
Packing Charge		22,700
7% Commission (on initial cost)		52,500
Shipping Charge		55,200
		857,900
Duty 30% (estimated) on goods purchased		
plus packing charge		225,060
		1,082,960
Other Expenses (storage, etc)		91,000
	Total Landed Cost	1,173,960

This figure is then translated into American dollars.

As has been examined in the preceding chapter, several forces necessitate the purchase of merchandise abroad. Whether the purchase is achieved directly through negotiation between the store buyer and supplier, or it is arranged through a commissionaire, there are a number of factors to which attention must be paid to ensure that a profit will be possible.

There has always been a fluctuation of foreign currency in relation to the American dollar. Today, the situation is even less stable. Each day the worth of our dollar on foreign markets fluctuates, sometimes in considerable degrees. The buyer must make certain that the terms of purchase include language that provides for protection of price. That is, if the cost due to dollar devaluation presents a risk to profit once the merchandise is delivered, the buyer should insist upon some protection. Such caution is significantly more needed where there is a wide time gap between purchase, production, and eventual delivery. The inexperienced could lose a great deal if these price considerations aren't carefully explored.

While the initial price might seem low, the bonded cost should always be figured to determine the real cost to the store. Such factors as packing charges and duty charges must be carefully examined to ensure that the product is worth the real cost.

Merchandise from abroad frequently includes selling features not found in domestic goods. Similarly, the merchandise might bring with it quality features that are detrimental to the merchandise. For example, European fit might be narrower than that which is appropriate for Americans. Often, the sample and the delivered goods bear little resemblance to each other. A buyer, prone to purchase imported merchandise, must be careful to set guidelines for the merchandise that is bought in foreign countries. Returns are difficult and time-consuming, and subquality goods could present problems.

Although it is generally conceded that goods from abroad are necessary to many merchandising plans, care must be exercised in their purchase. The foreign resident representative must be completely instructed as to the requirements of the purchase. Although dollars are important, other factors might prevent successful sale of the goods.

CHOOSING A CAREER AS A RESIDENT BUYER

In most retail operations the working hours of people with managerial status (buyers, department managers, and so forth) are hard to define. Stores are open for business for long hours and managers must always be available to make decisions and play all the roles they are called upon to perform. The resident buying office, while it has many important tasks to perform, is not directly concerned with the store's operation. Its main function is advisory. The

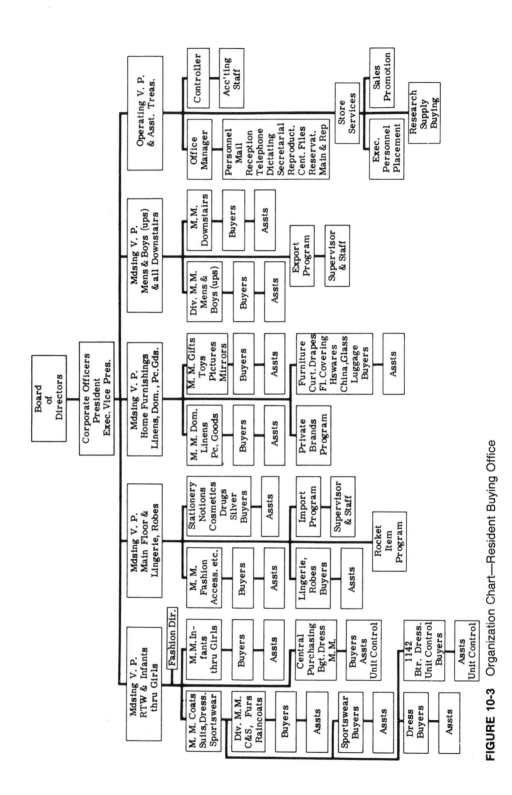

FIGURE 10-3 Organization Chart—Resident Buying Office

resident buyer's chief concern is supplying the right information. Responsibility for crowds during the peak selling periods in the store, store hours which often run to 9:45 on five evenings a week, and special promotions to sell slow-moving merchandise are the concern of the store's buyer. The resident buyer's job is typically that of an office worker: 9:00 A.M. to 5:00 P.M. and no Saturdays. Many people would find that a career in a resident buying office affords a good challenge, a salary a little less than a store buyer, but a work week that might be more to their liking.

The buying office, in addition to those positions primarily concerned with purchasing, also offers positions in personnel management, advertising, accounting, sales promotion, display, and secretarial work. An examination of an organization chart (Figure 10-3) of a leading office should give insight into the many tasks performed and careers available in the resident buying office.

Action for the Independent Retailer

The counterpart of the independent retailer is the independent resident buying office. For a nominal fee, the retailer can receive a wide variety of service assistance as well as a market representative to do some purchasing. Without investing in specialists to participate in the management of the store, the independent retailer can be satisfactorily served through resident office affiliation.

One should join an office that provides only those services that are sought. For example, if market representation is all that is required, a more expensive office that offers other services would be a wasteful cost.

Joining a resident office will not only provide pertinent information, but it can also free the store buyer from making many trips to the market and thus permit more attention toward the store. Thus, although membership involves a cost, it can also provide a savings by allowing the buyer to perform other in-store functions sometimes necessitated by hiring part-time personnel. If soundly used, a resident office could provide the professional advice generally out of the independent's reach.

IMPORTANT POINTS IN THE CHAPTER

1. *A resident buying office is an organization located in the heart of the wholesale market. It performs many buying services for small stores and stores whose geographic locations make coming to the market difficult.*

2. *Since there are a wide variety of sizes and types of resident buying offices, a retailer must select an office that is uniquely fitted to its buying needs.*

3. *Among the functions of the resident buying office are placing and following up orders, arranging adjustments, locating new resources and items, helping prepare displays and special events, and preparing for the buyer's periodic visits to the market.*

4. *Foreign resident buying offices serve domestic retailers who are unable to shop foreign markets.*

5. *Merchandise brokers are paid a commission by manufacturers for the orders they bring in.*

REVIEW QUESTIONS

1. In what ways can it be more advantageous for a large retailer to be part of a group owning a "semiprivate" office than to operate a completely private office?
2. Define the term "independent buying office."
3. Which type of office is generally associated with the giant retail organizations?
4. On what basis are members charged for the services of an independent office?
5. Why is it emphasized that retailers should not belong to the same office as their competitors?
6. Of what importance is the merchandise specialization of the resident office to the retailer?
7. Do resident buyers ever actually purchase merchandise? In which cases?
8. Is it likely that the resident office can more easily arrange adjustments with vendors than can the individual retailer? Give an example.
9. Where are the resident buying offices located? For what reason?
10. Are resident buyers ever located abroad? What purpose does this serve the store?
11. If the resident buyer is able to easily locate new resources, why isn't it as easy for the store buyer?
12. How can the resident office satisfactorily notify a member store of a "hot" fashion item?
13. Is window display work a part of the resident buying office's job, if there is not direct store responsibility? Explain your answer.
14. In addition to the use of brochures and pamphlets, describe two techniques used by the resident offices to help train retail stores' salespeople.
15. Where are notices of "buyers' arrivals" published? What purpose do they serve?
16. Does the resident buyer accompany the store buyer to market? Why?
17. Define "private brand" merchandise.
18. What are some advantages of carrying "private brand" merchandise?
19. Compare the duties of the store buyer with the resident office buyer.
20. In addition to the buying positions, in what other capacities do people work in resident buying offices?
21. Differentiate between the manner of payment for resident buying services and merchandise broker services.

CASE PROBLEMS

CASE PROBLEM 1

Clement's, Inc. is a large department store chain with 35 full-size department store units. They are located in the Middle Atlantic States, with their main store, from which top management operates, located in Philadelphia. The organization has been functioning under the control of its original founders, the Clement family. Their policies over the years have been rather conservative, and sales are beginning to decline. After complete analysis it was recommended that the organization either affiliate with a few other stores to organize a somewhat private buying office, or form its own completely separate buying office with branches in all the major resource markets. As strange as it might appear, Clement's has until now completely depended upon its store buyers to make purchases and scout the market. The research report suggests that their problem concerns merchandise selection and other merchandising matters.

The Board of Directors have met for several weeks, convinced that they must use resident buyers, but have reached a stalemate concerning which type of organization to develop.

QUESTIONS

Keeping in mind that Clement's is a very large conventional department store carrying the full complement of hard goods and soft goods, in prices that range from budget to high price:
1. What are the advantages of forming a completely private office?
2. Which benefits will Clement's lose if they have their own office?
3. After considering their present position, which type of structure would you recommend? Why?

CASE PROBLEM 2

ATC, the American Trading Company, is an independent resident buying office specializing in children's wear. They have been in operation for five years and represent about 200 small children's retail shops throughout the country. They offer many of those services typical of resident buying offices, but their main problem has been their inability to provide enough personal attention for store buyers during market week. The total volume of the member stores combined does not warrant a larger number of resident buyers, and during market week it is impossible to assign every member a resident buyer. The rest of the time store buyers are busy at their respective stores and only occasionally come to market.

ATC charges less than the large offices with full staffs, which makes it possible for these small stores to afford membership in the group. An increase in their fees would eliminate most of their clientele.

In an effort to keep the fees low and service at a level necessary to satisfy their members, ATC is looking for a plan to put into operation only during market weeks to ensure customer satisfaction.

QUESTION

1. Present a plan that would allow ATC to maintain its present buying staff but would solve the problem it faces every market week.

11 *merchandise pricing*

BEHAVIORAL OBJECTIVES

Upon completion of this chapter the student should be able to

1. *Define markup and achieve the grade of 70% on an examination requiring the calculation of markup based on cost and on retailing, inventory turnover, and markdown percent.*
2. *List eight factors that affect pricing.*
3. *Explain the advantages and limitations of merchandise inventory turnover.*
4. *Define price lines, listing four advantages of their use.*
5. *List and discuss five reasons for markdowns.*
6. *Discuss the timing of markdowns, including automatic markdowns.*

INTRODUCTION

There are as many different policies involving merchandise pricing as there are types of retail operations. Top management usually decides on a general policy to be followed by those responsible for the departmental operations. Although policies are generally set, each buyer may exercise some freedom in pricing his or her merchandise. For example, the misses' coat and suit department might work on an average markup (the difference between cost and selling price) of 42 percent. This does not prevent buyers from putting a 50 percent markup on merchandise they feel has great appeal or a 33⅓ percent markup on something that will attract more customers at that price. Top management is more concerned with the total profit picture for each department than individual prices and markups.

In addition to being concerned with how much to mark goods, retailers must establish the type of prices they are going to use. For example, traditional department stores generally end their prices with "95"; that is, $5.95, $10.95, $22.95, and so on. Most prestige Fifth Avenue retailers use the whole dollar figure, such as $10 or $25. On the other hand, many discounters end their prices with "99." The image of the store usually plays a part in determining which type of pricing to use.

Whatever the pricing policy is for a retail organization, it rarely changes. Customers expect certain prices at certain stores. Once these are set in the minds of customers, a change is unlikely unless the entire organization is to undergo change.

MARKUP

Markup is the difference between the amount that is paid for goods, and the price for which the goods are to be sold. In retailing, where profits are only made through selling, the markup must be high enough to provide for all of the expenses of operating the store plus a profit. For example, a store with merchandise on hand that cost $100,000 and operating expenses of $25,000 must sell the goods for $125,000 to break even. The store's profit would depend upon the amount in excess of $125,000 for which the goods can be sold.

Whatever the selling price, the markup will be the difference between cost of the goods and its selling price, or:

$$\text{Selling Price} - \text{Cost} = \text{Markup}$$

A dress purchased for $25 and offered for sale at $40 would have a markup of $15.

$$\text{Selling Price } \$40 - \text{Cost } \$25 = \text{Markup } \$15$$

The determination of the cost of the goods frequently requires calculation.

Illustrative Problem

A store purchases 100 sweaters at $10 each. They must pay incoming freight on the order of $12, and they are entitled to a quantity discount of 10% and a cash discount of 2%. What is the cost per sweater?

Solution

Cost of goods purchased 100 × 10 =	$1,000.00
Less quantity discount 10%	100.00
	$ 900.00
Less cash discount 2%	18.00
	$ 882.00
Add freight costs	12.00
Actual cost of 100 sweaters	$ 894.00
÷ 100 = Actual cost per sweater	$ 8.94

Note that the cash discount is taken before freight is added on, and after the quantity discount has been taken. The reason for this is that the cash discount is given for prompt payment of the amount of cash due on the merchandise, and vendors do not allow discounts on freight. The rule in determining costs is to adjust the price by all additional costs and reductions.

Although it is important to know the dollar markup, buyers and merchandisers whose responsibility it is to set markup are more concerned with markup percentage.

The markup percentage can be based on either retail (selling price) or cost. Markup expressed as a percent of retail is used primarily by department stores and fashion merchandisers. Retailers of perishables and hardware lines usually figure markup as a percent of cost.

Based on Retail

Formerly, markup was always based on cost. However, thanks to the efforts of the National Retail Merchants Association, retail research bureaus, and many universities, department stores and other alert retailers are presently using a system of markup based on sales. These are the advantages:

1. Since sales information is much more easily determined than costs, a markup based on sales greatly facilitates the calculation of estimated profits.
2. Inventory taking requires the calculation of the cost of merchandise on hand. The "retail inventory method" used by most retailers is based on markup at retail and provides a shortcut for determining inventory at cost.
3. Most retailers calculate markup based on retail. This provides interstore comparisons of such vital information as gross profit and net profit.
4. To the consumer, the smaller the percent of markup, the more reasonably priced the store. Markup based on retail provides a smaller percentage.
5. Salespersons' commissions, officers' bonuses, rents, and other vital operating data are based on sales. It is reasonable to base markup on sales as well.

To find the markup percentage based on retail, the dollar markup (the difference between the cost and the retail price) is divided by the retail price.

Illustrative Problem

A shirt that cost $13 retails for $20. Find the markup percentage based on retail.

Solution

To find the dollar markup:

$$\text{Markup} = \text{Retail} - \text{Cost}$$
$$= \$20 - \$13$$
$$= \$7$$

To find the markup percentage based on retail:

$$\frac{\text{Markup}}{\text{Retail}} = \text{Markup \% on retail}$$

$$\frac{\$7}{\$20} = 35\% \text{ markup on retail}$$

Illustrative Problem

A retail store buyer purchases a jacket for $35 and sells it for $42. What is the dollar markup? What is the markup percentage based on retail?

Solution

To find the dollar markup:

$$\text{Markup} = \text{Retail} - \text{Cost}$$
$$= \quad \$42 \quad - \quad \$35$$
$$= \quad \$7$$

To find the markup percentage based on retail:

$$\frac{\text{Markup}}{\text{Retail}} = \text{Markup \% on retail}$$

$$\frac{\$\ 7}{\$42} = 16\tfrac{2}{3}\%\text{ markup on retail}$$

If we compare the markups in both illustrative problems, we find they have the same dollar markup. By computing the percentages and comparing them, we see the importance of markup percentage to the retailer. The first markup percentage, 35 percent, was certainly better than the second, $16\tfrac{2}{3}$ percent.

Based on Cost

Although basing markup on retail has become common during the past decade, there are still retailers who use a markup system based on cost. While this is frequently the result of inertia and resistance to change, some establishments are better served by calculating markup on cost. Typical of this is a dealer in produce whose costs of fruits and vegetables vary from day to day, according to the supply and demand at the wholesale produce markets. Under such conditions, where the cost of inventories is unimportant (they completely sell out every few days) and the profit and loss figures can be easily determined, the use of markup based on cost is preferable.

To find the markup percentage based on cost, the dollar markup is divided by the cost.

Illustrative Problem

A camera cost the retailer $33 and sells for $44. Find the markup percentage based on the cost.

Solution

To find the dollar markup:

$$\text{Markup} = \text{Retail} - \text{Cost}$$
$$= \quad \$44 \quad - \quad \$33$$
$$= \quad \$11$$

To find the markup percentage based on cost:

$$\frac{\text{Markup}}{\text{Cost}} = \text{Markup \% on cost}$$

$$\frac{\$11}{\$33} = 33\frac{1}{3}\% \text{ markup on cost}$$

Hand-Held Calculators

When visiting the market to make purchases, the buyer often finds it necessary to determine the individual markup on an item, the markup percentage, the unit price, and so forth. Possibly the best tool to come along in recent years to perform these quick calculations is the hand-held calculator. For as little as ten dollars, and sometimes even less, calculators are available to perform these arithmetic chores. Not only can individual markup be derived, but so can calculations for average markup, cumulative markup, and markdowns.

FACTORS AFFECTING PRICING

As we have seen, the selling price of an item consists of its cost plus a markup that will be sufficient to yield a profit after covering the operating expenses. The prime function of management is to maximize profits. The pricing policy is the key to profit determination. This does not mean that the higher the prices, the greater the profit. It does mean, however, that management must choose a pricing policy that will result in the greatest profitability. The alternative pricing schemes range from the discounter who feels that the additional business brought into the store by low pricing will more than offset a smaller profit margin, to the high-fashion store that offers many services and a prestigious label in return for a higher price. Before a pricing policy can be selected, there are many factors that must be considered.

Buyer's Judgment of Appeal of Goods

It is unusual to find a store that uses a uniform percentage of markup for all of its goods. Even within a department, the percentage may vary from style to style. A good merchant should have a feel for pricing. This person should know what customers are willing to pay for an item, and mark up accordingly. In fact, there is frequently little relationship between the cost of an item and its customer appeal. Within certain established minimums and maximums, a buyer should set prices at what he or she thinks the goods should bring in. Bearing in mind what the competition is doing, the retailer can frequently improve the overall markup of a department by pricing certain styles in excess of the average markup. The department's average markup, rather than individual markup, is most important to the store.

If all buying decisions could be automated, it would not be necessary for retail operations to employ buyers. Most professionals, however, agree that buyers and their judgment provide in great part for the success or failure of the store. If buyers' skills were measured, their abilities to judge the appeal of goods would lie at the top of the list.

To retail an item at a fraction lower than is possible is a potential threat to profit, while marking merchandise too high could possibly result not only in lower sales, but also conceivable markdowns. It is the keenly aware buyer whose ability permits the proper price for the greatest sales potential.

Competition

One consideration to bear in mind when setting prices is the pricing policy of competing stores. Decisions must be made as to whether or not to set prices above, at, or below those of a competitor. If the services, conveniences of location, and other factors are such that consumers will pay a higher price for goods from our store than from a competitor's, perhaps we should use a high pricing policy. On the other hand, a high price policy would certainly drive some business away. How much? Does it pay to set high prices? These are the sort of problems management must face. This is an area for market research specialists.

Whatever the pricing policy selected, it is vital that a store know the prices and quality being offered by its competitors. For this purpose, stores employ comparison shoppers—people who spend their working hours studying the competition and reporting on prices, hot items, services, and other vital information.

To emphasize the importance of competition in pricing, it should be pointed out that some retailers advertise that they will meet all prices of competition. Some go as far as to refund the difference if it can be shown that merchandise purchased at their store could have been purchased cheaper elsewhere. (This is usually checked by the comparison shopper.)

To have customers find that they can buy the exact item at a lower price in a competitor's store is damaging to a retailer's image. The customers' impression is that not only were they overcharged on the item in question, but that overpricing may be the general policy of the store. To overcome this situation, retailers are forced to find, in addition to their regular goods, items on which they can mark up liberally with no fear of being undersold by a competitor. This merchandise is available as private branded items and exclusively offered goods.

Private Brands

One way to minimize competition is to sell an exclusive item, which cannot be compared in another store. It is only when a customer can find the same item, exact in every detail and carrying the same label, in two stores that prices can logically be compared. If the items are dissimilar, the higher-priced item can always be claimed to be of better quality and worth more. It is for this reason that the use of private brands is becoming increasingly important. Such stores as A & P, Sears, Roebuck and Co., Macy's, and many others do a significant amount of their total sales in brands that are exclusive to their own stores. Consider this example: A & P offers a nationally advertised brand of detergent for $.52. A nearby store charges $.47 for the exact same package. Clearly, A & P has been undersold. Now suppose that A & P arranges with the detergent manufacturer to have the merchandise packaged under an A & P brand label. Now the prices cannot be compared since, from the consumer's point of view, they are for two different items.

This illustration should not be understood as indicating that the use of private brands is a means of increasing profits at the consumer's expense. Since private brands are sold in large quantities and require no manufacturer's advertising, the retailer is able to buy the goods more inexpensively than standard brands. A & P claims that the use of private brands enables the food chain to sell for less while at the same time increasing profits.

Exclusivity

Another method of limiting price competition by the principle of exclusivity is by agreement with the manufacturer. In such a case, a dress shop in a small town gets an agreement from the manufacturer that the manufacturer will not sell to any of the shop's competitors in that town. A customer is then unable to compare prices between stores. Agreements with manufacturers are not limited to small users. In large cities with many competing department stores one can often find a style only in one store.

Characteristics of Goods

The amount of profit that various classifications of merchandise must bring in depends in large part on the specific characteristics of the goods. For example, staple goods, which are not subject to styling or seasonal losses, may be sold at a smaller markup than goods that are seasonal or perishable. Similarly, some goods are bulky and require large amounts of floor space, whereas others require expensive selling personnel. In large part, it is the nature of the goods that dictates pricing policy.

High-Risk Merchandise

High-risk merchandise is items that because of their perishability, seasonable nature, or high styling are almost certain to suffer some markdowns before finally being sold. The markup on such goods must be sufficient to cover such eventuality. This merchandise can be best described as fashion, seasonal, or perishable goods.

Fashion Goods. When we speak of fashion goods, highly styled ladies' wear comes to mind. The characteristics of this merchandise can be explained by example. The buyer of the ladies' dress department has a hot style. Ten of the initial order of fourteen were sold in two days. Since then the buyer has brought 200 pieces into the store, of which 180 have been sold. The number is now beginning to slow down and it appears that the buyer will have to mark down about ten dresses. Although the style has been highly successful, some markdowns must be taken. The markup will have to be high enough to cover both this style and other less successful numbers. Contrast this with sales in the hardware department, where staples are sold and markdowns are negligible. It is obvious that high-risk fashion goods are subject to markdowns and that to be successful, their selling price must be sufficient to cover these losses.

Seasonal Goods. Another type of high-risk goods for which the selling price must be high enough to cover future losses is seasonal goods such as bathing suits, furs, and toys. Characteristic of such goods is the fact that once the season is over, the retailer is faced with the choice of either cutting the price drastically or putting the goods aside until next year. Holding merchandise until the following season ties up capital that should be used for salable merchandise throughout the year. Moreover, held-over merchandise must eventually compete with newer styled goods; further, it has been handled, and customers may remember it from the previous year. Also, the merchandise may no longer be desirable. When retailers of seasonal goods walk around with a worried expression on their faces during an unusually rainy spring, there is good reason for it. Many stores charge high prices at the beginning of the season, under the assumption that customers who shop early are willing to pay more. This provides a cushion for the markdowns that will come later in the season.

Perishable Goods. Consider florists. They run businesses without markdowns. Once a rose is withered, it's unsalable. Florists can't sell out to the last piece, since they do not want to lose trade by not having goods available to be sold at any time. Here again we find retailers with built-in inventory losses who must price their goods at a level that will cover such losses.

A produce market where fruits and vegetables are sold faces a similar problem. These retailers, too, cannot be in business without taking inventory losses. Every day a certain percentage of produce must be drastically reduced in price or actually thrown away. This must be taken into account when prices are set.

Tradition

Traditionally, some goods command a higher markup and selling price than others. This is true despite the fact that they may be less risky, perishable, or seasonal. Men's shoes, although they are much more of a staple item, usually afford a better markup than the much riskier ladies' shoes. Apparently people are accustomed to paying certain prices for certain articles, and the retailer is able to set a price accordingly.

High-Overhead Merchandise

Certain classifications of goods, by their nature, require an unusual amount of overhead. In pricing such goods, provision must be made for any unusually high overhead costs so that a normal profit will remain after the additional expense is paid. Merchandise of extreme bulk or high value is part of this group.

Bulky Merchandise. Such merchandise as furniture and carpeting, because of its size, requires an unusually large amount of floor space, and consequently, rent expense. In marking up such goods, the selling price must be high enough to cover the excessive rent charges. As a result, traditional furniture stores usually double their costs to arrive at the selling price (50 percent on retail). Failure to set a high enough selling price would result in losses.

Precious Jewelry. The additional expenses that are required to carry a line of precious jewelry are considerable. A vault must be built to store the goods overnight. Highly paid salespersons are necessary, since the items are expensive and a knowledge of the subject matter is required. However, some of the additional overhead is counteracted by the fact that less rental area is required for a jewelry store or department than for displaying many other goods.

Merchandise Turnover

Of great importance to the pricing policy of a store is the effect that lower prices will have on sales. In a competitive economy, as selling prices decline, sales rise. Suppose store "A" does $100,000 per year at a 40 percent markup on sales. The cost of operation is $20,000. This is its income statement for the year 1980.

Sales	$100,000
Cost of goods sold	60,000
Gross margin (40%)	$ 40,000
Less: operating expenses	20,000
net profit	$ 20,000

In the year 1981 the pricing policy is changed, reducing the markup to 33⅓ percent of sales. The 1981 income statement follows:

Sales	$150,000
Cost of goods sold	100,000
Gross margin (33⅓%)	$ 50,000
Less: operating expenses	25,000
net profit	$ 25,000

A comparison of the two statements indicates that the decrease in markup resulted in an increase in sales. The larger sales required a relatively small increase in operating expenses since the rent, heat and light, advertising, and many other expenses do not vary directly with sales.

Certain merchandise is slower-moving than others. Retailers describe this by saying the stock turns over fewer times per year. A produce market sells (turns over) its stock every few days, whereas a furniture store's turnover is rarely more than a few times per year. A store with a quick turnover can afford a small markup and low prices because it will receive that markup many times during the year. This is another reason for the variation of pricing policies among various classifications of merchandise.

In Chapter 16, *Merchandise and Expenses,* a more careful look will be taken at merchandise turnover.

Promotional Activities of the Store

Another factor affecting retail pricing policies is the amount of promoting and advertising a store does. This sort of activity is expensive, and the cost of getting the customer into the store must be included in the selling price of the goods. This is not meant to indicate that the stores with the highest advertising budgets are those with the highest markup. Quite the reverse. Frequently the biggest promoters are those stores that depend upon small markups to increase their turnover and in this way pay for their promotional activities. The point is that whatever the pricing policy of the store, the markup must be sufficient to cover the advertising budget. Should each individual department's pricing policies be sufficient to cover its individual advertising budget? This becomes slightly more difficult since a store might be willing to break even on a department (such departments are called leaders), or even sell below cost (loss leader department), as a promotional means of getting people into the store. It is felt that a customer who is brought into the store by a leader or loss leader is likely to buy other items from more profitable departments.

Leaders and Loss Leaders

Several fundamental requirements of a good leader follow:

1. It must be an item that would interest a large number of customers. Since the purpose of the leader is to bring customers into the store, to be successful the item must appeal to a large segment of the buying public. R. H. Macy and Company uses their drug department in this fashion.
2. It must not be an item used as a leader by a competitor, since this would reduce the number of customers brought to the store.
3. The price cut must be important enough to bring the customers to the store in quantity.

There are disadvantages to the use of leaders. For one thing, the shopper may not buy anything but the leader, resulting in a loss. Some stores featuring leaders in their promotional schemes advise their salespeople to try to sell the customer regular goods. This frequently leads to customer resentment. Leader merchandising is unfair to competitors who charge a legitimate price for the same item. This last aspect is so important that many states have laws making it illegal to sell goods below their cost.

Store Image

It is wrong to assume that all purchasers are price-conscious. Many stores, particularly in the higher price ranges, are able to attract customers despite a higher than normal markup. The store's "name," for example, is more important to some customers than the prices it charges. Many shoppers willingly pay a premium to have a Lord & Taylor, Saks Fifth Avenue, or Brooks Brothers label on their garments. Other customers are willing to pay more to these prestige stores for the extra services offered, or because they like the wide assortment of merchandise, the way it is displayed, and so forth.

Prestigious stores, although they benefit from their higher than normal markup, are not necessarily more successful than their opposite number, the discounters. The prestige factor often requires a very high cost of operations. Improved sales service means more and higher-priced sales help. The store's furnishings, fixtures, displays, and so on are more expensive, as are many of their other operating expenses. Since massive clearance sales would be detrimental to their image, they have serious problems in disposing of their slow-moving goods. Consequently, although they have to some degree taken themselves out of the rat race of price competition, it is only at the cost of a new set of problems.

Other Nonprice Competition

Small neighborhood stores can often charge a little more for their merchandise in return for the convenience they offer. It is frequently worth a little more to the consumer to shop locally rather than travel downtown for a bargain. Similarly, by being open evenings and sometimes Sundays, when their competitors are closed, neighborhood stores can generally get away with higher than normal prices without losing customers.

Discounting

While prestige stores and neighborhood stores fight price competition by offering "label-appeal" and special services, the discounters are squarely in the center of the price battle, and that is exactly where they want to be. They reason this way: The one most important element in selling is price. The great majority of customers are not interested in frills. When the price is right, they'll buy. Moreover, they'll buy so much, and the merchandise will be turned over so quickly, that small profits per sale will be more than offset by the increased number of sales. The operation, then, is designed such that all expenses are held to a minimum with the exception of advertising. Since one of the functions of markup is to cover the operating expenses, less markup is required, and the goods may be sold less expensively.

In the typical discount operation one finds bare walls instead of expensive furnishings, and a minimum of customer services. Not all of a discounter's merchandise is sold at a low markup. Like more conventional retailers, the discounter sells many high-profit items. These items, of course, must be off-brands that cannot be comparison-shopped elsewhere.

Discount stores are presently found in all types of retailing. During the last decade their growth has been enormous and their impact on American retailing has been considerable.

Alterations

Once the decision on pricing policy has been made, the question of whether or not the customer is to be charged for alterations has been answered. That is, stores that have decided on an above-normal markup in return for additional services generally consider the cost of alterations as one of the services that is offered to their customers. On the other hand, a discount store that has curtailed services so that it can employ a less-than-normal markup would be unlikely to offer free alterations. There is room for compromise in this area. For example, a menswear department does not charge for shortening sleeves or cuffing trousers. However, it either refuses to do or charges extra for major alterations. In the event that alterations are to be freely given to customers, the selling prices must be adjusted to reflect this additional expense.

Goods Easily Soiled or Damaged

Toys, white gloves, and a host of other merchandise classifications become shopworn in a short period of time. They frequently require special handling on the shelves and special care from the sales personnel. Markup, by definition, must be sufficient to cover the costs of the item and provide a profit. If no provision is made in the markup for possible soilage or damage, the profit on fragile goods will be below the amount expected.

Pilferage

In recent years losses through pilferage have increased at an alarming rate. This has occurred despite a substantial increase in the cost of security maintenance. It is unfortunate that honest shoppers are forced to pay for the losses incurred through dishonest people. If a store is to be successful, its markup policy must be one that will cover the high cost of security, as well as the merchandise losses that result from shoplifting. A full discussion of pilferage was found in Chapter 8.

PRICE LINES

Most stores are not large enough to carry merchandise at all prices. Very few are able to offer a full assortment of goods that suits the needs of both the low-income and high-income family. In an effort to present a wide range of merchandise to satisfy their specific group of customers, retailers select certain "price lines" of merchandise. For example, ladies' shoes might be limited to $22.95, $24.95, and $27.95; men's gloves at $14.98, $16.98, and $18.98. Only the giant department stores and specialty chains generally offer merchandise in many price ranges.

Some advantages of setting specific price lines are

1. A wider assortment of merchandise can be offered than could be if many price lines were carried.
2. Customers are not confronted with merchandise at so many prices. Thus, selecting may be easier.
3. Customers know about how much an item will cost before they enter the store.
4. Planning purchases is easier for the store buyer.

There is no definite trend in price lines today. On one hand there are stores being established that sell only $22 and $24 dresses, a very limited price line. On the other side, there are the super department stores with a range from budget department prices to custom-made designer costs, with various price ranges in between.

MARKDOWNS

Markdowns are reductions in selling price. To fully understand the nature of markdowns one must start with the concept that the original price is nothing more than a temporary estimate of what the customer is willing to spend.

Reasons for Markdowns

Markdowns may be caused by faulty sales price, buying errors, selling and merchandise handling errors, and other reasons not related to human mistakes. When the original selling price is set at too high a level, or at a level above competitors' prices, markdowns inevitably result. Generally these price reductions are such that the final selling price is lower than the amount that the goods could have been sold for if they were properly marked originally.

Buying Errors

Many markdowns are the result of buying misjudgments. Overbuying is probably the principal cause of markdowns. It may come about through large initial orders instead of small lot ordering to test consumer appeal. Overoptimistic sales planning is another common cause of overbuying.

The inability to perfectly forecast the buying habits of a store's clientele frequently leads to markdowns. Often, goods that would be readily saleable in the proper colors and sizes cannot be sold because of these errors. This, of course, results in markdowns.

Markdowns are frequently the result of ordering goods too late in the season. Goods bought too late often cannot be sold because the customer is no longer interested.

Selling Errors

Faulty sales practices result in markdowns. Merchandise that could have been sold with proper display or salesmanship or departmental neatness is sometimes marked down and this decreases profits.

Lazy sales personnel, who take the line of least resistance by selling the fast-moving numbers instead of taking the time to sell the slower movers, cause markdowns.

Overeager salespersons whose high-pressure tactics end up in returns late in the season are a cause of markdowns.

Nonerror Markdowns

Not all markdowns are the result of errors. Some are beyond human ingenuity, others are actually planned. Occasionally, new products reach the market that make the older goods obsolete. In such cases the entire stock of obsolete merchandise must be marked down drastically and quickly.

No matter how competent a buyer is or how talented the salespeople, there will always be odd sizes and styles and shopworn merchandise that cannot be sold without markdowns.

High Opening Prices

Reasoning that a person willing to purchase early in the season will be willing to pay a premium for their purchases, some buyers set higher than normal opening prices on their goods. This both helps to make up for future losses and gets a good price from those shoppers who wait for markdowns before making their purchase.

Weather

Seasonable goods depend upon the weather. A store stocks a certain amount of merchandise in anticipation of certain weather conditions. If the weather does not behave as expected, the goods are not sold and customers must be lured in by markdown prices. In New York City, spring is short and uncertain. After a particularly rainy spring, markdowns follow as certainly as summer.

Poor Assortment

It is a bad policy for a store to offer a limited assortment of goods at any time during a season. Future sales depend on a customer's confidence in being able to always find an abundance of goods to choose from. Many merchandisers will protect the store's image by buying goods, to provide a rich assortment, late in the season. They do this knowing full well that many of the goods are destined for eventual markdown.

Timing Markdowns

Markdown or Carry Over

When the markdown required to sell merchandise becomes excessive, a merchant is faced with the decision of whether or not to carry the goods over to the same season of the following year. Frequently, the goods will bring a higher price at the beginning of the season in the following year than at the end of the current season. This fact must be weighed against the following disadvantages of carrying over:

1. The money tied up in the carried-over inventory will not be available for new styles for a full year. This will have the effect of reducing the assortment of new styles until these old goods are sold.

2. It is expensive to carry over in terms of warehousing costs, insurance, warehouse labor, and interest on money borrowed to carry additional inventories.
3. Carried-over goods tend to become shopworn or broken.
4. The store's image will be damaged in the eyes of those shoppers who remember the goods from the previous year.

Generally, well-managed stores limit their carry overs to those staple goods that are packaged in such a fashion that they will retain their fresh look in the following year. Fashion merchandise should never be carried over.

Early versus Late Markdowns

Of principal importance in the timing of markdowns is whether to reduce prices early in the season on an individual basis, or to hold the prices firm until late in the season and then have a storewide sale. There is considerable difference of opinion among retailers on the issue of when to mark down. The arguments favoring early markdowns are

1. Goods that are reduced early in the season while the customers are still in a buying mood can generally bring in more money than they would at the end of the season. Thus, the amount of markdown will be less.
2. The money brought in by early markdowns can be used for newer and better styles that may be turned over many times.
3. End-of-season sales frequently require additional sales personnel and therefore raise the cost of operations.

Arguments favoring late markdowns are

1. Customers become aware of a store's early markdown policies and will wait to make their purchase, knowing they can buy reduced merchandise early in the season.
2. Some goods that do not sell well early in the season suddenly take off and do very well. If these goods are marked down early, they will not bring in as much money as they should.
3. Prestige stores prefer not to have bargain hunters in their stores until they need them. A policy of limiting markdowns to season-ending sales accomplishes this.

Many stores compromise between early and late markdowns. When the sales of an item slow down, and the quantity on hand is excessive, it will be reduced for quick sale. At the end of the season a clearance sale will be used to clean out all of the unsold goods.

Automatic Markdowns

The policy of automatic markdowns is best illustrated by the basement store of Filene's of Boston. Filene's marks down all goods that have been in the store for a specific number of days, by a specific percentage. Goods that fail to sell after two weeks are marked down 25 percent. They are reduced an additional 25 percent each successive week. At the end of five weeks all unsold goods are given to charity.

How Much to Mark Down

Because the purpose of markdowns is to move goods, the amount of price reduction must be enough to satisfy customers. A $19.75 item marked down to $18.75 will probably not increase its sales appeal; shoppers willing to pay $18.75 would probably pay $19.75 as well. To sell the goods, a reduction to $16.75 would probably be necessary. When markdowns are taken early in the season, there is frequently time for a second markdown before the season ends. Consequently, early markdowns are usually smaller than late-season reductions. Markdowns are usually taken on an individual basis, depending on quantity, original price, and time of markdown.

Calculating Percent of Markdown

An important aspect of markdown is the markdown percent based on actual sales. The markdown percent may be calculated when the markdown from the original retail (selling price) is known.

Illustrative Problem

A retail store buyer decides to reduce the price of her entire inventory 15%. The inventory is $5,000 at retail. What is the markdown percentage based on sales, assuming she sells the entire inventory?

Solution

1. Determine the dollar markdown

$$\text{Original Retail} \times \text{Reduction Percentage} = \text{Markdown}$$
$$\$5,000 \times .15 = \$750$$

2. Determine the actual sales

$$\text{Original Retail} - \text{Reduction} = \text{Sales (New Retail)}$$
$$\$5,000 - \$750 = \$4,250$$

3. Determine the markdown percentage on sales

$$\text{Markdown \%} = \frac{\text{Markdown}}{\text{Sales}}$$

$$= \frac{750}{4,250}$$

$$= 17.6\%$$

Action for the Independent Retailer

Too often, misunderstanding the way in which markup and other factors affect pricing has adverse effects on small retailers in particular. In order to realize a profit, it is imperative to have a working knowledge of pricing principles. Retailers must cover their expenses before they can achieve profits.

Independents often cater to a narrower market than their chain store counterparts. They have the advantage of direct customer contact and should gear their merchandise purchases accordingly. Knowing firsthand the needs of the customer results in fewer markdowns.

Areas of caution include the timing of the markdown and the amount of the reduction. Smaller retailers too often wait too long and mark down at too low a rate. If a larger, earlier reduction were implemented, it would make room for newer and perhaps faster-moving merchandise. The early, substantial markdown motivates more customers to buy, freeing up "dead capital." Whereas the large chain must wait for a more bureaucratic decision, the independent has the advantage of quick action.

With the enormous expenses of the giants, it is often possible for the independent to compete on price. While services probably cannot be on the same level as those of the giant retailer, the price, if lower, could motivate the customer. Size, often an advantage in retailing, doesn't have to hinder the independent's chances for success. If all aspects of pricing are carefully explored and properly acted upon, the independent can successfully compete.

IMPORTANT POINTS IN THE CHAPTER

1. *Markup is the difference between the amount that is paid for goods and the price for which the goods are to be sold.*
2. *Although markup may be based on either cost or retail price, retailers generally base their markup calculations on retail price. This enables them to estimate gross profit when the sales for a period are known.*
3. *To make a profit, a retailer must sell goods at a price in excess of the cost of the goods and the expenses required to run the organization.*
4. *The price for which goods are offered for sale is influenced by competition, the characteristics of the goods, the risk involved in carrying the goods, and the overhead expenses required by the goods.*
5. *The rate of merchandise turnover is a tool for judging managerial effectiveness by determining the amount of inventory required to produce a certain volume of sales. Various categories of merchandise have different turnover rates.*
6. *Some stores are able to set prices above competitive levels by offering their customers such services as convenience, a high-prestige name, and alterations.*
7. *Markdowns are reductions in selling price that may be necessitated by buying errors such as overbuying, wrong color or size selection, or poor timing.*

8. Markdowns can also be caused by selling errors such as poor departmental management or a weak sales force.

9. Not all markdowns are the result of errors. Price reductions frequently are needed to move shopworn, obsolete, or oddly sized goods.

10. The problem of whether to mark down goods or to carry them over to the following season and offer them at regular price is a serious one. Most stores limit their carry overs to staple goods that are packaged in such a fashion that they will retain their fresh look in the following year.

REVIEW QUESTIONS

1. The buyers for a particular department know more about pricing their particular goods than any other person in the store. Why aren't they allowed complete freedom in setting pricing policies?

2. Define markup.

3. An invoice of $810, including $10 freight, must be paid. A quantity discount of 12% and a cash discount of 2% are allowed. Calculate the amount of the check.

4. A poker table and four chairs cost $95. If the buyer retails it for $150, what markup percentage on retail will the store achieve?

5. Lamps that cost $25 retail for $45 at the Atlas Furniture Shop. What is the store's markup percentage on retail?

6. The swimsuit buyer for Brandt's Specialty Shop buys a dozen swimsuits for $156. If the suits are marked up 48% of cost, what would each suit retail for?

7. A supermarket purchasing agent buys a gross of potted plants for $432. At what price should each plant be retailed if the agent wants a markup of 35% of cost?

8. Explain the effect of competition on pricing.

9. Explain the effect on retail prices of an "exclusive agreement" between the retailer and the vendor.

10. Why must special pricing consideration be given to seasonal goods?

11. Discuss the pricing of precious jewelry. Why should it be different from the pricing of regular merchandise?

12. Discuss inventory turnover as an indication of sound inventory control.

13. Explain the effect of pricing on a store's "image."

14. Some very successful retailers set prices above those of their competitors. Why are some consumers willing to pay these higher prices?

15. Give three examples of markdowns that could have been avoided by proper buying decisions.

16. Discuss two instances of markdowns that are the result of inefficient department management.

17. Buyers are frequently faced with the alternative of marking down or carrying over until the next year. Discuss this in relation to high fashion goods and staple goods.

CASE PROBLEMS

CASE PROBLEM 1

Liquor stores are a unique type of retail operation in that, with the exception of a few private labels, all stores carry the exact same merchandise. In New York State liquor stores are privately owned and the retail prices suggested by wholesalers yield a gross profit rate of about 25%.

Carl's Wines and Liquors has operated successfully for 35 years as a small neighborhood store. Retail prices have been set at the levels suggested by wholesalers, and Carl has saved enough money to retire in the next few years.

A recent change in the state laws enabled a competitor with a cut-price policy to open a store within a block of Carl's. This has resulted in a shrinkage of Carl's annual sales by 40%. Carl has maintained his pricing policy in the belief that his old customers would stand by him. His competitor has been operating for two years, and Carl has reason to believe that he is losing money. Carl is barely breaking even at his reduced volume, and any cut in prices without increasing volume would put his store into the "red" and require money he has set aside for his retirement.

Carl would like to sell his store and retire now, but at the present sales level the store is unsalable.

QUESTION

1. What might Carl do to remedy this situation?

CASE PROBLEM 2

Eight years ago the Buy-Rite Sales Corp. opened a large discount store in a rapidly growing suburban area. It sells appliances and housewares at discount prices, and its clientele consists of homeowners who are attracted by the store's low prices. Since most of the new homeowners in the area are price-conscious, the store is very successful.

The store's aggressive management is constantly searching for areas in which to expand and is presently considering a suggestion from the houseware buyer that it take in a nationally advertised line of kitchenware that will not be sold at a reduced price. The buyer argues that the line is very successful in other stores and that Buy-Rite's heavy customer traffic would ensure success. Moreover, the customers are changing from price-conscious new homeowners to more established homeowners who are more selective in their buying habits.

QUESTIONS

1. What effect will carrying these items have on the store's reputation for underselling?
2. The kitchenware is too expensive to be bought on impulse. Would a customer planning to buy the goods be more likely to go to a traditional store?
3. The merchandise is frequently bought as a gift, and the store does not maintain a wrapping department. Will that hurt sales?
4. The store is doing better than ever, indicating that there is no lack of price-conscious customers. Are these people interested in that type of goods?

IV building and maintaining the retail clientele

12 *advertising*

BEHAVIORAL OBJECTIVES

Upon completion of this chapter the student should be able to

1. *List four outside organizations that offer advertising services to the small retailer.*
2. *List in sequence the steps required for a buyer in a large retail organization to place an advertisement.*
3. *Differentiate between promotional and institutional advertising.*
4. *Give four advantages and three disadvantages of newspaper advertising.*
5. *Discuss magazine advertising, explaining the type of retail organizations that use this media and why they do so.*
6. *Understand the legal aspects that affect advertising.*

INTRODUCTION

Retailers make the consuming public aware of their organizations and merchandise offerings through any number of devices. Most professionals agree that advertising, in one form or another, is the key to spreading the word. The sums spent for advertising vary, of course, from company to company, with such factors as size, merchandising philosophy, location, competition, and business conditions being given consideration before a budget is decided upon. It should be understood that advertising is only one part of an overall promotion budget that management must apportion, which includes display, special events, and publicity. Advertising, though, is considered to be the heart of the retailing promotional package.

As defined by the American Marketing Association, "advertising is any paid for form of nonpersonal presentation of the facts about goods, services, or ideas to a group." By comparing advertising with some other promotional techniques, its concept is more easily understood. Publicity is free, while advertising is paid for; display actually shows the merchandise, but advertising merely tells about the goods through words and illustration.

RESPONSIBILITY FOR ADVERTISING

Large stores generally have their own advertising departments. They may be independent departments or a part of a larger sales promotion department. Small retailers, who are either unable to afford their own advertising departments or find it unnecessary because of the limited amount of advertising they do, make other arrangements to satisfy their needs.

Store-Operated Advertising Departments

The size of the advertising department varies according to the size of the organization and the type of advertising it engages in. Figure 12–1 shows a typical advertising department in a large retail organization. Figure 12–2 is a chart that would be appropriate for a giant in the field, with advertising spread over various media.

Whatever the organizational structure of the advertising department (and these examples are by no means the only ones in operation), their functions are the same. They are completely responsible for the planning and preparation of advertising. Planning includes all the research necessary to ensure successful results (discussed more fully in Chapter 19). The preparation of the advertisement includes such areas as the following:

1. *Writing copy.* Copy is the written text that is usually found in the advertisement.
2. *Artwork.* This involves the creation of the illustrations, either by photographers or by artists who prepare sketches.
3. *Production.* After the creative aspects such as the illustration and copy have been arranged and presented in a layout (the overall arrangement of the ad), the next step is to set it up for printing. The people involved in this part of advertising must have complete knowledge of the various printing processes. Since retailing managers rarely become involved in it, the more formal aspects of production will not be discussed.

The smaller advertising department depends upon a limited number of persons to perform all of the advertising responsibilities. Therefore, each per-

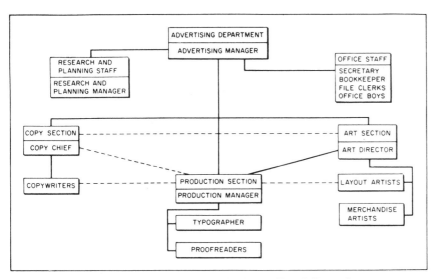

FIGURE 12-1 Advertising Department of a Large Retail Operation

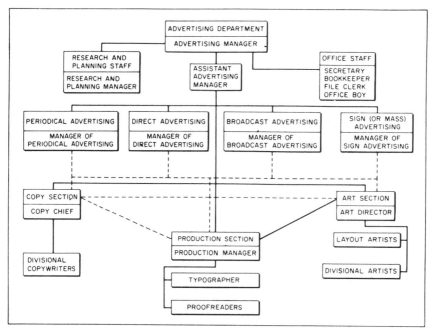

FIGURE 12-2 Advertising Department of a Giant in the Retail Field

son must be proficient at more than one advertising task. For example, one person might create the artwork and the accompanying copy. In the very large department, specialization is prevalent.

Small Store Advertising Arrangements

It would be impossible for a small store to afford its own advertising department. Such a department would be completely unnecessary because of the limited amount of advertising it would be required to generate. There are a number of outside organizations that offer advertising services to the small retailer.

Advertising Agencies

The advertising agencies offer complete service ranging from the execution of a single advertisement to a complete advertising campaign. Remuneration to the agency can be in the form of an allowance or a discount on the space they purchase for their customer from the various media (that is, they receive the difference between what the store would pay directly to a newspaper and the price they actually pay for the space), or it can be a flat fee.

Wholesalers and Manufacturers

The wholesaler and manufacturer, who are only as successful as the retailers to whom they sell, sometimes offer advertising assistance. Most commonly, manufacturers offer advertising mats (paper composition printing plates) to their customers with complete layouts of artwork and copy, and space for the retailer to insert the store's name.

Free-Lancers

A free-lancer is an individual who will prepare a complete advertisement. The free-lancer is generally experienced in one aspect of advertisement preparation, such as layout, and engages others to execute the artwork and copy, which the free-lancer then arranges in the ad. Free-lancers usually specialize in one type of merchandise, such as children's clothing or groceries.

Media Services

Generally the media, in addition to selling space or time, offer complete advertising service to their retail customers. Their services range from the planning stages to the actual preparation of the advertisements. The media are continuously involved in research so as to better service the needs of their clients. For example, their research will offer such information to retailers as characteristics of a newspaper's subscribers. This is invaluable information when selecting the proper newspaper in which to advertise.

PREPARATION OF THE ADVERTISEMENT

In stores where there are advertising departments, the advertising specialists are responsible for the preparation of the advertisement. The buyer, though, determines which merchandise is to be advertised. In some large operations the buyer works in conjunction with the merchandise manager in making the decision. Since advertising cannot sell merchandise that people don't want but *can* improve the sale of desirable goods, only the buyer, with more knowledge about the goods than anyone else in the store, should select the items to be promoted. Small, inexperienced retailers often waste promotional funds by advertising slow-moving merchandise in the hope that these goods will sell.

In the small store the proprietor usually provides all the pertinent information concerning the merchandise to the outside agency. This information includes merchandise specifications such as price, color, fabric, sizes, and anything else peculiar to the specific item. The remainder of the advertising tasks are performed by the company charged with the creation of the ad; final approval rests with the proprietor.

In large retail organizations, a procedure along these general lines is followed:

1. The buyer fills out a request form similar to the one pictured in Figure 12–3.

   The buyer only completes the form after carefully checking to see that there are sufficient funds available in the budget for the advertisement. In the appropriate areas on the form the buyer fills in the information about the item and lists other features of the goods that are important enough to be mentioned in the ad. For example, noting that a suit is "wash and wear" might make it more appealing for travel. Similarly, if a dress was designed by a famous European couturier, it probably would be attractive to a high-fashion clientele.

   Before becoming committed to the advertisement of a particular item, it is extremely important that the buyer make certain there will be sufficient quantities available in the department when the advertisement is printed. Many times buyers have found themselves in the embarrassing and aggravating position of having a successful advertisement only to find that the goods are out of stock. Besides being inconvenienced, customers often become disillusioned and do not respond to the future advertising of the store. Generally a loan slip accompanies the item to be advertised, and the completed form is nothing more than a receipt to be completed by the advertising department and returned to the buyer. In this way the buyer has a record of all goods that are temporarily out of the department.

2. The buyer sends the item to be advertised and the accompanying forms to the advertising manager. The advertising manager checks the request form to see that all the pertinent information has been provided. The advertising manager also verifies that the department has sufficient funds to produce and run the ad. Then staff members are notified of their roles in the construction of the impending advertisement. In a small company-run advertising department, the advertising manager might be responsible for copy and layout, and only the artwork would be executed by someone else. In the very large departments, different specialists in layout, copy, and art work as teams to complete an advertisement. Whatever the situation, those responsible for the advertisement consult the request form for information and often discuss ideas with the buyers when additional assistance is needed.

3. After the layout is completed and is approved by the advertising manager and the buyer, it goes to the production department. The production manager is responsible for following the orders indicated on the layout, such as the selection of type that is to be used. It is the production manager who marks instructions on the layout and sends it to the newspaper or magazine.

4. The newspaper prepares a proof (a sample of the printed advertisement) and sends it to the store. All the interested parties examine the proof and make notes on it wherever changes are necessary. Proofreader's marks, which are easily understood by everyone in advertising, are used to note such changes. The corrected proof is then returned to the newspaper.

5. After receiving the returned proof and making the corrections, the newspaper sends a final proof to the store for authorization. At this point the store gives permission to run the ad. (After the ad has been run, a "tear sheet" [actual copy taken from the publication] is sent to the store.)

6. It is at this time, if the advertisement is to be fruitful, that all the divisions of the store must work as a team. Stockpeople should be notified to replenish the advertised item's inventory, and salespeople should be made aware of the advertised

ADVERTISING REQUEST

CIRCLE ONE	Z	DI	X

THIS FORM WILL NOT BE ACCEPTED UNLESS INFORMATION IS COMPLETE

DEPT. NO.

	DATE	SIZE			DATE	SIZE
☐ TIMES			☐ COLONIE			
☐ NEWS			☐ AMSTERDAM NEWS			
☐ POST			☐ SUFFOLK SUN			
☐ L.I.P.			☐ OTHER (LIST)			
☐ NEWSDAY			☐			
☐ WEST. GRP			☐			
☐ N. H. REG.			☐			

MERCHANDISE FOR NEW ART WORK IS DUE IN 15th FL. LOAN ROOM WHEN PINK SHEET IS DUE

EXCEPTION: Ready-to-wear merchandise is due directly after weekly Merchandise Review Meeting. Bulk merchandise should be available on the floor for movement to studio, or for sketching, when called for. Merchandise in LOAN ROOM? ☐ Yes ☐ No

Do not request New Art Work BEFORE checking file FOR OLD ART.

No. of Illus.	Illustrations to be featured. Points to be emphasized
No. of New	
No. of Old	Date and medium in which old art ran last (attach proof)

OTHER MEDIA. ☐ MAGAZINE NAME_____ ISSUE_____ ☐ SALE BOOKLET ☐ OTHER DIRECT MAIL ☐ RADIO ☐ TV

MAIL ORDERS Yes ☐ No ☐   PHONE ORDERS Yes ☐ No ☐   COUPON Yes ☐ No ☐

TOTAL AMT. OF MDSE. AT RETAIL $_____ NO. OF UNITS_____ DAY SELLING IS TO BEGIN_____ NUMBER OF DAYS ON SALE_____

ON SALE AT: (CIRCLE) ALL STORES - H. S. - R. F. - HUNT. - B. S. - JAM. - W. P. - PARK. - FLAT. - NEW HAV. - QUEENS - COLONIE - NEW ROCHELLE - SM. HAV.

ABOUT THE MERCHANDISE: (NOTE: Please complete the following IN DETAIL.)

	ITEM	STYLE NO.	CURR. RETAIL	ADV. PRICE	QUOTE PHRASE & PRICE*	SIZES	COLORS
1.							
2.							
3.							
4.							
5.							
6.							

MOST IMPORTANT SELLING POINTS (from customer's view) AND SUPERIORITY TO COMPETITIVE ITEMS. (Use other side if necessary.)

IMPORTANT: PINK SHEETS WILL NOT BE ACCEPTED UNLESS THE FOLLOWING INFORMATION IS PROVIDED.

1. TEXTILE FIBER PRODUCTS	2. NON TEXTILE PRODUCTS	3. ELECTRICAL ITEMS
List all information on the product label. If available, a fiber identification tag may be stapled in place.	Copy from label or tag all information relative to composition of parts of product including finishes.	Copy all name plate ratings including volts, amps, watts, horsepower, BTU, CFM, etc. Indicate if UL approved.

THIS IS A ☐ SALE   LAST PREVIOUS DATE_____   LAST PREVIOUS PRICE_____

☐ CLEARANCE   ☐ SPECIAL PURCHASE   ☐ MFG'S CLOSE-OUT   ☐ OTHER

INFORMATION ON COMPARATIVE PHRASES: (Note: Complete in detail as applicable.)

1. ☐ "REGULARLY" - means temporary reduction. Refers to price immediately before sale and price to which merchandise will return following sale.
   (a) period during which merchandise was selling on floor at regular price_____
   (b) approximate number of units_____ Is this the normal selling rate?_____
   (c) Is stock to be augmented with merchandise which is not identical?_____

2. ☐ "ORIGINALLY" - means first price during the recent course of business. (Recent course of business is current selling season for seasonal merchandise such as apparel and sporting goods, etc. and not more than 12 months for non-seasonal merchandise such as furniture, appliances, etc.).
   (a) period during which merchandise was selling on floor at original price_____
   (b) approximate number of units_____ Is this the normal selling rate?_____
   (c) Is stock to be augmented with merchandise which is not identical?_____

3. ☐ "COMPARABLE VALUE" - merchandise of equal grade and quality in all material respects,
   OR
   ☐ "VALUE" - identical merchandise selling in other stores.
   Indicate stores at which merchandise is likely to be found._____
   If in Macy's stock, indicate style # and price_____

BUYER OR ASST. BUYER_____   MDSE. ADM. OR V.P._____   COMP. OFFICE REPRESENTATIVE_____

PART 1 ADVERTISING DEPT. COPY

FIGURE 12-3 Advertising Request Form—Macy's, New York

merchandise through a meeting with the buyer or a copy of the ad on the employee bulletin board. Even elevator operators should be notified of the whereabouts of the advertised goods if unusual traffic is expected to be generated. The display department should be contacted to arrange an interior display of the item to make it more easily located and eye-catching. Any other interested departments should be alerted, to guarantee a successful promotion.

7. Advertisements should be evaluated after they have run. Some stores carefully compare an item's sales before it was advertised and while it was being advertised. This evaluation is important to future advertising and can be checked by employing any number of research techniques, some of which are discussed in Chapter 19.

ADVERTISING TERMINOLOGY

Although it is not necessary for management to be fully knowledgeable about the technical aspects of advertising, an understanding of some of the terminology used in advertising is desirable. Comprehension of these terms will improve a buyer's relationship with the advertising department.

Point. A unit of measurement describing the height of type is the point. One point is equal to $\frac{1}{72}$ of an inch. Type that is one inch high is 72 points.

Pica. A unit of measurement describing the width of type is called a pica. One pica is equal to $\frac{1}{6}$ of an inch in width, or 12 points. Two picas would be $\frac{1}{3}$ of an inch or 24 points.

Type Face. The term *type face* refers to the style or shape of the specific type used. Different *type faces* convey different moods. For example, *Old English* is very ornate and is similar to the lettering used in old manuscripts, while *Sans Serif* offers a modern impression.

This is Futura Bold, a Sans Serif face.

This is Futura Medium, a Sans Serif face.

This is Old English Text.

CLASSIFICATIONS OF
RETAIL ADVERTISING

The type of advertising a store uses depends on the clientele served, the merchandise offered, and the image the store wishes to project. Basically there are two types of advertising, institutional and promotional. Institutional advertising (as defined here) is used to project an overall image rather than to sell a specific item. A store that advertises something other than merchandise or that promotes its numerous customer services is engaging in institutional advertising. Figure 12-4 is a Lord & Taylor institutional ad. The object of pro-

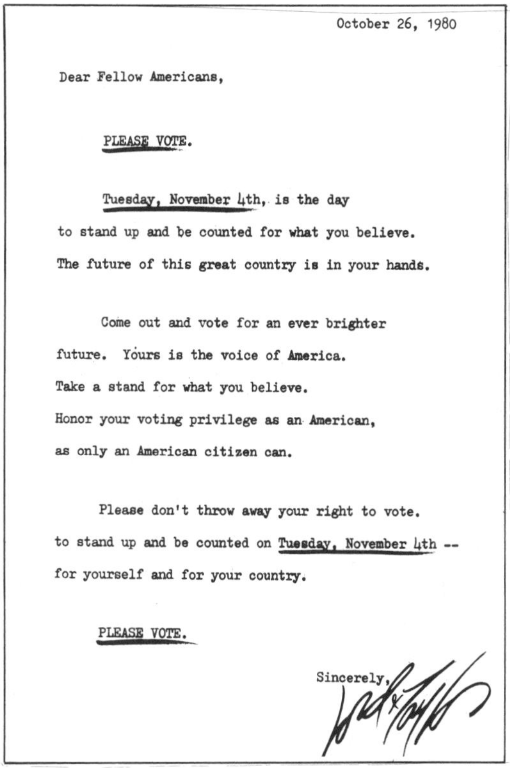
October 26, 1980

Dear Fellow Americans,

PLEASE VOTE.

Tuesday, November 4th, is the day
to stand up and be counted for what you believe.
The future of this great country is in your hands.

Come out and vote for an ever brighter
future. Yours is the voice of America.
Take a stand for what you believe.
Honor your voting privilege as an American,
as only an American citizen can.

Please don't throw away your right to vote.
to stand up and be counted on Tuesday, November 4th --
for yourself and for your country.

PLEASE VOTE.

Sincerely,

FIGURE 12-4 Institutional Advertisement

motional advertising is to promote particular items. It is promotional advertising that results in immediate business for the store. The effectiveness of institutional advertising is more difficult to measure. Figures 12-5 and 12-6 show promotionally oriented types of retail advertising.

Whichever method is used, and many organizations use both, it is important to bear in mind that neither type of advertising, if used very sparingly or irregularly, will be beneficial to the store. Advertising must be used on a continuous basis so that customers can become familiar with a store's ads and learn to recognize them quickly.

ADVERTISING MEDIA

The advertising media available to the retailer include newspapers, magazines, shopping publications, radio, television, direct mail, hand-distributed circulars, signs and billboards, car cards, and even skywriting. Some organizations make use of all those media listed (plus others), while some limit their use to one type.

Calvin Klein

for the body...for the soul.
A fragrant cologne bonus
with your Calvin Klein jeans!

Calvin Klein makes 'em sexy. Sleek, chic, western jeans. In a sensational, body-conscious shape to wear with everything from soft silk shirts to beautiful, bulky sweaters. And, to complement your dazzling image, Calvin gives you 1 ounce of his poetic, signature Natural Spray Cologne. A special gift with your purchase of this 4-pocket, western style jean (style* 1111). Navy cotton denim for sizes 4-14. $42. Designer Jeans (367)

Abraham and Straus

Brooklyn • Queens • Hempstead • Manhasset • Babylon • Huntington • Smith Haven • Monmouth • Paramus • Woodbridge • White Plains

FIGURE 12-5 Promotional Advertisement

Courtesy of Abraham & Strauss

Newspapers

The medium that receives the greatest share of retail advertising is the newspaper. Stores run the gamut of advertising from such widely distributed papers as *The New York Times* to small local publications. The decision as to which newspapers are best suited to the needs of the store can be determined through independent research or, more commonly, by calling upon advertis-

FIGURE 12–6   Combination Institutional and Promotional
Advertisement

ing agencies or the newspapers themselves for advice. Both have considerable
data on newspaper readership.

Some of the advantages of newspaper advertising are the following:

1.   The newspaper's offerings are so diversified that it appeals to almost every member of the family. Even a child looking for the funnies can be attracted by an advertisement that is of importance to him or her.

2. The cost is low when the number of prospects reached is considered. The cost per consumer is lower than any other medium.
3. The newspaper can be examined at one's leisure and therefore its life is greater than broadcast advertising. A moment away from the television set and the commercial won't be seen.
4. Newspapers enter into almost every home daily and therefore easily reach a large consumer market.

There are also some drawbacks to advertising in a newspaper:

1. Some of the readers are too far from the retail store for the advertisement to be meaningful. This problem has been lessened somewhat with the continued growth of phone order business.
2. The life of the message, while longer than radio or television, is only for a short period of time. Sometimes it's for only part of the train ride home from the office.
3. The quality of the stock (paper) used often limits the attractiveness of the item being offered for sale. Color is rarely used because of this reason.

Cost and Placement of Newspaper Advertisements

The cost of running an advertisement varies from newspaper to newspaper, depending on the size of the paper's circulation. Space is sold on the basis of the number of lines used for the ad. To determine the true value of the money spent on newspaper space, stores must figure the cost of the ad per reader. The cost per reader is determined on the basis of the "milline rate." The following formula is used to determine the milline rate:

$$\frac{\text{Rate per line} \times 1{,}000{,}000}{\text{Circulation}} = \text{Milline Rate}$$

If the rate per line is 30 cents and a paper's circulation is 300,000, then the milline rate is:

$$\frac{.30 \times 1{,}000{,}000}{300{,}000} = \$1$$

By applying this formula to the various newspapers' rates and circulation, a store can determine whether a higher line rate might actually cost less per reader.

In addition to the cost per line in newspapers, the costs vary according to placement or position of the ad. The least expensive method of advertising placement is called "ROP," "run of paper," or "run of press." This means that the advertisement will be placed at the discretion of the newspaper. "Regular position" guarantees that a store's advertisements will be placed in the same position all the time. It is costlier than ROP, but readers eventually know where to find a store's advertisements. "Preferred position," the most costly, locates the advertisement in the most desirable spot in the newspaper for that particular ad. The position may be adjacent to a pertinent newspaper column. For example, men's sporting goods advertisements would be more effective if placed next to a sportswriter's daily column. This positioning guarantees exposure to the appropriate readers.

Taking all of these factors into consideration, a retailer is often wise to run a smaller advertisement in a newspaper with a larger circulation positioned in the best location than a larger ad without these important features. After a careful examination of all the variables, the actual rate per line might not be the most important consideration.

Magazines

The magazine is infrequently used by retail stores. Only those organizations operating such prestige outlets as Saks Fifth Avenue make some use of this medium. One of the principal reasons magazine advertising is limited is that the store's trading area is generally much smaller than the market reached by the magazine and thus the store is spending (and magazine advertising is very costly) a considerable amount to reach people who are unable to become customers. Some magazines, however, overcome the disadvantage of reaching past the market. By publishing regional editions, publishers enable retailers to reach a narrower market and, thus, advertise at a lesser cost. Also, most magazines take many weeks to prepare before their publication date. Most retail stores cannot plan to advertise particular items so far in advance. Such stores as I. Magnin, Bonwit Teller, and Lord & Taylor, who do participate in long-range magazine advertising, feel that magazine advertisements in such periodicals as *Harper's Bazaar* and *Vogue* lend prestige to their operations and do bring a certain return. Also, stores such as Sears, with sufficient outlets and catalog customers available across the country, advertise in magazines. This type of advertising is more institutional than promotional and can therefore be planned well in advance of the publication date.

Independent Shopping Publications

In many cities periodicals are published primarily for the purpose of retail advertisements. *The Pennysaver,* pictured in Figure 12-7, is an example of such a publication. It is almost completely devoted to the advertising of the local retail stores. It is extremely attractive to this segment of retailing in that it is less expensive than regular newspaper or broadcast advertising and reaches a clearly defined market in which the store's customers live. These publications are either mailed to prospects in a particular area or are hand delivered to the home free of charge. Their success can be evidenced by the increasing number of shopping publications now in print.

FIGURE 12-7 Shopping Publication

Courtesy of *The Pennysaver*

Radio and Television

By comparison with the other media, broadcast advertising is still sparingly used by retailers. There is much evidence, however, that the dollar amounts spent by retailers on radio and television have increased.

Radio is showing a spurt, particularly with localized commercials. It is not unusual to hear local merchants advertise their goods as "spot" commercials on the airwaves. It should be understood that they do not sponsor complete programs but purchase commercial time throughout the day at the most appropriate time slots and on the most suitable programs for their products. For example, retailers of teen-oriented merchandise would generally choose as sponsors radio stations and programs that feature rock music.

Television is in two ways being used considerably more than before. Retailers are paying for "spots," as in the case of radio. When such TV programs as the *Merv Griffin Show* or the *Tonight Show* starring Johnny Carson pause for station identification or break for a commercial, it is often the retailer who purchases the spot. These spots are localized and perfect for the retailer who can present merchandise to a preselected, limited audience. The giant retailers are beginning to sponsor complete television shows. It is not unusual for Sears or J. C. Penney to sponsor entire television specials. Although it is costly, it serves two purposes. First, it reaches the largest market possible in the shortest amount of time, and second, it provides the retailers with a medium to replace the dying magazine field. It should be noted that only retailers with national organizations invest in complete sponsor arrangements.

Direct Mail

One of the most effective methods used to bring a particular advertisement to specific individuals is direct mail advertising. Nationally, direct mail is the third largest of the advertising media. In some retail organizations it is first. Using the mail, retailers are able to send, to both regular customers and prospective customers, a variety of direct mail pieces such as merchandise brochures, sales announcements, letters, catalogs, booklets, and circulars. At the beginning of the Christmas selling season, most major retailers distribute sales booklets that rival the production quality, size, and cost of many magazines. So successful are these pieces that many of them feature as many as 100 pages and well over 1,000 items. Not only are typical merchandise offerings made available through this advertising medium, but the unusual is also featured. The Neiman-Marcus annual Christmas book is a production that not only satisfies the needs of its affluent clientele, but also, with its unusually selected merchandise, delights other retailers and those studying retailing. In retailing circles these publications are collected and as carefully saved as many regular magazines.

Usage of both general types of direct mail continues to grow—separate

Now That You're Travelling as Two

FIGURE 12-8 Examples of Direct Mail Pieces

mailers and statement enclosure supplements. So successful is their use that retailers continue to set aside larger sums each year for direct mail production. Figure 12-8 shows some examples of direct mail advertising.

A summary of the reasons for direct mail's popularity is as follows:

1. Direct mailing pieces may be enclosed with end-of-month statements to charge account customers without incurring any additional mailing expense.
2. It permits the retailer to appeal to a particular group of people. Mailing lists can be compiled from names of satisfied customers or purchased from commercial list houses that categorize the population according to such classifications as occupation, income, education, religious background, and so on. Stores can then mail their advertisement to the group that most closely identifies with what the store offers for sale.
3. In comparison with periodical advertising, direct mail affords the retailer the undivided attention of the reader. A newspaper reader is offered many advertisements that compete for his or her eye.
4. The direct mailing costs can vary according to the budget allowance of the store, whereas the rates charged for newspaper space or television time remain constant. An announcement of a private sale to steady clientele need be nothing more expensive than a printed post card.

One of the pitfalls of direct mail is poor maintenance of mailing lists. If these lists are not continuously updated, a percentage of the mailing pieces will not be delivered. Customers who have moved are the main reason it is necessary to alter the list. If the postage is guaranteed, the post office will return all undelivered mail to the retailer. Thus, the retailer who makes use of this service can easily "clean up" the store's mailing lists. Stores often, in an attempt to solicit new customers, prepare a mailing addressed to "occupant." This directs mail to a particular address but no particular person. This system is employed, for example, when a new store begins operation and wishes to announce its opening.

Hand-Distributed Advertisements

Some of the forms used by the direct mail medium may also be hand-delivered to a store's prospects. The supermarket in particular makes extensive use of this medium. Many supermarkets distribute circulars to announce the store's weekly "specials." Since prices fluctuate rapidly in the food industry, it is important to notify the customer at what prices their "key" items are being sold during a particular period. Many shoppers carry these circulars to the supermarket as a guide to purchasing.

It should be noted that some communities have passed legislation that no longer allows hand-delivered advertisements. They consider them to be "eyesores." In these areas, merchants must distribute through the mails.

Billboards

Retailers make some use of billboard advertising. Billboards are either permanently painted or are covered with prepared advertisements that can be frequently changed. Billboard space is generally available on a rental basis, the cost being dependent upon size and location of the billboard. While it is an inexpensive medium, as the cost per observer is little, the audiences attracted are usually moving quickly (in an automobile, for example) and are not selected on any scientific basis. Newspapers, for example, have particular audiences and a retailer can select the most appropriate one. The billboard medium does not allow for such precise selection. Since the reader is aware of the billboard for such a limited period, the message must also be brief. Thus billboards are used by retailers more in an institutional manner than a promotional one. Billboard examples are pictured in Figure 12-9.

Car Cards

Car cards are advertisements that are displayed inside buses and trains. Since the number of people traveling the many public transportation systems across the country is enormous, and the time spent in these vehicles is extensive, the car card is of value to some retailers. The desired audience is easily reached by the cards being placed in the appropriate spots. For example, a high-fashion

The Spring Stuff is ready for picking at Stewart's

NOSEY BACK TO SCHOOL IN POLKA DOTS FROM STEWART'S

Santa Claus   D.J. Stewart

Our 101st Christmas Together.

FIGURE 12-9 Billboards

Courtesy of the Institute of Outdoor Advertising

ladies' shop seeking the proper clientele would locate its car cards in a commuter train originating in an affluent community.

Car card space is purchased in "runs"—full, half, quarter, and often double runs. A full run would place one card in every car, and so on.

Messages should be brief, printed in color, and lettered sufficiently large to be seen by most people in the car. Since passengers usually remain in one place for an entire trip, careful planning is necessary to guarantee a maximum amount of exposure.

Miscellaneous Media

Although the previously mentioned advertising media account for most of the advertising budget, there are additional media used by retailers. Among them are skywriting or airplane banners used to advertise nearby restaurants to people on the beach, in-store loudspeaker systems to call attention to special merchandise, station posters, neon signs, and telegrams.

Whichever and to what extent the various media are used is a challenge faced by management. Most important is that extreme care should be exercised in making these decisions.

COOPERATIVE ADVERTISING

The cost of advertising is usually alarming to the newcomer to retailing. In spite of the bite it takes from the promotional budget, advertising is necessary if a company is to be successful. One of the avenues an organization has available for expanding its advertising dollar is cooperative advertising. By definition, cooperative advertising is an arrangement in which the retailer and supplier share the advertising expense. A cooperative advertisement is easy to recognize. Not only does the retailer's name appear in the ad, but the manufacturer's or wholesaler's name is also prominently displayed.

In practice, two parties generally share the expense for cooperative advertising. The amount usually made available by the manufacturer or wholesaler is a percentage of the retailer's purchases from that company. For example:

Retailer A buys $200,000 from a manufacturer who offers a cooperative advertising allowance in the amount of 5 percent of total purchases. The allowance would be:

$$\$200,000 \times .05 = \$10,000$$

Retailer A then would receive $10,000 in advertising allowances toward $20,000 of the store advertising, or *50 percent* of the cost of the ad.

Not all suppliers offer advertising allowances, but if they do, under provisions of the Robinson-Patman Act, they must make the same offer to all of their customers.

THE LAW AND ADVERTISING

As are other industries, retailers are under the constant scrutiny of a number of governmental agencies that regulate advertising practices. Although many businesses chose to operate in the vein of caveat emptor, let the buyer beware, government at all levels has become the watchdog for the unsuspecting consumer. There are any number of practices through which retailers can color advertisements by subtly using words, or blatantly deceiving customers, with enticing offers. Whatever the reason and however the approach is taken, governmental agencies regulate retail advertisements.

Bait-and-Switch

Probably the oldest ploy for luring customers into stores is to offer attractive merchandise at lower than expected prices. In this practice a store advertises a particular product at a very low price to bait customers and motivate them to come to the store. Once the customer arrives, high-pressure selling takes over, with the store hoping to switch the customer's original want to a higher-priced product that brings in a larger profit.

Bait-and-switch advertising is illegal and carries penalties in the form of fines. Retailers who not only understand the legal ramifications of such deception, but also understand that the frustration of the disgruntled customer can lead to a negative store image, are unwise to use bait-and-switch tactics. Not only will the penalty pose an immediate cost to the company; customer unhappiness it causes could also spread through word of mouth.

Deceptive Terminology

Key words or phrases are often part of advertisements that tend to mislead readers and listeners. Comparative terminology such as *regularly, originally,* or *comparable value* are extensively used, with customers being misled about their real definitions. Generally the local governmental agency polices the use of these terms and serves notice on the retailers who abuse their placement in ads. *Regularly* indicates only a temporary reduction in price, *originally* indicates the opening or first price of an item, and *comparable value* is an indicator of a product's value in relation to similar products.

The last term is the one generally responsible for customer confusion, as it is incorrectly interpreted to imply the same meaning as *regularly* and *originally*. As in the case of bait-and-switch, misuse of terms can result in fines and customer decline.

Media Regulation

Many newspapers, magazines, television, and radio networks regulate proposed advertisements before they are accepted for production. They do this not only to comply with government regulations, but also to protect their subscribers from unscrupulous practices and to avoid any consumer backlash. Although the advertisement is the responsibility of the store, and the copy is their creation, any customer unhappiness may be attributed to the media in which the ad appeared. Media managers are aware of the problems associated with unethical practices and generally choose to police themselves.

Whether it is the Federal Trade Commission, the local department of consumer affairs, or the local better business bureau (the latter without legal bite), retailers are wise to engage in self-regulation. With the enormous amount of direct competition each retailer faces, unethical practices can only turn customers into angry bad will ambassadors.

Action for the Independent Retailer

Few independents, although aware of the benefits of advertising, pay any attention to it. Most often the reason given is the lack of available funds. Given this, enlightened independent retailers can involve their stores in advertising that requires imagination rather than a significant dollar commitment. There are many avenues available to make the appeal to customers meaningful, without spending large sums.

Independent shopping publications provide, at relatively low cost, a format that reaches the independent's target markets. Users generally agree that the returns are amazing. For the space fee alone, which is generally minimal, the publication's staff will create the copy for the advertisement. To stretch the dollar even further, cooperation from suppliers, sometimes to the extent of sharing 50 percent of the cost, is often available.

Many small retailers transact a good part of their business with private charge accounts. In those cases, adding customer notices to the end-of-month charge statements in order to announce special sales or merchandise features makes use of advertising without adding considerable expense. Since the postage is already required for statement mailing, the extra cost is only attributed to the statement enclosure. In small stores a handwritten note is often considered a perfect way to personalize this advertisement.

IMPORTANT POINTS IN THE CHAPTER

1 Retailers engage in advertising programs to make the consuming public aware of the store and the merchandise it offers for sale.

2. Advertising is any paid form of nonpersonal presentation of the facts about goods, services, or ideas to a group.

3. Large stores, which can afford to hire specialists, generally have their own advertising departments. Stores whose advertising budget is too small to support their own departments use advertising agencies for their needs.

4. Frequently suppliers and the advertising media, by supplying materials and services, help to reduce advertising costs.

5. Large retailers use carefully prepared procedures to ensure cooperation between the buyer and the advertising department. This includes follow-ups to evaluate the advertisement after it has been run.

6. Institutional advertising is used to project the image of the institution. Promotional advertising has the purpose of promoting specific items of merchandise.

7. Of all the media, newpapers receive the greatest share of retail advertising nationally. They are widely read and the advertising is inexpensive when calculated on a cost-per-reader basis.

8. Direct mail, third in importance nationally as a retail advertising medium, permits users to reach specific customers and affords the customers undivided attention.

9. Cooperative advertising is an arrangement in which the supplier and retailer share in the cost of the advertisement.

10. With many retailers engaging in unethical and illegal advertising practices, government at all levels has become the watchdog for the unsuspecting consumer.

REVIEW QUESTIONS

1. How does the retailer prospect for customers?
2. Is advertising too costly for the small retailer? Explain.
3. Why do stores advertise?
4. Who is responsible for advertising in a large retail organization? In a small organization?
5. Preparation of an advertisement includes three major areas. Discuss them.
6. In what way can a manufacturer help the retailer with advertising?
7. With whom does the advertising request begin? How does it gain the attention of the advertising manager?
8. What is an advertising "proof"? Why is it important?
9. Define pica and point.
10. How does institutional advertising differ from promotional advertising?
11. Determine the milline rate if a newspaper's line rate is 40 cents and circulation is 200,000.
12. In which newspaper position must an advertiser spend the most money? Why might the advertiser choose this space?
13. What are the advantages to a large retailer of advertising in independent shopping publications?
14. What sort of stores advertise in magazines? Why?
15. Explain the disadvantages of radio advertising for retailers.
16. Discuss the types of television advertising used by retailers.
17. Describe the method by which retailers can stretch their advertising budget.
18. What is meant by bait-and-switch advertising?
19. Differentiate between the advertising terms *regularly, originally,* and *comparable value.*
20. How is advertising regulated?

CASE PROBLEM

CASE PROBLEM 1

Carter's Emporium is a newly established retail organization that plans to open its doors to the public in approximately three months. Carter's is a ladies' specialty store, occupying two stories, with a sales expectancy of $8 million for its first year of operation. It is considered to be semipromotional in that the bulk of its merchandise will be regular-priced and sold with the aid of salespeople, while it is anticipated that about 30% of sales will result from special purchases (merchandise bought at less than the regular cost) and offered at a savings to customers.

Although the policies governing general store management procedures and merchandising have been established, there is great concern regarding the store's advertising practices. Several suggestions have been forthcoming from the general management as well as the store's own advertising department. At the present time an impasse has been reached concerning the advertising approach. General store management is of the opinion that promotional advertising would bring immediate results to the store and that the advertising should follow that route. The advertising manager strongly advocates the use of institutional advertising so that the store would be established as somewhat different from the other semipromotional stores, most of whom employ only promotional advertising. She feels that at this time, three months prior to opening their doors, institutional advertising would afford a proper response and would continue to do so on a regular basis.

QUESTIONS

1. Do you agree with either side completely? Defend your position.
2. Develop the approach that you would employ in publicizing the store through advertising.

CASE PROBLEM 2

Advertising dollars have been hard to come by for the sportswear buyer at Elayne's Department Store. The organization is a single-store operation carrying a wide variety of goods, and it grosses approximately $2.5 million per year. Since the store does more than one-half of its business in hard goods, the owner, Mr. Ellen, spends most of his advertising budget on those items. Ms. Sheri, the sportswear buyer, argues that additional money spent on promoting her merchandise would result in more than enough increased sales to warrant the expenditure. Her protests have fallen on deaf ears, while at the same time her sales have fallen slightly. Mr. Ellen, before expanding his original operation to its present structure, carried only hard goods. Since his orientation to soft goods is limited and his personality one of stubbornness, he refuses to change his position regarding the advertising budget.

QUESTION

1. If you were the sportswear buyer, what arguments might you use to change Mr. Ellen's position?

13 *display*

BEHAVIORAL OBJECTIVES

Upon completion of this chapter the student should be able to

1. *Write an essay on the three functions of a display.*
2. *List and discuss four types of window display.*
3. *Differentiate between overall lighting and highlighting, giving examples of each.*
4. *Explain the use of monochromatic, analogous, and complementary colors in display.*
5. *List five types of theme displays.*
6. *Discuss the importance of balance, emphasis, contrast, and space in merchandise arrangement.*

INTRODUCTION

Once the retailer has been successful in attracting customers to the store through advertising, it is often the visual presentation of the merchandise that convinces the customer to come in and make a purchase. For many years merchants have referred to the displays as "silent salesmen." With retailers often relying on customer self-selection, greater emphasis is being placed on display, or "visual merchandising," than ever before. What is to finally whet the customer's appetite once at the store? Good creative display is the answer for many retail stores.

In the past, the large retail organization traditionally employed a display staff. The smaller merchant arranged for periodic help from the itinerant "window trimmer." Today, with the growth of chain organizations, branch stores, franchises, and so on, a knowledge of display is a must for every store department manager and staff, since display services are not always available. Anyone entering the retail field should have some knowhow of arranging merchandise on a counter and of preparing a complete window. It is not uncommon today for managers of specialty stores, supermarkets, and other types of stores to be responsible for the execution of their displays.

A display should perform the following functions:

1. It must attract attention of the buying public. This may be achieved by the exciting use of color, dramatic lighting effects, and in-motion display. The great annual event at Lord & Taylor New York, at Christmastime, with the dancing dolls in the window or a live Santa coming down the chimney, are examples of in-motion displays.
2. A satisfactory display must hold the individual's interest, much as a newspaper advertisement must. It is not enough to stop the reader; it must make the reader investigate further. Interest is held by the display's timeliness, the merchan-

dise's appeal, and information contained in the message on the accompanying show card.

3. The display must be exciting enough to arouse the desire to further examine the merchandise (by asking to see it, try it on, and so forth). Retailers have long argued over whether display creates or arouses desires. The shopkeeper should settle for the awakening of the individual's desire to purchase.

When the window display achieves these ends, the customer will enter the store. Then, either creative interior displays will take over, or perhaps the salesperson will answer those questions still unanswered by the window display.

		Window Schedule – January	
Date	Window	Merchandise
Jan. 5	14	Avalon antron prints, Daytime Dresses.
	15	Art deco print jersey, Bobbie Brooks, Juniorite, Jr. Sportswear.
	16	Men's polyester knit slacks, Hagar, knit shirts. (12/22)
Jan. 9	1	Furniture & Accessories
	2	"
	3	"
	4	Lamps
Jan. 12	5	Bridal Lingerie
	6	Guest at the Wedding: Chiffon costumes, Young Modes, Don Sophisticates, Gold Room.
	7	Bridal Registry with Lenox.
	8	Bridal gowns: Priscilla, Pandora, Bride's Boutique Collection.
	Stage	Polyester knit dresses, long torso, moving skirts, Moderate Dresses.
Jan. 26		What a Bright Idea!
	1	Crinkle patent suits & sportswear – battle jackets, skirts, Jr. Suits & Sportswear.
	2	Crinkle patent handbags, gloves, Spring brights.
	3	Linen coatdresses, melon, brown, Sue Brett, Colette, Jr. Dresses.

FIGURE 13-1 Window Schedule—January

WINDOW SCHEDULES

All stores, no matter what their size, should develop a schedule for the display that will be presented. Through careful advance planning, each department of the store will have an opportunity to feature its desired merchandise at the most productive times of the year. In large stores, the development of such a schedule or calendar is even more important since many buyers compete for the assignment of the available windows. Similarly, the smaller the organization, the lesser the competition for display space in windows. Whatever the situation, early planning permits greater display efficiency.

Window schedules are planned as far as six months in advance, with almost every window assigned at that time. Some stores leave a small percentage of their display space unassigned to take care of last minute requirements. For example, an extended cold spell might warrant additional window space for outerwear, skis, snow shovels, or other such cold weather goods. The remainder or bulk of the windows are assigned as determined by the store's director of promotion.

The forms used vary from store to store but always include the dates of the display, the assigned window number, and the merchandise or department featured in the window. Figure 13-1 depicts a window schedule for the month of January for a large department store.

Some stores also include in the schedule the type of props to be used, requirements for the sign shop, and so forth.

Many retailers, in addition to the calendar type schedule, also publish a floor plan of the various windows and indicate in each window space what is

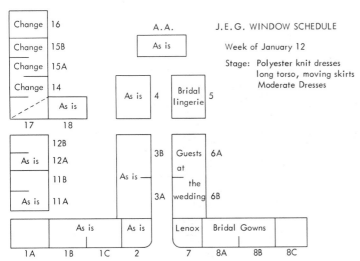

FIGURE 13-2 Window Floor Plan—January 12

to be displayed, what is to be changed, and what is to remain as holdovers from previous displays. Figure 13-2 shows such a window floor plan for the same department store as featured in Figure 13-1. Close examination shows its conformity to the week of January 12 on the window schedule.

TYPES OF WINDOW STRUCTURES

There are about a half dozen different types of window structures presently being used by retail stores. While it is unlikely that many department managers will have a voice in determining which type their store should have (since most will be in existence long before you begin your job), nevertheless, a familiarization with the various types is important as background. Perhaps, with the tremendous growth of branch stores and with chains opening so many additional units, managers will have increasingly meaningful input concerning the structure of the store windows.

Enclosed Mall Windows

The dominant trend of enclosed shopping malls has dictated a continued growth of a new type of window for stores in the mall. By its nature, the mall structure eliminates the formal physical barriers necessitated by stores built as free-standing units where doors separate the store interior from the outside, and formal windows, later discussed, are used to display the merchandise.

FIGURE 13-3 Parallel-to-Sidewalk Window

FIGURE 13-4 Arcade Windows

In the enclosed malls, there is a tendency for retailers to build a large opening, or doorway, for ease in customer access. This opening, sometimes very large, often uses the space previously allocated for windows. In such situations, the interior of the store itself serves as the "window" for the customer to see. Although this arrangement is being used with considerable success by many merchants in malls, others continue to use the more traditional structures as discussed next and featured in the accompanying illustrations.

Parallel-to-Sidewalk

The straight front or parallel-to-sidewalk window is most typical of large department stores. This type features a good deal of frontage on the street. (See Figure 13-3.)

Arcade Windows

The arcade window extends from the building, with the store's entrance set back between two windows. This arrangement allows the store with less frontage to increase its window space in which to show merchandise. It is a quite popular structure for small stores. (See Figure 13-4.)

FIGURE 13-5 Corner Windows

FIGURE 13-6 Island Windows

Corner Windows

This type is usually considered the most desirable by retailers. Since the window actually faces two streets, it allows for the greatest amount of converging traffic. (See Figure 13-5.)

Island Windows

Stores with very large vestibules, formed by locating two arcade windows facing each other, often build island windows in the center of the vestibule or lobby. These are windows, either built down to the ground or elevated, with glass on all sides. They permit shoppers to walk completely around and see the merchandise from all angles. They often present the display person with problems in showing the merchandise. (See Figure 13-6.)

Angled Windows

This window usually follows a slight angle from the building line of the store to the entrance, which has been set back from the street. It is actually a variation of the parallel-to-sidewalk window but allows for more interesting design. (See Figure 13-7.)

FIGURE 13-7 Angled Windows

The heights of the windows vary, as do the heights of the superstructures (the height between the ground and the base or floor of the window), depending upon the type of merchandise the store sells. Typically, women's ready-to-wear, furniture, menswear, and appliances have the highest windows, ranging from eight to eight and a half feet, with superstructures about twelve to eighteen inches off the ground. Jewelry shops usually are at the other extreme, with window heights of from four to six feet, with their bases about three feet from the ground. This permits shoppers to get a closer view of the merchandise. Other lines of goods usually fall somewhere between the two extremes. There are no specific rules attached to the determination of a window's height, except that small goods usually occupy a shorter window height and large merchandise a greater height.

INTERIOR DISPLAY

In recent years, especially with the "no-window" concept seen in the enclosed malls, more and more attention and money has been earmarked for interior display. Stores, especially the larger institutions, have made significant efforts to dress up their interiors. Great sums are usually expended to transform the entire store into a particular seasonal or holiday atmosphere. This responsibility is generally that of the display department.

In addition to the overall display theme, individual departments are pay-

FIGURE 13-8 Mannequin and Merchandise Rack

Courtesy of D. G. Williams, Inc.

ing considerably more attention to the display of merchandise within the confines of their allocated space. A variety of new and unique display props is available to artistically feature merchandise on walls, counters, display cases, floors, and so forth. Some incorporate mannequins into the display. Figure 13-8 depicts an interior display piece that features a mannequin wearing an item, and accompanying merchandise that the customer can easily select. Such a display immediately satisfies the customer's need for the particular item.

DISPLAY FIXTURES

These fixtures are the devices on which merchandise can be shown to its best advantage. The fixtures can be either forms that simulate the human figure or parts of the figure, or various types of stands, platforms, pedestals, and discs, which are used to drape and elevate the merchandise. In order to prepare a display, one must be familiar with these fixtures.

Human Form Fixtures

Mannequins are used to display an entire outfit. Men's, women's, and children's forms are available in a variety of materials, such as plastics, plaster of paris, burlap, velvet, raffia, papier maché, rubber, and wood. They range in design from lifelike replicas of humans, complete with imaginative hair stylings, to stylized forms, such as mannequins without facial features or with strawlike hair. In selecting the proper mannequins for a retail store, the store's image should be kept in mind. For example, a store catering to teenagers would hardly select conventional lifelike mannequins. Similarly, the typical ladies' shop located in a Midwestern shopping center most probably wouldn't pick the stylized variety. Large department stores, some with hundreds of mannequins, often have all the types mentioned. Their wide variety of merchandise necessitates this collection of human forms. The retailer with a display budget that only occasionally allows for the purchase of new mannequins, and with a narrower assortment of merchandise than the department store, should select those forms that most typify the store's image. The greatest percentage of human forms purchased today are plastic and lifelike. The plastic is lightweight and chip-resistant, and the lifelike variety is more easily accepted by the majority of consumers. Figure 13-9 shows some of the realistic as well as stylized heads available today. Figure 13-10 features the newer action-type mannequin. Figure 13-11 displays a variety of children's mannequins.

In addition to the full figure mannequin, the following human forms are

FIGURE 13-9 Realistic and Stylized Heads of Mannequins

Courtesy of D. G. Williams, Inc.

FIGURE 13-10 Action Mannequins—Joggers

Courtesy of D. G. Williams, Inc.

FIGURE 13-11 Children's Mannequins

Courtesy of D. G. Williams, Inc.

also used extensively in display. All come in the same materials as do the mannequins.

1. *Woman's torso or ¾ form.* Used for bathing suits, jackets, suits, lingerie, blouses, and skirts.
2. *Man's suit form.* Used for suits and sports jackets. Traditionally, this form is used a great deal more than a full man's mannequin.
3. *Woman's shoulder head form.* Used for millinery, scarves, jewelry, and hair ornaments. (Usually these forms are abstract or stylized.)
4. *Woman's blouse form.* Used to display blouses, sweaters, and lingerie.
5. *Woman's hand.* Used to display gloves, jewelry, scarves, and watches. It is also used extensively to drape merchandise such as blouses, skirts, slacks, and sweaters.
6. *Hosiery legs.* Used to display hosiery and socks.
7. *Shoe form.* Used for shoes and slippers.

Figure 13-12 shows some typical forms.

Adjustable Stands

These stands are devices that can be adjusted to various heights and to which several attachments can be secured for displaying dresses, blouses, lingerie, hosiery, textiles, table linens, and so on. The stands come in several sizes and can be adjusted as follows:

> 9-inch adjusts up to 18 inches
> 12-inch adjusts up to 24 inches
> 24-inch adjusts up to 48 inches
> 36-inch adjusts up to 72 inches

To these stands the most frequently used attachment is the "T" rod. When used in combination, it is called a "T" stand. Blouse forms and display hangers are also used for displaying with these stands.

In Figure 13-13 are examples of interior display units that attractively feature gloves, millinery, and scarf displays. These units permit customer "touching," which often contributes to the motivation for buying. One important aspect of these units is the ease with which anyone can dress them. A professional display person is not needed for changing the items as often as necessary.

Pedestals and Platforms

To achieve a variety of heights, pedestals and platforms in various sizes and shapes are used. These devices elevate the merchandise to the desired height to enable the merchandise to be shown to advantage.

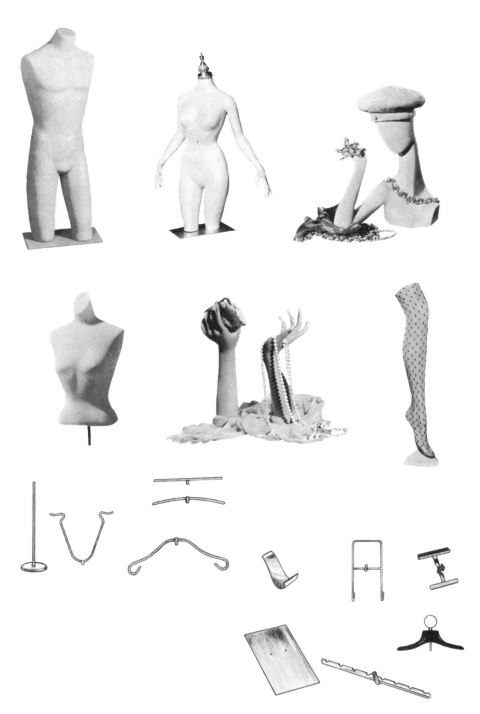

FIGURE 13-12 Human Forms and Adjustable Stands Used Extensively
Courtesy of Selrite Corp.

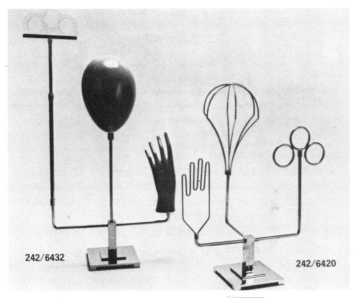

242/6432

242/6420

**242/6432 Scarf, Millinery,
and Glove Displayer**

**242/6420 Glove, Millinery,
and Scarf Displayer**

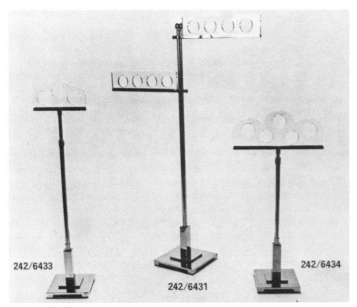

242/6433

242/6431

242/6434

**242 / 6433 Adjustable
Chrome and Lucite
Scarf Displayer**

**242 / 6431 2 Arm
Scarf Displayer**

**242 / 6434 Adjustable
Chrome and Lucite
Scarf Displayer**

FIGURE 13-13   Scarf, Millinery, and Glove Displayers

Courtesy of D. G. Williams, Inc.

The pedestals are generally available in clear plastic, wrought iron, wood, chrome, and brass. The majority of platforms (the fixture used atop the pedestal) are made of glass or clear plastic.

A complete understanding of the display fixtures previously discussed and the infinite variety of combinations achieved by assembling and reassembling them is of utmost importance in display. Not only are the stands adaptable to different devices (hangers, "T" bars, and so on); mannequins' arms can also be interchanged, positions can be adjusted, wigs can be changed to fit the merchandise, and so forth. One need only to go down to the local department store and watch the display people manipulate the fixtures in preparation for a new display to realize the many ways in which these fixtures can be used.

Most important in the interior display is that the featured merchandise be available for purchase. While windows often cannot be changed to coincide with the sale of all of the displayed items, since a display person's services might be required, interiors can be changed more frequently. Department managers, assistants, and sales personnel can easily make the changes as needed. A simple knowledge of the workings of such display properties as mannequins, stands, pedestals, and other props can make almost any store employee adept at interior display. Featuring merchandise that is no longer available is a waste of valuable display space.

LIGHTING

To carefully prepare the most beautiful merchandise, display fixtures, and background materials and then not pay attention to proper lighting is to completely destroy a display. Without lighting effects, the theater could never achieve the desired moods. Similarly, displays cannot be complete without good lighting.

Overall Lighting

To add general light (overall light) to a display satisfactorily, either incandescent or fluorescent lighting may be used. In both cases, the fixtures should be recessed into the ceiling. These lights should be used both in daylight and evening hours. In addition to illuminating the display, the overall lighting can overcome any glare. This general lighting should use only white bulbs. Colored lighting effects should be achieved through highlighting with adjustable spotlights, but such special effects must always be used with extreme care to get proper results.

Highlighting

Spotlights, either mounted behind a valance or frame in a window or placed on the floor, should be used to highlight the focal point of the display. This will set the mood and bring attention to an explanatory show card. For the novice, white spotlights are best. They throw a direct, bright, colorless, narrow beam in the direction pointed. Color, while most effective in display, can be disastrous if not employed correctly. Use of the wrong color light will change the color of the merchandise. In the theater you may have seen, purposely staged, the colors of costumes changed many times with lighting. For theatrical showmanship this is useful, but a customer entering a store and asking for the color seen in the window should find that color.

The important rule to remember when using colored light (achieved by using colored bulbs or, more commonly, by attaching colored gels, or colored transparent sheets, over white bulbs) is to use only lights of the same color as the merchandise you wish to highlight. A red light on a red dress will intensify the color; a different light will change the color.

With attention paid to these simple lighting fundamentals, a display can be well lighted and exciting enough to attract customers. With some experience and experimentation, more dramatic effects can be achieved. And drama is an attention-getter.

COLOR

Whether you are preparing to display merchandise in a showcase, on a counter top, or in a window, the correct color coordination of merchandise is necessary for an eye-catching presentation. In addition, the colors selected for the copy cards (poster giving pertinent information, accompanying the display) must be those easiest to read.

An intensive survey of color is not intended in this book. Our discussion will be limited to just enough information to permit the department manager or buyer to select the appropriate color combinations for use in the display. It is the individual department's responsibility to select the merchandise; the display department's job is to show it to its best advantage.

Basically there are six colors, plus the neutrals, black, brown, and white. Three are primary colors: yellow, red, and blue. Orange, violet, and green are secondary colors.

There are unlimited color combinations that can be achieved by using these colors, but the person attempting to create an attractive display, perhaps on a platform in her department, should stay with some of the simpler color combinations.

Monochromatic Color

Monochromatic (*mono,* meaning one, and *chroma,* signifying color) arrangements center around the use of one color. Therefore, the merchandise would consist of all yellows or all reds, for example; for interest and variety, different values (lights or darks of the one color, such as light yellow to dark yellow) and different intensities (brightest to dullest tones of the same color) are used. Thus, a manager might select a wide range of blue merchandise, avoiding monotony by choosing light blues, dark blues, dull blues, and bright blues. Blacks, browns, and whites, technically not colors, can also be used, still maintaining a monochromatic scheme. In seasons where there is a particular, universally accepted "fashion color," the monochromatic arrangement is perfect in a display.

Analogous Color

The incorporation of more than one color in a window can be achieved by selecting colors that are analogous (next to each other on the color wheel). For example, yellow and orange is an analogous color scheme; likewise, blue and green, green and yellow, and so on. As was true in the monochromatic arrangements, different values and intensities plus black, brown, and white are added for interest and variety. An entire display might be worked around a two-color printed piece of merchandise (blue and violet, as an example) as a central or focal point in a window, with various other pieces in blues and violets. In this way, prints, if popular, done in analogous combinations (artists' designs and color sections are often based on the same arrangements taken from the color wheel) can be attractively displayed in both window and interior displays.

Complementary Color

Again, one must go back to the basic color wheel. By definition complementary colors are direct opposites on the wheel. Yellow and violet, blue and orange, and red and green are complementary colors.

There are many, many other combinations, both usual and unusual, that can be used. The department manager who knows the job will automatically select creative combinations. Until that time, staying within the simple guidelines will allow for safe color combinations of merchandise displays.

MATERIALS AND PROPS

The materials selected and the props used are important in enhancing the merchandise for sale. Window floors and platforms are covered in a variety of fabrics, carpets, paper, stones, plastics, simulated grass, sand, and other materials, while backgrounds employ from the simplest to the most elaborate papers, wood, or fabrics, depending upon the nature or theme of the display. A visit to the local display center (most cities have them so that trimmers can select their background materials) will show the enormous variety of available materials. Props can vary from simple household articles such as chairs, ladders, and room divider screens to elaborate displays built by the store's display department. Displays are also available, either by purchase or lease, from display houses. One needs only to visit a display house when planning a Christmas presentation to see the wondrous creations for use in windows and interiors. Santas, fully moving, dancing elves, and skating children are just a few of the props available.

The selection of the display materials and props without the assistance of a professional displayperson is often difficult. Keeping in mind the message you are trying to project plus the merchandise you are planning to sell will help you select the right materials. Aid is always available at the display houses. The modern retailer wishing to keep abreast of what is current and available in display should faithfully read the National Retail Merchants Association's (NRMA) publication, *Stores,* which continuously features innovative window and interior displays executed by the country's leading retailers.

SELECTING A THEME

The selection of a theme or topic for a display is generally a simple task. The approaching season, a local event, a President's birthday, the opening of school are just some examples of ideas. Generally, themes of displays are usually one of the following types:

Seasonal Display

A seasonal display requires the arrangement of merchandise in a seasonal setting. The use of snow to emphasize winter, with a display of winter jackets, ski pants, skis, and bulky sweaters, is typical of a seasonal display. (See Figure 13-14.)

Ensemble Display

This is a display designed to show a complete outfit. An example is a display showing a man's tuxedo, shirt, shoes, vest, and hat. (See Figure 13-15.)

FIGURE 13-14 Seasonal Display

FIGURE 13-15 Ensemble Display

Unit Window Display

To emphasize the importance of an item, it is shown in abundance, alone in a window—for example, twenty-five one-gallon cans of paint, many colors of the same pair of women's shoes, or many patterns of textured hosiery. (See Figure 13-16.)

Theme Display

Any theme can be chosen, such as a beach scene showing swimwear, a camp scene showing campers' needs, or a church scene showing a bridal party. (See Figure 13-17.)

General Display

This presents unrelated merchandise. Such a display is becoming less frequently used by display people. (See Figure 13-18.)

Institutional Display

Institutional display is used periodically by retail stores to sell the store's image rather than specific merchandise. A window devoted to "Boy Scouts of America in Action" or "The Heart Fund" or some other event of public interest tends to show that the store is dedicated to the good of the community. Many retailers agree that the occasional use of institutional displays, void of

FIGURE 13-16   Unit Window Display

FIGURE 13-17 Theme Display

FIGURE 13-18 General Display

FIGURE 13-19 Institutional Display

merchandise, often brings more customers into a store than the conventional displays. (See Figure 13-19.)

EXECUTION OF A DISPLAY

An orderly plan should be followed in preparing a window or interior display. Generally, a window display is a more difficult task, but the suggestions previously discussed should be adhered to in the preparation of any display.

Selecting Merchandise

Although a great deal of emphasis is placed on background materials and props, the merchandise to be displayed is the most important consideration. Too often the display person overpowers the merchandise to be sold by paying excessive attention to the nonmerchandise factors. The merchandise should be timely, clean, carefully pressed (if this applies), and desirable in every way. A limitation of display often ignored by some retailers is the fact that display does not sell unwanted merchandise. But it does help to sell greater quantities of desirable merchandise. So, select those goods that will make the customer come through the door to purchase. Perhaps consumers will buy some unwanted merchandise once they are inside.

Selecting Display Materials and Props

For floor covering, fabric is easier to handle than paper. In addition, fabrics have a longer useful life. Stores frequently invest in neutral carpeting for windows and interior platforms, eliminating the necessity of frequent change.

Whatever is used, care should be taken to eliminate wrinkles and creases and to conceal staples.

Walls can be painted or lined with paper, fabric, or other material. The most important consideration in the selection of floor and wall coverings is that they must not overpower the merchandise, but enhance it. With attention paid to careful color selection in background materials as well as the merchandise, there will be color harmony.

The props should be consistent with the theme selected. For example, a back-to-school display might make use of chalkboards, school desks, rulers, erasers, and so on. A beach scene might employ such props as sun umbrellas, lifeguard chairs, beach chairs, and water wings. The props are important in setting the stage on which the merchandise is to be presented. Consequently, they should be carefully selected.

Some props are functional in addition to being decorative and permit an interesting display of merchandise. A dress draped over a settee, clothing suspended from a clothesline, and shoes arranged on a ladder are examples of imaginative ideas from a creative display designer.

Selecting Fixtures

Mannequins, "T" stands, blouse forms, and other fixtures should be selected next. If a wide choice of mannequins (or changeable wigs) is available, select those that best fit the merchandise. The youthful-looking, casual, standing female mannequin with a long, simple hair style is certainly better in a teen swimsuit window than is a sophisticated one with an elegant hair style.

If the props selected provide for the display of merchandise, fewer fixtures will be needed. The reverse is also true.

An overcrowded display leads to confusion. Select only those fixtures appropriate to the merchandise. Fight the tendency to include even one more than is absolutely necessary.

Preparation of Component Parts

The preparation of the physical parts of the actual display centers around a program of "cleaning." In a store window, glass should be carefully washed before each display is executed. A film settles after a while on the inside of the glass because of gases, soot from heating devices, and so forth. Anything that distorts the viewer's ability to clearly observe the display must be eliminated. Care should be exercised in avoiding "streaks" from washing; handprints, often left by display people on the inside glass, should be removed.

The floors and walls of the window should be cleared of staples, nails, wire, and soil marks left from the previous displays. All fixtures, including mannequins, should be cleaned. This not only guarantees a perfect picture for the customer, but also it avoids soiling the fresh merchandise being displayed.

Light bulbs should be replaced where burned out. A display window is worthless without lighting. Colored bulbs or "gels" used to change white bulbs to color should be prepared if they are to be used in the display.

Planning the Merchandise Arrangement

Perhaps the most difficult task for a person with no display experience is the problem of where and how to place the merchandise in an interesting and attractive arrangement. Following are some of the most important factors to consider in arranging the merchandise:

Balance

There are basically two types of balance in display, symmetrical and asymmetrical. The symmetrical is frequently referred to as formal balance. This is an arrangement in which, if the window were divided down the center, each side would have equal weight. This is pictured in Figure 13-20. This balance often tends to be dull, unoriginal, and monotonous to the viewer. An asymmetrical or informal balance is achieved by placing merchandise arrangements without a central axis. These displays are more difficult to execute and, while more exciting, should be left for later attempts. An example of an asymmetrical display is shown in Figure 13-21.

Emphasis

Each display should have a point of emphasis, or focal point. This can be achieved through using a spotlight, setting the main item apart from the rest,

FIGURE 13-20 Symmetrical Balance

FIGURE 13-21 Asymmetrical Balance

featuring one item in a contrasting color while the remainder of the display is another color, and many other methods. Experience teaches different ways to achieve emphasis.

Contrast

This can be achieved by use of more than one color, various sizes and shapes of merchandise and fixtures, and so on.

Space

Avoid overcrowding a display. Separating the various pieces in a window is important. If one piece of merchandise overlaps another, without being part of an ensemble, the eye doesn't know which belongs with which. The eye is incapable of absorbing very large segments. By allowing floor space to be visible between objects, the eye can outline each piece of merchandise separately. Raising merchandise from the floor, on pedestals, can help achieve separation and add interest to the display.

Preparation of a Graphic Plan

Large retail organizations with many separate units, in order to save the costs of large display staffs and to aid their store managers in executing window

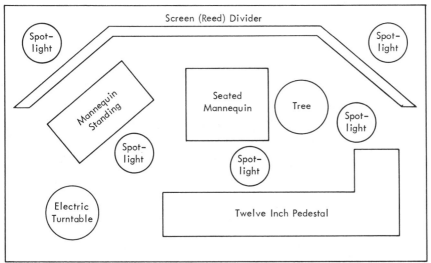

Notes:
1 Merchandise Suspended from Tree Branches
2 Spotlights Are All Floor Variety
3 Turntable for Small Wear
4 Twelve-Inch Pedestal for Small Wear

Scale: One Inch = One Foot

FIGURE 13-22 Window Planned to Scale on Graph Paper

displays, prepare graphic presentations of proposed windows, for distribution. Planning in advance on paper saves time and labor in the installation. For those who must plan a display without professional help, a similar plan should be used. Although different procedures may be used, the following one should be satisfactory for organizing most window displays.

1. Prepare on graph paper the floor of your window. A one-inch to one-foot scale is suggested. However, any other scale suited to your needs would be adequate.
2. Indicate, to scale, the position of props, mannequins, and other fixtures, keeping in mind the importance of balance.
3. Attach to the plan, or indicate in writing, the floor covering and wall materials to be used.
4. Show the position of display cards. Figure 13-22 shows an example of a window planned to scale on graph paper.

Trimming the Window

At this point, the actual arrangement of merchandise on the floor, stands, platforms, pedestals, and mannequins takes place. The proper planning, with attention paid to all of the points discussed, should result in an attractive, well-coordinated window. An additional basic principle, which can be practiced by the display person only while actually "trimming" rather than being indicated on a layout plan, is the placement of the various items. Small items should be placed up front. If they are placed in the rear of the window, they will not be seen. Generally, merchandise is arranged with the smallest in the front and the largest in the rear. Naturally, mannequins should not be placed in front of other merchandise that is displayed in the window.

The actual draping, pinning, and folding of window merchandise cannot be mastered by reading about it. This ability comes with the understanding of materials, shapes, and forms. A trip to a large store's display department to watch how it's done, or instruction in this area, will show how simple this part of display is.

Preparing Price Tags and Copy Cards

The attractiveness of the merchandise in the proper setting will surely get a customer's attention. In the case of window displays, the store wants to bring the right customer inside to make a purchase. Since few consumers are knowledgeable enough to determine the prices and pertinent facts about the merchandise such as material content, the written part of the display is important. Without the price, at least, departments could become overcrowded with consumers who are not real prospects. In today's world of retailing only the inexperienced retailer avoids the use of prices and copy cards to accompany their displays. Figure 13-23 shows an example of a copy card that gives pertinent information to potential customers.

Before the preparation of the written material, the colors to be used for this purpose should be carefully selected. A safe choice, appropriate for any display, is black lettering on white stock. This combination is neutral and easy to read. Other easy-to-read color arrangements are black on yellow, green on white, red on white, blue on white, and white on blue. In using these colors, make certain that they do not clash with the display's color scheme.

After selecting the stock (cardboard, oaktag, construction board, or other material) and the ink to be used, execution of the message and price tags takes place. Lettering, while a highly specialized job, can be simply performed. The

---

Tri-Color Scheme
BREAKFAST CLOTHS

pure linen crash
fast colors
51″ × 51″

$3.79

HOME ACCESSORIES BASEMENT

FIGURE 13-23 Display Cards

CO ccccccccccc
ciacldeeqqcjguu
acdeqg acdeqg cc
ooooobbbpphhnnm
abcdefghijklmnco
pqrsstuvwxyyz
AaBBbCcDdEFG
HIJjKkLIMNOP
QRSTUuVWXYZ
ABCDEFGHIJKLMNOPQRSTU
VWXYZ SINGLE STROKE GOTHIC

FIGURE 13-24   Samples of "C" Curves and Gothic Stroke

practice of three simple strokes will enable even the most untalented artist to create a written card. Figure 13-24 shows samples of two "C" curves and one single gothic stroke. From these three strokes, any letter or number can be achieved. With a few hours of practice anyone can prepare price tags and copy cards.

Action for the Independent Retailer

Display, to be effective, must be timely. To have appeal and properly motivate purchasing, a display need not be overwhelmingly expensive. If the independent keeps in mind both of these points, the displaying of merchandise could bring increased sales.

A waste of valuable display space occurs in both the store's window and its interior if the theme of the display has passed. For example, a Valentine's Day display that lingers a few days after the holiday is valueless. Large stores that have separate display personnel and adhere to window and interior display calendars are usually on target. It's the independent who often exhibits a stale display. A little planning could alleviate such a problem without requiring lots of money.

Since the sums spent by the larger companies cannot be expended by their smaller counterparts, the independent retailer's display dollar must be wisely spent. Itinerant or free-lance display persons are available for single displays. Often their fees include the use of their own props. If the store is fashion oriented, displays could be professionally executed once for each season and some of the important sales-related holidays. In between, with a little effort, the featured merchandise in the display could be changed by the owner or an employee, without changing the background props. With a completely different color scheme each week, the display could have a fresh look. If this approach is used, it is best to ask the display free-lancer to install neutral display props that can easily be adapted to a variety of merchandise.

In situations where hiring a professional display person is too costly, even on a periodic basis, the retailer could use permanent background materials that could be slightly accented with seasonal additions. For example, a men's shop might install a permanent wooden wall in the window; carpet the floor; and use sturdy glass, wooden, or chrome display fixtures. A sprinkling of autumn leaves might be sufficient to indicate a change in season.

By constantly scanning the windows and interiors of larger stores, the independent with even the smallest store can become "display educated" and satisfactorily execute the store's window and interior displays.

IMPORTANT POINTS IN THE CHAPTER

1. *The function of interior display is to attract customers' attention and arouse enough interest to make them want to investigate the merchandise more fully.*

2. *A window schedule should be prepared to properly apportion space as well as give management the proper amount of time for specific displays.*

3. *An important element of window display is the size, shape, and location of the windows. Different types of merchandise are displayed in different types of windows.*

While the department manager has no control over the size and shape of the windows, the pattern of the display is frequently dictated by these factors.

4. *Devices on which merchandise can be shown to its best advantage are called display fixtures. Fixtures may be forms that simulate the human figure or parts of the figure. Various types of stands, platforms, and pedestals are used to drape or elevate the merchandise.*

5. *Human form figures are available in a variety of materials that range in design from lifelike human replicas to stylized figures. The type of figure used depends in large part on the image of the store and the merchandise to be displayed.*

6. *Adjustable stands, pedestals, and platforms are used to provide a space on which merchandise can be displayed at a variety of heights.*

7. *The imaginative use of color and lighting are vital if a window display is to be a provocative, eye-catching device. Color and lighting provide the dramatic possibilities that make effective window display an art.*

8. *Since the theme of the display must be easily recognizable by all shoppers, most themes are simple and obvious. An approaching season, the opening of school, or an important local event are typical themes.*

9. *In the execution of the display, selecting the merchandise to be displayed is the most important consideration. The merchandise should be appropriate, clean, carefully pressed, and desirable in every way.*

10. *The actual preparation of the display should begin with a scale drawing on graph paper of the display, indicating all the materials and merchandise that will be used.*

11. *The selection and arrangement of the theme, merchandise, materials, and display fixtures should be carefully fitted to an overall scheme that will attract customer attention to the store and the merchandise displayed.*

REVIEW QUESTIONS

1. Who prepares the display in retail stores?
2. What are the important functions of display?
3. What are the purposes of interior display?
4. List and briefly describe five types of window structures. Which one allows for the greatest amount of converging traffic? Which one is most difficult to trim? Why?
5. Of what materials are mannequins manufactured? Which would give the store the longest service without repair? Why?
6. What are some attachments used with the adjustable stand?
7. For what purposes are colored lights used?
8. What kind of care must be exercised in selecting the colored lights to be used on merchandise?
9. Define intensity and value as they relate to color.
10. What is a monochromatic color scheme? How can the display person avoid monotony with this color arrangement?

11. Which type of window theme is generally used to project to the customer great depth in a particular type of merchandise? Give an example of this type of display.
12. What is an institutional display? Why do stores use this form of display?
13. What is the most important part of any display?
14. What is the difference between symmetrical and asymmetrical balance?
15. What is a focal point? How can this be achieved in a display?
16. Why must a display person plan a window before executing the display?
17. Are price tags always important in a window display? Defend your position.
18. Why, with all the merchandise attractively shown in windows, is a copy card generally deemed important?
19. In which area inside the stores is it not necessary for department managers to get permission for displays?
20. How can the independent retailer cope with the high cost of display?

CASE PROBLEMS

CASE PROBLEM 1

Frank Rogers and Peter Daniels have decided to open the first of what they hope will be a number of ladies' specialty stores. This first store is located in the middle of a large shopping center and has overall dimensions of 18 feet by 100 feet. It caters to a clientele generally in the $18,500 to $35,000 income bracket. There are a great number of stores in the center carrying the usual diversification of merchandise. Rogers and Daniels, after much planning, have decided to appeal to the young woman of 20 to 40 years of age. Their merchandise assortment will be fashionable, but not "way out." The price range will be moderate. For example, dresses will retail from $30 to $75, pants and sweaters from $20 to $25, and so on.

The two partners have decided on all policies, assignment of responsibility, store hours, and so on. Two decisions haven't been settled thus far: what type of window structure the store should have and what types of mannequins should be purchased. Many suggestions have been offered, but the two partners can't come to a final decision.

QUESTIONS

1. What factors should be considered in determining the type of mannequin to use?
2. Which type would you select? Why?
3. Which window structure is best suited to their needs? Why?

CASE PROBLEM 2

Each year at Hagelman's Department Store the buyers and department managers are asked by the store's display director to submit those dates that are important to their respective departments for space in the store's windows. Since there isn't enough window space for each department to display its merchandise all the time, the space must be allocated in order of importance. For example, a toy department might be given preference at Christmastime. Generally window displays are left intact for one week.

Hagelman's, like most department stores, has many departments, such as Misses' Coats and Suits, Junior Sportswear, Lingerie, Bridal Clothing, Menswear, Toys, Appliances, Shoes, Hosiery, and Sporting Goods. The window space is limited to six windows that are parallel to the sidewalk, three on either side of the main entrance. Traditionally, departments have requested and received all six windows at one time. It has been felt that in this way a department could really show the public its wide selection of goods.

At this time all departments' requests are in for window space. There is duplication of the dates needed by various departments. The display manager now has the task of making the window assignment.

QUESTIONS

1. List those dates or events that you would submit to the display department for each department mentioned in the case.

2. What factors would you consider in assigning space if more than one department requested the windows for the same period?

3. Do you believe it sound for one department to occupy all six windows at one time? Choose a position and defend it.

4. Prepare a window calendar, listing the departments (from those given) you would assign space and for which dates they would be assigned.

14

sales promotional activities

BEHAVIORAL OBJECTIVES

Upon completion of this chapter the student should be able to

1. *Write a brief essay on "special events," including three examples.*
2. *Explain the use of trading stamps as a sales stimulating device. Include the drawbacks of such plans.*
3. *Define publicity and give several examples of it.*
4. *Discuss the aspects involved in the multimedia concept.*
5. *Understand the purpose of storewide celebrations.*

INTRODUCTION

No matter what the time of year, those responsible for promoting the store's image to the customer are constantly searching for new promotional ideas and techniques. Countless dollars are expended to make certain that the store reaps its fair share of both regular and prospective customer attention. As we have seen, advertising and display command a considerable amount of dollars and time to reach the consuming market. By coupling these activities with a variety of special events and other promotional tools, the store management hopes that the media will be sufficiently enticed to provide free publicity, extoling the store's virtues. Creativity is the key to planning promotions that will not only increase sales immediately, but will also help to cement lasting relationships between the store and its clientele.

THE SALES PROMOTION DIVISION

In most large retail organizations there is a division that is separate from the others, with responsibility for creating the store's promotional activities. Figure 14-1 illustrates the typical departmental structure within the division. It is headed by an overall expert in promotion, whose task it is to manage all of the division's activities. Although each department is headed by its own manager, the promotion manager has responsibility for ultimate approval of advertising and display, and coordinates events that involve all of the areas of promotion. For example, in cases where a storewide special event is being presented, it is the sales promotion director who must make certain that each aspect of the event complements the others. Only with cooperation among the various departments within the division will a successful campaign be realized. In contemporary retailing, where the multimedia concept is prevalent, a spirit of cooperation is necessary to totally convey the store's desired image. Major events such as the Bloomingdale's "China," and Carson Pirie Scott "Futurescope," as explored later in the chapter, exemplify the importance of the sales promotion division.

FIGURE 14-1 Organization of a Sales Promotion Department

THE MULTIMEDIA CONCEPT

In advertising, professionals generally agree that the use of one particular medium exclusively is insufficient to reach all customers. Just as it is unwise to involve the store solely in newspaper advertising, it is also unwise to limit promotion to one tool. Sophisticated promotional campaigns require the blending of all worthy and available promotion techniques to reach the desired sales goals. A melding of advertising, through the various media, displays, and special events will achieve better results. Where advertising informs the customer of the promotion or event, display continues to whet the appetite as the customer enters the store. By rounding the package out with appropriate demonstrations and so forth, the flavor of the campaign will be constantly absorbed by the store's clientele. Relying on the multimedia or multipromotional concept, most retailers agree that increased sales will be achieved.

SPECIAL EVENTS

Whatever the type of retail organization, special events are tools that can be used to increase volume. Supermarkets, discount operations, traditional department stores, and specialty shops alike all have avenues available to them for reaching their customers. The breadth and depth of these endeavors depend considerably upon the available promotional dollar commitment as well as the experts employed to achieve the desired results. Larger companies employ sales promotion directors whose responsibility it is to coordinate and manage the various promotional departments. Without proper leadership to ensure a joint effort by all departments, the money set aside for promotion will not bring about the best results. In promotion, as in any other aspect of retailing, cooperation is essential to success. Special events are often major undertakings, with many planning months needed before the presentation. Sometimes outside agencies are called upon to assist with the promotion if its magnitude is too much for the regular staff to handle, or if the staff's capacity is just sufficient to handle regular advertising and display.

As does merchandise, special events come in all sizes, shapes, colors, and prices. Typical as well as specific store promotions will be explored in this chapter to give insight into how retailers of all sizes and classifications participate.

Fashion Shows

The display of fashions on live models has been a regular sales promotion device for both large and small retail stores. Although some executives feel that the presentation of a fashion show is primarily for prestigious purposes, stores can achieve immediate business from them. One need only watch customers rise from their chairs to rush over to the racks of clothing right after an Ohrbach's showing of European fashions to realize the instant success of the showing in terms of immediate sales. The partly emptied racks surely dispel the theory of prestige value exclusively. Even if a fashion show presentation doesn't result in immediate sales, it is valuable in that it exposes the store's fashion merchandise to potential buyers in a lively and exciting manner that is unobtainable in any other media. If the production is properly conceived and executed, appetites are likely to be whetted for future patronage.

Types of Shows

Fashion shows are by no means limited to women's wear. At a rapidly increasing rate the male model is becoming important in fashion shows. It is not unusual to see menswear take up about one-third of the merchandise shown at what was once "a woman's fashion show." Although it might be considered wasteful to include menswear, since fashion shows are almost exclusively attended by women, stores feel it is practical, because a large proportion of purchases are either directly made or influenced by women.

To be considered a fashion show, the presentation needn't be an extravaganza. Shows run the gamut from informal modeling to elaborate productions staged in imaginative settings.

Fashion Parade. The fashion parade is perhaps the easiest show to produce and also is the least costly. This type of production simply presents a succession of models displaying their outfits on a runway in the store (Ohrbach's follows this procedure at their "haute couture" fashion shows) or on the floor of a restaurant, in and around the tables, while patrons are dining. This type of show doesn't make use of any particular theme but simply presents the store's most timely merchandise. The staging doesn't lend itself to complicated backgrounds or space for the models to do intricate turns. Music is generally limited to a pianist.

Formal Fashion Show Productions. The major production requires a great deal of preparation. This show is presented in an auditorium or theater and is truly theatrical in nature. Generally the fashion coordinator (the person responsible in most large retail operations for the show's production) selects a theme for the show. It might be travel, back to school, or the wedding. After the theme has been established, background sets are constructed, a script complete with commentary is written, and appropriate music is selected to be played by a band.

Production Costs

A fashion show can be presented with very little cost to the retailer. Small retailers with limited promotional budgets, and even large retailers who do not wish to make heavy investments on fashion shows, can give successful shows for a nominal amount. The greatest expense incurred is the payment of modeling fees. College students may be used as models in a show directed to the attention of the campus set. This serves a double purpose. First, college students participating in such a production, particularly those majoring in retailing, find the involvement an excellent learning experience. For the store, this arrangement eliminates the cost of the professional model while guaranteeing an audience of the model's friends. Involvement with a college (or even a high school) provides students who will build sets, write and deliver the commentary, and work out other production problems in addition to modeling. Often the school band will play accompanying music, free of charge. Similarly, large fund-raising organizations are excellent sources for the presentation of fashion shows. As in the case of the student shows, these fund-raising groups use their own members for modeling as well as for the performance of the other necessary tasks. The use of the group's members provides models to whom the audiences can relate. For example, a size-14 housewife model is more meaningful and realistic to a group of homemakers than the "perfect" size-8 professional models.

If a store decides to have a more professional show, many local modeling agencies can provide a sufficient number of male and female models to fulfill its needs. These agencies also have lists of commentators, bands, and so on, to make the show a success.

Whatever the budget of the store, a little ingenuity can guarantee a successful presentation.

Parades

An institutional device that is used by a number of large retailers is the presentation of a parade to mark some occasion. For example, an annual event costing thousands of dollars is Macy's Thanksgiving Day parade in New York

City. The occasion is the official opening of their Christmas season. The show provides entertainment for the public while reminding them that it is time to begin shopping for Christmas gifts. Similar parades are presented throughout the United States. Even in small towns, groups of independent retailers often collaborate on similar presentations. This cooperation spreads the cost among the participating businesses.

Storewide Celebrations

Every so often, store organizations make a commitment to promote a special event, which encompasses almost all of their selling departments. Not only does it require the cooperation of each of the store's divisions, but also an investment far more than the amount usually budgeted for the typical special event. Such a happening was evident in Bloomingdale's undertaking to promote the treasures of China (Figure 14-2). With an investment of $10 million and an effort that took years to assemble, the extravaganza opened in the flagship store and its branches on September 23, 1980. Rarely, if ever, has a retail organization so fully transformed its selling floors into a combined cultural as well as shopping experience. Creativity is probably the hallmark of the Bloomingdale's China adventure. And an adventure it was with its flags, banners, art exhibits, craft demonstrations, ceremonial robes, Chinese delicacy snack bars, silk scrolls, and special shops surrounding the merchandise for sale. The special shops, created solely for the event, give an indication of the scope of the undertaking. The Palace of Spring featuring lingerie, The Temple of Perfect Harmony for accessories, The Kingfisher Pagoda for jewelry, The Friendship Store for collectibles, Marco Polo's Caravan for fabrics, and The Great Wall Gallery for art were just a few of those that were specially created. The success, in Bloomingdale's own words, was bigger than ever anticipated for its six-week run.

Another storewide celebration was that mounted by Carson Pirie Scott. Annually, the store presents a major spring promotion. For a two-week period in May 1980, the company presented a "Futurescope" event that took a look at how Americans' lifestyles would change during the 1980s. Planning the event took three months and involved a total consistent look throughout each of the store's floors and individual departments. Special shops, demonstrations, window displays, and advertisements were created to give a total picture. As with the Bloomingdale's China event, the increased traffic and media coverage surpassed what had been expected.

One special event that has had a far-reaching effect for its organization is the race called Macy's Marathon, sponsored by Macy's, Kansas City (Figure 14-3). The event is a one-day affair that attracted 1100 runners from twenty-four states for its first race and has become an annual event. Although the actual event is for only one day, the race, as indicated by Macy's management,

FIGURE 14-2 Bloomingdale's Storewide Promotion

FIGURE 14-3 Macy's Special Promotion

Courtesy of Macy's, Kansas City

has had tremendous influence in establishing Macy's as a community leader in the Kansas City area. The race has worked positively as a public relations tool for the entire year. While no merchandise is sold specifically because of this special event, its impact on the public is one that promotes community involvement. This type of event is akin to institutional advertising, which is intended to bolster the store's image, but sales increases cannot be immediately measured.

Other Special Events

There are many other types of special events that both large and small stores take advantage of to attract customers and increase good will. These range from small store support of little league and bowling teams to major art exhibits and lecture series offered by large institutions. The variety of these events is almost unlimited. While special events may be tied to the sale of specific merchandise, many such programs are intended solely to attract customers to the store and build good will by promoting the idea that the store is a kind of community center that supports cultural and athletic programs. Large stores that have the necessary facilities often reinforce the community center idea by offering their tearooms, dining rooms, and auditoriums to such consumer organizations as women's clubs and parent-teacher associations for meetings and special events.

SPECIAL DEMONSTRATIONS

In recent years there has been a resurgence in the use of live demonstrations in retail stores. Demonstrators showing how easy it is to manipulate wigs, apply cosmetics, clean rugs with miracle solutions, or prepare meals in a matter of minutes are often found in the high-traffic selling areas of medium and large stores. Some of these demonstrations last for one day and are confined to perhaps one counter. Others are major special events requiring a large space and a number of demonstrators. An example of a major demonstration was one that took place at Gimbels, New York, to promote Corningware, pyroceram cooking utensils, manufactured by Corning Glass. Counters were equipped with demonstrators who prepared food in Corningware equipment for the shoppers to taste. They also showed the ease with which the objects can be transferred from extreme cold to extreme heat without breakage and displayed the simplicity of cleaning the Corningware. Closed-circuit TV was employed to show the Corningware's resistance to breakage, with a brief film of a bull in a china shop knocking over the Corningware without damage to it. In addition to the special demonstration of the product, complete success was guaranteed by the involvement of the entire sales promotion division. The advertising people brought customers to the store; the display people and sign shop brought the customer to the appropriate selling floor, where the demonstrators took over. Without the cooperation of all the promotional staff's departments, the selling of goods isn't likely to be successful.

SAMPLING

A method of promoting sales that is very closely related to demonstrating is the use of samples. Sampling is similar to demonstrating in that it shows the customer how to actually use the merchandise. The major difference between the two methods is that in the one case, the merchandise is used by a representative of the store, and in the other, the customer uses the product. The decision on whether to sell by demonstration or sample is based upon the characteristics of the merchandise. Expensive merchandise that requires skill to operate is sold by demonstration. Products that can be inexpensively sampled, and the use of which requires no previous training, can be effectively sold by means of samples. Where sample selling is used, it is not unusual to have the producer of the goods share in the retailer's sampling expense.

The important characteristic of the sample method is that it allows customers to actually "get their hands on" the product. Depending upon the merchandise, sampling can effectively take place on the selling floor or in the customer's home. Food products, stationery, candies, and yard goods are generally given out by salespeople in the selling departments. Soap powders, razor blades, and swatches of material for shirts, bedclothes, sheets, and a variety of other uses are frequently mailed to the customers' homes. As long as the cost of the sample is relatively low, sampling is an effective way for a store to sell merchandise and get publicity.

SCHOOLS AND CLASSES

Many stores carry the concept of demonstrations far beyond the usual expert demonstrating a product to a small group on the selling floor. Certain products require consumer skills that cannot be taught in a simple demonstration period. For instruction in such products, classrooms and teachers are provided, with classes in many cases extending over a period of weeks. The Singer Sewing Machine Company is a typical example. Since sewing machines are of value only to people who can operate them, Singer offers its customers courses in the use of sewing machines that extend over a considerable period of time. Unquestionably, such classes are of considerable help in selling machines. Other stores, frequently with the cooperation of utility companies and appliance manufacturers, offer courses in gourmet cooking. Home decorating, baby care, and beauty culture are also taught over extended time periods. That this sort of continuing instruction is also typical of small retailers is evidenced by the amount of teaching that takes place in knitting shops, hobby stores, and many other small retail establishments. Frequently, courses are given in churches and women's clubs as a convenience to customers.

The use of instructional classes promotes both sales and good will. The sales are made by requiring the students to purchase the materials at the store. In addition, bringing the people into the store to attend classes results in purchases that might not otherwise be made at the store.

PREMIUMS

Premiums—that is, the process of giving special merchandise (products that are not regularly offered for sale by the retailer) as an inducement to buy goods—have been popular during the past ten years. The premiums may be awarded for single transactions (a box of Ivory Flakes with each washing machine bought), or for multiple transactions (a drinking glass for each twenty gallons of gasoline purchased). Premiums may be free, as in the two cases just mentioned, or if not free, the buyer is offered the premium at a substantial savings, as in the case of a one-dollar pair of nylon stretch stockings for $.50 plus a coupon from a Kraft cheese package. Whatever the premium plan, and there is a constantly growing variety of plans, when properly handled, premiums offer an important means of stimulating sales.

Trading Stamps

Although the use of trading stamps has been declining, it still is by far the most important use of premiums as a sales-stimulating device. Under this system, customers are given stamps when they pay for their merchandise, usually at the rate of ten stamps for each dollar of purchase. These stamps are pasted in books provided by the store, along with a catalog of premium merchandise, listing hundreds of valuable items that can be obtained for a specific number of stamps. (See Figure 14-4.) Although the use of trading stamps has declined in recent years, it is estimated that between 12 and 18 percent of all retail sales are made at stores offering trading stamps.

FIGURE 14-4 S&H Green Stamps *Idea Book of Exciting Gifts*

The cost of trading stamps to the retailers is about .002 to .003 cents per stamp plus the time involved in handling. While this can be a fairly high cost to high-volume stores, the use of trading stamps builds sales volume by attracting customers who might otherwise shop at a competing store.

To the consumer, trading stamps offer a means of saving to get premium merchandise in a somewhat painless fashion. Studies have proved that the books have a definite value—$3.21 in traditional stores or $2.82 in discount stores.

The question most often raised among customers of stores that feature trading stamps is, "Am I paying for these stamps through higher prices?" The answer, of course, is yes. On the other hand, the customer pays for all store promotions, such as advertising, with no questions asked.

Whether or not a store should handle trading stamps is a problem that requires careful analysis. However, it is likely that of two equal stores, the one handling trading stamps will attract more customers.

PUBLICITY

In this chapter publicity refers to the promotion of the store without cost. Free publicity is the result of a store's advertising, display, special events, or other promotions that are noteworthy enough for a publication or commentator to mention without cost to the retailer. For example, a store might present a fashion show that is so outstanding that the local newspaper's fashion editor will review it in a column (Figure 14-5). A store's holiday parade might get attention on a television news broadcast. The larger stores employ a public relations person, who is charged with the responsibility of preparing releases about the store's activities that might attract media and, therefore, customer interest. The free publicity a store receives is not always kind, and could work adversely. For example, the recent newspaper exposure of incorrect weights on meat packages in some New York supermarkets certainly hurt sales.

Free publicity can be in the form of favorable comments concerning the store's community activities, merchandise promotional activities, or place in the business community. The purpose of free publicity, like all other sales promotional activity, is to create sales by presenting the firm's name in the most favorable light. An advantage of free publicity over conventional advertising (in addition to the cost savings) is that promotional material found in advertising is presumed to be biased and is not taken as seriously as the same material would be if it were found in the nonadvertising section of the newspaper.

The term *free publicity* is somewhat misleading. In fact, large firms spend a considerable amount of money on publicity. Large stores frequently assign the responsibility for publicity to one or more members of their sales promotion department to spend their full time in reporting newsworthy information to the local media. These people establish contacts with local newspa-

Here Comes the Bride

The bride on her day of days will reflect a traditional point of view in the organza and peau 'dange lace gown with lace bordered and applique train, left, or, she may prefer the organza gown with re-embroidered lace accents and fiction pearls in a flower motif. Both styles are part of the Gertz spring and summer bridal collection to be unveiled Saturday in Gertz Bay Shore; Jan. 17 in Gertz Hicksville; Jan. 24 in the Flushing store and Jan. 31 in Gertz Jamaica. All showings will get underway at 11 a.m. in the Bridal Salon. Reservations may be obtained by contacting the individual stores.

FIGURE 14-5 Example of Publicity

pers and radio stations and actually write the articles and comments that, if acceptable by the media, appear in the news sections. Smaller stores employ the services of free-lance writers or public relations agencies for this purpose.

The newspapers and other media are well aware of the fact that their audience, particularly women, is interested in news concerning merchandise. Newspaper editors are constantly on the lookout for stories that supplement their advertising pages. Such information as the opening of a new season's fashions or a fashion show are important to readers, and editors are pleased to accept stories and photographs concerning such events. Many newspapers appoint special editors and writers to cover fashion events and report such news as a regular feature.

Studies have shown that there is a direct relationship between the amount of advertising space a company buys and the amount of free publicity it receives. This is probably due, in part, to the newspaper's willingness to please their good customers. It is also likely that a store with a large advertising budget probably engages in many newsworthy promotional activities.

Action for the Independent Retailer

Major promotions are usually reserved for the giants of industry. This does not, however, preclude the independent from promoting the smaller retail establishment.

Although production of a fashion show can cost large sums, the independent can get great mileage from a show while spending virtually nothing. The fashion retailer of men's, women's, and children's wear might contact a charitable or religious organization for the purpose of presenting a fashion show. By using organization members or their children as models, and their premises for presentation, the cost would be minimal, if anything at all. Not only does such an undertaking promote specific merchandise; it also serves as a good public relations tool, much the same as institutional advertising.

Another promotional endeavor to be used by the independent, with little cost, is the offer to contribute a small amount, say 10 percent, of sales for a specified period to a particular charity. The announcement could be made essentially through letters to citizens' groups and signs in the store's window. Such a promotion could increase volume while, at the same time, offering a positive store image.

Often a company is willing to send a representative to demonstrate a product. A food store might contact one of its suppliers to prepare a particular food for free customer tasting.

Promotion effectiveness need not be expensive. With a little creativity, independents can produce cost-free promotions.

IMPORTANT POINTS IN THE CHAPTER

1. *Retailers use special events to improve their store's image as well as to sell goods. Typical of this is a fashion show, which brings many customers into the store to buy goods while improving the store's reputation as a style center.*
2. *Other special events, such as art exhibits and support of teams and clubs, are used to attract customers and improve good will.*
3. *Live demonstrations and samples are used to increase customer interest in merchandise by demonstrating its use. Where goods are expensive or complicated to use, demonstrations are a better promotional device than samples. For products that require a considerable amount of consumer skills, series of classes are frequently arranged.*

4. The use of redeemable trading stamps as a sales stimulant is widespread. Under such a plan, customers receive a specific number of stamps per dollar of purchase. The stamps are redeemable for a wide variety of consumer goods.

5. Publicity refers to the promotion of the store without cost. Noteworthy events such as parades and fashion shows are frequently interesting enough to be reported by media in their regular news stories. This may result in an improvement in good will toward the store, at no cost to the retailer.

6. The multimedia promotional concept involves the coordination of all promotional tools, such as display and advertising, to promote the store.

REVIEW QUESTIONS

1. Describe the job of the sales promotion director.
2. Define *multimedia concept*.
3. What is a special event?
4. Compare a special event with a storewide celebration.
5. What purpose is served by a store's Thanksgiving Day parade?
6. Contrast the fashion parade with the formal fashion show.
7. How valuable is the use of demonstrations in retail stores? Discuss in terms of a particular item.
8. What sort of goods lend themselves to sampling?
9. Explain the use of premiums in sales promotions.
10. Discuss the procedures by which trading stamps are used in sales promotion.
11. What are the advantages to the store of the use of trading stamps?
12. List several types of information concerning a retailer that a newspaper might print in its regular news columns.
13. Discuss the relationship between a store's advertising budget and the amount of free publicity it receives.
14. Is free publicity always an asset to the store?
15. How might the small retailer, with a limited budget, carry out a special promotion?

CASE PROBLEMS

CASE PROBLEM 1

The Buy-Rite Company operates a chain of 120 supermarkets in the southwestern United States. It is a highly successful, well-established chain whose annual sales volume has grown steadily since the inception of the business. In part, the firm's success is due to an aggressive advertising and sales promotion policy, which operates with a higher-than-usual budget.

Recently, a new woman was appointed to the position of vice-president in charge of advertising and sales promotion. After a careful study of her department's operation, she suggested many changes in sales promotion policies.

Among her proposed changes is a plan to do away with the chain's trading stamp promotion (Buy-Rite gives trading stamps through a nationally advertised trading stamp company). The vice-president offers these arguments in support of her stand:

1. The money spent on the trading stamp operation would be more productive if spent in other areas.
2. Freeing the checkout counters of the necessity of handling stamps would shorten the customer's delay at the checkout counters and improve customer relations.

QUESTIONS

1. Can you think of any other arguments to support the vice-president's argument?
2. Give reasons for retaining trading stamps.
3. Discuss the effect of giving up trading stamps on customers who save stamps and on customers who do not save stamps.

CASE PROBLEM 2

A large New York City department store has been running a fashion show for many years. Owing to the excellent promotion of the event, the show has become an important fashion event of the city. The free publicity the store receives from the showing is excellent, with all of the important newspapers giving prominent space in their fashion columns to the occasion. In addition to the excellent publicity, the show produces a very important boost in sales volume. The customer attendance at the show is standing room only, with many interested people being turned away because of insufficient space.

The format of the show is ladies', men's, and children's clothing. This year a proposal has been made to have three individual showings, one each for ladies', men's, and children's clothing. It is reasoned that by dividing up the shows, there would be more publicity, more sales, and more seats for interested customers. In addition, each line of goods can have more time for display and show more merchandise.

QUESTIONS

1. Can you think of any more arguments favoring the split?
2. List the arguments opposing the split.
3. As merchandise manager, what would you do? Why?

15 *personal selling*

BEHAVIORAL OBJECTIVES

Upon completion of this chapter the student should be able to

1. *Discuss five personal characteristics essential to a successful salesperson.*
2. *List five areas of merchandise with which a salesperson must be familiar.*
3. *Write a brief paragraph on the selling of additional merchandise after a sale has been made. At least three methods should be included.*
4. *List six sources of product information that are available to a salesperson.*

INTRODUCTION

In a time when most of management's attention is focused upon the scientific determination of merchandise needs with the aid of such sophisticated tools as the computer, the activity that is often the lifeblood of the store, being a good salesperson, is in danger of being neglected. It is necessary only to enter various selling floors to note the lack of attention paid to upgrading selling techniques. It is true that to a certain extent retailers are making more extensive use of self-service. While customer selection without the aid of a salesperson is perhaps suitable for particular types of merchandise, self-service is not the answer for all goods. Items such as furs, higher-priced apparel, major appliances, carpets, and furniture generally require the services of trained sales personnel. The demand for personal attention is certainly not as important in the discount operations, where price is deemed more important than service, but in the service-oriented, conventional department and specialty stores personal ability to sell goods is a service necessary to the achievement of satisfactory sales. It should be stressed that, to be meaningful, the personal method of selling used with the customer must be efficient. Efficient personal selling by no means requires a hard sell, "fast-talking" approach. With today's more sophisticated and better educated consumers, this type of selling can only lead to customer dissatisfaction, an increase in merchandise returns, and a poor image for the retail store.

ESSENTIALS FOR THE SALESPERSON

Too much emphasis cannot be placed on the importance of the salesperson's ability. The image of the store is directly affected by the impression that person makes on the prospective customer. It is important to remember that until the individual shopper makes a purchase, that individual can only be considered a prospect. Personal selling ability, more than any other type of selling aids such as advertising and display, is the main activity in retailing that builds or destroys the shopper's confidence. Normally the salesperson is the store's only representative. To the public the salesperson *is* the store and many times a customer purchases or does not purchase because of him or her. Often when a shopper states, "I don't like that store," it is the salesforce that is being referred to. With the enormous amount of competition facing the retailer, the store's main liaison with the public, the salesperson, must be properly prepared.

Appearance

Before helping shoppers with their purchases, the salesperson must make an impression that is conducive to purchasing. The first impression is the result of the salesperson's appearance. The prospective customer isn't apt to be receptive to the advice of someone who isn't appropriately attired.

In small stores dress regulations are not as stringent as they are in the larger organizations. Most small storekeepers deal with only a few salespeople and can supervise their dress habits informally. In some larger stores, where management often deals with several hundred salespeople, a uniform dress code is established. For example, such colors as black, brown, navy blue, and gray may be prescribed. The main reason for this regulation, often frowned upon by employees, is that it makes certain the salesperson's attire will not detract from the merchandise, and shocking colors and patterns will be avoided. The simple statement that "employees should dress in good taste" is not adequate. Taste is too personal to be left to chance. The salesperson should avoid wearing any type of outfit that might be offensive and could discourage a customer from asking for sales help. For example, the younger employee working in a conservative men's shop should avoid wearing "way-out" styles. If salespersons choose to dress in a manner unlike the atmosphere of the store, the potential customers might not seek their advice.

Salespeople at Abraham & Straus, a department store with branches in New York State, receive a copy of a booklet called "Your Appearance Counts," which serves as a guide in the selection of appropriate styles and colors for business use. The following questions are posed in the booklet, which when answered affirmatively, contribute to proper appearance:

Ladies . . .

Is your hair neatly combed?
Is your skin clear?
Are your hands clean and well manicured?
Makeup just right . . . not too heavy . . . not too light?
No runs in your stockings?
Are you wearing neat, well-heeled (and comfortable) shoes?
Is your attire businesslike and fresh looking?

Gentlemen ...

Is your hair trim and clean?
Do you shave daily?
Hands well scrubbed ... nails clipped and clean?
Are your shoes well shined?
Is your shirt or uniform clean and pressed?
Are your collar and shirt fresh?

Enthusiasm

The term *enthusiasm* does not imply that a salesperson should be overly aggressive and should "come on strong." Being too aggressive may lead to overpowering the customers and convincing them to buy items they might not really want. An enthusiastic salesperson is one who shows a real feeling for the merchandise and stimulates the customer's emotions. If the salesperson discusses the merchandise enthusiastically, the enthusiasm may transfer to the customer. Too often, shoppers are helped by lethargic salespeople who encourage a poor frame of mind.

Voice and Speech

A voice that is sufficiently audible and speech that properly uses diction are important to good selling technique. Salespersons do not, by any means, need theatrical training to make a clear presentation to customers, but they should exercise care in the manner in which they speak and in their choice of words. The salesperson who speaks properly will more easily establish rapport with the shopper.

Tact

Being tactful is essential to selling in the retail store. The salesperson's job is to help satisfy the customer's needs. Should the salesperson allow the customer to purchase something that the salesperson knows is wrong, even though the customer wants to make the purchase? Allowing this purchase to be made might lead to criticism (by the customer's friends) and eventual return of the goods. On the other hand, the salesperson's suggestion that the shopper's choice is a poor one might be an affront. For example, if a stout woman would like to purchase a dress that accentuates her figure in the wrong places, extreme care must be taken not to offend the customer, but to direct her tactfully to something more appropriate. Tactfulness is something that comes only with extreme caution and experience.

Self-Control

It is unlikely that even the most even-tempered salesperson hasn't had the desire to punch a customer in the eye. Prospective customers' personalities and attitudes are not all the same. A salesperson who is to be successful must keep in mind that "the customer is always right" and must control emotions even when this quoted statement seems intolerable. Abusing the customer will only lead to the loss of sales. The individual who is easily excited by the shortcomings of others shouldn't pursue a sales job, or for that matter any career in retailing.

In addition to the previously mentioned essentials for good selling technique, a prospective salesperson should show initiative and sincerity, and be cheerful, knowledgeable, and resourceful. It may be unusual for one person to have all these qualities, but the more that are possessed, the greater are the chances for success in a sales position.

HOW TO SELL

Perhaps the most difficult job to learn from a textbook is how to sell. Salesmanship can be improved by many techniques, such as role-playing, but there are basic steps in the selling process that should be learned before refinement can take place.

Know the Merchandise

Salespeople who say that they can sell anything without knowledge of the product are either naive or do not have an understanding of good selling methods. The ability to sell merchandise in a way that will gain the customers' confidence and satisfy their shopping needs requires an understanding of the merchandise for sale. The inability to answer the shoppers' specific product questions tends to make salespeople bluff, or avoid the queries. Using proper technique may result not only in an immediate sale; it may also lead to future customer purchases. While it is not really possible for a salesperson to be completely knowledgeable in all areas of hard goods and soft goods, it is important to have some fundamental information about the merchandise. Complete unfamiliarity with the goods (in the case of a new employee or a transfer from another department) necessitates getting the necessary product information. (The sources of product information will be discussed later in the chapter.) The following areas should be completely familiar to the salesperson.

Merchandise Location

Not all merchandise is arranged in shelves or on racks that are easily accessible. Some goods are kept in reserve (under counters or in stockrooms, for example) and the knowledge of their exact location is important. The need to search for merchandise detains customers and wastes time. Even for merchandise that is exposed, it is important to know the exact location.

Merchandise Uses

While it is obvious what purpose a dress or a suit serves, some goods have less obvious uses, or numerous uses. For example, a vacuum cleaner, in addition to cleaning rugs, may be adapted for upholstery and drapery cleaning, and perhaps even for spray painting. Even in soft goods some items might be adapted for various uses. With a different blouse, an outfit can be used for daytime or evening wear.

Styles

The shapes of things (styles) vary from season to season. Besides knowing which styles are fashionable or suitable for a particular purpose, salespeople should know the appropriate styles for their customers. For example, the lines of a double-breasted jacket are arranged in such a manner that they somewhat conceal a "bulging midsection." Knowledge of styles and their uses can help in closing a sale more quickly. Style is not limited to soft goods. Refrigerators, ranges, dining room tables, and chairs are examples of other types of merchandise that are available in a variety of styles. It is important for a salesperson who sells refrigerators to have sufficient knowledge of that department's various models and their advantages to satisfy the most discriminating customer. For example, a customer might want to know the advantages of a double-door refrigerator-freezer as compared with a conventional model.

Sizes

In addition to clothing and accessories, other merchandise comes in a variety of sizes. Sofas, chairs, dishwashers, television sets, and pool tables, just to mention a few, come in different sizes. Salespersons should have an understanding of the sizes in their departments so they can quickly help customers choose the right items. Some years ago a person selling women's clothing was concerned only with misses' and junior sizes. In an attempt to approximate the female figure more closely and eliminate costly alterations, manufacturers have introduced many new size ranges. In addition to the two already mentioned, sales personnel must know the differences among junior petites,

TYPICAL SIZE RANGES FEMALE FIGURE										
DEPARTMENT	SPECIAL INFORMATION					SIZES				
Junior	Short waisted, narrow figure	3	5	7	9	11	13	15		
Junior Petite	5'2" and under	3	5	7	9	11	13			
Missy	Average female figure	8	10	12	14	16	18	20		
Missy Petite	5'5" and under	8	10	12	14	16				
Half Sizes	Full figure, short waisted	14½	16½	18½	20½	22½	24½	26½		
Womens	Full figure, average height	38	40	42	44	46	48	50		

FIGURE 15-1   (Left) Size-Range Chart   **FIGURE 15-2**   (Right) Special Size Tag

misses' petites, diminutives, half sizes, junior plenty, and women's sizes. (See Figures 15-1 and 15-2.) Sizes for the male figure run an equally wide gamut.

Price and Quality

Aside from just remembering the prices, a salesperson must often justify them. Remembering the prices without consulting the price tags gives a customer the impression that the salesperson is familiar with the merchandise. This knowledge, while it might seem insignificant, often establishes confidence. In those areas where prices vary according to changes (the use of one fabric instead of another on a chair), it is less likely that a salesperson will remember all the prices.

Justifying the price requires a knowledge of quality and the recitation of the product's salient features. Quality can be impressed upon the customer with the intelligent discussion of such information as materials ("this is linen, which is one of the costlier fibers"), construction ("this glove is made with an outseam, which eliminates stitches on the inside and allows for maximum comfort"), guarantees ("this refrigerator is unconditionally guaranteed for three years"), and workmanship ("the lapel is handsewn, which provides for a neater look").

Care of Merchandise

The special care or the ease in caring for an item is important to good selling. A statement indicating that a suit is unconditionally washable and dries without wrinkles just about convinces the travel-minded customer to buy. Similarly, the customer purchasing a garment that requires special cleaning attention, such as a suede coat, is apt to receive longer wear if he or she is familiar with the care of the coat. The salesperson should be absolutely certain about how to care for such goods because mistakes can lead to unnecessary returns and customer dissatisfaction.

Approaching the Customer

After becoming familiar with the merchandise to be sold, the salesperson is ready to greet prospective customers. Customers should be greeted with a friendly smile. The greeting used to begin a conversation is most important. One should not begin with a question that might bring a negative response. For example, approaching a customer by asking, "May I help you?" might bring a reply of "no." Although this is typical of retail store selling, it is a poor way to begin a sales presentation. Preferably a salesperson might begin by saying, "Good morning, I'm Mr. Smith. I'd like to help you with your purchasing needs." Another desirable approach is to strike up a conversation regarding an article of merchandise that a shopper is examining—for example, "That chair is as comfortable as it is good-looking. Try sitting in it." When a customer approaches a salesperson for help, the greeting is less difficult because the customer sought assistance. A mere "Good afternoon" is sufficient. Even "May I help you?" is acceptable, since in this situation it will not bring the possibility of a "no" response.

At this early point in the sales demonstration, it is time to determine the shopper's needs. Certainly, approaching the customer who is examining an item gives the salesperson an idea of what is desired. In cases where the customer isn't studying the merchandise, a determination of what is needed is a little more difficult. Some brief questions (which become second nature with experience) pertaining to style, color, size (if applicable), and so on will guide the salesperson in the selection of appropriate merchandise. Keeping in mind what the store has available for sale, the salesperson is now ready to show the merchandise to the customer.

Presentation of the Merchandise

Telling the customer about the merchandise, the salesperson should include all of those features that make it distinctive. Such factors as construction, materials, and uses are generally discussed. To make the item more desirable to the customer, an outstanding feature should be stressed. For example, the mention of the name of the designer, if he or she is one of renown, would probably be more meaningful to a fashion-minded customer than any other information. Similarly, to shoppers who are interested in easing their household chores, the mention of completely "wash and wear" should be most meaningful. It is beneficial to invite the customer to "try" the merchandise. A piece of jewelry becomes more exciting if it is tried on rather than being viewed on a counter. The person interested in a lounge chair should be invited to sit in it rather than to merely admire it. The comfort achieved (if it is comfortable) will help close the sale. How many suits and coats would a man purchase if he didn't try them on? Whatever the item, the customer's involvement is extremely important for closing the sale.

If an item can be demonstrated, it should be. What could be more convincing than the demonstration of a vacuum cleaner in action? Would stores sell as many color television sets without showing them in operation? Some other examples of the power of demonstration are the purposeful dropping of an unbreakable dish or the crushing of a wrinkle-proof blouse. There are very few types of merchandise that do not lend themselves to customer involvement or demonstration.

Handling Objections

There are many hints that indicate when a customer is getting ready to purchase. These hints are usually in question form. "How much does it cost?" "Does it come in other colors?" "Are alterations included in the price?" "How soon could it be delivered?" "Is the installation cost included in the price?" These are but a few of the signals that a customer might be ready to purchase. Even after spending time considering a purchase, the shopper might hesitate and raise objections. These objections might be excuses telling the salesperson that the customer isn't going to buy, or they might be sincere objections that need further reassurance. Whatever the reason for the objections, the salesperson must overcome them to close the sale.

Some of the more common objections are those involving price, the product's features, inadequate guarantees, the delivery time, and poor fit. Even the salesperson's attitude might deter buying. The experienced salesperson is prepared to handle these objections and does so in a number of ways. One technique is to agree with the customer but then to offer another selling point. For example, Mrs. Jones shows interest in the dress she is trying on but declares, "The price is high." The salesperson might reply, "Yes, but the fit is so perfect the cost generally involved in alterations will be eliminated." Aside from the use of "yes, but" to handle objections, these phrases may be used:

> I agree with you, sir, but another factor to consider . . .
> You're right, Mr. Peter, however . . .
> One of my customers felt exactly as you do, but she finally made the purchase because . . .
> It certainly is a long time to wait for the table, Miss Adams, but . . .

The above statements are by no means the only ones to be used but are intended to serve as guides for the new salesperson.

Another technique employed in handling objections is to ask questions of the customer. In this way a salesperson can separate excuses for not buying from real objections. Examples of some questions to use are:

> What color would you prefer?
> Why do you object to the style of this refrigerator?
> What would you consider an appropriate price for a sofa?

Still another technique to be used, but with caution, is to deny the objection. Salespersons must be absolutely certain of their information when employing this method.

Customer's Objection	Salesperson's Response
I think the fabric will shrink.	Oh no, madam, the shirt has been preshrunk.
The Elite Shoppe sells it for $5 less than your price	Our store always sells that item at a price lower than the Elite Shoppe.
I don't think the rug will be delivered in time for the party.	I guarantee the delivery date, Mrs. Reihing.

If the salesperson uses this method but doesn't provide truthful information, the customer will be dissatisfied upon learning the truth and probably will never again trust the store's sales personnel.

Closing the Sale

After presenting the information necessary to answer all the customer's questions and any objections have been overcome, the salesperson should try to close the sale. The recognition of the appropriate time to close comes with experience. The seasoned salesperson looks for signals that indicate that the prospect is about to become a customer. Only the naive or inexperienced salesperson expects to hear from the customer something like, "O.K., I'm ready to buy." Some of the closing signals are

How long will it take for the alteration to be completed?
Can I charge this purchase?
When can I expect the merchandise to be delivered?
Are these items exchangeable?
Is the guarantee for one year?

The salesperson who recognizes what he or she believes to be the opportune moment should then proceed to close the sale. Choosing the right words at this time might seem difficult to the student of retailing. Using the question "Are you ready to buy?" is certainly not the correct approach. The use of questions and statements such as these prove to be effective:

Shall I gift-wrap it for you?
Would you like to wear the shoes out of the store?
Which would you like, the blue one or the brown one?
Will that be cash or charge?
Would you like it delivered or will you take it with you?

> After today this item goes back to its original price.
> This is the last one in stock; a special order will take four weeks.

Even the most experienced salespersons sometimes find that they have not chosen the appropriate time to close the sale. It make take several attempts before a sale is finalized. Retailing students should keep in mind that not everyone is really a customer, and also that not every shopper can be satisfied with the store's offerings. The customer's words in refusing to buy should be evaluated. For example, a definite "no" might indicate that the customer can't be satisfied. Reactions such as "I'd like to see another style" or "no, I'm still uncertain about the fit of this garment" are signals that perhaps more selling effort is necessary. Whatever the degree of negativism, a seasoned salesperson should not give up after the first attempt. How many attempts should be made? Too few might let the customer "slip away." Too many tries might tend to make shoppers feel they are being high-pressured. The right number of times before one gives up will eventually be perceived through experience.

After making an unsuccessful attempt, a salesperson must be able to proceed again to a point that will result in success. In order to do this, the salesperson must keep some information in reserve that will perhaps whet the customer's appetite. For example:

> If you purchase today, you will be entitled to buy a second pair at a 20 percent reduction.
> This is the last day of our special sale; tomorrow the price will increase by 10 percent.
> Did you know that these shoes are *wear-dated* and are guaranteed, under normal use, for one year?

If consecutive attempts to close are unsuccessful and it is felt that the customer still might purchase the product, some salespeople resort to what is called a T.O. or turnover. This technique involves turning the customer over to a more prestigious department member such as the manager or buyer. Customers might respond more affirmatively to these people and thus the department will benefit.

It is important to keep in mind that even a customer who does not make a purchase at this time is still a prospect for future business. Courtesy is extremely important to guarantee that the customer will return at another time. It is at this time that many stores lose their favorable image. A disagreeable or disgruntled salesperson can bring disastrous results.

Some stores provide their new sales employees with printed suggestions on how to sell. The training department of the Personnel Division of Abraham & Straus provides its employees with a card entitled, *"How to Sell to Close the Most Sales."* (See Figure 15-3.)

HOW TO SELL
TO CLOSE THE MOST SALES

Step No.1—*KNOW*	Step No. 2—*SHOW*
Know The Merchandise—	*Show Alertness—*
Location, use, type or style, size, price, quality, care.	*Contact* customers promptly. Greet customers positively.
Know How To Stock It—	*Show Courtesy—*
Arrange for ease in selling. Assort and keep neat.	Customers expect a friendly attitude, a pleasant smile, and help in selecting.
Know that *the more customers you approach, the more you will sell.*	*Show Merchandise—*
	Determine customer needs in relation to stock. Show medium price first. Display to best advantage—dramatize, demonstrate use. Be enthusiastic.

KNOW	*SHOW*	*TELL*	*SELL*

HOW TO SELL
TO CLOSE THE MOST SALES

Step No. 3—*TELL*	Step No. 4—*SELL*
TELL:	SELL:
the facts or distinctive features of the merchandise.	benefits—something that the merchandise does for the customer which appeals to pride, pleasure, profit, protection.
Size, type or style, use, construction, manufacturer's name, care.	There is a sell point for every tell point.

CLOSE THE SALE
NARROW THE SELECTION
ASSUME THE CUSTOMER IS BUYING — ASK HER TO BUY.
SUGGEST ADDITIONAL MERCHANDISE.
ASSUME TAKE-WITH.   THANK CUSTOMER.

TRAINING DEPARTMENT   ABRAHAM & STRAUS   PERSONNEL DIVISION

FIGURE 15–13 How to Sell to Close the Most Sales

Courtesy of Abraham & Strauss

SUGGESTING ADDITIONAL MERCHANDISE

Although the salesperson should be pleased with having closed the sale, it is at this point that the experienced employee tries to tempt the customer with additional merchandise. The customer is in a buying frame of mind and with some expert selling effort it might be possible to build the sale. Suggestion selling should in no way be considered as high pressure, but rather as a way of assisting the customer. There are a number of ways in which this can be accomplished.

1. The suggestion of accessories to be used in conjunction with the purchase. For example, an alert salesperson having sold a customer a suit could suggest such items as shirts and ties with which the suit could be coordinated. Instead of asking whether or not the customer is interested in these other items, the creative salesperson selects the accessories that are most appropriate and demonstrates to the customer how perfectly they blend. Even if the shopper has no intention of purchasing a shirt and tie, their display might be tempting. Accessories need not be limited to soft goods. At the close of a vacuum cleaner sale, attachments and disposable bags might be suggested. Similarly, the sale of a phonograph might result in a larger total purchase if records and record cases are suggested to the customer.

2. The suggestion of more than one of the items sold. For example, a customer having selected a pair of stockings might consider buying additional pairs if the salesperson can offer an advantage of the multiple purchase. In practice you can convince a customer to buy a second pair of stockings by saying, "If you buy a single pair and one stocking becomes damaged, you'll have to dispose of the other. By buying two pairs, you will still be left with one pair even if a stocking from the second pair is destroyed." Similarly, upon completing a sale, you might suggest additional yardage for stress areas (stairs) that might wear away before the rest of the carpet.

3. The suggestion of a special offer. Very often purchasing one item may entitle the customer to take advantage of another item at a reduced price. In a dollar sale, a customer who purchases one item at the regular price may buy a second item for an additional dollar. Service contracts are offered to customers having just purchased an appliance, at a price less than the customary price.

SUGGESTIONS TO PROMOTE FUTURE BUSINESS

Although completing the sale is extremely important, once having done so, the resourceful salesperson takes the opportunity to guarantee the customer's return for future purchases. Retailers seek to establish a reputation that will encourage other transactions. Spending a few extra moments with the customer at this time will promote good will and encourage that individual to return. Some suggestions for achieving these ends are

Here's my card, Mrs. Bennett. It has been a pleasure helping you with your purchases. I'd like to do so again in the near future.

Mrs. Avidon, I'd like your telephone number in case something special comes in that I feel would be appropriate for you.

Rushing to the next customer without the use of these important courtesies is not as important as the few moments spent to solidify a customer relationship. This time might establish a rapport that the customer will recall when ready to shop again.

SOURCES OF PRODUCT INFORMATION

There are a great number of sources salespersons can investigate for information pertaining to the merchandise in their departments. Some of these sources are easily found within the store; others demand that the salesperson look elsewhere.

The Buyer

The most knowledgeable person in the department in regard to the product is the buyer. Buyers generally specialize in a particular type of merchandise, such as junior dresses, sweaters, or produce. In the larger organizations the buyer's range of merchandise is highly specialized. In the smaller store the buyer's purchases may be more diversified. The continuous exposure to merchandise coupled with a sound education in retailing provides the buyer with the needed know-how.

In stores where the buyer has the overall responsibility for the department's operation and thus comes into direct contact with the sales staff, the buyer is the best source of information for salespeople to tap. In organizations such as the larger chain operations, where the buyer is not easily accessible to the sales personnel, salespeople must resort to other sources of merchandise information.

Assistant Buyers

In some stores where buyers spend a great deal of time in the market, their assistants are often actually in charge of the sales staff. While perhaps not having the buyer's experience, the assistant is an excellent source for merchandise information. This job requires a limited amount of purchasing and thus demands a good deal of product knowledge.

Managers

In organizations where the buyer operates from a central location, store managers and, in larger stores, department managers are about the most knowledgeable merchandise experts in the store. They often select the merchandise their stores will feature from lists made available to them by the central buyers, and they have a working knowledge of the merchandise. Salespeople working in the large chain operation will find that their managers can provide the information necessary to make them knowledgeable sales personnel.

Vendors' Salespeople

Most retail stores (certainly the main store in large organizations) are visited by manufacturers' and wholesalers' representatives. These representatives (salespeople) call upon the retailers to show their lines of merchandise. If the retailer cannot conveniently visit the market, these people must visit the retail store. After purchases have been made, it is not uncommon for them to offer selling suggestions to the store's salesforce. Particularly in areas in which merchandise fit and care are important factors, this salesperson can be extremely helpful.

Other Vendor Aids

In addition to the informal knowledge a manufacturer's or wholesaler's salesperson can provide, vendors sometimes provide brochures and even recorded lectures about their merchandise's features. Some years ago a swimsuit manufacturer prepared a recording that was mailed to retailers; it discussed fabrics, construction, quality, fitting suggestions, and style information. The use of the record gave salespeople firsthand information about the vendor's products and made the selling of them easier.

Merchandise Tags and Labels

A good many items have tags and labels affixed that offer some information that may be helpful to the sales personnel. For example, in this era of wash and wear, every garment that falls into this category will surely have an at-

FIGURE 15-4 Merchandise Tag with Washing Instructions

tached "hangtag" stating this information. Likewise, tags often suggest methods of caring for the garment, such as washing instructions or directions to guarantee maximum use of the product. Fiber content, type of leather, and special size restrictions (as shown in Figure 15-4) are just some of the items that can be found on garment tags. In hard goods it is common to find tag attachments that include such information as colors available, guarantees, warranties, delivery dates, and construction features.

Formal Study

Colleges and universities offer courses in product information, which can be invaluable for salespeople. Such courses and the highlights covered are

Textiles. The study of all types of fabrics, their uses, the necessary care, the life expectancy, and the government regulations concerning textiles. This course is valuable for every salesperson selling soft goods.

Fashion Accessories. The study of leather, gloves, shoes, jewelry, furs, handbags, and neckwear. Styles, methods of construction, and the care of garments are discussed.

Home Furnishings. The study of dinnerware, glassware, silverware, furniture, clocks, and other household accessories.

TELEPHONE SELLING

Some people consider telephone selling a personal appeal to customers. Since it is not the same as in-person salesmanship we believe it deserves discussion. The suburban migration of customers and the growth of traffic congestion in downtown areas have led to a considerable increase in the use of the telephone as a means of ordering merchandise. Telephone ordering is generally in response to advertisements, but it is by no means limited to advertising responses. Since customers ordering by phone frequently require answers to questions, some large stores set up special departments for telephone selling. Selling by telephone requires special characteristics on the part of the salesperson, who has contact with customers only by voice. The salesperson under such conditions requires a good vocabulary, a thorough knowledge of the total selling stock, and a strong imagination. This person must be carefully trained and be aware of the following:

1. Inquiries must be converted to orders.
2. Long pauses while the salesperson gets information are bad. The salesperson must have up-to-date knowledge of the stock.
3. Orders may be increased by the suggestion of additional quantities, higher-priced merchandise, related goods, and price specials.

If the level of telephone sales is to be encouraged, the following procedures should be followed:

1. The store's telephone equipment should be increased to a point at which there will be minimal delays because of busy signals.
2. Provision should be made for the service of incoming calls for a long period of time during the day. It is not unusual for stores to maintain telephone service beyond the hours in which the store is normally open.
3. Telephone selling specialists should be trained so that satisfactory service will be ensured.
4. The fact that the store offers telephone service should be prominent in all advertising and other sales promotional devices.

Those stores that promote selling by telephone report that as much as 13 percent of their total sales come to the store by means of the telephone. Moreover, research indicates that these are sales that would not have been made had telephone service not been available, since many people shop in person at stores other than those to which they called their orders. Average telephone sales are usually 40 percent larger than average floor sales.

Soliciting by Telephone

Selling by telephone need not be limited to instances in which a customer calls the store. Sales are frequently made by a call from the store to a customer. For example, a salesperson may call a customer with information of new merchandise or special sales. This sort of solicitation is usually done with established customers. Many stores frown upon telephone solicitation, since they feel that the annoyance to customers results in more loss of good will than increase in sales.

The amount of "blind" soliciting—that is, calling people who are not regular customers—has grown in use in recent years. While it may be productive to small retailers who are not trying to build a repeat business, it may lead to a serious loss of good will and the destruction of a carefully built up store image.

CAREERS IN SALES

The salesforce in a store is generally made up of two groups of people. One group is comprised of part-time salespeople who are looking for a limited amount of work without the intention of moving into a managerial position. The other group is made up of people who are interested in management careers. The job as salesperson provides these people with the foundation necessary to achieve the goal of manager. Those qualifications required of the former group for sales positions include neat appearance, dependability, sincerity, and good speaking habits. The latter group generally must have those qualifications discussed earlier in the chapter, in addition to a college degree, since their future aspirations are beyond that of salesperson. Salaries for salespeople vary according to the merchandise they sell and their previous experience. The methods of remuneration for salespeople are discussed in Chapter 5.

Action for the Independent Retailer

If there is one area in which the independent can compete with the large company, it is in personal selling. Being able to recognize and relate to individual customers has been the secret of success for many smaller retailers. While the large stores experience a high rate of salesperson turnover, the independent generally has a much better record. Many customers who patronize the independent retailer do so because of the attention they receive from the salespeople.

Without the need for complicated training in such areas as the various methods for recording sales, the independent retailer has the advantage of being able to train salespeople on the floor and observe their performances. Continuous informal training about greeting customers, assisting customers, building sales, and so forth encourages improved performance. In large stores, where management is often preoccupied with other tasks, selling practices are usually given less attention than is necessary. Through efficient selling, the independent can gain customer loyalty.

IMPORTANT POINTS IN THE CHAPTER

1. *The trend toward scientific retailing controls and automation must not be permitted to de-emphasize the importance that management gives to personal selling.*

2. *The image of a store is directly affected by its salespeople. To impart the proper image to customers, salespeople should be neat, tactful, enthusiastic, and should possess a good voice and grammatical speech patterns.*

3. *Capable selling technique requires a thorough knowledge of the merchandise, including its location in the store, uses, sizes and styles, and prices.*

4. *The effective salesperson is friendly in approaching customers, presenting the merchandise in its best light, and being certain to point out the outstanding features of the goods. Since customers will always raise objections, the salesperson should be prepared for them.*

5. *As salespersons gain experience, knowing the method and timing of closing the sale becomes easier. After the sale is safely closed, a good salesperson should suggest additional merchandise for immediate or future sale.*

6. *The product information that is required by salespeople may be obtained from the buyer, manager, vendors' salespeople, and merchandise tags and labels.*

REVIEW QUESTIONS

1. In which type of operation might the salesperson's job be eliminated? For what reason?
2. What adverse effect can the "hard sell" approach have on customers?
3. When a customer says, "I don't like that store," to whom is the customer often referring?
4. Why is the salesperson's appearance important?
5. If dress regulations merely stress "good taste," might there be some problems?
6. For what reasons do stores forbid their sales personnel to wear loud prints and stripes?
7. How can a salesperson's enthusiasm or lack of it play an important role in selling ability?
8. Define tact. Why must a salesperson be tactful?
9. Discuss the various factors the salesperson should know concerning merchandise.
10. Besides remembering the prices of merchandise, for what other purpose may the salesperson be called upon in regard to price?
11. Why, besides making it a selling point, must the salesperson be certain of special care requirements of merchandise?
12. "May I help you," although commonly used by salespeople, is not a preferred approach. Why?
13. Is it important to demonstrate the merchandise that can be demonstrated? Defend your answer.
14. State some of those objections a customer may have for not making a purchase.
15. In addition to the "yes, but" technique of overcoming objections, describe another commonly used method.
16. Describe some of the signals that indicate a closing attempt should be made by the salesperson.
17. Should a salesperson try to close again if the first attempt was unsuccessful? Why?
18. Define suggestion selling by giving some examples of its use.
19. Why are the few extra moments spent with the customer after the sale has been made important to the retail store?
20. Who in the department store is the best source of product information?

CASE PROBLEMS

CASE PROBLEM 1

Recently, Ellen Frances was watching television and saw a commercial advertising a sale on "fun furs" at Stevan's Department Store. The commercial indicated that the selection, specially priced, included rabbit, muskrat, raccoon, and mink paw. The price range for this special sale was from $200 to $575.

Tempted by the advertisement, Mrs. Frances visited Stevan's and was further excited by the store's elegant window displays featuring the fur coats. With her appetite whetted, she rushed to the fur department to make her selection. Because she was unfamiliar with fur, she sought the assistance of a salesperson who could help her choose a coat. No salesperson approached her, so Mrs. Frances made the first overture. The conversation that followed went something like this:

Mrs. Frances:	"I'd like some assistance with a fur coat.
Salesperson:	Oh, they're all on sale. Look through the rack.
Mrs. Frances:	I'm not familiar with some of these furs—could you help me?
Salesperson:	I'd like to, but I'm really not that knowledgeable about furs, myself.
Mrs. Frances:	(After looking through the rack and choosing one to try on) Do you think it fits right?
Salesperson:	It looks O.K.
Mrs. Frances:	Does this coat require any special care?
Salesperson:	I'm not sure.
Mrs. Frances:	I don't think I'm going to purchase a coat today.
Salesperson:	At these prices, we wouldn't really worry.

Mrs. Frances, thoroughly disgusted, left the store without making a purchase.

QUESTIONS

1. Do you think the salesperson had those qualities essential for good selling? Which were lacking?
2. Did the salesperson have enough knowledge of furs to sell them effectively? How might this knowledge be gained?
3. What could the store do to improve such a salesperson's ability?

CASE PROBLEM 2

Mr. Ben, a small chain organization featuring conservative men's clothing, has ten units located in the suburbs of New York City. Its salespeople do not receive any special training because the company feels that the cost involved to do a meaningful job is prohibitive. Besides that, with the increased trend of self-selection, management rationalizes that even though its salespeople are not specifically trained, their help is better than complete self-selection.

The following is the essence of a conversation between a salesperson and customer at Mr. Ben's:

Customer:	I'd like to see a gray suit.
Salesperson:	(Selecting the least expensive first) This is a good number.
Customer:	May I try it on?
Salesperson:	Yes.
Customer:	(Returning from the dressing room) It seems to fit right. How much is it?
Salesperson:	$59.95.
Customer:	That's less than I anticipated. I'll take it.
Salesperson:	Cash or charge?
Customer:	Cash.

The suit was packed, and the customer paid for it and left the store.

QUESTIONS

1. Do you think the salesperson was effective? More effective than self-selection in this case?
2. Was the customer sold the right-priced suit?
3. How could the salesperson have increased the final amount of the sale?
4. Is management's attitude correct regarding training of salespeople? Defend your answer.
5. What methods could be employed to better prepare salespersons at Mr. Ben's?

V

retail information systems, functions, and controls

16 merchandise and expenses

INTRODUCTION

Simply stated, management's prime responsibilities lie in the area of earning the highest possible profits while safeguarding the company's assets. The control of merchandise inventory and expenses is concerned with these managerial duties. The proprietor of a small firm may control its inventory by watching the shelves, and with a little wisdom, can minimize expenses. As a firm grows in size, it becomes impossible for management to know the details of the inventory or weigh the necessity of each expense. Under such conditions, careful control procedures become mandatory for successful operations.

MERCHANDISE CONTROL

In most retail enterprises the amount of money invested in merchandise inventory represents a large part of the organization's total capital. Both the profitability of a store and the capability of its high and middle management can be judged, in large part, by its inventory. Inventory must be large enough to ensure a high level of sales, but not so large as to result in excessive losses or expenses. It is relatively simple to carry a large enough inventory to satisfy every customer. However, the markdowns, handling costs, rental expense, insurance expense, and so on that go with a large inventory make it uneconomical. To find the proper balance of inventory requires careful control that can be achieved only through a careful analysis of purchases and sales.

All retail stores need inventory controls. The small retailer who merely watches the store's shelves can maintain a proper balance between inventory and probable customer demand. However, that retailer's buying will suffer through lack of information concerning color, size, trends, and other customer preferences. To cite an example of the importance of trends to a small retailer, the Puerto Rican migration to New York City resulted in a gradual change in the clientele of many small popular-priced women's shoe stores. This change required a completely new sizing pattern. Stores that had habitually ordered shoes in sizes ranging from 6 to 9 found that their new customers needed sizes $4\frac{1}{2}$ to 8. Since these small stores kept no inventory records, many sustained considerable losses. Sales of small sizes were lost, and the larger sizes could not be sold.

Generally, the necessity for merchandise control can be summarized as follows:

1. *Matching the stock on hand to customer needs.* A well-run store must have in stock the item that the customer has in mind. While no store can please every customer, any store that expects future traffic must please a substantial number of customers. This can only be achieved through a careful study of the needs and preferences of the store's clientele.

2. *Minimizing markdowns.* The prompt reporting that is a principal feature of a sound merchandise control system brings attention to situations in which there are goods in excess of customer needs. By carefully analyzing sales, a relationship between stock on hand and estimated customer demand can be determined. Conditions in which the stock is in excess of the expected demand may indicate the necessity for immediate markdowns. The timeliness of markdowns is important, since the earlier the markdown, the higher the selling price.

3. *Controlling shortages.* Effective merchandise control indicates the amount of merchandise that should be on hand. When the actual amount on hand is less than the amount predicted, shrinkage has occurred. Sound merchandising control can quickly pinpoint the specific area of shortage. Once the location of the shortage is known, effective security procedures can frequently be initiated.

4. *Controlling the investment in inventory.* The inventory carried by a retail store represents a considerable portion of the store's net worth. When the inventory on hand exceeds the amount required to satisfy customers, money is unnecessarily tied up. Merchandise control, by keeping the investment in inventory in check, frees money for expansion, improvements, and so on.

5. *Reducing stock carrying expenses.* There are many expenses involved in carrying inventory. These include the retail cost of floor space, personnel for handling, insurance premiums, and other overhead costs. Carrying unnecessary stock results in an increase of these expenses. The careful control of merchandise minimizes these expenses. In most retail stores, a reduction in the size of the stockroom, which results from carrying a small inventory, increases the available selling space, a vital factor in a store's success.

6. *Improving purchasing procedures.* The buyer's decisions about what to buy, when to buy, and how much to buy can spell the difference between the success or failure of an operation. It is important that these decisions be based on up-to-date, efficient information about the sizes, styles, and colors the customers require. The best source of such information is a history of past customer requirements. The end product of merchandise control includes detailed analyses of stock, sales, and merchandise on hand and on order. While this does not free the buyer from decision making, it offers vital data upon which the decisions must be based.

Merchandise may be controlled in two ways. The first, dollar control, requires an analysis of all sales and purchase transactions and yields information in terms of dollars. In other words, it produces merchandise information in terms of dollars, or "how much." The second method, unit control, analyzes merchandise transactions in terms of units. The output of unit control is in terms of specific pieces of merchandise, or "what." Both types of information are important, and many stores control merchandise by using both methods.

Dollar Control

The method of accounting for merchandise in terms of dollars may be accomplished by using the cost of the merchandise or, in most cases, its selling price. Dollar control may be used for determining inventory at cost (see Retail Inventory Method—Chapter 17), or the method may be extended to a complete system of merchandise control.

Classification of Merchandise

Since merchandise control in a small store may be nothing more than the proprietor looking over the stockroom and shelves, dollar control for the store as a whole may be adequate. In such a case, dollar control will indicate the total inventory picture. As stores grow in size and become departmentalized, merchandise control in terms of totals becomes ineffective. The very purposes of merchandise control require specific information concerning specific merchandise. For example, it is of little value to the menswear buyer in Macy's to know the total sales, purchases, and inventory of the total R. H. Macy operation.

Departmental Classification. When merchandise transactions are analyzed by departments rather than totals, the information given by a merchandise control system becomes far more useful to top management and to buyers. Classification by departments does not, however, give to the buyers information about the individual items of merchandise that make up their departments. For example, a menswear buyer must make a decision about buying dress shirts for next season. Departmental dollar control indicates that the department was very successful last year. However, since the control figures are for the total department, including suits, ties, and sportswear as well as dress shirts, the information is not specific enough for making decisions about individual items.

Price Line Classification. As the classification of merchandise narrows down and becomes more specific, the value of the system's informational output becomes more useful. Buyers who are given merchandise information by price line are able to spot the relative importance of the various categories of merchandise in their departments. The menswear buyer mentioned above now is able to use the merchandise information concerning the effectiveness of the various price lines of dress shirts the store carries, and the buying decision becomes more scientific. It should be pointed out that the buyer still knows nothing of colors and sizes.

Computerized Classification. As the classification of merchandise used for dollar control narrows down and becomes more valuable, the system becomes more detailed, more prone to error, and more expensive to operate. While there is some question about whether or not the computer can actually save money in the operation of a merchandise control system, it is the perfect tool for this sort of application. The computer is designed to deal with the mass of repetitive data that is the raw material for merchandise control. In addition to all of the previously mentioned classifications, computerized merchandise control is capable of producing information about size, color, vendor, and other merchandise characteristics. Data processing is no substitute for buyer judgment, but it is a great source of information, and the more information buyers have, the more likely they are to make correct decisions.

Procedures

Two methods may be used to analyze merchandise by the dollar method. These are the perpetual inventory method and the periodic inventory method.

Perpetual Inventory Method. The perpetual inventory method is used to calculate the amount of merchandise on hand at selling price without physically counting the actual stock on the shelves. By adding the selling price of the goods that came in during the day (purchases) to the selling price of the goods on hand in the morning (opening inventory), the selling price of total goods that were handled (available for sale) can be determined. Deducting the sales from this figure will leave the selling price of the unsold goods (closing inventory). An accountant presents this information as follows:

Opening inventory (goods on hand in the morning)	$ 9,000
Purchases	18,000
Merchandise available for sale (total goods handled)	$27,000
Less: sales	15,000
Closing inventory (goods on hand at closing)	$12,000

The illustration was based on one day's transactions, but the procedure may be used for any period up to one year. In addition, the illustration may be taken to be for one specific price line or, in a sophisticated data processing system, for one particular style, size, and color. When markdowns occur, they must be added to the sales. Failure to do this would result in an overstated closing inventory. In addition, the closing inventory must be reduced by any estimated shrinkage of stock.

The advantage of the perpetual inventory method is that it yields information quickly. As a result, not only are reports to buyers prompt, but income statements can be produced frequently.

The weakness of the system is in its accuracy. The classification of the goods must be correctly indicated on the sales slip for the system to work effectively. Life on a hectic sales floor does not lend itself to careful clerical work. Of course, those computerized systems that employ a prepunched sales tag that includes classification information are not as subject to clerical error.

Periodic Inventory System. The perpetual inventory system was used to determine the closing inventory by arithmetic calculation. The periodic inventory system requires the closing inventory to be determined by actual physical count, and it is the sales figure that is arithmetically calculated. By adding the selling price of the goods on hand at the beginning of the period to the selling price of the purchases made during the period, the selling price of the total goods handled may be determined. From this total the goods on hand at the end of the period (as determined by actual count) is deducted. The remainder, the difference between the amount that was available before sales were made, and the amount after sales were made, is the amount of sales and markdowns. An accountant states this as follows:

Opening inventory (goods on hand at beginning of period)	$ 9,000
Purchases	18,000
Merchandise available for sale (total goods handled)	$27,000
Less: closing inventory (goods unsold at end of period)	12,000
Total sales and markdowns	$15,000

The total sales and markdowns must be reduced by the amount of the markdowns to determine the sales.

The advantage of the periodic inventory system lies in its simplicity and reduced paperwork. Its principal disadvantage is that an actual physical inventory must be taken. This is costly and time-consuming, and disrupts the normal operation of the business. For this reason physical inventories are rarely taken more than twice a year. This severely limits the number of income statements and other informational reports that are made available under the physical inventory method.

Dollar Control—An Evaluation

Although our discussion of dollar control extended down to the narrow classification of size and color, dollar control is more frequently used to afford top management an overall financial view of operations. A disadvantage of using broad classifications for decision making is indicated in the following illustration.

The chief financial officer of a large department store correctly decided that a department's inventory was too high in relation to its sales. The store used dollar control of merchandise, classified by departments. The department, whose inventory–sales ratio was high, was ordered to cut its inventories by 10 percent. The simplest way to reduce inventories is by limiting purchases, and this was done by the department in question until the desired inventory level was achieved. The department's sales fell drastically. A careful analysis of the figures showed that the cut in new purchases and reorders had the effect of reducing the department's good selling items, since those were the items requiring replenishment. The drop in sales was due to the fact that while the inventory was at the proper level, it was to a large degree comprised of slow-moving items. The point of the illustration is that the financial officer was correct. The buyer, lacking narrowly classified merchandise control, simply did not know which items to cut. It would seem that dollar control at the mid-management level is not effective unless the classifications are very specific. Since unit control offers an excellent means of specific classification, this method is generally used at the mid-management level.

Unit Control

As is the case with dollar control, unit control is a system of analyzing merchandise transactions and producing informational reports. The difference between the two methods is that unit control information is kept in units rather than in dollars. In other words, instead of reporting the sales of a particular price line as $1,000, the report would read that 100 units were sold. The advantages of this method of record keeping, particularly to mid-management, are considerable. The following information, unavailable under dollar control systems, may be found in unit control reports:

1. *Vendor information.* Unit control systems can be designed to include information on vendors. In such cases the buyer is given information on the salability of the vendor's products, the number of sales returns for each vendor, the vendor's success in meeting delivery dates, the markdowns taken on a particular vendor's goods, and other vendor information of value to mid-management.

2. *More accurate information.* The stock-on-hand items listed in unit control reports are easily spot-checked. That is, a salesperson can easily check the inventory report of six pieces of a certain style on hand by going to the shelf and counting the units. This sort of checking should be done constantly and results in more accurate reporting.

3. *Better control of shortages.* The ease with which a unit control inventory may be checked not only turns up shortages easily, but also reveals the specific area in which the shortage occurred. This is helpful in designing security procedures.

4. *Time-in-store information.* Since the merchandise is accounted for by units rather than dollars, specific information concerning the units may be kept. The date of arrival is one such bit of information. Dating provides a buyer with information on slow-moving goods that should be marked down or placed on sale.

5. *Size and color information.* Of great value to the buyer for future ordering and reordering is data on customer preferences in colors and sizes. Armed with this information, the buyer is more likely to make correct decisions, which will minimize future broken-lot markdowns.

6. *Model stock information.* The determination of the ideal model stock requires constant evaluation and updating. An analysis of sales by units sold provides the information for such checking.

7. *Automatic reordering information.* Once the model stock has been determined, reorder levels can be established for staple merchandise. For example, the buyer can decide that one dozen pairs of men's black socks should be ordered whenever the stock falls below two dozen. This becomes an automatic procedure that can be done by a computer or buying assistant. In this way, the buyer may be relieved of a time-consuming task.

8. *Other buying information.* Data on out-of-stock conditions, the timing of purchases, promotions, and markdowns are quickly and readily available under a unit control situation.

Operating a Unit Control System

The operation of a unit control system is simple. However, as the information required increases, the amount of clerical work needed grows. Basically, a card or page is required for each item, showing the units on hand at the beginning of the day, the units that came in during the day, the units that left the store during the day, and the balance on hand at the end of the day. The following is a simplified form that might be used in a shirt department:

SHIRTS—STYLE 127

Date	On Hand	Received	Sold	Balance
1	10	—	2	8
2	8	—	3	5
3	5	12	2	15
4	15	—	4	11
5	11	12	6	17

As the information required by the system increases, so do the clerical problems. Sales returns and purchase returns data would require separate columns. Size and color information necessitates separate pages and cards. As the system's informational value increases, so too does its complexity and cost to operate. This is the biggest disadvantage of unit control. Today, large retailers are making extensive use of the computer to keep track of their merchandise units. In Chapter 20, *Electronic Data Processing,* the new methods will be explored.

Physical Inventories

The most important feature of any system of merchandise control is the inventory. The stock on hand is the heart of the system, and the effectiveness of a retailer's merchandise control can be checked by comparing the inventory predicted by the system with the inventory found to be on hand by actual count. The taking of a physical inventory—that is, the counting and tabulation of the value of the goods on hand—serves functions other than checking the merchandise control system.

1. Firms with no systems of merchandise control can only determine the value of the merchandise on hand by actually counting the stock.
2. Shortages may be determined by comparing the inventory shown by the merchandise control system with the amount indicated by physical count.
3. The financial statements prepared by accountants require the high degree of accuracy that is the result of actually counting the inventory.
4. The taking of a physical inventory requires "looking into corners" and calling attention to slow-moving and neglected stock, which might otherwise go unnoticed.

Frequency of Physical Inventories

Physical inventories should be taken as frequently as possible. However, the problems involved with inventory taking are so great that an inventory count is rarely done more than twice a year, and frequently only once a year. The efforts involved in taking an inventory, in terms of time, expenses, and interference with regular procedures, are so great that many stores take inventory only when required for the accountant's financial statements.

Physical Inventory Procedures

There are probably as many procedures for taking a physical inventory as there are businesses. These methods vary from the proprietor of a small store listing the store's merchandise on a sheet of paper, to the carefully planned large store method, which includes an instruction booklet. The system to be used must be designed to ensure absolute accuracy. A map of the entire store may be made, to ensure that each bin, shelf, and counter is included. Care must be taken to include the goods in the receiving department, shipping department, stockrooms, and window displays. Most inventory procedures include the use of two-person teams that count the stock, check the count, and make entries of the count on specially designed forms. After the counts have been entered on inventory sheets, the costs of each item of stock must be looked up and multiplied by the number of items on hand. The value of each of the items is then added, and the total cost of the inventory is determined.

Computerized Inventory Systems

Inventory taking may be greatly simplified with data processing systems. Such systems include a duplicate of the sales tag, which is affixed to each item in the store. These tags are prepunched with all of the information required for inventory purposes. They are removed from each item by the inventory taker and are then fed into the computer, where they are sorted and tabulated. The computer's output consists of a detailed listing of the merchandise on hand.

Stock Turnover

The function of inventory is to generate sales. Ideally the amount and makeup of the inventory carried should be matched to the maximum amount of sales planned. When more inventory is carried than is necessary for sales, markdowns and excessive capital investment result. Too little inventory results in loss of sales. The most important test to determine the effectiveness of the stock on hand is the stock turnover rate. This test indicates, for a specific period of time (usually one year), the number of times the inventory has been completely sold out and repurchased.

Calculation of Stock Turnover Rate

Stock turnover rate may be calculated at cost, at retail, or in units. Given the following information, turnover rates may be determined as follows:

	Units	Cost	Retail	
Sales 1,400 units				$14,000
Opening inventory	800	$ 6,000	$ 8,000	
Purchases	1,600	12,000	16,000	
Merchandise available for sale	2,400	$18,000	$24,000	
Less: closing inventory	1,000	7,500	10,000	
Cost of goods sold	1,400	$10,500	$14,000	

1. To find the stock turnover rate at retail:

Opening inventory at retail $ 8,000
Closing inventory at retail   10,000
$18,000 ÷ 2 = $9,000 Average inventory at retail

$$\frac{\text{Net sales}}{\text{Average inventory at retail}} = \frac{14,000}{9,000} = 1.56 \text{ Stock turnover rate at retail}$$

2. To find the stock turnover rate at cost:

Opening inventory at cost $ 6,000
Closing inventory at cost   7,500
$13,500 ÷ 2 = $6,750 Average inventory at cost

$$\frac{\text{Cost of goods sold}}{\text{Average inventory at cost}} = \frac{10,500}{6,750} = 1.56 \text{ Stock turnover rate at cost}$$

3. To find the stock turnover rate in units:

Closing inventory in units	800
Opening inventory in units	1,000
	1,800 $\div$ 2 = 900 Average inventory in units

$$\frac{\text{Net sales in units}}{\text{Average inventory in units}} = \frac{1,400}{900} = 1.56 \text{ Stock turnover rate in units}$$

As can be seen in the preceding illustrations, when the markup is consistent throughout the period, all of the methods result in the same turnover rate.

A more exact turnover rate can be determined by improving the accuracy of the average inventory. This could be done by adding the beginning inventory for each of the twelve months in a year, plus the closing inventory for the twelfth month, and dividing by 13.

Turnover by Merchandise Classifications

Different classifications of merchandise will have different turnover rates. For example, food stores generally have a turnover rate of about 16, while shoe stores rarely go above 4. Since turnover rates are used for comparison purposes, there is little to be learned by calculating the storewide rate. This is to say, a large department store might achieve the excellent turnover rate of 4, while its toy department has the poor turnover rate of 1.5. For maximum use, the turnover rate should be calculated by merchandise classifications or, at the very least, by departments. Some typical turnover rates are listed in Figure 16-1.

FIGURE 16–1 TYPICAL TURNOVER RATES
FOR CERTAIN RETAILERS

Gasoline stations	11
Grocery stores	16
Women's ready-to-wear	7
Department stores	6
Discount stores	5
Variety stores	4
Jewelry stores	3

The Use of Stock Turnover Rates

The effectiveness of a store's or department's inventory management can be determined in part by comparing its turnover rate with that of similar stores, industrywide averages, and the turnover rates of the same store in prior periods. It must be emphasized that a store's turnover rate is only part of the story. Turnover rates can be improved by reducing prices, carrying only fast-moving merchandise, and devising promotions. In other words, a higher-than-average turnover rate does not necessarily guarantee higher-than-average profits.

EXPENSE CONTROL

When the amount for which goods are sold is greater than the cost of the goods and the operating expenses, a profit results. Of the three factors—sales, cost of goods, and expenses—the first two are more subject to control by competition than by the management of a retail establishment. Even in the most carefully controlled buying and selling system, prices are in large part set by vendors and customers. The control of expenses is another matter. In this area the retailer is in full command, and it is this extremely important area that frequently spells the difference between retailing success and failure.

It should be understood that expense control does not mean expense reduction. Frequently, careful expense control can indicate the advantage of increasing some expenses, such as advertising, in order to improve the profit position. Expense control is the process by which expenses are analyzed and set at a level that will maximize profits.

Classification of Expenses

In part, expenses are controlled by comparing the expenses of one retailer with those of a similar store, an industrywide average, or prior periods within the same store. Such comparisons are used to indicate weaknesses, which are then subjected to further study. For example, if a competitor with a similar operation is able to make more sales with less sales salaries, expense control would point out this fact and provide a basis for further study.

Obviously, if comparisons are to be made, it is important that they be made between exactly the same expenses. It would be impossible to compare the sales salaries expense of two stores if one included fringe benefits and the other did not. To assist in the uniformity of expense classification, the National Retail Merchants Association suggests the following titles, which they call Natural Classification:

1. Payroll
2. Fringe benefits
3. Advertising
4. Taxes
5. Supplies
6. Services purchased
7. Unclassified
8. Traveling
9. Communications
10. Pensions
11. Insurance
12. Depreciation
13. Professional service
14. Donations
15. Bad debts
16. Equipment costs
17. Real property rentals

Expense Allocations

Once a sound system of expense classification has been established, the next step in expense control is to distribute these expenses to the various selling departments. This will enable management to check the effectiveness of each of the departments. Expense allocation can be relatively simple, as in the case of selling salaries, which are charged to the department in which the salesperson worked. The case of rent expense or heating expense is more difficult.

The distribution of expenses is facilitated by dividing the expenditures into two broad classifications: the direct expenses, those that occurred only because the department was in existence (sales salaries); and indirect expenses, those that occur whether or not the department exists (officers' salaries). The allocation of direct expenses is simple. There are several theories as to how indirect expenses should be divided.

Methods of Allocation

All methods of allocation agree that direct expenses should be allocated to the department receiving the benefit of such expenses. The methods differ in the manner in which indirect expenses are to be allocated, or if they should be allocated at all.

Net Profit Method

The net profit method requires that all expenses, direct or indirect, be allocated to selling departments so that a net profit may be determined for each department. The distribution of direct expenses should be made according to the department receiving the benefit of the expense. The indirect expenses should be allocated in a logical manner. For example, rent expense may be allocated by floor space.

The prime advantage of the net profit method is that, by showing the net profit of each selling department, it permits judgments to be made as to the department (and department head's) effectiveness. In addition, by taking indirect expenses into account, it indicates to the department head the importance of providing profits to cover these expenses. Finally, the total departmental operating statement is an aid in setting selling prices, since the retail price must be high enough to cover the direct and indirect expenses.

The problem with the net profit method is that the allocation of the indirect expenses is not only expensive, but so complicated that it cannot be accurate. If rent expense is to be allocated on the basis of the feet of floor space used by each department, should main floor front be considered as valuable as fifth floor rear? What is an accurate way for dividing the store president's salary among the various departments? Holding a department head responsible for indirect expenses, which are likely to be inaccurate, and over which the department head had no control, is a serious disadvantage.

Contribution Method

The contribution method attempts to overcome the disadvantages of the net profit method by limiting expense allocation to direct expenses. The final result from this method is controllable profit (only those expenses that the department head controls are deducted). Controllable profit is the department's contribution to the amount required to cover the indirect expenses and net profit.

This method does, in fact, answer the most serious objections of the net profit method. What it does not do is help in price setting, or involve the buyer with indirect expenses.

The Expense Budget

A common and effective method of controlling expenses is by means of an expense budget. This may be defined as a carefully planned estimate of future expenses for a specific period of time. Expense budgeting offers these advantages:

1. *Makes financial provision for future expenses.* By knowing the financial requirements of future expenses, management may make provision for such expenses and be prepared for them when they arise.
2. *Enables planned expenses to be balanced against planned sales.* To achieve a planned net profit, it is necessary to estimate expenses as well as sales and costs. Successful planning requires careful estimates of expenses, sales, and costs.

3. *Provides standard against which to measure performance.* Upon completion of the period for which the expense budget was prepared, a comparison is made between the actual expenses and the estimated (budgeted) expenses. Any significant differences may then be analyzed to determine the reasons for such variations. In this way, weak spots are frequently uncovered.

4. *Fixes responsibilities.* By identifying specific expenses with specific departments, a particular person may be held responsible for seeing to it that the amounts expended are within the budget. It is important that the person held responsible has the authority to approve or disapprove expenditures.

Preparing the Expense Budget

Typically, the expense budget is prepared as part of the overall planning. By adjusting past periods' information with the coming period's expectations, estimated sales, costs, and expenses may be determined. For example, if last year's sales of $100,000 is expected to be increased by 10 percent, then the budgeted sales will be $110,000. Should no change be expected in last year's 30 percent gross margin, the budgeted gross margin will be $110,000 $\times$ 30%, or $33,000. If the only change expected in last year's total expenses of $20,000 will be an additional $1,000 for salaries, then the budgeted expenses will be $21,000. The budgeted net profit is $12,000. This can be stated in income statement form as follows:

	Prior Period	Future Period Budget
Sales (to be increased by 10%)	$100,000	$110,000
Gross margin (30% both periods)	30,000	33,000
Less: expenses (to be increased by $1,000)	20,000	21,000
Net profit	$10,000	$12,000

After the total estimated expenses have been determined, the total is broken down into the various types of expenses such as rent, advertising, utilities, and so forth. Then the various types of expenses are split up among the departments. Department heads are involved in this procedure. The final step in preparing an expense budget is to break down the department budget into short-period budgets.

Action for the Independent Retailer

One of the great advantages large retailers have over their smaller competitors lies in their ability and willingness to keep intensive inventory control records. This gives them a clear picture of customer demand and improves their buying accordingly. This advantage results from the availability of trained personnel and computer service. The growing popularity of relatively inexpensive, simple, *small computers seems to be changing this. Now all but the smallest retailers can have access to speedy accurate inventory and sales analysis. A new generation of small computers that sell for about $5,000 is achieving nationwide success and is extending the advantages of computerization to all but the smallest retailers.*

For the vast number of retailers who cannot afford these small devices, inventory control is a serious problem. Too often the inventory problems are handled by a glance at the shelves. Generally speaking, this is simply not enough. While shortages can be determined in that fashion, details on customer preferences in color, size, and style are more difficult to determine. Small retailers should make an effort to keep inventory records, if not for the whole store, then at least for fast-moving, highly styled goods. A careful physical inventory should be taken periodically. Even in the smallest store, looking into corners and actually counting merchandise frequently brings surprises. In addition, it is impossible to calculate accurate profit figures without a physical inventory.

IMPORTANT POINTS IN THE CHAPTER

1. In order to ensure high profits and minimize losses, it is vital that management keep careful control of merchandise inventory and expenses.

2. Since the investment in inventory represents a large portion of an organization's capital, it must be carefully and constantly studied. Too large an inventory results in markdowns; too small an inventory results in lost sales. Management's effectiveness depends, in large part, upon how closely inventory is balanced against customer demand.

3. Control of inventory requires an exact knowledge of the various items that make up the total inventory at any specific time. This information can be determined in dollars or units.

4. When dollar control is used as the method of accounting for inventories at retail price, for maximum effectiveness, information on merchandise should be broken down by departments. This enables management to make judgments concerning the operations of each individual department.

5. The inventory of a large retailer is so large and varied that inventory control is enormously complicated. To overcome this difficulty, most large retailers use electronic data processing. This enables them to get prompt information on the specific items that make up their inventory.

6. Whatever the method of inventory control used, a periodic physical inventory must be taken at least once a year to check the accuracy of the control inventory.

7. Dollar control indicates the position of each department in broad terms. As such, it is an excellent tool for top management. Unit control, by giving specific information on vendors, the amount of time goods are in the store, size, colors, and so on, is extremely useful to the departmental buyer.

8. *Stock turnover, by indicating the number of times the inventory has been completely sold out and repurchased during a period, is another means of determining departmental effectiveness.*

9. *Expense control requires that judgments be made on the amount of expenses by comparing the amount of expense a department had in two separate periods, or comparing its expenses within a period with those of a similar department in another store. For comparisons to be effective, expenses must be classified in the same way for all periods. The National Retail Merchants Association has published a list of expense titles that are widely used among retailers.*

10. *The allocation of expenses to departments requires that expenditures be divided into two broad classifications: direct expenses (those that occur because the department was in existence) and indirect expenses (those that occur whether or not the department is in existence). Direct expenses, such as salespersons' salaries, are much easier to allocate among the departments than indirect expenses, such as officers' salaries.*

11. *The expense budget is a means of controlling expenses by predicting future expenses for a specific period and then comparing the actual expenses with the predicted expenses.*

REVIEW QUESTIONS

1. Discuss the advantages of balancing inventory and customer needs.
2. Small retailers know every piece of stock in their individual stores. Is it necessary for them to keep inventory control records? Why?
3. How does inventory control assist in reducing shortages?
4. Explain the advantages of inventory control to the sportswear buyer at the beginning of a new season.
5. Dollar control becomes more valuable as the classification of merchandise narrows. Discuss.
6. The buyer of menswear in a department store must decide on reordering cashmere sweaters. The merchandise is controlled in dollars with goods classified by departments. How will dollar control help the buyer to make a decision?
7. How does the periodic inventory method differ from the perpetual inventory method?
8. What are the advantages and disadvantages of the perpetual inventory method?
9. Given the following information (all at retail), calculate the sales:

Markdowns	$ 2,000
Closing inventory	24,000
Purchases	25,000
Opening inventory	18,000

10. Why is dollar control a better tool for top management than it is for mid-management?
11. Discuss the advantages to mid-management of unit control over dollar control.

12. Of what value is vendor information to a buyer?

13. Discuss the control of shortages under unit control and dollar control. Which is the better method?

14. Calculate the units on hand:

Opening inventory	12 units
Sales	7 units
Purchases	3 units

15. At the time the physical inventory is being taken, the receiving department has undistributed goods on its floor. Should these goods be included in the inventory?

16. What are the advantages and disadvantages of a physical inventory?

17. Discuss the purposes of calculating stock turnover. How can turnover rates be improved?

18. Calculate the rate of stock turnover at cost:

Sales	$15,000
Purchases (at cost)	10,000
Opening inventory (at cost)	12,000
Closing inventory (at cost)	8,000

19. What are the problems involved with allocating indirect expenses to selling departments?

20. Differentiate between the net profit method and the contribution method of expense allocation.

CASE PROBLEMS

CASE PROBLEM 1

Prell's, Inc., is a large department store in a metropolitan southeastern city. It is a very successful high-image store blessed with alert, aggressive management and the latest in data processing equipment. The merchandising committee of top management meets monthly to survey the inventory situation of the various departments. It uses dollar control to compare the inventory and sales of each department with the inventory and sales position of the same department during the corresponding period of the prior year. At such meetings, any department with an inventory that is out of line is ordered to reduce its stock. The January meeting resulted in an order to the men's haberdashery department to reduce its stock by 15%.

The men's haberdashery department at Prell's controls inventory by unit control. Upon receipt of the inventory directive from the merchandising committee, the buyer and the two assistants made a careful study of their unit control system to determine the specific areas in which they were overstocked. The study indicated an excess of inventory in white shirts, socks, underwear, and handerkerchiefs, all staple items that did not meet Christmas selling expectations. The buyer suggests that the only way inventory can be reduced is by a special promotional sale of overstocked items.

A high-image store such as Prell's does not have promotional sales.

QUESTIONS

1. As a member of the merchandising committee, what would you suggest?
2. What would be the attitude of the men's haberdashery buyer?

CASE PROBLEM 2

The operating statement for a discount store is as follows:

Sales, 15,000 units	$750,000
Cost of goods sold, 15,000 units	600,000
Gross margin	$150,000
Operating expenses	125,000
Net profit	$ 25,000

The owner of the store feels that by decreasing the average selling price by 10%, the number of units sold will be increased by 20%. The increase in sales will cause operating expenses to increase by 30%.

QUESTIONS

1. Prepare a budget for next year based on the changes indicated above.
2. Which operating expenses will increase as a result of the added business? Will any of the operating expenses not be affected?

17 *accounting concepts*

BEHAVIORAL OBJECTIVES

Upon completion of this chapter the student should be able to

1. *Define accounting and explain the responsibilities of that function.*

2. *Achieve a score of 70% on an examination that includes a simple income statement and the retail inventory method of estimating inventory.*

3. *List and discuss five advantages and three disadvantages of the retail inventory method.*

4. *Define and solve simple problems in costing inventory by LIFO, FIFO, and weighted average.*

INTRODUCTION

Among the most important tools available to all retailers are accounting services. Basically, these services consist of setting up systems for recording business transactions, interpreting their results, and giving advice based upon the interpretation. Large retailers are well aware of the important role of the accountant. They maintain large accounting staffs and buy the expensive service of independent accounting firms as well.

Each day bits of financial information flow into a retail firm. This may be in the form of sales, receipt of cash, payment of cash, purchases, and expenses. To arrange this information in a logical, orderly fashion from which reports can be made requires a system. This system is set up by the accountant and usually consists of bookkeeping records such as journals and ledgers. The records are tailored to the needs of the individual store and usually consist of the following:

1. *Cash receipts.* Cash that the retailer receives.
2. *Cash payments.* Cash that the retailer pays out.
3. *Sales.* The revenue from sales.
4. *Purchases.* The merchandise bought for resale to customers.
5. *Payroll.* The salaries paid to employees and any deductions made from salaries, such as social security and withholding tax.
6. *Inventory.* The retailer's investment in merchandise that is to be sold to customers.
7. *Accounts receivable.* The information concerning the amount charge customers owe the firm.
8. *Accounts payable.* The amount that the store owes its creditors and suppliers.

Accounting has often been referred to as the "language of business." As such, some understanding of accounting is necessary for the success of anyone engaged in any area of business. The degree of accounting understanding necessary to a specific job is keyed to the level of the job. Thus, high management requires a considerable knowledge of accounting principles, while less know-how is required as the job level decreases. Since an introductory retailing course is pitched at about a mid-management level, this text will limit the retail applications of accounting to that level.

FUNCTIONS OF ACCOUNTING

The responsibilities of the accountant include the following areas.

Summarizing the Results of Operations

Simply stated, the accountant supervises the recording (entering on books), classifying (sorting business transactions into similar groups), and summarizing (preparing reports for management). Every financial transaction is taken into account, and its effect on profits, loss, and values is periodically shown on a variety of reports. In this way, the effect on profits and the value to the business of every dollar coming into or going out of the business will be reported to management.

Aiding Future Planning

Since the major part of future planning is involved with projecting past history, summaries of past performance become a vital starting point for future planning. How, for example, can the purchasing budget for the coming season be planned without knowing last year's sales of the same period? Other information necessary for budgetary planning, such as the inventory on hand and the trend (have sales been increasing?), is the responsibility of the accounting function.

Facilitating Managerial Control

By comparing the results of the present operations with the results of past years, management can get valuable insights into the effectiveness of its policies. For example, if the total sales have increased while the sales of a particular department have declined, the accountant's reports would provide a basis for further study of this discrepancy. Similarly, expenses can be compared, the effectiveness of advertising evaluated, and so on.

Other Accounting Functions

The accounting function is responsible for a host of other operations that are of no significance to this text. Important among these are complying with government regulations and safeguarding company assets.

COMPUTERIZED ACCOUNTING

There is probably no field of business that has been more widely adapted to electronic data processing systems than accounting. There are few, if any, large businesses that have not computerized at least a portion of their accounting systems. The massive volume of repetitive clerical accounting chores required of a large business is a perfect match for the capabilities of a computer. As a result, the high cost of data processing is more than offset by the savings in time, accuracy, and clerical salaries. Even smaller establishments that cannot afford to purchase or lease computers of their own are renting time from computer-servicing companies that rent time to small users on an hourly basis.

It should be pointed out that the accounting principles discussed in this chapter are applicable to all institutions, including those that make extensive use of computers.

INCOME STATEMENT

Among the informational statements prepared by the accountant, the income statement is the most important for managerial control. It may be defined as a summary of the results of doing business for a specific period of time (such as one month or one year). It is a formalized way of taking the total revenue (sales) and deducting from it the various costs and expenses of doing business. When the total revenue exceeds the total costs and expenses, the results of the operations are profitable. When the total costs and expenses are greater than the revenue, a loss occurs.

The following is an example of an income statement:

Ideal Ladies Shop
Income Statement for the Year Ended June 30, 19____

Net sales	$100,000
Cost of goods sold	60,000
Gross margin	$ 40,000
Operating expenses	30,000
Net profit	$ 10,000

1. The *net sales* of $100,000 were determined by deducting from the total merchandise sold, the amount of goods returned by customers.

Total Sales − Sales Returns = Net Sales

2. The *cost of goods sold* ($60,000) indicates the cost to the store of the goods that were sold for $100,000. It includes the cost of the goods sold that were purchased

this year as well as the cost of the goods that were sold out of inventory. A more detailed analysis of the determination of the amount of cost of goods sold will be presented later in the chapter.

3. The *gross margin* (or gross profit) of $40,000 indicates the excess of the selling price over the cost of the goods that were sold. During this period merchandise that cost $60,000 was sold for $100,000. The term gross profit (margin) is used because the $40,000 is not the final profit; there are still other expenses to be deducted from the $40,000.

$$\text{Net Sales} - \text{Cost of Goods Sold} = \text{Gross Profit (Margin)}$$

(Note: Gross profit is frequently referred to by retailers as gross margin.)

4. The *operating expenses* include all expenditures other than the cost of the merchandise. These consist of such items as rent, salaries, heat, light, advertising, and so on.

5. After the cost of the goods sold and the operating expenses have been deducted from the net sales, the amount left is the *net profit*. In our example, goods that cost $60,000 were sold for $100,000. In addition there were expenses of $30,000. Therefore, the operations for the period resulted in a profit of $10,000.

$$\text{Net Sales} - (\text{Cost of Goods Sold} + \text{Operating Expenses}) = \text{Net Profit}$$

COST OF GOODS SOLD

The determination of the cost of goods sold is relatively easy for a retailer of fine jewelry or a furrier, who sell only a few items a day. They have merely to total the purchase invoices of the goods that were sold. Now consider a supermarket or a large department store. To find the purchase invoice and total the cost of every item sold during the day is obviously an impossible task. Accountants handle it this way: To the cost of the merchandise on hand at the beginning of the period, they add the cost of the purchases made during the period. This total is the merchandise available to be sold during the period. From this total they deduct the cost of the merchandise still on hand at the end of the period. The difference, the amount of the merchandise missing, is the cost of the goods sold. In other words, if we know the amount of goods we began with and the amount of goods that came in, by deducting the amount of goods still on hand, we can determine the amount of goods sold. An accountant expresses it this way:

Opening inventory (on hand beginning of period)	$40,000
Purchases (amount that came in during period)	50,000
Merchandise available for sale	$90,000
Closing inventory (on hand at end of period)	30,000
Cost of goods sold	$60,000

All the figures required for the preparation of an income statement, with the exception of the closing inventory, are readily available to the accountant. The sales are available from the cash registers, the purchases from the purchase invoices, the operating expenses from the check stubs that paid those bills, and the opening inventory from the physical inventory taken at the beginning of the period. Only the closing inventory presents a problem (the opening inventory has already been taken). As we have seen in a previous chapter, taking a physical inventory is costly and time-consuming and disrupts the store's regular procedures; therefore, it is rarely done more than twice a year. On the other hand, management, for effective control, must have income statements much more frequently. Obviously, a method of accurately estimating the closing inventory at cost is needed. The retail inventory method of estimating inventory presents such an estimate.

RETAIL INVENTORY METHOD

The retail method of estimating inventory at cost can be accomplished in three steps. (It must be borne in mind that it is the *cost* of the closing inventory that we are trying to determine.)

1. *Determine the relationship (percent) of the cost of the merchandise to the selling price of the merchandise.* This can be done by keeping records in a manner that will indicate both the cost and selling price of the goods. To do this, all purchases are recorded at cost as well as at selling price. Similarly, all inventories, physical and otherwise, must also be kept at cost and selling price. When this is done, our books of account yield the following information:

	Cost	Retail
Opening inventory	$20,000	$30,000
Purchases	40,000	50,000
Merchandise available for sale	$60,000	$80,000

In other words, we had goods that cost $20,000 on hand at the beginning of the period. We bought additional goods during the period for $40,000. In all, we offered our customers goods costing $60,000, during the period. Figured the same way, the goods that cost $60,000 during the period had a retail value of $80,000. To determine the percentage of the cost of the merchandise to its selling price we divide:

$$\frac{\text{Cost}}{\text{Selling price}} \quad \frac{\$60,000}{\$80,000} = 75\%$$

We have now determined that, on the average, our cost is 75 percent of selling price. Now, we can determine the cost of any lot of merchandise by taking 75 percent of its retail price.

2. *Determine the inventory at retail.* Since we know the value of the merchandise available for sale at retail (from step one), by deducting the sales actually made, we can determine the amount unsold (the inventory) at retail. In other words, if we assume sales of $50,000 we can do the following:

Merchandise available at retail	$80,000
Less: sales	50,000
Inventory at retail	$30,000

If we had $80,000 at retail available to be sold, and we sold $50,000, we must have $30,000 left (inventory) at retail.

3. *Convert inventory at retail to inventory at cost.* Having determined the closing inventory at selling price (retail) and the percent that cost bears to selling price, we can convert the inventory from selling price to cost by applying the percent.

Inventory at retail	$30,000
Percent cost bears to retail	× 75%
Estimated inventory at cost	$22,500

Illustrative Problem

During its first year of operation, the Acme Department Store bought merchandise costing $300,000 that was marked to sell for $500,000. The year's sales totaled $200,000. Find the estimated cost of the inventory at the end of the year.

Solution

1. To determine the percentage of the cost of the merchandise to its selling price:

$$\frac{\text{Cost}}{\text{Selling price}} \quad \frac{\$300,000}{\$500,000} = 60\%$$

We have found that the cost is 60 percent of the selling price. Now if we can find the inventory at selling price, we can convert it to cost by taking 60 percent of it.

2. To determine the inventory at selling price:

The total amount of merchandise available for sale had a selling price of	$500,000
Of this, the amount sold was	200,000
The amount left on hand (inventory) at selling price	$300,000

3. To convert the inventory at selling price to inventory at cost: We have already determined that cost is 60 percent of selling price. Therefore if the inventory at selling price is $300,000,

$$\$300 \times 60\% = \$180,000 \text{ Inventory at cost}$$

While some large retailers with extensive data processing systems might have their closing inventory at cost readily available to them at all times, the vast majority use the retail inventory method described above. Without this method, and the income statements that are dependent upon it, retail management would have to operate under severe handicaps.

It should be understood that the problems presented were somewhat simplified. Sales returns, purchase returns, additional markups, markdowns, and so forth would have to be taken into account in estimating the cost of the inventory under the retail method.

The reasons for the wide acceptance of the retail inventory method include the following:

1. *Provides frequent income statements.* Since the closing inventory at cost can be estimated by a relatively simple calculation, income statements (by department as well as for the total store) can be prepared when required. This is usually done monthly. By contrast, a store depending on physical inventory taking to determine the cost of the closing inventory is limited to one or, at most, two income statements a year. Efficient managerial control, both for top and middle management, is severely handicapped if income statements are not produced promptly and frequently.

2. *Simplifies physical inventories.* The retail inventory method permits the prices to be taken as they are ticketed on the merchandise. Retailers not using the retail inventory method take physical inventories by style number. The cost of each individual style must then be found to determine the cost of the merchandise on hand, a costly and time-consuming job.

3. *Turns up shortages.* When a physical inventory is taken, the estimated inventory (calculated by using the retail method) can be compared with the actual inventory (inventory determined by actual physical count). Where the physical inventory is less than the estimated inventory, the difference may be due to shortages. This may indicate ineffective control over the merchandise.

4. *Assists with insurance coverage and claim adjustment.* Insurance on inventories is based upon the value of the inventory. The bigger the inventory, the higher the coverage, and the larger the premium. Since insurance is expensive, it is vital to have the proper coverage at all times. Retailers, because of the seasonal nature of their businesses, have constantly fluctuating inventories. Using the retail inventory method, they are able to adjust their insurance coverage to their actual needs on a monthly basis. Moreover, insurance companies accept the records of the retail method in settling claims. For example, in the case of a complete inventory loss due to fire, it is often impossible to determine the amount of the loss any other way.

5. *Furnishes basis for dollar control.* If dollar control is to be employed, as it must for any efficient retailing operation, the retail method of estimating inventory must be employed. There can be no effective dollar control without it.

6. *Ensures accurately valued inventory.* Merchandise inventory is an asset. That is to say, it represents a value that the retailer owns. The amount of that value is sometimes lower than its cost. Take, for example, a situation in which goods are marked down. This usually indicates that they can be replaced at a value less than their cost. To include such goods at cost would overstate the inventory, since the goods are worth less than their cost. Under the retail inventory method

the goods are listed at retail prices that take markdowns into account. When the cost percent is applied to this marked down amount, the result is an amount less than cost for marked down merchandise. This accurately represents the true value of such goods.

Some disadvantages of the retail inventory method are as follows:

1. *Averaging.* A serious disadvantage is that it depends upon an average cost percent. When the total merchandise available for sale at retail is divided into the total merchandise available for sale at cost, the resulting percent is the average throughout the store. Since not all sales of merchandise follow the same average, errors occur. In fact, low markup goods generally sell better than the higher marked-up variety. This results in an actual markup on sales that is different from the cost percent. Retailers using different markups and special sales have these problems magnified.
2. *Not for all departments.* In some departments it is impossible to estimate the selling price of goods in advance. These generally are departments in which the merchandise is bought as raw materials and changed before sales can be made. Restaurants, pharmacies, and bakeries are typical of such departments. Department stores that insist upon uniformity among all departments find this a disadvantage. It would seem that insistence upon uniformity under these conditions is a high price to pay for disregarding so beneficial a system.
3. *High operating cost.* The additional records required by the operation of the retail inventory method are considerable. As a result, the cost of the system is high. In addition, accuracy is vital, and expensive checks and counterchecks are necessary.

The determination of whether or not to use the retail method requires the careful comparison of the advantages versus the disadvantages. On balance, the advantages of the system seem to outweigh its disadvantages, as evidenced by the fact that the vast majority of large and medium-sized retailers employ these methods. Many large organizations that use other accounting methods for their income tax returns and reports to stockholders use the retail method, for the efficiency of managerial control that it provides.

COST METHODS OF DETERMINING INVENTORY

Most retailers (including those using the retail method for managerial control) use the lower-of-cost-or-market method for determining the value of their inventories. This requires the periodic physical count of each item on hand and the identification of the cost of each item. The cost to replace each item is then determined, and the lower-of-cost-or-market (replacement value) is used to determine the value of the inventory. Failure to use the replacement value would result in an overstatement of the inventory, an overstatement of the profits, and an overstatement of the income tax liability. Since the value of the inventory is important, the calculation of its worth is critical. There are several methods of determining the cost per unit of inventory, as will be shown in the following illustrative problem:

Illustrative Problem

During the year, a furniture store made the following purchases of bridge chairs:

Feb. 10	100 chairs @ $10
June 20	200 chairs @ $12
Sept. 14	60 chairs @ $ 8
Dec. 12	100 chairs @ $14

On December 31, the date on which the inventory must be determined, there were found to be 120 bridge chairs on hand. Since it is the policy of the store to stock all bridge chairs together, it was impossible to ascertain the specific purchase lots from which the 120 chairs came. Calculate the value of the 120 chairs in the merchandise inventory.

Solution

To solve this problem, we must first make certain assumptions concerning the merchandising policy of the store. If the store is operated in such fashion that the first merchandise to come in is the first to be sold, then the inventory at December 31 must be valued at the cost of the last purchases. If the reverse is true, and the last goods to come in are the first to be sold, then the merchandise remaining on hand at December 31 must be valued at the cost of the earliest purchases. Another method of valuing the inventory would be to use an average cost per chair. We shall solve the above problem using all three of these methods.

1. *FIFO.* FIFO is an abbreviation for the first-in-first-out method of pricing inventories. It assumes that the first chairs purchased by the store were the first that were sold. That is, the first chairs to be sold were those purchased on February 10, the second group sold were those purchased on June 20, and so on. Therefore, the 120 chairs remaining on hand on December 31 consisted of the last chairs purchased and the inventory should be valued as follows:

$$
\begin{array}{ll}
100 \text{ chairs @ } \$14 = \$1,400 \\
\underline{20} \text{ chairs @ } \$8 = \underline{\$160} \\
120 \hspace{2.5cm} \$1,560 \text{ FIFO Inventory Value}
\end{array}
$$

2. *LIFO.* LIFO is an abbreviation for last-in-first-out. It is the opposite of the first-in-first-out method. That is, it assumes that the last chairs purchased were the first to be sold. Therefore, the first chairs sold were those bought December 12, the next sales were the chairs purchased on September 14, and so on. Using the LIFO method, the chairs left on hand on December 31 were from the earliest purchased, thus:

$$
\begin{array}{ll}
100 \text{ chairs @ } \$10 = \$1,000 \\
\underline{20} \text{ chairs @ } \$12 = \underline{\$240} \\
120 \hspace{2.5cm} \$1,240 \text{ LIFO Inventory Value}
\end{array}
$$

3. *Weighted average.* Another method of determining the value of the inventory is the weighted average method. This method assigns the average of all of the costs of all of the purchases to the units remaining in the inventory. It is necessary to use a weighted average, one which takes the number of units of each purchase into account, since in a simple average the purchase of one unit would have as important an effect as the purchase of 1,000 units. The 120 chairs in the above problem would be valued as follows:

a. Find the weighted average cost per unit.

Feb. 10	100	chairs @$10	=	$1,000
June 20	200	chairs @$12	=	$2,400
Sept. 14	60	chairs @$ 8	=	$ 480
Dec. 12	100	chairs @$14	=	$1,400
	460			$5,280

$$\frac{\$5,280}{460} = \$11.48 \text{ Weighted average cost per unit}$$

b. Multiply the weighted average cost per unit by the number of units in the inventory.

Units on hand on December 31	120
Weighted average cost per unit	$\times$ $ 11.48
Weighted average inventory value	$1,377.60

A comparison of the three inventory methods discloses the following:

FIFO inventory	$1,560.00
LIFO inventory	1,240.00
Weighted average inventory	1,377.60

Since such important business considerations as the amount of net profit and the amount of income taxes are directly related to the value of the inventory, it is easy to understand that the method of evaluating inventory is of great importance to business people.

The preceding problem has been oversimplified for teaching purposes. Regardless of the order in which the goods are sold, retailers are entitled to choose any of the above methods for evaluating their inventories. They are all acceptable to the accounting profession as well as the taxing authorities, as long as the method chosen is used consistently for all years. Since a comparison of the three methods results in different inventory values, the amount of profits and taxes will be affected by the method chosen.

FIFO

Most retailers attempt to sell their oldest goods first. This is particularly true in the case of goods that are perishable or subject to style changes. FIFO is a logical method for valuing inventories since it most perfectly fits the actual flow of goods from the receiving department to the customer.

During an inflationary period, when purchase prices are constantly rising, the FIFO method results in a high markup. The assumption that the first goods in (the cheapest during an inflationary period) are the first sold results in a low cost of goods sold, and high profits and taxes. Since these goods will have to be replaced at higher costs, FIFO causes problems in a period of rising prices.

LIFO

In recent years there has been a trend among large retailers to offset the high taxes resulting from FIFO, and by so doing, have funds available for the increased cost of maintaining inventory. LIFO offers such a solution. It became available as the result of a Bureau of Internal Revenue ruling in 1947 and has been growing in use since then.

By assuming that the most recent purchases (most expensive in an inflationary period) are the first sold, LIFO results in a high cost of goods sold and low profits and taxes. Similarly, LIFO provides that the inventory be priced at the oldest (cheapest) prices. The resulting tax savings help provide funds for the increased cost of purchases.

While most large retailers are presently taking advantage of the tax savings available through LIFO, smaller stores are slow to make the change. Among the reasons for the hesitancy on the part of the small store are:

1. A complicated accounting system is required to operate the LIFO system.
2. Once LIFO is chosen, it must be used continuously. In times of a declining price level, its effect would be high profits and taxes.

Weighted Average

The weighted average method of inventory valuation is essentially a compromise between LIFO and FIFO. The effect of price level changes (inflation) is averaged in the determination of inventory value and profits. Since the records and calculations required to determine the inventory value using this method are considerable, it is less frequently used than LIFO or FIFO. It is likely that the growing use of computers to minimize calculation and record keeping problems will result in an increase in the use of the weighted average method.

Action for the Independent Retailer

To the small retailer, particularly one who is just beginning a business and is anxious to keep expenses down, the cost of an accountant's services seems like an unnecessary luxury. That an accountant provides a necessary service rather than a luxury is evidenced by United States Department of Commerce records indicating that 84 percent of the retailers who fail do not have adequate accounting records.

Much of the work an accountant does is clerical and can easily be done by anyone who has been given a brief explanation of the requirements. In small firms, where the expense of an accountant may be a burden, many of the simpler accounting functions can be handled by the proprietor, or a part-time bookkeeper whose time is considerably less costly than that of an accountant. It is important, however, that only a trained accountant perform the part of the work that cannot be delegated to an untrained individual.

Many small retailers who employ accountants get far less than the full service available to them. Using an accountant solely for keeping records and preparing tax returns is a serious mistake. The accountant should also be called upon to arrange credit, advise on expansion, forecast sales, and perform a host of other chores. The financial area is complicated and important. Few small business owners and managers are trained for it, and they should lean heavily on their accountants for advice.

IMPORTANT POINTS IN THE CHAPTER

1. *The function of accounting is recording business transactions, interpreting the results of the transactions, and giving advice based upon the interpretation.*

2. *The accountant provides systems of recording and summarizing financial information. These systems involve the use of bookkeeping records, such as ledgers and journals, which are tailored to the individual needs of each retailer.*

3. *Since accounting provides an important tool to the operations of a business, it is vital that managers have a sound understanding of the various reports that are the end product of an accountant's work.*

4. *Because the accounting function requires an enormous number of repetitive transactions, it is ideally suited to electronic data processing. Large retailers rely heavily on the computer for the operation of their accounting departments.*

5. *The most important report supplied by the accountant is the income statement. It is a summary of the results of doing business for a specific period of time, which indicates the profit or loss of the business for that period.*

6. *For effective managerial control, income statements must be provided frequently. Preparing an income statement requires the cost value of the inventory at the end of the period. Since taking a physical inventory is too costly and time-consuming to be done frequently, accountants use the retail inventory method to estimate the cost value of the inventory.*

7. *When a physical count of the merchandise inventory is taken, it is necessary to determine the cost of each unit counted. This can be difficult since similar goods are bought*

at various costs. First-in-first-out, last-in-first-out, and weighted average are methods of determining the cost of the inventory.

REVIEW QUESTIONS

1. Indicate the functions of an accountant that are most important to the owner of a small retail store.
2. What benefits can a department store buyer of highly styled merchandise get from the store's accounting department?
3. Prepare an income statement in good form from the following information: Operating expenses $4,000, Sales $12,000, Cost of goods sold $6,000.
4. Why is the computer considered "the perfect accounting tool"?
5. Determine the cost of goods sold from the following information: Closing inventory $60,000, Opening inventory $80,000, Purchases $100,000.
6. Explain the necessity of estimating the inventory on hand at the end of the period.
7. If purchases that cost $10,000 are marked up to sell for $15,000, what percentage of the selling price is the cost?
8. The following information was taken from the books of account of the Fit-Rite Clothing Store:

	Cost	Retail
Opening inventory	$14,000	$21,000
Purchases	49,700	77,000

Calculate the cost percent.

9. The Fit-Rite Clothing Store described in Question 8 sold $70,000 worth of goods. Determine its inventory at retail.
10. From the information given in Questions 8 and 9, calculate the estimated cost of the closing inventory of the Fit-Rite Clothing Store, using the retail inventory method.
11. Why is managerial control improved when the retail inventory method is used?
12. Explain how the retail inventory method simplifies the taking of a physical inventory.
13. How are shortages discovered by the retail inventory method?
14. The treasurer of Blake's Inc. claims that the use of the retail method will reduce insurance costs. What information is this statement based on?
15. A serious disadvantage of the retail method is that it is based on an averaging of markups. Explain this.
16. Discuss other disadvantages of the retail inventory method.
17. Given the following information, calculate the inventory value, using the FIFO method. There are 19 units in stock.

Opening inventory	14 units @ $ 8
1st purchase	8 units @ $ 9
2nd purchase	12 units @ $10
3rd purchase	6 units @ $12

18. Using the data given in Question 17, calculate the inventory, using the LIFO method.
19. Using the data given in Question 17, calculate the inventory, using the weighted average method.
20. During an inflationary period would you expect a higher inventory using the FIFO method or the LIFO method?
21. During an inflationary period, income taxes may be saved by using the LIFO method. Why?

CASE PROBLEMS

CASE PROBLEM 1

The Evans Dress Shop, a moderate-priced specialty store, had a serious fire in September. As a result of the fire a large portion of the merchandise was completely destroyed. Merchandise with a retail value of $12,000 was undamaged by the fire and considered completely salable. The balance of the goods was completely destroyed, with the individual garments unidentifiable.

The accounting records were kept in a fireproof safe and were available after the fire. A study of these records indicated the following facts:

	Month	Cost	Retail	Actual Sales
Opening inventory	January 1	$25,000	$45,000	———
Purchases	January 31	12,000	18,000	$15,000
Purchases	February	12,000	25,000	15,000
Purchases	March	16,000	30,000	25,000
Purchases	April	14,000	20,000	26,000
Purchases	May	6,000	10,000	25,000
Purchases	June	12,000	16,000	14,000
Purchases	July	4,000	8,000	6,000
Purchases	August	6,000	12,000	4,000
Purchases	September	12,000	16,000	20,000

The insurance company agrees that they have a financial responsibility, but since the garments cannot be identified, the cost of the destroyed goods cannot be determined. They have offered $10,000 in full settlement of the claim.

QUESTIONS

1. Is the $10,000 acceptable?
2. How much should Evans get?

CASE PROBLEM 2

Trueman's Inc. showed a profit of $46,312 for the fiscal year just ended. Since its overall tax rate is about 50%, its tax liability will be considerable. The inventory used in determining its profit was valued, by the FIFO method, at $44,840. The accountant claims that a tax savings would result from a change to the LIFO method of evaluating inventories.

The details of the inventory and purchases are as follows:

Style	Opening Inventory	First Purchase	Second Purchase	Third Purchase	Closing Inventory
127	50 @ $ 74	50 @ $ 80	100 @ $ 81	———	40
216	30 @ 90	100 @ 90	60 @ 93	50 @ $ 96	60
318	30 @ 160	40 @ 170	50 @ 170	30 @ 180	20
426	———	100 @ 250	50 @ 265	30 @ 267	50
731	60 @ 200	40 @ 210	60 @ 210	50 @ 222	30
812	10 @ 180	30 @ 188	40 @ 190	———	30
914	50 @ 300	60 @ 300	50 @ 320	40 @ 330	20

Note: As the inventory increases or decreases, the profit increases or decreases by the same amount.

QUESTIONS

1. Calculate the profit, using the LIFO method of inventory valuation.
2. Determine the tax savings if the LIFO method is used.
3. Do you feel a change to LIFO is warranted? Why?

18 *credit and other customer services*

Upon completion of this chapter the student should be able to

1. *Write a brief essay on consumer motives for owning credit cards.*
2. *Discuss three methods of credit extended by retail operations.*
3. *Describe the five major responsibilities of the credit department.*
4. *List the steps in a collection system.*
5. *Define the federal laws of Truth-in-Lending and Regulation Z.*
6. *Discuss the various types of services found in stores.*

INTRODUCTION

Consumers are motivated to make their purchases at particular stores for a variety of reasons. While for many, the chief factor is price, a significant number of shoppers head for particular retail establishments because of the services offered. Recent years have witnessed the demise of discount-oriented companies, such as Korvettes, and an increase in the number of service-oriented stores.

With price very often the same at many competing operations, and similar merchandise available in more than one store, customers may be appealed to via attractive services. The most widely offered service is customer credit. While there are benefits to the retailers who grant customers the right to buy now and pay later, few prefer credit in place of cash purchases. Thus, credit must be considered a service. Many other services are offered to the shopper. Some are widely available, while others are less apt to be found in many stores.

In this chapter credit and its far-reaching effects on retailing will be explored, as well as other services that retailers offer to the consuming public.

CREDIT

Of the many changes in American lifestyle that occurred at the end of World War II, none was more dramatic than the enormous expansion of consumer credit. From a total of about $4 billion in 1945, total consumer credit had surged to about $100 billion by 1975. It is likely that at present some 80 percent of all American families use at least one type of credit card. This increase in the use of credit has been one of the prime factors in the success of our economic system. It has had the effect of making goods available to consumers that they would not otherwise have been able to purchase. Credit has allowed people to purchase merchandise that they can afford but for which they are unable to save. For most of us it has acted as a kind of forced savings. The economic result has been an enormous demand for goods and services, which has kept our industrial activity at a high level.

Those people who warned that the expansion of credit would lead to eventual collapse have been shown to be wrong. So far, at least, credit losses have been minimal, and the vast majority of American families have shown great responsibility in their use of credit buying and have kept this kind of buying at a level they can afford. Unquestionably, there are limits beyond which credit buying becomes treacherous, but the great majority of us are aware of this. We are in the habit of living on credit and are careful to keep our debts at a level we can easily handle. This enables us to have the use of merchandise we can afford, but have difficulty saving for.

Of the total amount of credit purchases, retail credit accounts for a major share. It is likely that some 40 percent of our retail purchases are on credit. Naturally, this varies with the type of store. About 70 percent of all department and specialty stores' sales are to credit customers. The most important retail segment that does not use credit is the supermarket. Where credit has been tested in this area, the markup has been found to be insufficient to cover the costs of credits and collections.

Customer Motives—Owning Credit Cards

Successful retailing depends upon an understanding of customer motives. This is true in the selection of merchandise categories, the choice of styles within the categories, and, because credit buying is so important, the reasons the customer has for buying on credit.

Convenience

A charge card identifies the buyer as a good store customer. This improves service, makes it easier to exchange and return items, and facilitates mail and telephone shopping. In addition, charge customers get advance notice of special sales.

Cash Is Unnecessary

Many people dislike carrying the large amounts of cash required for big-ticket sales. A charge card eliminates fear of theft or loss.

Customers without charge accounts who lack immediate funds frequently request C.O.D. shipments. This requires the payment of C.O.D. charges and waiting at home for deliveries.

Credit Rating

Because we live in a largely noncash business environment, establishing a credit rating is important. Having a charge account with one store is an aid in securing other credit. Similarly, a charge card is a good identification for check cashing.

Bookkeeping

Having a charge account reduces home record-keeping problems. One check per month covers all of a specific type of purchases and the monthly statements provide a record of purchases.

Prestige

A charge account from a prestigious store is considered by some to be a status symbol.

Customer Motives—Not Owning Credit Cards

Some people oppose credit cards. Their reasons are numerous—sometimes logical, often illogical. Wise or foolish, the retailer should know them. There are those who feel that it is immoral to go into debt; others say that it is too easy to buy on credit and they would rather wait and pay cash. Many feel that credit cards are only for the rich and that there are service charges involved. Still others simply cannot get another charge plate into their wallets, or object to the questions on the application.

Whatever the customer objection to charge accounts is, logical or illogical, a wise retailer should know customers' motives.

Why Retailers Give Credit

Bluntly, retailers give credit because they have to. It is expensive and time-consuming, and involves the use of floor space that could be put to better use. With today's buying habits, there is simply no other way of maintaining sales. Certainly there are side benefits, but considering the costs involved, many retailers would drop charge accounts if they could.

Customer Preferences

As we have seen, customers have many valid reasons for demanding credit. Many will simply not patronize a store that does not offer charge accounts. Some years ago, discount retailers were enormously successful. Their operation included reduced selling prices in return for a cutback in customer services. For a while they were very successful, but with the increase in customer demand for charge accounts, they have been forced to offer this service also. This necessitated an increase in selling prices, which narrowed the difference between their offerings and those of their more conventional competitors. At present, many discounters are being forced, to some extent, to change their operations. In other words, competitive pressures are such that a store that does not offer credit will have difficulty maintaining its share of the market.

Customer Relationships

Although it would be difficult to prove, most retailers believe that a charge customer is a loyal one. Tests have shown that charge customers are more likely to read the advertising of stores with which they have accounts. Other research indicates that the charge account buyer is a better customer, in terms of volume, than the cash buyer. It is likely that this "customer loyalty" view of charge accounts is an exaggeration. Given the present wide use of credit, most buyers carry credit cards for competing stores and are hardly "loyal" to any individual retailer.

Direct Mail Selling

An important benefit that charge accounts bring to a store is a mailing list consisting of persons that have shown a fondness for the store's specific type of operation. This type of list is valuable and difficult to come by. (Most commercial lists include many names of totally disinterested people.) These lists, when carefully used, may be an important source of mail order business. This can be accomplished either as direct mail or, more frequently, with enclosures that are inserted along with the monthly charge account statement. When the latter method is used, there is no additional mailing cost and the expense of printing the enclosure is frequently borne by the supplier rather than the retailer.

Salespeople and Credit

To salespersons, the use of credit offers an excellent means of closing sales. An important feature in any sales training program should be the use of credit and the encouragement of customers to open charge accounts. Credit customers are in a position to buy impulsively, add accessories, and buy larger amounts than originally intended. Armed with this information, the salesperson should try to increase both unit sales and higher-priced items. One expert has estimated that most stores lose hundreds of sales each day for lack of a timely credit suggestion. The shoe salesperson who has not suggested a matching pocketbook, the appliance salesperson who has not pointed out the advantages of the more expensive model, and the white goods salesperson who does not suggest a dozen towels instead of six are all guilty of not using credit as a selling tool.

An important portion of the expansion of consumer credit is that offered by retail stores to their customers. There are four major types of retail credit, and individual retailers offer many variations of these basic kinds.

Charge Accounts

Charge account credit is the most important type of credit offered by department stores. Customers receive their merchandise at the time of purchase without being required to give a down payment or a pledge of collateral. Upon receipt of a monthly statement, the customer is expected to pay within 30 days. There is no charge for this kind of credit, although customers who fail to pay within the 30-day period are charged interest or a service charge. Under this arrangement the store has no right of repossession, and collection of late accounts may require expensive legal proceedings. Such credit is expensive in terms of bad debts, collection costs, and the expenses involved in carrying customer accounts. Frequently, stores must borrow money to cover their outstanding receivables. As is the case with all other customer services, a store's markup must be sufficient to cover these expenses. Some years ago, open account credit was offered only to the most affluent customers, minimizing bad debt risks. More recently, charge account requirements have been liberalized and at present almost anyone with a job is encouraged to open such an account.

Installment Accounts

Installment credit is much more formal than charge account credit. It has the following characteristics:

Down payment. At the time of purchase, the customer is required to make an immediate payment of a percentage of the total sale. The amount of down payment varies with the type of merchandise and the particular store.

Periodic payments. Installment account customers agree to make a specified number of equal payments over the life of the loan. These payments are usually made monthly with the number of months varying, frequently at the customer's option.

Finance charges. Unlike charge account customers, installment customers are required to pay interest and other finance charges for the extended life of their loan. These costs are frequently so high that the seller can make a larger profit on the financing costs than on the sale itself. Some retailers, such as credit jewelry stores, are often described as finance companies first and retailers second.

Repossession rights. Installment sellers retain, as security for their loan, the right to take back the merchandise sold, in the event of nonpayment of an installment when it comes due. In the event that the repossessed goods, when later sold, do not bring in enough money to satisfy the remaining debt, the seller may go back to the defaulted customer for the difference.

Formal contract. The installment purchaser must sign a formal contract setting forth the conditions of the sale and the rights of both parties at the time of purchase. This serves two purposes. It both clearly outlines the terms of the complicated transaction and permits the seller who so desires to get immediate cash. Installment contracts can be sold and can serve as collateral for loans.

Revolving Credit

Revolving credit is a combination of charge account and installment credit. Installment credit is usually reserved for such expensive items as jewelry, furniture, and appliances. Revolving credit permits installment paying for small purchases. It works this way: A customer is given a credit limit by the store—for example, $500. In addition, the customer has to pay $50 per month whenever there is an outstanding balance to the store until the debt is wiped out. At the same time more merchandise may be purchased whenever the debt to the store is less than $500. Like that of the installment buyer, this buyer's monthly payment is $50 (unless less is owed), and like the charge customer, this customer can freely buy on credit up to the credit limit.

Revolving credit usually carries a service charge (about 1.5 percent per month). As is the case with installment credit, revolving credit can be profitable to the store.

Option Terms

Revolving credit requires a fixed monthly payment. A variation of this permits the customer the choice of paying in full or making some minimum payment (usually $\frac{1}{12}$). Most charge customers are automatically given option terms. Their monthly statement indicates the full amount due and the minimum option payment that will be acceptable if the customer prefers it. Because the option payment is a fixed fraction of the amount owed, it will vary with the size of the balance. Customers who prefer the option payment are billed service charges for the unpaid balance (usually 1.5 percent).

Revolving credit with option terms is growing in use. Stores like it because it increases interest income while reducing customer resistance to service charges. Customers like the method because they are given a choice of payments, which they can vary depending upon their budget for each month.

The Credit Department

As we have seen, the proper use of credit has become a necessary ingredient in successful retailing. The responsibility for managing credit lies with the credit department, under the supervision of the controller. This department is charged with the following:

1. Opening new accounts
2. Keeping credit records

3. Authorization
4. Billing
5. Collections

Opening New Accounts

Charge account customers are the store's best customers because they are responsible for a major portion of the store's sales volume. Consequently, every effort is made to have noncharge customers open accounts. This may be done by telephone solicitation, radio, newspaper, and direct mail advertising. Sales personnel are the most important source of new accounts and they are trained to suggest a charge account whenever possible. For new accounts, most stores use the following procedures:

Interview. The customer interested in opening a charge account is sent to the credit department, where an interview with a member of the department takes place. During the interview a credit application is filled out. (See Figure 18-1.) Through the questions on the application and others that the interviewer directs to the customer, the three "C's" of credit are determined: these are character, capacity, and capital. Character refers to the applicant's willingness to pay debts when they fall due. This characteristic cannot be determined by the interview alone and, as we shall see, further checking is required. The ability to pay debts out of current income is referred to as capacity. Total family income and the number of years the applicant has held the same job are the most important means of estimating capacity. Another method of determining an applicant's ability to pay is called capital. This is judged by the amount of assets, such as bank accounts and real estate, the individual owns.

An important part of the interview is spent promoting the store and explaining the workings of the store's charge account system.

Approval. The decision about whether or not an applicant should be granted credit is the responsibility of the credit manager. With today's easy credit, the vast majority of applications are approved immediately. Upon approval (the interview and approval rarely take longer than twenty minutes), many stores permit the applicant to make credit purchases at once. Other stores postpone the use of credit for a few days while checking outside sources. It should be noted that outside sources of credit information are used even when immediate credit is granted.

Retail Credit Bureaus

Most stores use retail credit bureaus where they are available. These organizations are usually cooperatively owned by the stores that use them. The stores involved send the credit bureau information on each of their credit customers. These data, which indicate maximum high credit and payment habits

GIMBELS

APPLICATION FOR CREDIT

DO NOT WRITE
IN SHADED AREAS

ACCOUNT NUMBER								
	1	2	3	4	5	6	7	8

OTHER GIMBEL ACCOUNTS
☐ OPTION ☐ CEP ☐ OTHER

ACCOUNT NUMBER

FIRST — LAST

NAME
9 10 11 12 13 14 15 16 — 18 19 20 21 22 23 24 25 26 27 28 29 30 31

HIGH BAL.	PRES. BAL.

STREET
33 34 35 36 37 38 39 40 41 42 43 44 45 46 47 48 49 50 51 52 53 54

HIGH AGE	PRES. AGE

NO. OF PLATES 1 ☐ 2 ☐

TYPE OF ACCT.
☐ OPTION "O"

CITY & STATE
55 56 57 58 59 60 61 62 63 64 65 66 67 68 69 70 71 72 73

12 ZONE CYCLE CODE
74

STATUS

OPEN 6 MOS.
☐ YES ☐ NO

☐ CEP "P"
☐ OTHER
75

ZIP CODE
76 77 78 79 80

HOME PHONE

NO. OF DEPENDENTS

DATE OF BIRTH MONTH DAY YEAR

RESIDENCE ☐ OWN ☐ RENT ☐ RM. HOW LONG? MONTHLY PMT. OR RENT FORMER ADDRESS HOW LONG?

PRESENT BUSINESS OR EMPLOYER

COMPLETE THIS BOX IF YOU ARE RELYING ON YOUR SPOUSE'S INCOME TO PAY FOR CREDIT GRANTED UNDER THIS ACCOUNT, OR IF YOUR SPOUSE IS AUTHORIZED TO USE THE ACCOUNT OR IF THIS IS AN APPLICATION FOR A JOINT ACCOUNT.

BUSINESS ADDRESS

POSITION INCOME HOW LONG? NAME OF SPOUSE OR JOINT ACCOUNT APPLICANT

BUSINESS PHONE SOCIAL SECURITY NO. **PRESENT BUSINESS OR EMPLOYER**

FORMER BUSINESS OR EMPLOYER **BUSINESS ADDRESS**

POSITION INCOME HOW LONG? **POSITION** INCOME HOW LONG?

CREDIT REFERENCES (OTHER ACCOUNTS OR LOANS) ACCOUNT NO. **BUSINESS PHONE** SOCIAL SECURITY NO.

FORMER BUSINESS OR EMPLOYER

POSITION INCOME HOW LONG?

BANK REFERENCE

CHECKING BRANCH ACCT. NO.

SAVINGS BRANCH ACCT. NO.

PLEASE READ AND SIGN THE AGREEMENT ON THE REVERSE SIDE

F.1605 REV. 4/76

RETAIL INSTALLMENT CREDIT AGREEMENT

In consideration of the extension of credit to me, I agree that with respect to all purchases made by me or others authorized to use my account:

I may, within 30 days of the closing date appearing on the periodic statement of my account, pay in full the "new balance" appearing on said statement and thereby avoid a FINANCE CHARGE; or, if I so choose, I may pay my account in monthly installments in accordance with the schedule appearing to the right hereof. If I avail myself of the latter option, I will, if I am a resident of any state other than Connecticut, incur and pay a FINANCE CHARGE, computed at a periodic rate of 1-1/2% per month (an ANNUAL PERCENTAGE RATE of 18%), on that portion of the previous balance which does not exceed $500.00 (subject to a minimum charge of 50¢) and 1% per month (an ANNUAL PERCENTAGE RATE of 12%) on that portion of said balance which exceeds $500.00. For convenience, however, there will be no FINANCE CHARGE on balances of $5.00 or less. The FINANCE CHARGE will be computed on the previous balance without deducting any payments or other credits and without adding current purchases.

If I avail myself of the latter option, and I am a resident of Connecticut, I will incur and pay a FINANCE CHARGE computed at a periodic rate of 1% per month (an ANNUAL PERCENTAGE RATE OF 12%) on the average daily balance of my account. No FINANCE CHARGE will be added in any billing period when there was no balance outstanding in my account at the beginning of that period. For convenience, moreover, there will be no FINANCE CHARGE on average daily balances of $5.00 or less. The average daily balance is computed by totaling the balances outstanding each day throughout the monthly billing period, and dividing the sum thereof by the number of days in the monthly billing period. The balance outstanding each day is determined by adding purchases and other charges to, and subtracting payments and credits from, the balance outstanding on the previous day.

All payments required under this agreement shall be deemed to have been made when received by Gimbels.

If I should default in any payment, the entire outstanding balance shall become immediately due and payable at Gimbels' option, and, if the account is then referred to an attorney for collection, I will pay an attorney's fee not to exceed twenty percent of the amount then due and court costs.

Gimbels can at any time amend any of the terms of this agreement upon proper written notice to me. Gimbels reserves the right to limit the extent of any customer's purchases.

I agree that the charge plate given by Gimbels to me shall remain the property of Gimbels and will be surrendered by me to Gimbels at any time upon Gimbels' request.

I hereby authorize Gimbels to investigate my credit record and to furnish information concerning my account with Gimbels to credit reporting agencies and others who may properly receive such information.

If your card is lost or stolen, please call Gimbels immediately at (212) 564-3300, extension 6268, or write us at Gimbels, Broadway at 33rd Street, New York, N.Y. 10001.

I MAY AT ANY TIME PAY MY TOTAL INDEBTEDNESS.

TAKEN BY: _____

DATE: _____

APPROVED BY: _____

DATE OF APPROVAL: _____

GIMBELS
Broadway at 33rd Street, New York, N.Y. 10001
Telephone: (212) PE 6-5100

Gimbel Brothers, Inc.
Seller

NOTICE TO THE BUYER

1. Do not sign this credit agreement before you read it or if it contains any blank space.
2. You are entitled to a completely filled in copy of this agreement.

RETAIL INSTALLMENT CREDIT AGREEMENT
APPLICANT'S SIGNATURE _____

ADDRESS _____

CITY _____ STATE _____ ZIP _____

JOINT APPLICANT'S SIGNATURE _____

ADDRESS _____ DATE _____ CITY _____ STATE _____ ZIP _____

MINIMUM PAYMENT SCHEDULE
GIMBELS OPTION ACCOUNT

If I owe:	My Minimum Payment Is:
$ 0.01 to $ 10.00	Balance
$ 10.01 to $ 60.00	$10.00
$ 60.01 to $ 90.00	$15.00
$ 90.01 to $120.00	$20.00
$120.01 to $180.00	$30.00
$180.01 to $240.00	$40.00
$240.01 and Over	1/5 of Balance (rounded off the nearest dollar)

MINIMUM PAYMENT SCHEDULE
GIMBELS CONTINUOUS EASY PAYMENT ACCOUNT.

Highest Balance	Monthly Payment:
$ 50.01 to $ 60.00	$ 5.00
$ 60.01 to $ 75.00	$ 6.00
$ 75.01 to $ 100.00	$ 7.50
$100.01 to $ 125.00	$ 9.50
$125.01 to $ 150.00	$11.50
$150.01 to $ 175.00	$12.00
$175.01 to $ 200.00	$13.00
$200.01 to $ 225.00	$14.50
$225.01 to $ 250.00	$15.50
$250.01 to $ 300.00	$18.00
$300.01 to $ 350.00	$19.00
$350.01 to $ 400.00	$22.00
$400.01 to $ 450.00	$24.00
$450.01 to $ 500.00	$25.00
$500.01 to $ 600.00	$27.00
$600.01 to $ 700.00	$30.00
$700.01 to $ 800.00	$35.00
$800.01 to $ 900.00	$40.00
$900.01 to $1000.00	$45.00
Over $1000.00	$50.00 plus $5.00 for each additional $100.00 or portion thereof

FIGURE 18-1 Credit Application

of customers, are available to all members. Upon request, the credit bureau furnishes its members with this information, which is used as a basis for credit decisions. The information given does not include the source of the data. In this way each store's list of credit customers is protected.

Credit Limits

After credit has been approved, a credit limit must be decided upon. That is, a decision must be made about the total amount a customer may be permitted to owe the store at any one time. Such information as general business conditions, unemployment prospects in the area, the credit bureau's report, and weekly earnings are taken into account. Many stores set a credit limit at twice weekly earnings. It should be understood that the limit set can be increased at the customer's request upon further investigation.

Keeping Credit Records

Record keeping for charge customers is one of the responsibilities of the credit department. This is more than a mere bookkeeping chore because customers' credit ratings change and a careful study of the payment records can frequently indicate the necessity of a reduction in credit limit. Some stores subscribe to rating books that are published by private credit bureaus. These periodicals indicate changes in ratings of consumer credit buyers. The use of the computer for credit record keeping will be discussed later in the text.

Authorization

Each charge customer is given an identification number that is displayed on a recognition device such as a charge card or metal plate. This card is presented at a sales cash register. In some stores further identification, such as a driver's license, is required to prove that the buyer is the true owner of the card. In other stores the charge card must be signed in advance by the customer. This signature is then compared with the signature on the sales slip for discrepancies before the sale is recorded.

In cases in which the charge customer wishes to take the merchandise with her or him, the problem of ascertaining the standing of the account comes up. That is, will the purchase put the account above the previously determined credit limit? This can be determined in a variety of ways. Some stores use a telephone connection between the cash register and the credit department. Others send a copy of the sales slip to the credit department by way of pneumatic tube. Stores that have computerized their credit record keeping get an almost instantaneous response by slipping the credit card into a slotted device that flashes the available credit in a visual display area. Whatever method is used, credit checking is time-consuming and frequently results in long lines at registers, much to customers' annoyance. This is overcome to some extent by many large stores that permit credit sales of up to $25 without credit approval. Another method used by large stores is to have separate registers for cash and charge sales. This relieves the cash customers of the problem of waiting for another customer's credit authorization.

When the authorization does not come through because of late payments or purchases in excess of the credit limit, the customer is requested to visit the credit department to try to work things out. Tact and courtesy must be used in these cases to try to keep the customer on a cash, if not a credit, basis.

Billing

The last step in credit sales transactions is sending the monthly statement to the customer. This is a list of the month's transactions showing the balance due the store.

Cycle Billing. When charge accounts were few and the volume of credit sales small, retailers were able to send all of their statements on or about the first of each month. With the great expansion of charge accounts, the volume has grown to such an extent that stores have found it impossible to cope with the tremendous workload if it is concentrated at the start of each month. Cycle billing is a procedure in which the accounts are divided into groups and mailed on different days of the month. Under cycle billing, accounts are due ten days after receipt of the statement rather than by the 10th of the following month.

Country Club Billing. A time-saving method of billing involves filing each sales slip in a packet and sending them all, along with a totaled listing of the bills, to the customer. This is called country club billing. Naturally, a photographic copy of each sales slip and the monthly statement is kept by the store for internal bookkeeping purposes. This is a labor-saving improvement over posting each slip to a customer's account and sending a copy of the account to the customer.

Descriptive Billing. Stores that have automated their bookkeeping use a computer-printed statement that indicates

1. Beginning-of-the-month balance
2. The dollar value of each purchase and the department (in code) from which the purchase was made
3. Total purchases
4. Payments and other credits
5. Service charges
6. Amount due and due date of payment

COLLECTIONS

Unlike most other services provided by the store, credit can have adverse effects. No matter how carefully the credit manager screens customers, there is little to prevent a proportion of people from not paying their bills. If the store operates its own credit system (credit card organizations will be discussed separately), it is they who bear the responsibility not only for the collection of bad debts, but also for the alienation of those who are upset by the store's actions.

A sensitive area in the system is how to collect what is owed without offending the customer. Contrary to common belief, the culprits are not always those who have real financial problems. Often times it is the store's better customers who are delinquent payers of their bills. Much caution must be exercised not to offend those people. Although the retailer has every right to collect, the value of the individual's future business must be weighed before the unpleasant task of collection begins. Most retailers would be quick to relate stories concerning good customers who severed their relationships with a store because of overdue bills.

Yes, credit is a service, but it often poses difficult problems.

Collection Policy

Any competent credit manager could cut collection problems drastically by allowing credit only to those accounts whose applications are credit-perfect. But such a policy will not do in today's retail market. The forces of competition (everybody offers liberal credit) and the fact that mediocre credit risks are an important source of sales volume force stores to extend credit freely. A store's credit policy is usually set by top management, and is almost invariably liberal. The collection problems caused by the credit policy chosen are the responsibility of the credit department.

The three factors that must be considered in setting a credit policy are capital, competition, and kind of goods.

Capital

Of great importance in determining the strictness of the credit policy is the financial condition of the store granting the credit. All retailers need their customers' money to pay their own debts. How quickly these funds are needed depends upon their working capital position, their ability to borrow from banks to carry their customers, and their willingness to pay the cost of such loans. Naturally, underfinanced stores must have a strict credit policy.

Competition

The force of competition is probably the deciding factor in determining credit policy. American buying habits would drastically limit the volume of any store that grants significantly less credit than its competitors.

Kinds of Goods

Perishable goods require stricter collection policies than hard goods. Customers are less willing to pay for goods that are no longer in use. In addition, hard goods can often be repossessed, and continued use by the customer requires timely payments of his or her account.

Collection Systems

Large organizations have collection systems, consisting of routines that are in all cases followed in prescribed patterns. The formulation of these systems must be geared toward prompt payment for the following reasons:

1. Customers take advantage of lax collection systems. Many will withhold payment until strong pressure is exerted. Moreover, a lax system is an indication of poor management and is damaging to the organization's image.
2. The older a debt is, the less likely it is to be paid. Prompt payment reduces bad debts.
3. Customers who are behind in their payments are likely to shop different retailers.
4. The older a debt is, the more drastic the steps in the collection policy and the greater the chance of losing good will.
5. Each succeeding step in the collection procedure is more expensive than the prior one. The cost of collections is reduced by prompt customer payment.

Steps in a Collection System

Customers have a wide variety of payment habits that range from prompt payment to no intention of payment. Because these customer classifications are impossible to determine in advance, a good collections system sifts out the various types with each step in the process. (The various steps outlined below are used after the end of the credit period.)

Impersonal. People who have failed to receive their statements on time, overlooked the payment, are in temporary financial straits, or are careless are generally sent an insert with the statement, a sticker (Figure 18-2), or a form letter. Good payers usually respond to these impersonal reminders, which are intended to retain customers by maximizing good will.

Impersonal Appeal. The second step is still devoted to a major effort of retaining good will. Form letters appealing to a sense of fair play, asking for

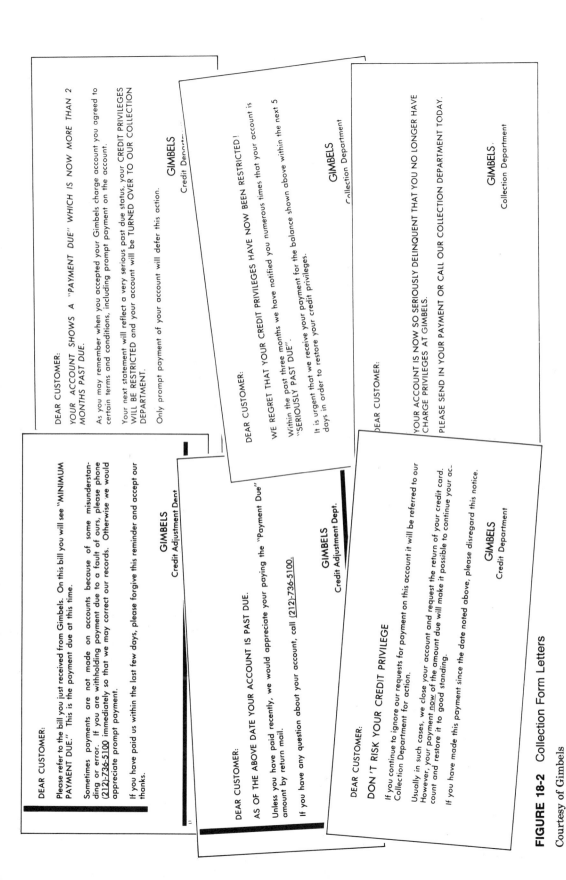

DEAR CUSTOMER:

Please refer to the bill you just received from Gimbels. On this bill you will see "MINIMUM PAYMENT DUE." This is the payment due at this time.

Sometimes payments are not made on accounts because of some misunderstanding or error. If you are withholding payment due to a fault of ours, please phone (212)-736-5100 immediately so that we may correct our records. Otherwise we would appreciate prompt payment.

If you have paid us within the last few days, please forgive this reminder and accept our thanks.

GIMBELS
Credit Adjustment Dept.

DEAR CUSTOMER:

AS OF THE ABOVE DATE YOUR ACCOUNT IS PAST DUE.

Unless you have paid recently, we would appreciate your paying the "Payment Due" amount by return mail.

If you have any question about your account, call (212)-736-5100.

GIMBELS
Credit Adjustment Dept.

DEAR CUSTOMER:

DON'T RISK YOUR CREDIT PRIVILEGE

If you continue to ignore our requests for payment on this account it will be referred to our Collection Department for action.

Usually in such cases, we close your account and request the return of your credit card. However, your payment now of the amount due will make it possible to continue your account and restore it to good standing.

If you have made this payment since the date noted above, please disregard this notice.

GIMBELS
Credit Department

DEAR CUSTOMER:

YOUR ACCOUNT SHOWS A "PAYMENT DUE" WHICH IS NOW MORE THAN 2 MONTHS PAST DUE.

As you may remember when you accepted your Gimbels charge account you agreed to certain terms and conditions, including prompt payment on the account.

Your next statement will reflect a very serious past due status, your CREDIT PRIVILEGES WILL BE RESTRICTED and your account will be TURNED OVER TO OUR COLLECTION DEPARTMENT.

Only prompt payment of your account will defer this action.

GIMBELS
Credit Department

DEAR CUSTOMER:

WE REGRET THAT YOUR CREDIT PRIVILEGES HAVE NOW BEEN RESTRICTED!

within the past three months we have notified you numerous times that your account is "SERIOUSLY PAST DUE".

It is urgent that we receive your payment for the balance shown above within the next 5 days in order to restore your credit privileges.

GIMBELS
Collection Department

DEAR CUSTOMER:

YOUR ACCOUNT IS NOW SO SERIOUSLY DELINQUENT THAT YOU NO LONGER HAVE CHARGE PRIVILEGES AT GIMBELS.

PLEASE SEND IN YOUR PAYMENT OR CALL OUR COLLECTION DEPARTMENT TODAY.

GIMBELS
Collection Department

FIGURE 18-2 Collection Form Letters

Courtesy of Gimbels

details of any disagreement and the like, are mailed. If there is no response at this time, many stores send telegrams, special delivery letters, or use the telephone.

Personalization. If there has been no response to any of the prior steps, telephones and letters take on a more threatening tone. At this point, the customer is not one the store is anxious to keep and good will is less important. Moreover, those credit customers whom the store wants to keep have already been sifted out, and those that are left are poor credit risks. This does not mean that no attempt is made to retain good will. To the contrary, the store needs cash as well as credit customers. However, some good will may have to be gambled when a customer has failed to respond to the first attempts at collection.

Legal Action. When all else has failed, long-past-due accounts are turned over to collection agencies or attorneys. This may result in wage garnishment or repossession.

Small Retailer Credit

It is likely that small retailers suffer greater credit losses than the larger organizations. In large part this is probably because personal sentiment is likely to play an important role in small business credit extension. Credit is often granted to old customers without proper research into their ability to pay; credit limits are also unscientifically determined; and collections, rather than being carefully systematized, are frequently haphazard and ineffectual.

CREDIT CARD ORGANIZATIONS

In recent years independent credit card organizations have become a major source of retail credit. Some, such as American Express, Diner's Club, and Carte Blanche are generally restricted in use to hotels and restaurants (although American Express is attracting many retail store members). Bank credit card systems, on the other hand, are widely used in retail stores. These are systems in which banks offer credit to their consumer customers. The two principal bank credit cards are MasterCard and VISA. Their growth as a factor in retail credit has been phenomenal.

Bank credit card operations begin with the customer applying to the bank for a card. (This is sometimes done at a retail store.) After a credit check, a card is issued that is acceptable in almost all retail stores. After making a sale, the store forwards the sales slip to the credit card organization, which remits the amount of the sale to the store after deducting from 4 to 6 percent, depending upon the store's volume.

The charge customer, under these plans, is the bank's customer. All of the responsibilities for credit decisions and collections belong to the bank. Banks usually allow small sales to be made without authorization. Large amounts are authorized by special telephone lines.

Bank credit is a boon to small retailers who lack the financial strength and know-how to engage in a credit business in any other way. It is widely used among large retailers also. With the growth in use of credit cards, customers prefer to carry a single card that may be used in many situations.

Retailers using bank credit card systems find that they have several disadvantages:

1. The cost of the system is considerable. If it cannot be added to the selling price (usually set by competition) it reduces profits.
2. The illegal use of lost or stolen cards is the store's responsibility. This is a serious factor in high-crime areas, and careful identification is required.
3. The close relationship between the store's credit card holder and the store is destroyed. The various advantages of store credit, such as mail order selling and special sales, are lost, along with customer loyalty.

GOVERNMENT REGULATIONS ON CREDIT

The granting of consumer credit is regulated by a variety of state and federal laws. These regulations are restrictive, and penalties may be severe. All retailers that grant consumer credit should be aware of the laws that affect their operations.

State Laws

State laws controlling installment and other credit sales vary from state to state. Generally, they require written credit contracts that specify the cash price, length of payment, down payment, fees and other credit charges, and so forth. In many states maximum interest rates are set. Some states permit the buyer to cancel the already signed contract within a few days.

Truth-in-Lending Law

In 1968 the Federal Consumer Credit Act (Truth-in-Lending Law) was passed. This law, along with Regulation Z, which was issued under the provisions of the act, required that lenders provide a great deal of information to their installment and charge customers. Among the information given is the time before finance charges are made, the amount of finance charge, and the method of computing the finance charge. Another disclosure must be the annual rate of the finance charge. Thus, a store charging interest at a rate of 1.5 percent per month must notify their customers that the annual interest rate is 18 percent.

OTHER CUSTOMER SERVICES

Stores offer any number of services that are free to the customer, and other services that carry an extra cost. Discount-oriented operations rather severely restrict the offering of services since customer motivation for shopping in these organizations is based upon price. The more traditional retailers, who usually work on a higher markup, appeal to their clientele with a variety of services. Whatever the type of retailing, all stores offer at least minimal services. It is management's task to select and offer those services that build customer good will and promote repeat business.

Merchandise Alterations

Clothing alterations are often referred to as a necessary evil. Many retailers confess that the service is costly and occasionally leads to complications. For example, a customer might love the garment, be displeased with the alteration, and refuse to pay for it, leaving an altered piece of merchandise that is potentially a complete loss. While some stores play down the alteration service for women's clothing, it is virtually impossible to eliminate it for menswear. Men generally do not buy unless the item can be altered. They simply do not have the time or desire to seek outside assistance in the tailoring of their clothing. Most menswear retailers would agree that without the alteration shop, sales would dramatically decline. Women, on the other hand, generally are not as demanding about on-premises alterations. Those with more time often seek outside services for their needs. Some stores, particularly those that cater to the working female, find that there is a need for tailoring in the store. Whether to charge extra for tailoring or include it within the price of the garment is a problem retailers must face. Traditionally, in the store that features both men's and women's clothing, the male customer's clothing is altered free of charge while the female must pay. Recently, a female customer who discovered a charge to women for alterations and none for men on an identical item took her complaint to court on discrimination charges. As a result of this complaint, stores such as Macy's have decided to study the impact of an equal system for males and females. Whatever the decision, unless the merchandise is severely discounted, store alterations is generally one service that is essential.

Gift Wrapping

Gift wrapping is provided by most stores that sell merchandise to be purchased as gifts. Some stores, because of their unique gift wrapping, gain a clientele who could otherwise make the same purchase elsewhere. The smaller retailers of boutique items and small giftware often include the cost of gift wrapping in the price of the merchandise. It is traditional that the larger retail organizations provide a free gift wrapping service, making use of less costly materials, and offering fancy packing for an extra charge that varies with the complexity and cost of the wrappings and decorations used. Gift wrapping is an excellent way to advertise a store's image. It is relatively inexpensive for a large store to operate a gift wrap department or for a small store to provide free gift wrap, when weighed against the enthusiasm often generated by beautifully decorated packages.

Delivery

There are a variety of methods by which stores may furnish customers with a service to deliver goods. When offered such a service, customers will often purchase gifts to be sent to individuals who live at distances from the purchaser. Some merchandise—such as furniture or appliances—is too cumbersome to purchase and take home. Most retailers, though, in store signs, encourage the taking home of the purchase. Delivery could be costly, especially if included in the price, and unnecessary deliveries are avoided. There are a number of delivery arrangements available to retailers. For small items, parcel post is often used. Other goods may be delivered through a store's own trucks or by means of a private carrier. Unless a store does a sufficient amount of business to warrant operating its own delivery system, an outside company is employed. Many of the large retailers who deal in bulk items and operate from warehouses, such as Levitz, the furniture discounter, offer the customer two prices—one including delivery, and one if the merchandise is carried by the customer. In such a situation an individual has the option to save money even on the traditionally delivered item. In some cases of bulky merchandise, delivery is required. In other cases, the retailer must weigh the advantages and disadvantages of providing delivery service, and whether or not the service should carry an extra cost to the customer.

Restaurants

More and more retailers are offering dining services to their customers. A restaurant might not be considered a service, but some retailers offer food at lower-than-usual prices in order to dissuade the customer from leaving the store at meal time. By retaining the customer on the premises, the store increases the chances for additional shopping after the meal. Some stores provide the management of these restaurants, while others lease space to experienced food companies to operate the eating facilities. The service runs the gamut from snack bar to the fanciest of establishments, such as the new Bloomingdale's gourmet railroad dining car restaurant in its flagship store. If a customer is kept in the store for an extended period, then the use of such space for a dining facility is worthwhile.

Additional Services

The extent and nature of other services are directly related to the store's image, the type of business it conducts, and the clientele served. The following is a list of some of the services offered across the country.

- Free interior design advice with furniture purchases.
- Use of strollers for toddlers.
- Foreign-speaking assistance for non-English-speaking customers.
- Personal shoppers to advise on purchases.
- Play areas for children.
- Special shopping days or hours for particular groups, such as the handicapped.
- Use of community room for organizations.
- Travel service departments.
- Expanded shopping hours at peak periods.

One of the more complete service programs is at Bloomingdale's in New York. In their flagship store they offer the following services, in addition to those normally provided by retail operations:

- *At His Service*—personal shoppers for men.
- *At Your Service*—personal shoppers for women.
- *Beatrice Dale*—for the shopper who wants to buy in great quantity and pay with one check.
- *Bridal Registry*—for customers who wish to check if prospective brides have indicated particular preferences in silver, china, and so on.
- *American Express Travel Service*
- *Le Train Bleu, The Greenhouse, Forty Carrots, Espresso Bar*—a variety of eating places, from gourmet dining to quick snacks.
- *Beauty Concept*—high-fashion beauty care.
- *Hair Place*—quick, young haircutting.

Action for the Independent Retailer

It is in the area of customer services that many people believe the independent is no match for the giants of the industry. This is not true. In just about every instance, the independent can provide service that, if not precisely the same as the large retail counterpart, provides as much motivation for the customer to purchase.

Smaller retailers can provide the "personal" service that is so often lacking in the big store. In how many large organizations can a customer get the buyer's advice and attention? In the independent store, the owner is usually available to provide the personalization that makes the customers feel important.

Also, just about every small retailer can provide credit, through "house charges" or credit card organizations such as VISA or MasterCard; deliver merchandise; gift wrap packages; provide extended convenience shopping hours at holiday times; offer alterations that are often better than those provided by the large organization, because of on-premises supervision by the store owner; and present promotions that involve customers, such as fashion shows.

The strength of the small business lies in the service it is able to provide only because of its size. Many shoppers find a more palatable atmosphere in the independent store than in the impersonal arena of the giant retail operations. If this were not true, the country would be void of the countless boutiques, small grocers, specialty stores, and restaurants that are found in every town and city throughout the United States.

IMPORTANT POINTS IN THE CHAPTER

1. *Since World War II the expansion of credit selling has been phenomenal. At the present time, most nonfood retailers offer some sort of credit.*

2. *Customers use credit because it is convenient; is prestigious; makes carrying large sums of cash unnecessary; provides a credit rating for more credit; and reduces home bookkeeping.*

3. *Retailers offer credit because customers prefer it; customer relationships are improved; and it provides the opportunity for direct mail sales.*

4. *Among the types of retail credit available are charge accounts, installment accounts, and revolving credit and option terms.*

5. *The credit department is charged with the following responsibilities: opening new accounts, keeping credit records, authorizing credit, and billing and collections.*

6. *In establishing a collection policy, consideration must be given to the financial condition of the store, competitors' policies, and the kinds of goods involved.*

7. *Large retailers follow carefully prescribed patterns for the collections of late accounts. These begin with gentle reminders and end with legal action.*

8. *Credit card organizations such as American Express are a major source of retail credit. They are particularly helpful to small retailers.*

9. *The granting of consumer credit is regulated by a variety of state and federal laws.*

10. *The variety of customer services often accounts for the amount of business transacted in retailing.*

REVIEW QUESTIONS

1. List six reasons why customers prefer to shop with credit cards.
2. Discuss the argument that too-liberal credit terms will bankrupt most American families.
3. Despite competitive pressures, some very successful stores *do not* give credit. How do they survive?
4. Discuss the relationship between a store and its charge customers.
5. How are credit accounts helpful in direct mail selling?
6. Explain the importance of teaching about credit in a sales training program.
7. Should a salesperson try to talk a customer out of a sale if the salesperson feels the buyer's credit burden will be excessive?
8. What benefits do stores get from a liberal credit policy?
9. List five characteristics of installment accounts.
10. Explain how revolving credit works.
11. What is revolving credit with option terms?
12. Discuss the responsibilities of the credit department.
13. Why is the interview important in opening a charge account?
14. What are retail credit bureaus? How are they organized?
15. Discuss the cash register operator's role in the granting of credit approval.
16. Differentiate among cycle billing, country club billing, and descriptive billing, giving advantages and disadvantages of each.
17. What is the effect of good will retention on collection policy?
18. List and define three factors that must be taken into account before a credit policy can be set.
19. Compare credit management in a small retail organization with that of a large store.
20. How do the independent credit card organizations operate?
21. Explain the requirement of the "Truth-in-Lending" Law and Regulation Z.
22. Should retailers charge for alterations?
23. How can the independent compete, in terms of service, with the giant retailers?

CASE PROBLEMS

CASE PROBLEM 1

The Smart Set, Inc. is a ladies' specialty store that started in 1950. The store is situated in a growing middle-class suburb of a large metropolitan area. During most of the organization's history, an influx of new homeowners and a lack of aggressive competition has led to steady growth in sales volume. In that period, the store has grown from a family-sized store to a relatively large and successful operation employing fourteen persons.

In recent years, major innercity department stores have begun following their migrating clientele into the suburbs. This, of course, has increased competition enormously. By tasteful buying and intelligent inventory control, Smart Set has been able to compete with the department stores in the area of merchandising. However, it has been forced to increase such customer services as the extension of credit.

Credit selling has expanded dramatically in recent years. Because the store is too small to afford a credit manager, store charge accounts (the only sort of credit offered) have been issued on a haphazard basis. Since the store is situated in a respectable, fairly affluent area, bad debt losses, although higher than normal, have been bearable. Collections, though, have been slow (customers seem to pay competing stores first). The result has been a fairly serious shortage of working capital.

The owner of Smart Set, Inc. has approached you to prepare a collections system for the store. The system given should include a step-by-step program for all late accounts.

QUESTIONS

1. Prepare the necessary collection program.
2. Have you any other suggestions?

CASE PROBLEM 2

A problem has come up in one of the largest, most successful department store chains in the country. The organization, Bloomcrest's, has major outlets in many major cities and wealthy suburban areas across the nation. The store's clientele consists of upper- and upper-middle-class patrons who flock to this prestigious organization because of the imagination and taste of the merchandising personnel.

Thanks to the uniqueness of the store's offerings, decor, and service, the markup is well above average, making it one of the most successful retail operations in the country.

As would be expected, top management is highly skilled and aggressive. Rather than rest on its laurels, it is constantly trying to improve the operation. One of management's programs is a periodic (every five years) evaluation of store procedures by a large, independent consulting firm.

One of the suggestions recently proposed by the consultants was that major independent credit cards be accepted. They argue that customers are weighted down by the number of credit cards they are forced to carry and many people have decided to replace their bulging wallets with a single, universally acceptable credit card such as Master-Card or VISA.

The corporate controller, responsible for chainwide credits and collections, objects.

QUESTIONS

1. Present the controller's arguments.
2. Which decision do you favor? Why?

19 *research*

BEHAVIORAL OBJECTIVES

Upon completion of this chapter the student should be able to

1. *List and discuss six areas of the use of research by retailers.*
2. *Differentiate between, and give examples of, primary and secondary information sources.*
3. *List three types of questionnaires. Give four advantages and four disadvantages of each.*

INTRODUCTION

Decision making is probably the most important aspect of a manager's job. The decisions of one in top management can affect the entire retail organization. Middle managers, such as buyers or those in charge of selling departments, are concerned with decision making that primarily affects their own departments. Nonetheless, considering the amount of competition in retailing today, decision making at every level must be sound in order to improve the store's position and make certain it receives its fair share of business. Those who prepare haphazardly or make decisions based upon "feeling" or "whim" are apt to be unsuccessful retailers.

Retailers are continually trying to "beat yesterday's figures." With the constant increase in costs, merely meeting last year's sales figures will result in smaller profits. In an attempt to achieve new goals, retailers are always involved in some type of research. *Marketing research* is a term that should be familiar to all students of retailing. Broadly, it involves the investigation of marketing problems and those recommendations necessary to solve these problems. Retailing is the last step in the marketing of most consumer goods (goods used for one's own personal satisfaction). Therefore, the problems that face the retail store confronted with purchasing merchandise from vendors and selling it to household consumers are often solved through marketing research or, since it is confined to retail organizations, *retailing research.*

To some students the term *research* is associated with the *scientific method* and is thought of as grand-scale laboratory investigations carried out by scientists in white coats. Needless to say, the research used in retail stores may be as sophisticated or as simple as the size of the store or the problem warrants. Research in retailing is not confined to the giants of the industry. The individual proprietor can also become involved in investigating and solving some areas of uncertainty without going to great expense. Naturally, the larger the organization, the more complex the problems and the more involved the research will be.

AREAS OF APPLICATION

Research is employed by retailers in a wide range of areas. It is used even before the retailer sets up shop to make certain it is situated in the right location. Research covers every conceivable area of operation, starting before the goods are purchased by store buyers and ending after the customer has them at home. Following are some areas in which management may find research helpful in solving its problems.

Store Location

Picking the right place to house the retail outlet is of primary concern. Without the proper location, the best merchants in the world cannot run a successful operation. Some of the areas of investigation researched in the selection of the store's location are

1. *The size of the trading area.*
2. *The backgrounds of those inhabiting the trading area.* This includes, among other things, income, size of the family, types of dwellings inhabited, and occupations.
3. *Transportation conditions.* Included are available public transportation and roads leading to proposed location.
4. *Store competition.* Is the area in need of this type of operation, or is there too much competition to warrant another shop of the kind proposed?
5. *Competing trading areas.* As an example, a store planning to open on a town's main street must investigate whether or not any other business section, such as a central shopping center, is more convenient for the customer.

The Customer

Whether the research is formalized by sending questionnaires to customers or carried on informally by having the salesperson determine customer needs through questioning, successful retailers know that satisfying the requirements of the customer is most important. Catering to the shoppers' demands makes it simpler to sell merchandise. Such areas as income, age, taste, education, and occupation must be studied to make certain that the customers' needs, such as style, color, and price, are being satisfied.

Advertising and Sales Promotion

Advertisements and displays and their creation are the result of much research. Whether a store engages in promotional advertising or institutional advertising is not left to chance. Even after a display is executed or an advertisement appears in one of the available media, its effectiveness should be measured. Another question answered through research is, "In which medium should we spend most of the sales promotion dollar?"; and if newspaper advertising is the answer, "Should we advertise in a morning or afternoon paper?"

Sales Methods

While some departments such as precious jewelry and expensive furs almost demand individualized service, other types of merchandise do not present so clear-cut a picture. Some stores offer both service and self-service. By studying the customers, potential customers, and the practices employed by competitors and noncompetitors, decisions regarding sales methods can be made.

Merchandising

Perhaps the most important part of retailing is merchandising. This is broadly defined as the entire buying and selling cycle, including all of the activities involved in the process. In addition to studying customer demands, the retailer is interested in the current market conditions, new sources from whom to purchase, prices, sales forecasts, and inventory analysis.

Analysis of Costs

Departments either operate on a standard markup for all merchandise or try to maintain an average markup for their entire inventory. Average markup allows for a department to vary the markup on individual items. Whichever method is employed, the markup needed to show a profit must be decided upon only after carefully studying all the costs involved. Markup cannot be a purely arbitrary amount, because of competition. Keeping this in mind, retailers are always trying to reduce costs and losses without pricing themselves out of their market; to accomplish this necessitates a good deal of research.

Customer Services

The amount and types of service to offer poses a problem to retailers. Some stores afford their shoppers such services as personal shopping (accompanying a customer through the store and making suggestions on what to purchase), baby-sitting, and free delivery. Other retailers may eliminate shopping services entirely. The practice to be followed is best determined by studying the customers through some form of research. Some retailers have found that customers are willing to pay a little more in order to have additional services. We need only to compare today's "discount" operations with those of ten years ago to see that the addition of delivery service and credit service resulted in higher prices.

Personnel

Finding and hiring the best available personnel, at all levels, is often a problem for the retailer. Which sources of supply produce the best applicants, what type of interview is most successful, whether or not testing is meaningful, are just some questions that need answers. The answers are often the result of research.

Certainly each of the areas briefly discussed opens up an infinite number of categories that are researchable and important to the proper overall functioning of the store.

THE RESEARCH PROCESS

Different problems require different research tools, but the research process, whatever the situation, is usually the following.

Identification of the Problem

A variety of factors might lead to the researching of a problem. One, perhaps, might be a gradual decline in sales for no obvious reason, either storewide or confined to a particular department. The reasons for the decline may not be obvious and therefore necessitate investigation. Another problem might be whether a retail store should expand the facilities at its present location or move to another location. Still another problem might concern the evaluation of the effectiveness of the store's advertising practices in relation to sales. Whatever the area of concern, it must be identified in order to be effectively researched.

Definition of the Problem

Business executives, unlike market researchers, tend to be rather general in describing the problems confronting their organizations. In order to successfully solve a problem, it must be clearly defined. For example, evaluating the effectiveness of advertising and its relation to sales is too vague a question for investigation. Careful analysis of exactly what sales level is expected to result from advertising and whether or not the advertising program is bringing this response is more specific.

Conducting the Study

After the problem has been defined and is considered practical to solve (sometimes the costs are too prohibitive), a study is undertaken.

Studying Secondary Information

Before an investigator becomes involved in original research, an examination of secondary data (data that has already been compiled) is in order. The secondary data might supply background information that could be helpful in solving the problem. Sometimes so much has been published relating to the problem to be solved, it might not be necessary to engage in "field research." Among the secondary sources of information that may be important to retailers are

Company's own records. These may include accounting reports such as the balance sheet and income statement; sales records of employees; unit control records (showing the activity of individual merchandise styles); records of returns, credits, and refunds; buyers' records; and records showing activity of charge customers' accounts.

Libraries. Just about every desired business publication is available in the public library. Those helpful to retailers include *Advertising Age, Chain Store Age, Women's Wear Daily, The Journal of Retailing,* and *The Journal of Marketing.* For a complete listing of pertinent business literature, most libraries have available a Business Periodicals Index. These publications are extremely important in that they often publish the results of surveys that might be similar to the one being initiated. In that case, an original research project may be unnecessary since the same type of problem has already been investigated.

Trade organizations. These groups are composed of businesses with common interests. The largest retail trade association is the National Retail Merchants Association, whose membership includes almost every important retail organization. These groups hold periodic meetings that result in forthcoming publications of interest to retailers. Some even publish their own periodicals.

Government. Much data is available from the federal government. *The Monthly Catalogue of U.S. Government Publications* contains a comprehensive list of government publications. Of particular interest to retail organizations are publications by the Department of Commerce, of which the Census Bureau is a part. Here all pertinent data, by different classifications, relating to potential business are available. For example, the census of housing, the census of business, and the census of population offer the retailer invaluable data.

Private services. There are several established agencies that have data that is otherwise unavailable without going into original research. Such companies as Dun and Bradstreet (credit information) and A. C. Nielsen Company (radio and TV measurement of audiences) can provide important information for retail research projects.

Colleges. Research studies are available at many colleges' business administration, marketing, and retailing departments.

Gathering Primary Information

If after exploration of the secondary data, the problem hasn't been solved (and it usually hasn't at this stage), then primary data must be collected. Primary data is simply defined as data that is compiled from firsthand sources. In retailing these sources include customers, vendors, advertising agencies, the advertising media, and employees of the organization.

There are several techniques employed by retailers in securing primary information. The nature of the problem generally determines the method to be used.

Counts (Observations). Traffic counts and fashion counts are frequently used by retailers. As the name implies, this method requires the counting and recording of people or things that may be important to the retailer.

Traffic counts may be used when top management, in trying to evaluate a new location for a branch store, is interested in how much traffic passes the proposed site. The traffic is generally broken down into categories generated by public transportation, automobiles, and pedestrian traffic. A simple form is devised to record the number of people passing the location within a given period. A count of this type might also be used when a retailer is considering billboard advertising. Counting the number of people passing the proposed site is relatively simple.

Middle management often engages in informal traffic counts within their own departments. These counts may be used to determine the peak selling period for that department in the day. This information can be a help in scheduling employees' work periods.

Fashion counts are used to determine the type of clothes customers are wearing. This information can be helpful to buyers of fashion goods, in planning additional purchases for the current season or in planning for a new season. These counts, which are merely recorded observations of people, are also helpful in recognizing trends. A survey of this type might be taken at periodic intervals in places where a store's clientele congregates. Checking a particular kind of merchandise by such a survey might reveal factors that would be of interest in future purchasing. For example, a shirt shop catering to the "Madison Avenue advertising executives" might want to determine the colors that should be replenished in inventory and the amounts to be purchased. First, by taking an informal count at places such as luncheon spots frequented by the advertising crowd, or perhaps at the entrances to the buildings that house the advertising agencies, the store owner can quickly learn what the store's clientele is wearing. Tabulation of the number of people observed (the number needed is determined by a statistical formula) will produce figures that can be translated into percentages. If, for example, 20 of the 100 men observed wore blue shirts, it might be wise for this retailer to carry 20 percent of the store's inventory in blue shirts.

If it is desirable to determine whether color preferences are increasing or decreasing, additional counts can be taken. A comparison of the data taken on two dates would show the trends in men's colored shirts. High fashion specialty stores often take fashion counts at social events, such as the opening of the horse show in New York City or the first night of the season at the Metropoli-

FIGURE 19–1 FASHION COUNT
ITEM COUNTED: LADIES' OUTER GARMENTS
LOCATION: _____

(Fill in Name of Theatre Where Count Was Made)

Style	Furs	Materials	Color (If Fabric)	Length
"A" Line	Mink	Brocades	Black	Short coat
Cape	Persian lamb	Flat wool	Blue (Navy)	Mid-calf coat
Chesterfield	Rabbit	Leather	Brown	Floor-length coat
Double breasted	Sable	Mohair	Gold	Jacket
Empire	Fox	Satin	Green	Other _____
Jacket	Chinchilla	Suede	Gray	
Mandarin	Seal	Tweed and plaid	Natural	
Redingote	Beaver	Velvet	Red	
Trench-coat	Muskrat	Other _____	White	
Wraparound	Sable		Yellow	
Other _____	Other _____		Other _____	

Place a check mark next to appropriate item. Place only one check mark in each column.

tan Opera House. Since these events are frequented by fashion leaders, it is wise to see what these people are wearing.

The fashion count is simple to organize, and in comparison with other methods used in gathering primary information, it is inexpensive. Stores often employ college students for this task since a great deal of research experience is not necessary. About the only really important point that must be impressed upon those who have not "counted" before is that they must have a perfect understanding of what is to be counted. An example of a form used for a fashion count taken by college students for a retailer's use is pictured in Figure 19-1.

Questionnaire. The most widely used method of gathering information is the questionnaire. This technique is more involved and more time-consuming than the count. Whereas counts require no cooperation from those being surveyed, the questionnaire must seek out those willing to be involved.

Retailers can select from three methods of collecting data: telephone, mail, and personal interview. Which method is the most appropriate depends upon several factors. Among them are

1. Geographic area to be covered
2. Number of people available to carry out the survey
3. Cost
4. Time available to gather information

Closer analysis of the three methods points up their advantages and disadvantages.

Telephone.   The advantages of gathering data by telephone are that

1. It is the quickest method for researching people.
2. The cost of making the calls is relatively small.
3. Questioning can be carried out from a central point without the need for sending people into the field.
4. Information is obtained quickly.

Following are some disadvantages of using the telephone:

1. Only those with telephones can be reached. Stores catering to the lower socioeconomic groups may not be able to contact their customers using this method.
2. Many people are reluctant to respond to interviewers they cannot see.
3. If the store's trading area is out of their normal call zone, those living in toll zones might not be called because of the high cost involved. This would present a limited picture of the store's clientele.
4. Calls might be annoying and resented by the store's customers.

Mail.   Advantages of sending questionnaires through the mail are that

1. Postage is relatively inexpensive.
2. Wide distribution (for trading areas of national chains) still affords the same cost to all persons being questioned. The telephone would require different costs because of toll calls.
3. More time is allotted for studying and answering questions.
4. The interviewer cannot influence the answer, as might happen in a personal interview.
5. A field staff is eliminated.

Some disadvantages of using the mail are the following:

1. The rate of return is very small. A 10 percent response is considered to be good.
2. Since the rate of response is so small, the cost per return is very high; the cost of those not returned must be considered part of the overall cost of the survey.
3. Questions might not be completely understood without an interviewer.
4. The time it takes to receive the responses is longer than either personal interview or telephone.
5. Those responding might not truly be representative of the sample.

Since the number of responses and the time factor involved are generally uncontrollable, retailers, in an effort to overcome these disadvantages, often offer premiums as an inducement for better results. Such inducements as courtesy discounts, special prices on particular items, and even cash are offered to those from whom responses are sought.

Personal Interview. The interview may take place at the individual's home, in front of the retailer's store entrance, or even in the store. This is the only method employing face-to-face involvement. The questions may be either of the short-answer variety (most commonly used by retailers) or open-ended with the respondent giving a complete reaction to the question.

Advantages of a personal interview are that

1. Trained interviewers have success in getting a high percentage of people to grant interviews.
2. Questions that are not completely clear can be explained.
3. Additional probing can be conducted using the open-end question. This is not possible via the mail.
4. Observations may also be recorded.

The following are disadvantages of personal interviewing:

1. Responding to an interviewer may cause the respondent to "color" responses because of embarrassment—for example, on such items as age and income.
2. Employment of experienced interviewers is costly.
3. Interviewers' biases might be reflected in the responses.
4. Interviews in the home might come at an inopportune time.

Preparation of the Questionnaire Form. The amount and type of response received from the questionnaire may be only as good as the questionnaire design. Therefore, great care must be exercised in preparing these forms to guarantee accurate results. Among those factors that must be considered are

1. The occupations of those being questioned.
2. Educational level.
3. Prejudices of those to be interviewed.

In constructing the form to be used, the following should be carefully considered:

1. Questions must be easily understood. The language must be compatible with the intelligence of those to be interviewed. This is particularly true in the case of the mail questionnaire, where there will not be an interviewer available to clarify questions.
2. Avoid generalities by eliminating such words as usually, generally, and occasionally. Such words tend to prohibit a clear-cut response from the respondent. For example, "Do you usually shop at the R & M Department store?" An answer to this question will not tell how often the customer shops at R & M or the percentage of purchases that are made there.
3. Questions should be arranged in sequential order so that each question makes for a smooth transition to the next one.
4. Questions should be concise and to the point.

5. The questionnaire should not be too long. This might discourage a response. A one-page form is most satisfactory for use by retailers.

6. The design must be organized in such a manner that recording is simple. Caution must be taken to provide enough space for responses, particularly if open-end questions are used.

7. The questionnaire should be organized in such a manner that tabulation of the results is simplified.

Examples of mail, personal interview, and telephone questionnaires are shown in Figures 19-2, 19-3, and 19-4.

Consumer Panels and College Boards. Some retailers have had success in organizing groups for guidance in such areas as merchandise selection, advertising evaluation, and customer services. The groups are selected from a cross-section of customers or potential customers, depending upon the information that is desired. The groups are either organized permanently to meet periodically and make recommendations, or are temporarily formed.

Most successful to stores selling back-to-school clothing have been the college boards. This group or panel is generally composed of representatives of those colleges attended by the store's customers. Panels of this nature might have as many as thirty colleges represented. The students (usually young women) advise buyers on the selection of styles most appropriate for their colleges and universities. They also can be found on the selling floors, prior to going back to school, to help those students interested in the appropriate selection of clothing for their particular schools. This panel both advises management and helps to sell the merchandise.

Another example of a consumer panel is one using potential customers. A newly opened retailer, in an attempt to increase disappointing sales, might organize a cross-section of individuals who comprise the store's trading area. The group, led by a trained researcher, discusses customer characteristics and needs. After a careful study of a recording of the discussion, recommendations for adjusting the situation can be made. If the data is still inconclusive, the employment of a questionnaire might be found worthwhile, with the questions to be answered formulated from the panel's responses.

Most important in the use of the panel is to make certain the individuals truly represent the group you are trying to learn about. For a very small cost, a marketing research firm can arrange any type of panel. In this way, proper participation will be guaranteed.

Sampling

After preparing the necessary forms to be used, a determination must be made regarding the number of people to be included for the survey to be meaningful. It is neither necessary nor practical to involve every conceivable individual in a group. For example, a retailer located within a trading area of

500,000 people need only investigate a small part of this population. The segment of the population selected is known as a sample. The sample is most effective when its members are truly representative of the group to be studied. The size and selection of the sample are based upon many considerations and should be carefully decided upon with the help of a statistician.

Collection of the Data

The actual collection of data depends upon the method to be used. Whichever technique or combination of techniques is employed, the investigators must be thoroughly trained. Stores employing the services of a professional research organization need not be concerned, but those using college students or their own employees to collect data must make certain that there is a thorough understanding of the investigative methods. A successful method used in training laypersons to conduct personal interviews is role playing. One individual assumes the interviewer's identity and the other the consumer's; in this way an individual trained in the art of questioning can observe, criticize, and make recommendations to improve questioning techniques. In the area of observations, investigators must be familiar with what they are observing and recording. The results of the fashion count in Figure 19-1, concerning women's outer garments, could not have been meaningful unless the observers were able to distinguish between such items as a floor-length coat and a calf-length coat. Similarly, those involved in recording information derived from consumer panels must be thoroughly trained in that procedure.

Processing and Analysis of Data

After the investigators submit the raw data collected, the data must be processed, that is, arranged in proper form for analysis. All the forms must be first inspected and corrected or modified to guarantee that the information is stated appropriately for tabulation. The data must then be classified into categories. This step is simplified if care was exercised in the preparation of the forms used. Without being classified into homogeneous groupings, the data cannot be analyzed. The next step, particularly if data processing machines are to be used for the purpose of tabulation, is coding. A code must be devised for each possible type of reply. For example, code 6 might mean blue and code 12 might stand for red. These codes can then be fed into the computer for quick processing. Coding can be eliminated if the questionnaire was precoded with each item having a number assigned to it on the original form. Actual tabulation can be done by machine, as mentioned, or by hand. (See Figure 19-5 for examples.) Small retailers often use small samples that can be tabulated by hand. More common is the machine tabulation, which mechanically and more quickly and efficiently performs the steps involved in manual tabulation.

After the data have been compiled and summarized, analysis takes

FIGURE 19-2 MAIL QUESTIONNAIRE

Dear Customer:

In our efforts to serve you better and to provide you with the best in shopping facilities, we periodically ask some of our valued patrons to answer a few simple questions. Your responses and suggestions guide us in some key decisions regarding store operations. Our sole objective is to give you the type of store that you can look forward to shopping in the year round.

Please fill in the form below. After completion, fold and insert the form into the attached self-addressed, stamped envelope.

As a token of our appreciation, on receipt of your questionnaire, we will send you a free premium for an attractive gift that may be redeemed at any of our branch stores. Please hurry since the supply is limited and the cutoff date is _____ .

May we thank you in advance for your answers, your comments and your advice.

(Tear off)

1. Do you find the store layout convenient?
   ☐ Yes   ☐ No   (If no, please suggest some changes you would like to see made. Comment in the space provided below.)

   _____
   _____
   _____

2. Are our salespeople always helpful?
   ☐ Yes   ☐ No   (If no, please mention some ways they can better serve you.)

   _____
   _____
   _____

3. Are you satisfied with our checkout counters, particularly in terms of speed, handling of credit cards and charge accounts, and wrapping?
   ☐ Yes   ☐ No   (Please comment below)

   _____
   _____
   _____

4. What other merchandise lines or service would you like to see added to our store?

   _____
   _____
   _____

5. Are you satisfied with our adjustment and refund policy?
   ☐ Yes   ☐ No   (If no, please suggest ways we can improve this policy)

   _____
   _____

FIGURE 19–2 MAIL QUESTIONNAIRE *(Continued)*

Classification Data

6. Please tell us approximately how often you shopped here in the past six months.
   Check the appropriate box below:
   None ☐
   1–3 times ☐
   4–6 times ☐
   7–9 times ☐
   10–12 times ☐
   15 or more times ☐

7. Of your total purchases what percent is:
   Cash _____%
   Charge Account _____%
   Credit Card _____%
   Other (specify) _____%
   _____ 100%

8. What is the occupation of the head of the household?

   _____

9. What is the last grade of school you completed?
   Grade school or less ☐
   Some high school ☐
   Completed high school ☐
   Some college ☐
   Completed college ☐

10. Was your approximate family income last year under $18,500 or over $18,500?

Under $18,500	Over $18,500
Was it - under $7,500	Was it - under $20,000
or $7,500–10,000	or over $20,000
or $10,000–12,500	
or $12,500–18,500	

11. Would you please indicate in which of these age groups you belong? Are you in your ...
   20's .....
   30's .....
   40's .....
   50's .....
   60 and over

Your Name (Please print) _____

Address (Please print) _____

City _____ State _____ Zip # _____
      (Do not abbreviate)

Pardon me . . . I am making a consumer survey for Brant's.

1. Did you buy anything at Brant's today? ___ Yes ___ No ___ Just passing through

    If respondent answers "yes," thank her for her patronage and tell her that

    the study you are making does not involve Brant customers.

    If she is just passing through the store, thank her for this information.

    If her answer is "no," go ahead with the rest of the questionnaire.

2. What departments at Brant's did you visit (indicate department and floor)?

3. Would you mind telling us your reason for not buying anything at Brant's?

Item	Didn't have what I wanted (size, color, brand, style, etc.)	Price too High	Salesperson not helpful	Out of Stock	Just looking	Other, specify
a)						
b)						
c)						
d)						

4. When you think of Brant's what is the first thing that comes to your mind?

Classification data –

   What part of town are you from? (Eastland, Riverview, etc.)

   Do you work downtown?   Yes   No

   Age (to be estimated by interviewer)   Under 30   30-44   45 and over

   Man   Woman

   Date and time

Store entrance (circle one)
   Walnut Street Cosmetics   Walnut Street Men's Furnishings   Walnut Street Blouse
   Euclid Street Purses   Euclid Street Hosiery   Main Street
   Euclid Street Men's clothing

FIGURE 19-3   Personal Interview Questionnaire

Robert H. Myers, "Sharpening Your Store Image," *Journal of Retailing*, Vol. 36, No. 3.

place. The amount and kind of analyses depend upon the research project. Some studies, such as the fashion count, might be used only to determine which colors are most popular and in what percentages. Other studies might require more sophisticated statistical analysis and interpretation. This phase of the research project is most important, since future decisions will be based upon it. Knowledgeable research analysts are best used to evaluate all possible courses of action and make final recommendations. If a retailer is conducting its own study, it is advisable for everyone in management connected with the project to review the recommendations of the chief researcher before implementing those suggestions.

RICHARD MANVILLE RESEARCH INC.
230 PARK AVENUE, NEW YORK, N.Y. 10017

WASHING MACHINE SURVEY

NAME:_____   TIME STARTED:_____

TELEPHONE
NUMBER:_____   DATE:_____

     Hello, we're conducting a survey and I'd like to ask you a few questions.

1.   Do you have a washing machine in your home?

        4-1 ☐ Yes

        -2 ☐ No   (IF NO, DISCONTINUE -
                   IF YES, ASK:)

2.   Did you buy it within the last six months?

        5-1 ☐ Yes

        -2 ☐ No   (IF NO, DISCONTINUE)

3.   Is it <u>filled</u> by one hose or by two hoses?

        6-1 ☐ One Hose

        -2 ☐ Two Hoses

        -3 ☐ Don't Know

4.   Where in your home or apartment do you keep the washing machine?

     In what room?

        7-1 ☐ Kitchen

        -2 ☐ Basement

        -3 ☐ Washroom

        -4 ☐ Hallway

        -5 ☐ Other (Specify)_____

5.   Is it on rollers or is it permanently installed?

        8-1 ☐ Rollers

        -2 ☐ Permanently Installed

        -3 ☐ Don't Know

     (IF ON ROLLERS, ASK QUESTION 6)

6.   Do you have to move the washing machine each time you use it?

        9-1 ☐ Yes   -2 ☐ No

7a   Is the washing machine regular size or compact size?

        10-1 ☐ Regular

        -2 ☐ Compact

        -3 ☐ Don't Know

  b   (IF A COMPACT WAS PURCHASED, ASK:) Why did you purchase a compact
      machine rather than a regular size model? (PROBE)

11-   _____

       _____

       _____

FIGURE 19-4 Questionnaire for Telephone Survey

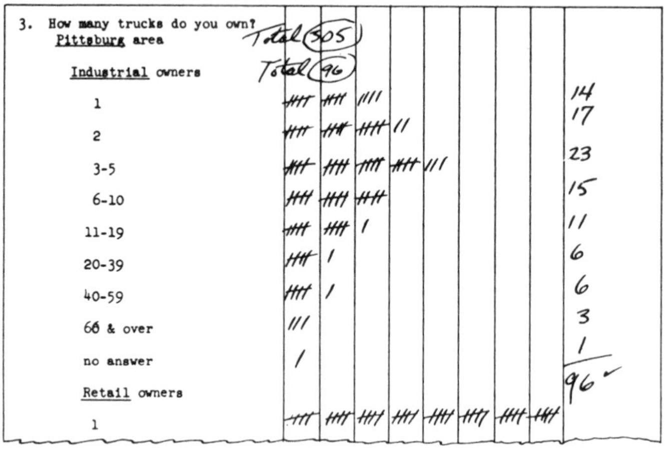

3. How many trucks do you own? Total (505)
Pittsburg area
Industrial owners Total (96)

1	~~||||~~ ~~||||~~ ||||	14
2	~~||||~~ ~~||||~~ ~~||||~~ ||	17
3-5	~~||||~~ ~~||||~~ ~~||||~~ ~~||||~~ |||	23
6-10	~~||||~~ ~~||||~~ ~~||||~~	15
11-19	~~||||~~ ~~||||~~		11
20-39	~~||||~~		6
40-59	~~||||~~		6
60 & over	|||	3
no answer			1
		96

Retail owners
1

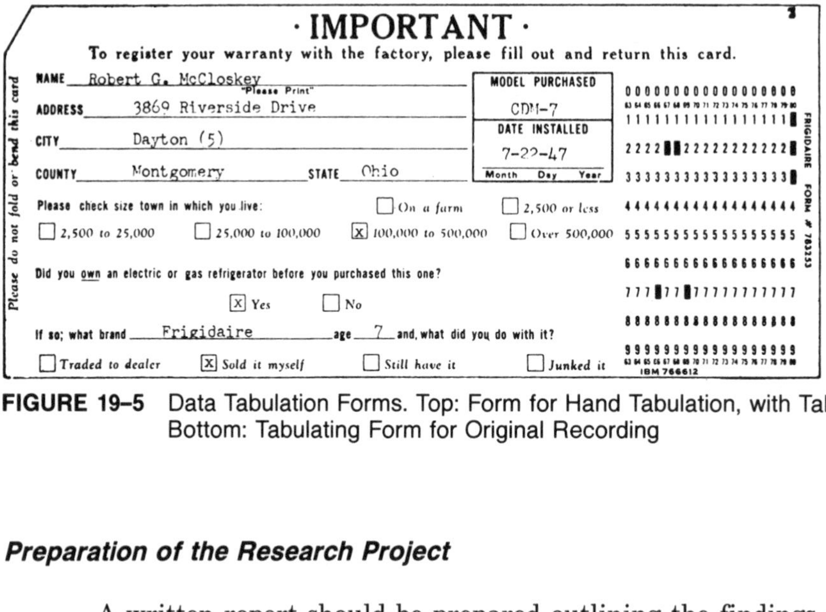

· IMPORTANT ·
To register your warranty with the factory, please fill out and return this card.
Please do not fold or bend this card
NAME Robert G. McCloskey "Please Print"
ADDRESS 3869 Riverside Drive
CITY Dayton (5)
COUNTY Montgomery STATE Ohio
MODEL PURCHASED CDM-7
DATE INSTALLED 7-22-47
Month Day Year
Please check size town in which you live: ☐ On a farm ☐ 2,500 or less
☐ 2,500 to 25,000 ☐ 25,000 to 100,000 ☒ 100,000 to 500,000 ☐ Over 500,000
Did you own an electric or gas refrigerator before you purchased this one?
☒ Yes ☐ No
If so; what brand Frigidaire age 7 and, what did you do with it?
☐ Traded to dealer ☒ Sold it myself ☐ Still have it ☐ Junked it
FRIGIDAIRE FORM # 783233
IBM 766612

FIGURE 19–5 Data Tabulation Forms. Top: Form for Hand Tabulation, with Tallies; Bottom: Tabulating Form for Original Recording

Preparation of the Research Project

A written report should be prepared outlining the findings of the investigation. It should include the data, analysis, and recommendations bound in some permanent form. This can serve for future reference and related studies.

Most complete research reports follow the areas covered in this chapter. They are

1. The problem defined
2. Methodology used in the study

3. Analysis
4. Recommendations
5. Appendices, to include data from both secondary and primary sources

CAREERS IN RESEARCH

The field of research is the fastest-growing phase of the marketing process. The retail store, one of the last marketing institutions to use research in solving problems, is fast becoming a firm believer in its merits. Because of this recent surge more graduates are needed to fill the managerial positions in retailing research as well as in the broader area of market research. Graduates with marketing degrees are afforded recognition by research firms at numerous career days. Graduates with backgrounds in statistics and marketing are considered to be properly prepared for entrance into the field. Initial employment generally involves participation in field investigations and data processing and analysis.

Action for the Independent Retailer

Research is often looked upon, especially by smaller retailers, as too time-consuming, involved, complicated, and, above all, too costly for their businesses. While it is true that many studies that are undertaken require large sums of money as well as trained specialists, there are areas of research that can benefit even the smallest retailer with a minimum of expense.

Some principles for independents to follow are

- *Read all of the available literature. Trade associations and periodicals provide a multitude of studies that might parallel even the smallest store's problems.*
- *Make available questionnaires to customers who could comment on merchandise assortment, price lines, and so forth.*
- *Prepare a fashion count, if appropriate. College classes could be approached to carry out the research as a class project. This gives the retailer information and the students practice.*
- *Provide a suggestion box for customers, and tally the suggestions. Those that are most prevalent and appropriate could be utilized.*

Research need not be costly. It provides a variety of pertinent information that could be collected with little or no cost at all to the retailer.

IMPORTANT POINTS IN THE CHAPTER

1. *Retailing research involves the investigation of retailing problems and the recommendations necessary to solve those problems. In practical terms, retailing research is an attempt to take some of the guesswork out of managerial decision making.*

2. *Research is used by retailers in a wide range of areas. These include determining sites for a store's location; gathering information concerning the tastes and needs of a store's customers; analyzing the effectiveness of a store's advertising and sales promotion; and studying merchandising policies, including resources, sales forecasts, and size and color analyses.*

3. *Before the methods of research can be decided upon, it is necessary to clearly identify and define the problem.*

4. *The necessary information upon which the research will be based may be taken from many sources. These include the company's own records, libraries, trade organizations and publications, governmental publications, and private research organizations.*

5. *Much retailing research is based upon counts. This method requires the counting and recording of people or things. Such information as the number of people wearing particular styles or colors is typical of research based upon counts.*

6. *The questionnaire, either by telephone, by mail, or in person, is essentially an involved, time-consuming method of gathering information needed for some research studies.*

7. *After the research information has been collected, it must be tabulated, analyzed, and reported. Recommendations based on the report are the final step in a research project.*

REVIEW QUESTIONS

1. Define retailing research and tell how it differs from marketing research.
2. Discuss some of the factors that should be researched in the selection of a store location.
3. Is top management or middle management more concerned with research in the area of store location? Defend your position.
4. What are some questions answered through research for the manager of a store's advertising department?
5. Identify those areas of investigation that might be helpful to the personnel manager.
6. Why must a problem be carefully and clearly defined in a research project?
7. Even after a problem is identified and defined, it occasionally is not researched. Why?
8. Define the term *secondary data*.
9. Where might a research investigator find invaluable information for a project without looking outside the company?
10. Which publications might be beneficial for retailers to use when they are conducting a study?

11. How might a trade organization help the retail store involved in a research project?

12. Using which type of research technique might a retailer gather information without permission or direct assistance from those being studied?

13. Describe the technique often used by retailers to assess the amount of traffic at proposed sites for branch stores.

14. Compare the advantages of the telephone and mail questionnaires.

15. Why do some consider the personal interview the best questionnaire method?

16. Does the writing of a questionnaire need the expertise of someone seasoned in research? Explain your answer.

17. What is a consumer panel?

18. Define the term *sample*.

19. How is the data, collected through questionnaires or counts, processed?

20. Discuss the reasons for preparation of a formal, written report to show findings and recommendations.

CASE PROBLEMS

CASE PROBLEM 1

Business in general is increasing at a reasonable growth rate in Alan's Department Store, located in a downtown metropolitan area. Alan's has been in operation for forty years. For the past three years the furniture department, in existence since the store's inception, has shown a decline in sales. Both the buyer, who has headed the department for the past twelve years, and the merchandise manager in charge of hard goods have been unable to stop the slump. A routine study of the situation shows the following:

1. There have been no significant changes in sales personnel (Alan's has a very low employee turnover rate).
2. The same vendors are being used as were used in the past.
3. The population in the trading area has been increasing.
4. No new competition has opened for business.
5. Store policy and service has remained the same.

The store's gross has shown a steady increase of about 6% annually (last year's sales for the entire store were $26 million) and the furniture department has been declining at a rate of 5% annually for the last three years. Since this department accounts for 15% of the store's total sales, top management has approved a research project to discover the causes of the problem.

QUESTION

1. Prepare an outline indicating and explaining the approach you would take to solve the problem. Include all the steps you would employ in your design. Your outline should be prepared as though you were a research consultant.

Teen-Rite is a specialty shop catering to teenage girls. It carries a complete line of dress-wear, sportswear, and accessories to outfit the teenage customer. The largest part of their operation is devoted to clothing worn for school. This past season Teen-Rite did not realize a profit. Traffic into the store was the same as it had been in past seasons, with the same customers comprising the shopping group. Another profitless season could lead to bankruptcy.

One salesperson suggested to Ms. David, the proprietor, that she contact a marketing research firm to help with the problem. Ms. David explained that her operation, which grosses about $200,000 annually, is unable to afford the expense involved. Instead, she decided to carefully study the situation to determine the causes of the problem. After informal talk with customers she discovered that school dress regulations in her community had changed and her merchandising practices would have to be updated. Although she discovered the reasons for poor business, she was still confronted with the problem of proper merchandise selection.

QUESTIONS

1. With a minimum of cost involved, what research techniques would you employ to determine Teen-Rite's merchandise needs?
2. Prepare the forms necessary to be used in the project.
3. Whom would you use to conduct the project?

20 *electronic* *data processing*

BEHAVIORAL OBJECTIVES

Upon completion of this chapter the student should be able to

1. *List and explain the contents of six computerized reports that large retailers issue to their buyers.*
2. *Discuss three areas of computer application for a major retailer.*
3. *Explain the use of sales tickets in a computerized operation.*
4. *Write a brief essay on the reasons for the growing use of point-of-sale registers.*

INTRODUCTION

The production requirements of World War II resulted in a surge of growth for American industry. The prosperity of the postwar years led to a near-constant period of business expansion. Throughout this time, technological advances led to improved production and marketing methods, which kept pace with the steadily increasing demands of the consuming public. However, since most business people consider office procedures to be a necessary evil, resulting in neither profits nor cost reduction, this era of marketing growth and production improvement saw practically no change in clerical procedures. Around 1950, the larger industrial organizations had grown to a point where the paperwork required to support their business activities was such that their poorly equipped office staffs were unable to keep pace. The bottleneck was so great that further business growth was threatened. Management was faced with the alternative of developing new office techniques or slowing down the industrial growth rate. Its decision was to spend money.

THE COMPUTER

As is frequently the case with industrial problems, when necessity is joined with the money required to solve the problem, the solution can usually be found. In this instance, the solution was the computer: expensive, difficult to change over to, with practically no trained personnel available to operate, but capable of handling an unbelievable amount of data. In short, the computer was the perfect answer to the paperwork bottleneck.

Although it is not the purpose of this book to fully explain computers, no understanding of their capabilities can be achieved without a brief explanation of the workings of an electronic data processing system. The devices use electrical impulses that can be added, subtracted, or stored. Since it is possible to store electrical impulses, the machine may be said to have memory. That is, the computer can be instructed to perform an operation at some future time.

For example, it can be instructed to multiply the hours Fred Smith works by $4, his hourly rate of pay. Then, at the end of any week, when told the number of hours Fred has worked, it can compute his week's earnings.

The electrical circuitry of a computer is enormously complicated. Its capabilities, on the other hand, are quite simple. It can add, subtract, transfer from one location to another, and store. Nothing more. It is essentially a moron, with one redeeming feature. It can perform these operations in millionths of a second. Thus, though it cannot even multiply, but must use repeated addition as a substitute (it computes 3×4 as $4 + 4 + 4$), it can find the product of two ten-digit numbers in a fraction of a second. A further illustration of computer speed is that it can print the results of its computations at the rate of better than nine $8\frac{1}{2} \times 11$ pages per minute. It is this blinding speed that has made the computer the perfect tool for handling massive amounts of data.

Business uses of the computer began in the offices. As we shall see, it was quickly adapted to other business functions in which instant, accurate information is vital. Before going into other applications of computers, let us briefly discuss the historical development of computers.

HISTORY AND DEVELOPMENT

It all began in 1812 when an English mathematician named Charles Babbage designed his "difference engine." This machine was so far ahead of its time that the technical know-how necessary to its manufacture was unsolvable. The device could do everything but work. It couldn't even be built.

It was not until the late 1880s that a workable, practical data-handling machine was built. It happened at that time because it was needed. The situation was this: the laws of the United States require that a census be taken every ten years to serve as a basis for reapportioning seats in the House of Representatives. By 1880 the population of the country had grown so rapidly that it was not until 1887 that the 1880 census had been completely tabulated. It was obvious that the 1890 census could not be completely analyzed in the required ten years. At this time, Dr. Herman Hollerith, a statistician with the Census Bureau, developed the punched card (the Hollerith card is still in use today) and the machinery necessary to handle it. Needless to say, the 1890 census was tabulated by Hollerith in record time and at a considerable financial saving. From then on data processing was off and running. By 1896 Hollerith organized the Tabulating Machine Company to manufacture and market the machines and cards. Through a series of mergers, the Tabulating Machine Company has become the International Business Machines Corp. (IBM), currently the world's leading producer of date processing equipment. From the time that Hollerith proved the value of data processing machines, their use in industry has grown steadily. This growth, coupled with technical improvements in the speed and adaptability of computers, has brought us to a point at which large establishments, to keep their competitive place in industry, find the use of the computer an absolute necessity.

THE COMPUTER AND RETAILING

As various areas of American business turned to electronic data processing, retailing lagged behind. There are several reasons for this:

1. Programming (instructing) a computer is a complicated process requiring considerable time and expense. Every step must be analyzed and procedures carefully mapped out. In a department store with as many as 2,000 different items in inventory, programming is a prohibitive task.
2. Retail transactions are complicated. They may be cash, charge, C.O.D., or layaway, taken or delivered, and so on. The computer is at its best in handling data in which each transaction is exactly the same as all others.
3. For the computer to operate effectively, the information going into it must be absolutely accurate. The retail operation makes wide use of part-time, imperfectly trained personnel who are prone to make mistakes.
4. Retail establishments depend upon data-handling personnel who receive relatively low wages. This often results in increased costs as a result of a changeover to electronic systems.

The factors that ultimately forced the large retailers to install computers are chiefly in the area of improved information.

1. Better inventory control can lead to large savings by reducing markdowns. Exact, prompt information keeps unnecessary buying, and subsequent markdowns, to a minimum. Similarly, the loss of business because a store is out of stock on an item can be controlled by prompt information on shortages.
2. The high cost problem was overcome by the fact that vital decision-making information is made quickly available by computerized installations. For example, a large ladies' wear chain rented a computer for inventory control. One day the buyer of ladies' sweaters decided she would like to know which sizes were most popular. This is a simple computer problem and the information was readily available. Then she wanted to know about the popularity of various colors, and was given the answer. Then she wondered if bright colors were better in small sizes than large. This goes on and on, until the buyer is so well equipped with information that she can perform with far greater efficiency. At this point it is foolish to compare the cost of the computer with the salaries of the clerks it replaced, since the information the device supplies is far more important than the job it was originally installed to do. This, incidentally, is also an example of why computers that were meant to work six hours a day are now working twenty-four hours a day.

To sum up, efficient retailing depends upon information. Much of the necessary knowledge has always been available in the sales records, but the job of analyzing such mountainous records and producing timely, accurate informational summaries is not possible without the use of the computer.

AREAS OF APPLICATION

As we have seen, the computer, originally installed as a kind of superclerk, has come into its own as a vital information source. Effective retailing, particularly in high fashion merchandise, depends upon prompt, accurate data. Since the computer is an excellent source of such information, the marriage between retailing and the computer has been a happy one.

To fully appreciate the value of the computer as an informational device, we will look at some specific retailing applications of electronic data processing.

Merchandise Inventory Control

The merchandise inventory on hand is probably a store's most important asset. In dollars, it requires a very large part of the enterprise's capital. In terms of profits and losses, the makeup of the inventory is critical. Having the wrong merchandise is disastrous. Having the right merchandise in too little quantity loses sales. Too much of the right merchandise results in markdowns. In addition to this, a large store has an inventory of thousands of items, frequently kept in many locations. The problems of inventory control are so vast in such an organization that decisions on what to buy, how much to buy, when to buy, and from whom to buy require a considerable amount of up-to-date information. These problems match perfectly with the capabilities of the computer:

1. Its capacity is so great that it can collect data from many departments and locations.
2. Its speed is so great that it can process an enormous amount of data rapidly.
3. It has the ability to print out reports in easily understood form.

Because the end product is the informational report, it is vital that the computer be given all of the information necessary to construct such a report. Basically, the required information is the merchandise on hand, the merchandise sold, and the merchandise on order. Moreover, to be usable, the data must be presented to the computer in a language it can understand. The following is the input necessary to the computer for comprehensive merchandise inventory control. (It should be pointed out that while many department stores are moving toward the following system, some stores work with considerably less information.)

1. Style number
2. Vendor

3. Sales
4. Goods on hand
5. Goods on order
6. Receipts from vendors
7. Returns to vendors
8. Cost
9. Selling price
10. Color and size
11. Markdowns
12. Customer returns
13. Shipments to branches
14. Shipments between branches

From this information, the computer can be instructed to provide as output a wide variety of reports at required time intervals. One department store furnishes its buyers with the following informational reports:

1. Information on sales of high-fashion merchandise is distributed every three days. Such reports allow buyers to make decisions on reordering or transferring stock between branches while the style in question is still new, available, and in demand. Such a report, since it is to be used by a buyer for reordering, would include (for each style, price, and color) such information as three days' sales, a week's sales, sales to date, sales in the various branches, number of pieces on hand, number of pieces on order, date the order is due, and so forth—in short, all the information needed by the buyer to make the reordering decision.
2. Reports on staple type goods, as for example, men's black socks, need not be nearly so detailed or frequent. Since staples don't run "hot," the decision based on the report is merely to reorder when the number of units on hand falls below a certain level. In many operations the computer is actually instructed to print out a reorder automatically whenever the stock on hand falls below a certain level.
3. The buyer, merchandise manager, and department manager frequently receive weekly unit reports of sales for the week, prior week, and month to date, as well as the on-hand figure for each style. From this report, trouble spots can be seen early and remedial action, such as transfers between branches and promotions, can be taken before markdowns become necessary.
4. Every ten days a dollar report furnishes information on the current total inventory, this month's and this year's sales, and markdowns for each store in the chain. From this the buyer can determine weaknesses, the amount of inventory in each store, and how well each store is doing.
5. Monthly, the buyer receives a report showing the relative importance of each price line in the various units making up the chain. This report shows a comparison between the prior year's units and dollars of sales and that of the current year. Future merchandising trends for each unit can be determined from these monthly reports.
6. Every six months the vendor analysis presents the buyer with information on total purchases, returns, markdowns, and the gross profit for each vendor. Excessive returns, markdowns, and so forth, that turn up in such reports are important for future vendor selection.

7. In addition to the reports already mentioned, special reports are constantly flowing from the computer to the buyer. These might include size and color analyses and the aging of the inventory to indicate the amount of time each unit has been in the store. In fact, almost any information that the buyer requests and that computer time can be found for can be produced.

Although large retail establishments have been operating successfully for many years, and the computer is relatively new, it is difficult to understand how buyers could ever have performed effectively without them.

Sales Forecasting

Essentially, sales forecasting is based on historical data. That is, a study of past reports on each item often reveals trends that may predict future sales. The computer is well suited to this form of operation. When properly programmed, it can review the information for past periods and predict future selling activities. As in all computer functions, the method it uses is the method it is told to use. Consequently, the sales forecast is as accurate as the person instructing the computer. Since forecasting future activities is inexact, the computer should not be expected to predict exactly.

Credit Authorization and Control

In Chapter 18, *Credit and Other Customer Services,* discussion centered upon the importance of consumer credit to contemporary retailing and the types of systems to which retailers subscribe.

It is important to understand, however, the role played by the computer in credit authorization and control.

Credit Authorization

Nearly all stores set a limit on the amount of a sale that a salesperson may make without checking to determine whether or not the purchase will increase the amount that is owed the store to a point beyond the purchaser's credit limit. This determination of whether a credit customer will be allowed to make a large purchase on credit is called credit authorization. Under some systems, this authorization must be obtained by a call to the credit department. Other systems permit the salesperson to go directly to the computer for the information. In any case, if the sale is to be permitted, a credit authorization number is issued. This number gives the salesperson authority to make the sale.

The most modern credit authorization systems require the salesperson to pick up a dial telephone and call the computer's credit authorization extension. When the ready tone is heard, the sales clerk dials the customer's account number and the amount of the sale to the nearest dollar. The computer checks this information with the customer's account, which it has in its memory bank. If the account is in order, the credit authorization number is given to the salesperson and the sale is completed. If the sale is not to be accepted, the customer is generally referred to the credit department for a review of his or her account.

Credit Control

For the computer, involvement in credit control requires input of the following information:

1. Sales on credit for each customer
2. Sales returns by credit customers
3. Payments by credit customers

With this information, plus the information of the customer's credit limit, the computer can be programmed to keep records of each customer's account and provide the following output:

1. Report the amounts purchased, returned, and paid by each customer, the dates of such transactions, and the balance due the store after each transaction.
2. Print out monthly bills to be mailed to each customer, showing all of the information described above. Since the printing of all the bills as of the first day of the month would tie up the computer, billing is usually staggered during the month, with different customers being billed as of different dates.
3. Print out a report of delinquent accounts. This report can be analyzed by the amount delinquent, days overdue, and so forth. Based on this analysis, the computer can select and print an appropriate dunning letter from a large selection of such letters it has in its memory.
4. Automatically turn certain past-due accounts over to an attorney or collection agency.
5. Keep track of all accounts turned over for collection and check the effectiveness of the collection agency.
6. Produce reports comparing bad debts with prior years' bad debts.
7. Produce from credit files information such as the area from which customers come to shop at the store, home ownership, number of children, and so forth. From this information, advertising and sales promotion can be designed to fit the specific characteristics of the customer.

SYSTEMS AND PROGRAMMING

The changeover from a manual to a computerized system requires a great deal of time, effort, and expense. First, systems must be set up. That is, decisions must be made on equipment, personnel, and other facilities that must be combined to operate under certain procedures to accomplish the objectives of the organization. After the overall systems and procedures have been developed, the computer must be programmed to handle its part in the total system.

In the area of systems and programming, the manufacturers of the computers are helpful. Generally they have in their files systems and programs that have been tested elsewhere, and can be modified to the requirements of the customer. The change to computers is still difficult, but the "canned" computer manufacturer's programs help.

Two canned programs evolved by IBM and of interest to retailers are SKU and IMPACT. Both are concerned with inventory control.

The SKU system is for staple merchandise such as men's shoes, linens, and hardware. No decision has to be made on reordering such goods. The only question concerns the stock level at which the reorder must be made. When that level is reached, the computer automatically prints a reorder.

The IMPACT system is a highly sophisticated example of an inventory management program for high fashion merchandise such as dresses, handbags, and ladies' shoes. In this case it is not only the stock level that is important to the reordering decision; of greater importance is the number of units sold last week and last year that week, markdowns on the item, and many of the other facts that are important to high-fashion merchandise.

INPUT DEVICES

As has been discussed, the great success of computers has been due to the speeds at which they can operate. Consequently, those parts of the computer system that work most slowly are the areas that are being subjected to considerable research. One great obstacle has always been the fact that data going into the computer must first be translated into a form the computer will understand. Several years ago this required that information be translated onto punched cards or magnetic tapes. Recently an optical reader has been produced. By means of this device, rather than needing a keypunch operator translating written information into machine language, the computer can do its own translating. As a result, translations are being done at computer speed rather than the speed of a keypunch operator. Future computer installations will feature even greater speed and efficiency.

It is in the area of input devices that the application of computerization to the area of retailing is undergoing the most rapid changes. At the time of this writing, every major retailer has changed or is in the process of changing to cash register input devices that automatically place sales information directly into the computer system. The new piece of equipment, illustrated in Figure 20-1, is called a point-of-sale cash register.

FIGURE 20-1 Point-of-Sale Register

Courtesy of NCR Corporation

Point-of-Sale Registers

As just mentioned, in addition to being able to perform all normal cash register functions, the point-of-sale register has the ability to place information directly into the computer system. Most manufacturers of point-of-sale registers offer the option of optical scanning, in which case the register has the capability of reading and abstracting information from the sales slip. Obviously, this is a considerable saving in operator time and efficiency.

To fully understand the advantages of the point-of-sale register, let us look at the procedures of an operation in which regular registers are used. A perforated portion of each sales tape must be removed from the ticketed merchandise and placed in a box. Every mutilated, poorly torn, or lost ticket results in an error or the chance of an error. Periodically, the torn-off portions of the tickets are sent to the data processing center. There, they are fed into a ticket-reading device that extracts the information from each ticket and transfers it into a computer language or a type of tape that is acceptable to the computer as input. Finally, the tape is periodically fed into the computer.

In contrast, the point-of-sale register with an optical scanner permits the operator to get the information directly into the computer as quickly as the sales invoice can be placed in front of the optical scanning device. Upon receipt of the information, the computer immediately updates its records. These new registers, then, provide a shortcut through several steps in the data processing system while improving accuracy by eliminating error-prone procedures.

The time savings offered by point-of-sale registers permits instantaneous updating of inventory. In the big-ticket departments such as carpeting and appliances, this is a vital factor, since under the old system salespeople could only tell customers the previous day's inventory position. The inventory could not be updated with the same day's sales. Another, and perhaps more important, advantage of rapid inventory correction is that informational reports, vital to the efficient operation of the high-styled departments, become more timely and consequently more accurate.

In addition to instantaneously updating the inventory, the credit files also are immediately corrected. In situations in which the credit accounts are not updated quickly, customers who make several successive purchases in rapid order can increase their accounts far beyond their individual credit limits. Where credit records are updated after each sale, this is impossible because the authorization requested for the second sale would be denied once the first sale's posting increased the account to the credit limit.

Point-of-sale registers are used to advantage by the supermarket industry where inventory control, because of the enormous number of items, is a constant problem. Optical scanning devices are, however, causing problems in this area of retailing. Companies that supply packaged goods to department stores are premarking their merchandise with a code that is compatible to computers. At the checkout counter, this code is passed over an optical scanner and the sales total is determined, with a considerable savings in checkout time. Another savings expected from this operation is that because the price for the article is coded onto the package, in-store marking is not required. The problem is that the customers do not like the system. They prefer that each item be clearly marked, so they can check each price as the operator rings it up. To offset this problem, the latest point-of-sale registers produce a tape of product descriptions and prices.

Universal Product Code

Many large retailers, particularly supermarkets, are adopting the Universal Product Code (UPC) as a means of getting information into the computer. The UPC is a Bar Code (see Figure 20-2) that is placed on the product by the manu-

FIGURE 20-2 Universal Product Code

facturer. A point-of-sale register can read the information in the code by use of a scanning device or a wand. The information is used to update the inventory while adding up the amount of the sale. Ideally, the point-of-sale system should save price marking on individual items, but this is meeting considerable consumer resistance.

TIME SHARING

An increasing number of small retailers are taking advantage of computer systems by renting computer time for their needs. Commercial computer centers are springing up throughout the country to service those businesses that are interested in obtaining computer output but are too small to be able to afford their own installation. These service companies supply programmers, operators, and computer time on an hourly basis. As a result, the computer, once only available to commercial giants, is now being used by their relatively small competitors. Since this trend is growing steadily, it is vital that all business people familiarize themselves with the capabilities of computers.

A little over twenty years ago the first electronic computer was profitably used by a retail store. Since then, more and more retailers have used this modern tool to solve their business problems with great efficiency and speed. Unquestionably, the future will see wider use of computers of all sizes by retail organizations of all sizes. Electronic data processing is no longer restricted to use by the retailing giants, but is in general use throughout a wide range of American businesses. The point is rapidly being reached at which any school that claims to train business people must require an introductory course in computers to be taken by all students.

SPECIFIC APPLICATION—A LARGE DEPARTMENT STORE

The store in this illustration is the parent store of a chain of ten department stores in the New York area. The chain is part of an ownership group that has annual sales in excess of $1 billion. The particular unit being discussed does $40 million in sales annually.

All shipments from vendors to the store are channeled through a particular freight company. This freight company has the responsibility of tagging all of the merchandise delivered to the various stores in the chain. The tag, affixed to each piece of merchandise, contains the following information:

1. Selling department
2. Type of goods
3. Vendor

4. Style number
5. Cost
6. Size
7. Date arrived
8. Selling price

This information is both printed for visual reading and punched in a code that can be read directly into the computer. Since there are only eight kinds of information going into the computer, the informational reports provided by the computer are summaries and interpretations of these data. As we shall see, these eight sources of data can produce a wide variety of vital information.

Figure 20-3 is an illustration of the type of tag that is used. It is called a Dennison Tag. It is one of a set of similar tags, perforated together for easy tear-off, that are attached to the incoming merchandise. The tags will be used as follows:

1. The data processing center uses one tag to increase the inventory by the amount of the incoming goods and to perform other bookkeeping functions.
2. When the goods are sold, the cashier punches the information into a point-of-sale cash register, which is connected to the data processing center. There the inventory will be reduced and other bookkeeping functions performed.
3. At inventory-taking time a tag is removed and sent to the data processing center for compilation of the stock on hand.
4. The remaining tags go with the customer. In this way, if goods are returned, they can be placed directly on the racks without the necessity of retagging.

In addition to the tag, there is other information necessary for merchandise control that must be fed into the computer, such as transfers between stores, price changes, and returns to vendor. Such data do not come from point-of-sale cash registers, and the information must be translated (keypunched) into a language the computer understands.

At this point all the necessary information is in the data processing cen-

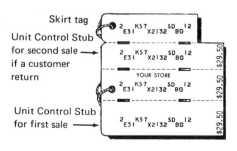

FIGURE 20-3 Dennison Tag

Courtesy of Dennison Mfg. Company

ter. An efficient way of feeding information into a computer is by magnetic tape, and the data must now be transferred from the various sources to tape.

Once all the information is in the computer, any illogical material is thrown out in the next step. For example, a child's sweater selling for $300 is simply not possible and is listed separately for further study.

The remaining logical material is now sorted, classified, and interpreted for the following informational reports:

1. *Unit-Sales Report.* This report is illustrated in Figure 20-4. The Unit-Sales Report is sent to each department in the middle of every week. As can be seen in

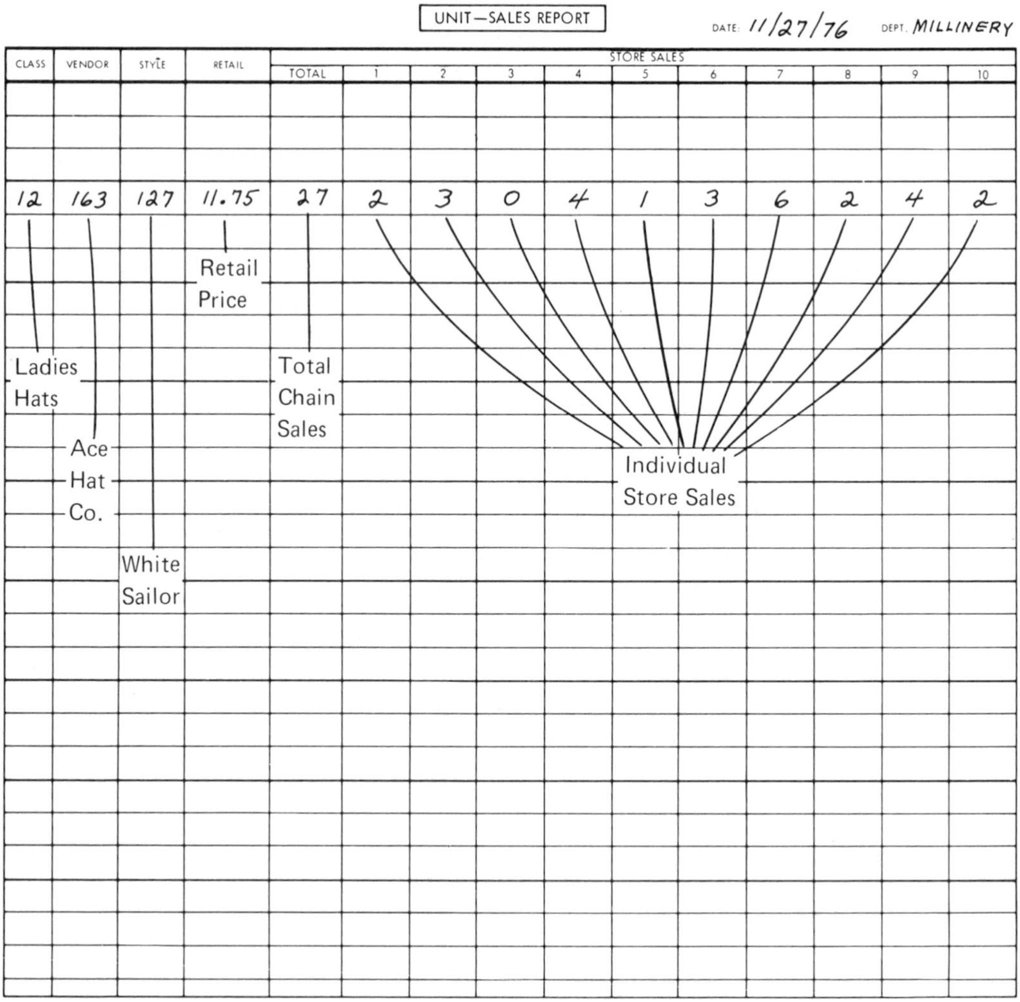

| UNIT—SALES REPORT | | | | DATE: 11/27/76 | | DEPT. MILLINERY | | | | | | | | | |

DATE: 11/27/76   DEPT. MILLINERY

CLASS	VENDOR	STYLE	RETAIL	STORE SALES										
				TOTAL	1	2	3	4	5	6	7	8	9	10
12	163	127	11.75	27	2	3	0	4	1	3	6	2	4	2

Retail Price — Total Chain Sales — Individual Store Sales — Ladies Hats — Ace Hat Co. — White Sailor

FIGURE 20-4   Unit-Sales Report

the illustration, the report indicates the class of goods, such as ladies' hats; vendor; style number; and retail price. It indicates the total chain sales in dollars for each of the above categories, and the amount each unit of the chain contributed to the total. This breakdown permits department buyers to know their own sales and that of other units.

2. *Sales and Stock Status Report.* This report is illustrated in Figure 20-5. The Sales and Stock Status Report is sent to each department at the end of every week. The report gives information in units (not dollars) on the class, vendor, style, and unit retail price for the total chain as well as the individual store. It indicates the first and last date of receipt of goods as well as the total units received, sales to date, and sales the previous week. The buyers may also determine the number of units on hand at the end of the week and the units sold during the week, both in their own stores and, for comparison purposes, in all the stores of the chain. To improve this report, the data processing center is presently working on a system to include in the format of the report the units on order.

3. *Size and Color Sales Report.* This report is illustrated in Figure 20-6. The Size and Color Sales Report is sent to selected departments every week. It indicates sales for each store in the chain. The sales are broken down into class, vendor, style, unit retail selling price, color, and size. It not only allows comparisons of the store's position in terms of the other stores in the complex but also indicates the important sizes and colors for each style sold. This is vitally needed information for reordering and future ordering.

4. *Classification and Price Line Recap.* This report is illustrated in Figure 20-7. The Classification and Price Line Recap is prepared monthly for the merchandise manager. It is a summary of the month's sales and the inventory and open-to-buy position at the end of the month. Listed according to the categories "class" and "price range" is each store's stock on hand, on order, and open to buy. In addition the report offers a means of comparing this month's sales with those of the same month last year. The previous year's sales of the next month and the second next month are given for the purpose of forecasting and determining the adequacy of the goods on hand.

The few reports indicated above are by no means the total output of the computer at the store. They are in fact only a small part of the computer's total usage. Although the examples given are specific to this particular store, they are far from standard. Data processing is relatively new to department stores, and the state of the art is in its infancy. As a result, new systems, newly designed reports, and new computer applications are constantly being implemented. It is not unlikely that within a few years the systems described here will be nothing more than a hazy memory to this store's data processing department.

Action for the Independent Retailer

Whether or not a small independent retail store should be burdened with the expense of an electronic data processing system depends upon several factors.

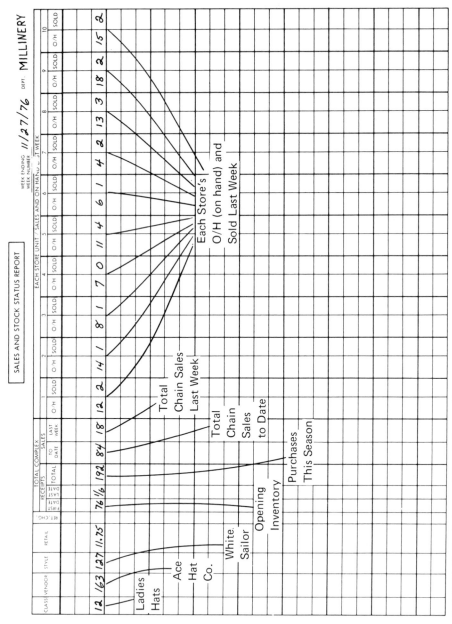

FIGURE 20-5 Sales and Stock Status Report

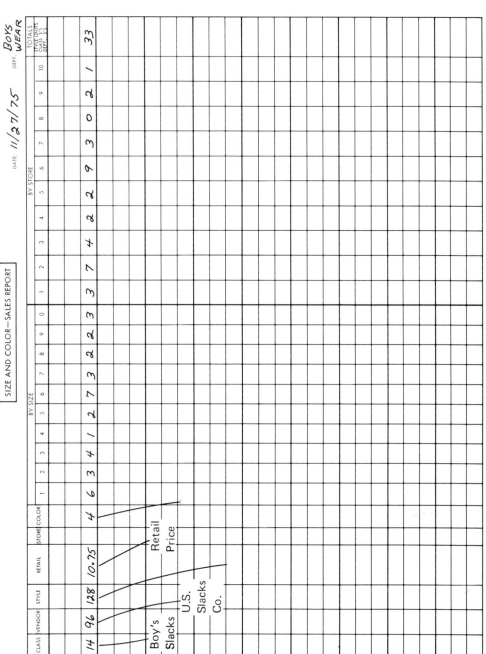

FIGURE 20-6 Size and Color Sales Report

CLASSIFICATION AND PRICE RANGE RECAP

MONTH & YEAR
WEEK NUMBER

DEPT.

CLASS	PRICE RANGE	STORE	TOTAL STOCK		SALES					OPEN TO BUY
			ON HAND	ON ORDER*	THIS YEAR	LAST YEAR				
					THIS MONTH	THIS MONTH	NEXT MONTH	2ND NEXT MONTH	3RD NEXT MONTH	

*FIGURES TO BE ENTERED MANUALLY

FIGURE 20-7 Classification and Price Line Recap

First, the size of the store and the availability of the required funds are important factors to consider. Obviously, a mom-and-pop grocery store has neither the finances nor the need for this type of equipment. However, there are a large number of retailers that are far from giant industry leaders and yet are big enough and profitable enough to afford an electronic data processing system. For these organizations, a determination must be made about whether or not the problem warrants the investment. For example, is the store frequently out of stock because timely reorders were not sent out? Are there excessive markdowns because of errors in the buying of styles, sizes, or colors? If the buyer had accurate, timely reports, would these markdowns be minimized? Another area to be considered is the office. Are customer statements going out on time? Are excessive errors being made?

If it is found that a computer would be advantageous, decisions must be made about the type of system to buy. Many medium-sized retailers rent computer time from a computer service company only for the areas that need help, for example, for payroll, customer accounts, or the control of high-style merchandise. This spot use of a computer is relatively inexpensive and often paid for by the savings in the personnel it replaces.

IMPORTANT POINTS IN THE CHAPTER

1. *The principal advantage of the computer is its ability to handle enormous amounts of data at speeds approaching the speed of light.*

2. *The computer's enormous speed and data-handling capability enable management to receive more information than was ever available before in much less time.*

3. *Retailers were slow to adopt the computer because the great variety of retail operations made programming complicated and expensive, and because retailers depended upon low-paid, imperfectly trained personnel who were prone to making mistakes that hampered data processing operations.*

4. *The factors that led to the adoption of the computer by retailers are chiefly in the area of improved information. For example, better inventory information minimizes markdowns.*

5. *The most important applications of computers in retailing are in inventory control, sales forecasting, credit authorization, and bookkeeping.*

6. *The computer is instructed by a coded system of controls called a program.*

7. *Information is put into the computer by means of input devices such as punch cards or magnetic tapes.*

8. *Electronic data processing is available to small retailers through computer service centers that provide time and know-how to businesses that cannot afford to have their own installations. In effect, they share computer time among many small users.*

REVIEW QUESTIONS

1. Discuss the major reason for the first business applications of the computer.
2. It has been said that "necessity is the mother of invention." How may this be applied to data processing?
3. What are some of the reasons that delayed the adoption of computers in the field of retailing?
4. Discuss the factors that led to the introduction of computers in retailing.
5. Explain the importance of prompt, accurate information to the successful operation of a high-style sportswear department.
6. Since the data were always available, why is the computer considered an improved informational system?
7. Explain the importance of inventory control in terms of profits and losses.
8. Why must informational reports on high-fashion merchandise be produced more frequently than similar reports on staples?
9. Can high-fashion merchandise be effectively ordered automatically by a computer? Discuss.
10. Discuss the advantages of using point-of-sale cash registers.
11. What is an optical scanning input device? What problems does it pose when used in a supermarket, which do not occur in in-store price marking?
12. Credit losses can be minimized by a strict credit policy. Why do stores not do this more often?
13. Discuss the future use of the computer by small retailers.
14. Why do most of the computer-prepared informational reports in the example indicate the vendor of the goods?
15. Explain the uses of each of the parts of the Dennison Tag as used in the example.
16. Since Dennison Tags are prepunched in a computer language, why must an extensive keypunch operation be maintained?
17. The semiannual physical inventory is used by management. Would you expect the report to contain the date the merchandise came into the store?
18. Will size and color sales reports be used in sales forecasting? How?

CASE PROBLEMS

CASE PROBLEM 1

Carlson's, Inc., is a large department store in a major midwestern city. The store does an annual volume in excess of $20 million and the trend seems to indicate constantly rising sales.

The data processing department is relatively new, having been in existence only five years. The effect of this is that many of the computer systems are not yet firmly established, with changes in format still being effected.

The treasurer of the corporation would like to have the cost of the goods included on the prepunched Dennison card. With this information in the computer, merchandise control and income statements would be more easily and more accurately prepared. Since the Dennison Tag is of limited capacity, including the cost would require dropping some other piece of information. The treasurer suggests that the information indicating the vendor be dropped and that the buyers keep their own records of this information.

The buyers are up in arms over this. They feel that they would lose speed and accuracy and that the demands on their time would be excessive.

QUESTIONS

1. Discuss this problem from the treasurer's point of view.
2. Discuss this problem from the buyers' point of view.
3. What would you do as general manager?

CASE PROBLEM 2

A fast-growing small supermarket chain opened its fourth unit this year. Each of its stores is very successful, and it expects to open another unit in about a year. Indications are that this year's profits will be about $150,000.

Inventory control has been done manually by a force of six clerks. They had been doing the job reasonably efficiently until the fourth unit opened. Since then, they have been working overtime to keep up with the work load.

Management is progressive and up to date. It realizes that it will eventually need a computer in the merchandise control department; the only question is when. A properly controlled system would cost about $2,000 per month rental, plus operation (programmers, operators, and so forth). Since this would represent an important part of the profits, the problem is a serious one. This is particularly true since so considerable an increase in expenses would probably postpone the opening of the next unit.

The problem simply stated is this: If the chain waits until the next unit opens, the expense will be easier to handle. On the other hand, should it expand without an efficient organization?

QUESTIONS

1. Support the position favoring immediate expansion.
2. What are the disadvantages of expanding without maximum efficiency?
3. As a member of the board of directors, what would you do?

index